ASCENT
CENTER FOR TECHNICAL KNOWLEDGE

Autodesk® Inventor® 2018
Introduction to Solid Modeling
Part 1

Student Guide
1ST Edition

AUTODESK.
Authorized Publisher

ASCENT - Center for Technical Knowledge®
Autodesk® Inventor® 2018
Introduction to Solid Modeling - Part 1
1st Edition

Prepared and produced by:

ASCENT Center for Technical Knowledge
630 Peter Jefferson Parkway, Suite 175
Charlottesville, VA 22911

866-527-2368
www.ASCENTed.com

Lead Contributor: Jennifer MacMillan

ASCENT - Center for Technical Knowledge is a division of Rand Worldwide, Inc., providing custom developed knowledge products and services for leading engineering software applications. ASCENT is focused on specializing in the creation of education programs that incorporate the best of classroom learning and technology-based training offerings.

We welcome any comments you may have regarding this student guide, or any of our products. To contact us please email: feedback@ASCENTed.com.

The following are registered trademarks or trademarks of Autodesk, Inc., and/or its subsidiaries and/or affiliates in the USA and other countries: 123D, 3ds Max, Alias, ATC, AutoCAD LT, AutoCAD, Autodesk, the Autodesk logo, Autodesk 123D, Autodesk Homestyler, Autodesk Inventor, Autodesk MapGuide, Autodesk Streamline, AutoLISP, AutoSketch, AutoSnap, AutoTrack, Backburner, Backdraft, Beast, BIM 360, Burn, Buzzsaw, CADmep, CAiCE, CAMduct, Civil 3D, Combustion, Communication Specification, Configurator 360, Constructware, Content Explorer, Creative Bridge, Dancing Baby (image), DesignCenter, DesignKids, DesignStudio, Discreet, DWF, DWG, DWG (design/logo), DWG Extreme, DWG TrueConvert, DWG TrueView, DWGX, DXF, Ecotect, Ember, ESTmep, FABmep, Face Robot, FBX, Fempro, Fire, Flame, Flare, Flint, ForceEffect, FormIt 360, Freewheel, Fusion 360, Glue, Green Building Studio, Heidi, Homestyler, HumanIK, i-drop, ImageModeler, Incinerator, Inferno, InfraWorks, Instructables, Instructables (stylized robot design/logo), Inventor, Inventor HSM, Inventor LT, Lustre, Maya, Maya LT, MIMI, Mockup 360, Moldflow Plastics Advisers, Moldflow Plastics Insight, Moldflow, Moondust, MotionBuilder, Movimento, MPA (design/logo), MPA, MPI (design/logo), MPX (design/logo), MPX, Mudbox, Navisworks, ObjectARX, ObjectDBX, Opticore, P9, Pier 9, Pixlr, Pixlr-o-matic, Productstream, Publisher 360, RasterDWG, RealDWG, ReCap, ReCap 360, Remote, Revit LT, Revit, RiverCAD, Robot, Scaleform, Showcase, Showcase 360, SketchBook, Smoke, Socialcam, Softimage, Spark & Design, Spark Logo, Sparks, SteeringWheels, Stitcher, Stone, StormNET, TinkerBox, Tinkercad, Tinkerplay, ToolClip, Topobase, Toxik, TrustedDWG, T-Splines, ViewCube, Visual LISP, Visual, VRED, Wire, Wiretap, WiretapCentral, XSI.

NASTRAN is a registered trademark of the National Aeronautics Space Administration.

All other brand names, product names, or trademarks belong to their respective holders.

General Disclaimer:

Notwithstanding any language to the contrary, nothing contained herein constitutes nor is intended to constitute an offer, inducement, promise, or contract of any kind. The data contained herein is for informational purposes only and is not represented to be error free. ASCENT, its agents and employees, expressly disclaim any liability for any damages, losses or other expenses arising in connection with the use of its materials or in connection with any failure of performance, error, omission even if ASCENT, or its representatives, are advised of the possibility of such damages, losses or other expenses. No consequential damages can be sought against ASCENT or Rand Worldwide, Inc. for the use of these materials by any third parties or for any direct or indirect result of that use.

The information contained herein is intended to be of general interest to you and is provided "as is", and it does not address the circumstances of any particular individual or entity. Nothing herein constitutes professional advice, nor does it constitute a comprehensive or complete statement of the issues discussed thereto. ASCENT does not warrant that the document or information will be error free or will meet any particular criteria of performance or quality. In particular (but without limitation) information may be rendered inaccurate by changes made to the subject of the materials (i.e. applicable software). Rand Worldwide, Inc. specifically disclaims any warranty, either expressed or implied, including the warranty of fitness for a particular purpose.

Contents Part 1

Contents
Part 2

Preface

The *Autodesk® Inventor® 2018: Introduction to Solid Modeling* student guide provides you with an understanding of the parametric design philosophy through a hands-on, practice-intensive curriculum. You will learn the key skills and knowledge required to design models using Autodesk Inventor, starting with conceptual sketching, through to solid modeling, assembly design, and drawing production.

Topics Covered:

- Understanding the Autodesk® Inventor® software interface
- Creating, constraining, and dimensioning 2D sketches
- Creating and editing the solid base 3D feature from a sketch
- Creating and editing secondary solid features that are sketched and placed
- Creating equations and working with parameters
- Manipulating the display of the model
- Resolving feature failures
- Duplicating geometry in the model
- Placing and constraining/connecting parts in assemblies
- Manipulating the display of components in an assembly
- Obtaining model measurements and property information
- Creating Presentation files (Exploded views)
- Modifying and analyzing the components in an assembly
- Simulating motion in an assembly
- Creating parts and features in assemblies
- Creating and editing an assembly Bill of Materials
- Working with projects
- Creating and annotating drawings and views
- Customizing the Autodesk Inventor environment

Note on Software Setup

This student guide assumes a standard installation of the software using the default preferences during installation. Lectures and practices use the standard software templates and default options for the Content Libraries.

Students and Educators can Access Free Autodesk Software and Resources

Autodesk challenges you to get started with free educational licenses for professional software and creativity apps used by millions of architects, engineers, designers, and hobbyists today. Bring Autodesk software into your classroom, studio, or workshop to learn, teach, and explore real-world design challenges the way professionals do.

Get started today - register at the Autodesk Education Community and download one of the many Autodesk software applications available.

Visit www.autodesk.com/joinedu/

Note: Free products are subject to the terms and conditions of the end-user license and services agreement that accompanies the software. The software is for personal use for education purposes and is not intended for classroom or lab use.

Lead Contributor: Jennifer MacMillan

With a dedication for engineering and education, Jennifer has spent over 20 years at ASCENT managing courseware development for various CAD products. Trained in Instructional Design, Jennifer uses her skills to develop instructor-led and web-based training products as well as knowledge profiling tools.

Jennifer has achieved the Autodesk Certified Professional certification for Inventor and is also recognized as an Autodesk Certified Instructor (ACI). She enjoys teaching the training courses that she authors and is also very skilled in providing technical support to end-users.

Jennifer holds a Bachelor of Engineering Degree as well as a Bachelor of Science in Mathematics from Dalhousie University, Nova Scotia, Canada.

Jennifer MacMillan has been the Lead Contributor for the *Autodesk Inventor Introduction to Solid Modeling* since 2007.

In this Guide

The following images highlight some of the features that can be found in this Student Guide.

Practice Files

The Practice Files page tells you how to download and install the practice files that are provided with this student guide.

FTP link for practice files

Chapters

Each chapter begins with a brief introduction and a list of the chapter's Learning Objectives.

Learning Objectives for the chapter

1.3 Working with Commands

Getting Started

Starting Commands

The main way to access commands in the AutoCAD software is to use the Ribbon. Several of the file commands are available in the Quick Access Toolbar or in the Application Menu. Some commands are available in the Status Bar or through shortcut menus. There are additional access methods, such as Tool Palettes. The names of all the commands can also be typed in the Command Line. A table is included to help you to identify the various methods of accessing the commands.

When typing the name of a command in either the Command Line or Dynamic Input, the **AutoComplete** option automatically completes the entry when you pause as you type. It also supports mid-string search by displaying all of the commands that contain the word that you typed, as shown in Figure 1-12. You can then scroll through the list and select a command.

Figure 1-12

You can also click [icon] (Customize) to display the Input Settings for the AutoComplete feature.

To set specific options for the **AutoComplete** feature, right-click on the Command Line, expand Input Settings, and select from the various options, such as the ability to search for system variables or to set the delay response time, as shown in Figure 1-13.

Figure 1-13

If you need to stop a command, press <Esc> to cancel. You might need to press <Esc> more than once.

As you work in the AutoCAD software, the software prompts you for the information that is required to complete each command. These prompts are displayed in the drawing window near the cursor and in the Command Line. It is crucial that you read the command prompts as you work, as shown in Figure 1-14.

© 2015, ASCENT - Center for Technical Knowledge®   1-9

Instructional Content

Each chapter is split into a series of sections of instructional content on specific topics. These lectures include the descriptions, step-by-step procedures, figures, hints, and information you need to achieve the chapter's Learning Objectives.

Side notes

Side notes are hints or additional information for the current topic.

Practice Objectives

Practice 1c | Saving a Drawing File

Getting Started

Practice Objectives
- Open and save a drawing
- Modify the **Automatic Saves** option

Estimated time for completion: under 5 minutes

In this practice you will open a drawing, save it, and modify the **Automatic saves** option, as shown in Figure 1-51.

Figure 1-51

1. Open Building Valley-M.dwg from your class files folder.

2. In the Quick Access Toolbar, click [icon] (Save). In the Command Line, _QSAVE displays indicating that the AutoCAD software has performed a quick save.

3. In the Application Menu, click [Options] to open the Options dialog box.

4. In the Open and Save tab, change the time for Automatic save to 15 minutes.

Practices

Practices enable you to use the software to perform a hands-on review of a topic.

Some practices require you to use prepared practice files, which can be downloaded from the link found on the Practice Files page.

Chapter Review Questions

Getting Started

1. How do you switch from the drawing window to the text window?
   a. Use the icons in the Status Bar.
   b. Press <Tab>.
   c. Press <F2>.
   d. Press the <Spacebar>.

2. How can you cancel a command using the keyboard?
   a. Press <F2>.
   b. Press <Esc>.
   c. Press <Ctrl>.
   d. Press <Delete>.

3. What is the quickest way to repeat a command?
   a. Press <Esc>.
   b. Press <F2>.
   c. Press <Enter>.
   d. Press <Ctrl>.

4. To display a specific Ribbon panel, you can right-click on the Ribbon and select the required panel in the shortcut menu.
   a. True
   b. False

5. How are points specified in the AutoCAD Cartesian workspace?
   a. X value x Y value

Chapter Review Questions

Chapter review questions, located at the end of each chapter, enable you to review the key concepts and learning objectives of the chapter.

Command Summary

The Command Summary is located at the end of each chapter. It contains a list of the software commands that are used throughout the chapter, and provides information on where the command is found in the software.

Autodesk Certification Exam Appendix

This appendix includes a list of the topics and objectives for the Autodesk Certification exams, and the chapter and section in which the relevant content can be found.

Icons in this Student Guide

The following icons are used to help you quickly and easily find helpful information.

New in 2018	Indicates items that are new in the Autodesk Inventor 2018 software.
Enhanced in 2018	Indicates items that have been enhanced in the Autodesk Inventor 2018 software.

Practice Files

To download the practice files for this student guide, use the following steps:

1. Type the URL shown below into the address bar of your Internet browser. The URL must be typed **exactly as shown**. If you are using an ASCENT ebook, you can click on the link to download the file.

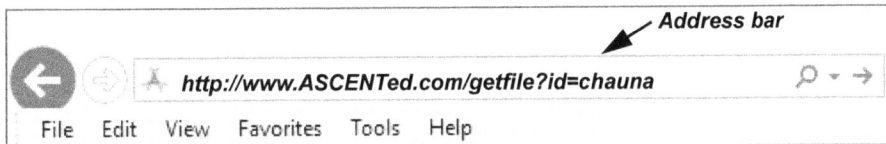

Address bar

http://www.ASCENTed.com/getfile?id=chauna

File   Edit   View   Favorites   Tools   Help

2. Press <Enter> to download the .ZIP file that contains the Practice Files.

3. Once the download is complete, unzip the file to a local folder. The unzipped file contains an .EXE file.

4. Double-click on the .EXE file and follow the instructions to automatically install the Practice Files on the C:\ drive of your computer.

   Do not change the location in which the Practice Files folder is installed. Doing so can cause errors when completing the practices in this student guide.

http://www.ASCENTed.com/getfile?id=chauna

Stay Informed!

Interested in receiving information about upcoming promotional offers, educational events, invitations to complimentary webcasts, and discounts? If so, please visit:

www.ASCENTed.com/updates/

Help us improve our product by completing the following survey:

www.ASCENTed.com/feedback

You can also contact us at: *feedback@ASCENTed.com*

Introduction to Autodesk Inventor

Understanding how Autodesk® Inventor® models are built and how they react to change is fundamental when designing robust and intelligent models. In addition, learning the working environment is important. The environment consists of many different components, including toolbars, panels, and menus. Learning to interact with all of the components increases your modeling efficiency.

Learning Objectives in this Chapter

- Understand how the Part, Assembly, Presentation, and Drawing environments enable you to create and document a 3D Digital Prototype.
- Understand how the five key Inventor attributes contribute to creating robust parts and assemblies that can be easily documented.
- Load and activate a project file.
- Open existing Autodesk Inventor files.
- Navigate the software interface to locate and execute commands.
- Use the model orientation commands to pan, zoom, rotate, and look at a model.
- Assign visual styles to your models.
- Use object selection techniques to efficiently select objects in your models.

1.1 Introduction

The Autodesk Inventor software takes you beyond 3D to Digital Prototyping by providing a comprehensive set of tools for 3D mechanical design that enables you to design, visualize, and simulate products before they are built. Digital Prototyping helps you to minimize the need for physical prototypes, design better products, reduce development costs, and get to market faster.

There are a number of tools available to design models in the Autodesk Inventor software. To begin, you must start with a foundation in solid 3D part design. Then you progress to placing the models relative to one another in an assembly, followed by creating drawings that document the 3D parts and assembly models in a 2D format.

Parts and assemblies are often referred to collectively as components, because of the similar manner in which they are treated. For example, a drawing file might reference either a part or another assembly file.

The following are the basic environments for 3D model design.

Environment (File Extension)	Description
Part (.IPT)	All part modeling, sketching, and complex design takes place on individual parts.
Assembly (.IAM)	Parts are added to assemblies to position and constrain them together to form a completed design. Parts are not stored in the assembly but their data is referenced from the original part model. The only modeling data stored in the assembly is the positional data that locates each part in the assembly.
Presentation (.IPN)	Used to document disassembled views in a drawing. Additionally, it can be used to animate tasks for visualization of component movement.
Drawing (.DWG & .IDW)	Used to communicate the 3D design in a 2D format. Views and annotations are used to document the design.

The part, assembly, and drawing files shown in Figure 1–1 illustrate how the original data created in the part model is passed to the assembly and finally used in a drawing to document a 3D design in a 2D format for manufacturing.

Models are placed relative to one another to create an assembly. If exploded views are required, a presentation is created.

Part models are initially designed

As with assemblies, part models can also be directly referenced to create drawing views.

Assembly and presentation files can be referenced to create a drawing.

Figure 1–1

Hint: Autodesk Inventor and AutoCAD Interoperability

There are several ways to incorporate AutoCAD® DWG files in an Autodesk Inventor file. The method you use depends on your project requirements. You can open the file directly in the Autodesk Inventor software for review. You can also import and convert the AutoCAD DWG into an Inventor DWG file, where all links to the original AutoCAD DWG file are lost. Alternatively, you can import and use an AutoCAD DWG as an associative underlay in an Autodesk Inventor file. These tools are discussed in detail in the *Autodesk Inventor 2018: Advanced Part Modeling* student guide.

1.2 Autodesk Inventor Fundamentals

The Autodesk Inventor software has the following five key attributes:

- Feature-Based Modeling
- Parametric Features
- Associative
- Assembly Management
- Model Documentation

Feature-Based Modeling

The Autodesk Inventor software is a feature-based modeling program, which means that a part evolves by creating features one by one until it is complete. Each feature is individually recognized by the software. A part model consisting of several individual features is shown in Figure 1–2.

Extruded features can either add or remove material from the model.

Figure 1–2

To start a design, create a simple extruded base feature that approximates the shape of the part. Continue adding features until the part is complete, as shown in Figure 1–3.

1st (Base) Feature: Extrude

2nd Feature: Drafts

3rd Feature: Fillets

4th Feature: Shell

5th Feature: Extrude

6th Feature: Hole

7th Feature: Copy

Figure 1–3

Sketched Features

A sketched feature is created by sketching and constraining a 2D cross-section on a placement plane. Then, the profile is used to create solid geometry, similar to the extrusion shown in Figure 1–4. Sketched features can either add or remove material.

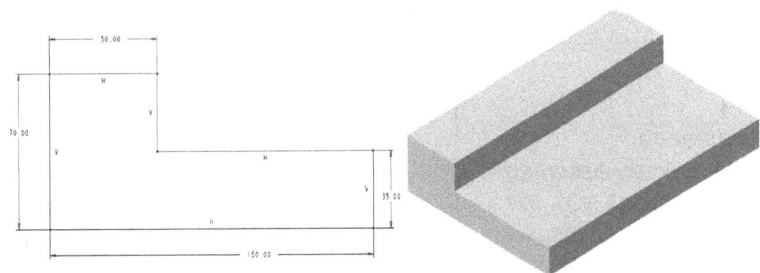

Figure 1–4

Pick and Place Features

A pick and place feature is a feature for which a shape has been predefined. For example, the cross-section of a Hole feature is a circle. To create a pick and place feature, you must define the location of the feature and the references required to locate it with respect to the existing geometry. An example of a pick and place Hole feature is shown in Figure 1–5.

The hole feature is located on this surface.

Figure 1–5

Feature Relationships

Feature relationships are formed between features as a model is created.

Feature-based modeling requires that features be added one by one. As a result, feature relationships are created as new features reference existing ones. For example, the hole shown in Figure 1–5 cannot exist without the cylindrical extruded feature because the hole's placement references exist in the extrusion. Feature relationships are created with all features.

Parametric Features

Parametric features are features that are created using dimensional constraints to define the feature's shape. The dimensional constraints are considered parameters: changes can be made at any time, and the features automatically update.

For example, the dimensional value that positions the cut feature shown in Figure 1–6 is changed. Therefore, the position of the feature updates to reflect the design change.

Names are automatically assigned to dimensions (e.g., d1 or d2). You can display either the name or value of the dimension, as required.

.300

.600

Figure 1–6

Dimensioning is an important step in the modeling process. When creating dimensions, use the following guidelines:

- Consider the dimensions that are going to be displayed in drawings and be aware of the resulting feature relationships.

- Consider changes that might need to be made to the model and how easily the dimensions facilitate these changes.

- Periodically modify dimensions to test *what if* scenarios. This is called *flexing the model* and ensures that the model behaves as expected.

Equations are user-defined mathematical relations.

Parameters and dimensions can be used in an equation to capture and control design intent. The ability to use equations in a model becomes extremely important in making a robust model.

Associative

The Autodesk Inventor software is fully associative, which means it operates in a concurrent engineering environment. You can work with the same model in different modes (e.g., Part, Assembly, or Drawing), and all modes are fully associative. Therefore, changes made to a model in any of the modes propagate to all other modes.

Assembly Management

Models built in Part mode can be used as components in an assembly. Assemblies are created by constraining components with respect to one another. The addition of constraints creates feature relationships between components and builds intelligent assemblies. Similar to features in Part mode, assembly constraints are assigned a unique internal identification number and can be used to establish relations between components.

Model Documentation

The tools available in the Drawing environment enable you to quickly create production-ready drawings for manufacturing. Drawings are created from part, assembly, or presentation models where their geometry and assembly specifications have already been defined. This information is used to create the required views in a drawing file. Adding details to your drawings enables you to communicate additional information about the design.

Drawing models are not actually contained in a drawing file. There is a link between the drawing file and the source model. If a change is made to the source model, all drawing views that reference it automatically update. The reverse, where a change made in the drawing also reflects in the model, can also be true if your workflow permits.

1.3 Getting Started

My Home

When you launch the Autodesk Inventor software, the *My Home* dashboard displays as shown in Figure 1–7. This default layout enables you to create a new file, activate a project file, or open a recently used file.

Figure 1–7

The default view for My Home is the Home dashboard which displays the *New*, *Projects*, *Shortcuts*, *File Details*, and *Recent Documents* areas. You can use this Home dashboard as follows:

- The *New* area enables you to create new part, assembly, drawing, and presentation files using the default templates provided with the software.

- The *Recent Documents* area lists previously opened files for the active project. When you hover the cursor over a file in the *Recent Documents* area, the following three buttons display, as shown in Figure 1–8:

    - 📂: Opens the document. Alternatively, double-click on the thumbnail to open the file.

    - 🗑: Removes the document from the *Recent Documents* area. This does not delete the local copy of the file.

    - ⚙: Accesses the options shown in Figure 1–8.

Figure 1–8

- Use the search field in the *Recent Documents* area to locate files.

- Use the filters on the left of the *Recent Documents* area to refine the files are that displayed in the list. You can refine based on project, file format, recently modified, etc.

- With a file selected in the *Recent Documents* area, the *File Details* area displays the details for the file (e.g., file format, location, modification date, etc.).

- Click ⊞ to add a recent document to the pinned list so that they are listed at the top of the *Recent Documents* area.

- Use the *Projects* area to activate any preloaded project by double-clicking on the project's name.

- Use the *Shortcuts* area to create a link to a folder or web page for easy access.

*The tools in the Home dashboard are also available in the Get Started tab, Quick Access Toolbar, or **File** menu.*

If you are using the Autodesk Vault software, a file's status in the Vault is displayed in the Recent Documents area.

Hint: Customizing the Home View

The Home view can be customized to refine how the default areas are displayed and used in the *My Home* dashboard. You can alter the display of the dashboard as follows:

- Resize the areas of the *My Home* dashboard by dragging each area's border to reposition it.

- Change the layout of the available areas using the buttons at the top of the dashboard to flip the locations of the available areas or maximize the *Recent Documents* area.

- Change the display style of the recent documents (i.e., tile, large, small, or list).

- The *My Home* dashboard can be set to display alternate information. The available options are located on the *Get Started* tab>My Home panel and enable you to create a customizable page or access help and training tools. Using ⇦ (Back) enables you to return to the previous My Home screen.

Project Files

If you work as part of a design team, managing access to the shared Autodesk Inventor data is crucial. Incorporating project files enables you to organize and access the files that are used. A project file is a text file that has an .IPJ format.

At a fundamental level, a project file specifies the locations of the files in the project and maintains all of the required links to the files. When you open a model, the paths specified in the active project are searched to find all of the referenced files. At a more advanced level, project files can specify library locations and set many options.

Project Files are discussed in more depth later in this student guide.

How To: Load a Project File

1. Use one of the following methods to open the Projects dialog box:

   - In the *Get Started* tab>Launch panel, click 🗁 (Projects).
   - In the New or Open dialog boxes, click **Projects**.
   - In the **File** menu, select **Manage>Projects**.

2. Click **Browse** and navigate to the location of the project file. Select it and click **Open**. The Projects dialog box updates and a checkmark displays next to the new project name, indicating that it is the active project.

3. Click **Done** to close the Projects dialog box.

Once a project has been loaded it remains listed as an available project. A previously-loaded project can be activated by:

- Double-clicking on its name in the Projects dialog box, or

- Selecting the check box adjacent to the project in the *Projects* area of the *My Home* dashboard.

New Projects cannot be loaded using the *My Home* dashboard.

Opening Files

Files can be opened using a number of different methods in the Autodesk Inventor software. Use one of the following methods to open an existing file:

- In the *Get Started* tab>Launch panel, click ⊳ (Open).

- Click ⊳ (Open) in the Quick Access Toolbar at the top of the interface.

- In the **File** menu, select **Open>Open**, or select a file from the Recent Documents list.

- In the *My Home* dashboard select a file in the *Recent Documents* area and click ⊳, or double-click on the thumbnail image.

For all but the **Recent Document** option, the Open dialog box opens. Navigate to the required file, select it, and click **Open**.

The ⊞ (Find) button in the Open dialog box can also be used to find a file to be opened.

Hint: My Home Tab

Once a file has been opened, the *My Home* tab displays at the bottom of the graphics window, as shown in Figure 1–9. The *My Home* tab can be closed. To reopen it, in the *Get Started* tab>My Home panel, click ⌂ (Home).

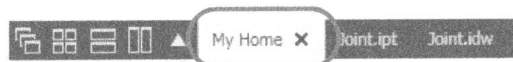

Figure 1–9

1.4 Autodesk Inventor Interface

Once a file has been opened, the interface updates to include additional elements. These are consistent among the various environments. The Part environment and many of the interface elements are shown in Figure 1–10.

Figure 1–10

Interface

The following interface elements exist in the Part environment and the other Autodesk Inventor environments.

Title Bar

The title bar at the top of the interface displays the name of the current active file.

Ribbon/Tabs/Panels

Many commands can also be accessed by right-clicking on a feature in the model or in the Model browser.

The ribbon provides access to commands and settings. The ribbon is divided into tabs and they are further subdivided into panels. The tabs that are available vary depending on the mode that is currently active. All commands are listed in panels. In Figure 1–11, the *3D Model* tab is active. Sketch, Create, and Modify are some of the panels in this tab.

Figure 1–11

Click ⬚ to pin a panel open. Select a second time to unpin it.

- Commands can be hidden into either compressed panels or commands. To expand hidden commands, click ▼ on the panel or command name, as shown for the *Modify* panel and Start Sketch command in Figure 1–12.

Figure 1–12

- Only commonly accessed Panels are displayed by default. To customize which panels are displayed, right-click on the ribbon, expand **Show Panels**, and then select a panel, as shown in Figure 1–13.

Alternatively, you can expand ⊙ ▾ (Show panels) at the end of each tab and select from the available list.

Figure 1–13

Graphics Window

Open files are displayed and can be directly manipulated in the graphics window. As individual files are opened, they display listed as tabs along the bottom of the graphics window. Select a tab name to display it. In the example shown in Figure 1–14, two models and the *My Home* dashboard are open. The active model is **Joint.ipt**.

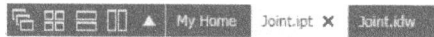

Figure 1–14

- Generally, maximizing each window provides the most modeling space, but you can also minimize and resize the windows or use ⬚ (Cascade), ⬚ (Arrange), ⬚ (Tile Horizontally, and ⬚ (Tile Vertically) which are next to the tab names.

Quick Access Toolbar

Commonly accessed commands are available at the top of the software window in the Quick Access Toolbar, as shown in Figure 1–15.

Figure 1–15

- Click ▼ on the right of the Quick Access Toolbar to customize the toolbar. Alternatively, you can right-click on any command on the ribbon and select **Add to Quick Access Toolbar**.

- The selection filter in the Quick Access Toolbar enables you to filter entities, features, or components so that you can only select that type of object. For example, if you select **Select Face and Edges**, you can only select the faces or edges on the model. The options that display in the drop-down list vary depending on the current mode. Part mode options display as shown in Figure 1–16.

To quickly access the filter options without having to use the Quick Access Toolbar, press and hold <Shift> as you right-click in the main window.

Figure 1–16

- The ⬅ (Undo) and ➡ (Redo) drop-down lists provide you with a list of previously-completed actions that were performed on the model. To jump forward or back to a point in the model's history, select it in from the drop-down list.

Model Browser

The Model browser lists all of the features or components in your models, in order of creation. The Model browser is a powerful tool that can be used to complete any of the following actions:

- Select features.

- Access commonly used options (e.g., **Delete**, or **Edit**).

- Search for features.

- Edit features.

- Display information on features.

- Change the order of features (click and drag).

- Open components in an assembly.

- Open drawings of components.

- Create drawings of parts and assemblies.

- Investigate relationships between features and components.

The Model browser can be displayed or removed from the interface. To control its display, enable or disable the tool in the User Interface drop-down list (View tab>Windows panel).

In the Model browser (shown in Figure 1–17), each feature is identified by its name and a symbol that identifies the feature type. Expandable nodes reveal additional information on the features.

Enhanced
in 2018

Figure 1–17

- The header of the Model browser indicates the active panel.

  Model is the panel that is displayed by default. Click ➕ to expand the list of available panels.

  - For part models, you can activate an iLogic or Favorites panel.
  - For assembly models, you can activate an iLogic, Favorites, or Representation panel to help view model information.
  - For assemblies you can also toggle between an Assembly or Modeling view.

- Click 🔍 in the Model browser header to access the quick search panel. A search is conducted as you type in keywords. In an assembly model, the quick search also provides access to the 🔲 and 🔲 icons, which enable you to filter unresolved and out of date data respectively.

- Click ≡ in the Model browser header to access options to expand and collapse the browser nodes, conduct an advanced search, set display preferences, or access help.

Status Bar

The Status Bar displays messages that are related to the active command. For example, in a Sketch, the Status Bar can display information related to sketching, dimensioning, and constraining an entity, while adding a feature the Status Bar can display Feature information.

Modeling Tools

The marking menu and feature creation controls are commonly used in the design process.

Marking Menu

The marking menu can be customized using Customize in the Tools tab.

The marking menu provides alternative access to commands. When you right-click in the graphics window, a radial marking menu and a vertical menu are displayed. Both menus provide quick access to commonly used, context-sensitive commands.

- The marking menu consists of eight wedges that contain different commands. To activate a marking menu command, move the cursor in the direction of the command so that it is highlighted (as shown on the right in Figure 1–18) and click it.

Figure 1–18

- As you become familiar with the marking menu commands, you can use gesturing behavior to initiate the commands. To gesture, click and hold the right mouse button, immediately drag the cursor in the direction of the marking menu wedge that is required to create a trail, and then release the mouse button. If these operations are completed in 250 milliseconds, the selected wedge is briefly displayed to confirm that the operation has been performed.

- To close the marking menu, you can start another command, select away from the marking menu, or press <Esc>.

Feature Creation Controls

Mini-toolbars are not available for all feature types.

When you create a feature, you must define a variety of elements or properties. You can define these using a Feature dialog box or mini-toolbar. In the example shown in Figure 1–19, an Extrude feature is being created and the Extrude dialog box and its mini-toolbar are displayed. Options can be selected in either location.

The elements that display in the dialog box or mini-toolbar vary according to the feature being defined.

By default, the dialog box is collapsed. Click the arrow to expand the dialog box.

Figure 1–19

New
in 2018

Hint: Mini-Toolbar Display

By Default, the display of the Mini-Toolbar is toggled off. To toggle on its display, on the *View* tab, expand **User Interface** and enable the **Mini-Toolbar** option on the list of interface items.

Accessing Help

A number of different tools are available to get help with the software:

- In any active dialog box, click 🔲 to access context-sensitive help (when available).

- Hover the cursor over a command name to display a tooltip, as shown in Figure 1–20. Some tooltips provide a video demonstration in place of a static image.

Figure 1–20

- If you are connected to the Internet, you can use Online Help. To access the Help documentation, click ⑦ (Help) in the top right corner of the interface, or press <F1>. Use the *Search* tab to enter a topic to search for or browse the available topics in the Help window.

- The Help documents can also be installed locally. This installation is done in the software load point to ensure that it located when required. Once installed, enable the **Installed Local help** option in the *General* tab in the Application Options dialog box.

- The *Get Started* tab in the ribbon contains help tools, including lessons, tutorials, and a What's New document which explains the new features that are available in the latest release of the software.

- Enter text in the *<Search Help & Commands>* field in the title bar to search for a keyword or phrase. The resulting list updates as you are typing and is divided based on the type of the result (e.g., commands, help articles, support articles, discussion groups, etc). If you press <Enter> after entering a keyword or phrase, the Help files are loaded.

Autodesk A360

The *Autodesk A360* tab in the ribbon provides access to Autodesk A360 online services. This service is available to all customers, but subscription customers have more storage space. It permits secured document storage and sharing. To use this service, you must create a user account and can then upload and share files.

1.5 Model Manipulation

When working with Autodesk Inventor models, being able to manipulate their orientation and display style helps you to better visualize them. The interface elements that control this are shown in Figure 1–21.

Figure 1–21

Model Orientation

A model can be oriented using the software's pan, zoom, rotate and ViewCube controls.

Pan a Model

The **Pan** command moves a model in the graphics window in any direction planar to the screen.

How To: Pan a Model

1. Click ⍟ (Pan) in the *View* tab>Navigate panel or in the Navigation Bar.
2. Press and hold the left mouse button.
3. Move the mouse to drag the model.

You can also pan a model by pressing and holding the middle mouse button while dragging the mouse, or by holding <F2> and panning with the left mouse button.

Rotate a Model

The **Orbit** command rotates a model around the center of the window, free in all directions, or around the X- or Y-axis.

How To: To Rotate a Model

You can also press and hold <F4> to rotate, or press and hold <Shift> and the middle mouse button.

1. Click ⊕ (Orbit) in the *View* tab>Navigate panel or in the Navigation Bar. The Rotate symbol (a circle) displays on the screen. The appearance of the cursor changes based on the location of the cursor relative to this circle.
2. Drag the cursor to the required orientation.

   • To rotate freely, move the cursor inside the circle. The cursor appearance changes to ⊕. Click and hold the mouse and then rotate the model in any direction.

   • To rotate about the horizontal axis, move the cursor to the top or bottom handle of the circle symbol. The cursor appearance changes to ⟠. Press and hold the left mouse button and rotate the model about the Y-axis.

   • To rotate about the vertical axis, move the cursor to the left or right handle of the circle symbol. The cursor appearance changes to ⊖. Press and hold the left mouse button and drag horizontally.

   • To rotate about an axis through the center of the circle symbol (normal to the screen), move the cursor to the rim of the circle symbol. The cursor appearance changes to

   ↻. Drag the mouse to rotate. To change the center of the rotation, click inside or outside the circle to set the new center.

   • To stop rotating, click ⊕ again to clear it. Alternatively, while still in the orbit circle, move the cursor away from the model until ↖ displays, and click in the graphics window.

Zoom a Model

The **Zoom** command zooms in and out on the model, on a specific entity, or on an area. The available zoom types are shown in Figure 1–22.

Figure 1–22

How To: Zoom in a Model

You can also press and hold <F3> to zoom.

1. Click (Zoom) in the *View* tab>Navigate panel or in the Navigation Bar.
2. Press and hold the left mouse button.
3. Move the mouse downward to zoom in and upward to zoom out.

How To: Zoom to a Specific Entity

1. Click (Zoom Selected) in the *View* tab>Navigate panel or in the Navigation Bar.
2. Select the entity.

- When zooming to an edge or vertex (not a surface), the order in which you select the entity and toolbar icon is important. Clicking the icon, and then clicking on a point on the entity positions the entity in the center of the screen, and maintains the current zoom level. Selecting the reverse (the entity and then clicking the icon), causes the software to zoom to the selected entity. When zooming on a surface, the order of selection does not have an impact.

How To: Zoom to an Area

1. Click (Zoom Window) in the *View* tab>Navigate panel or in the Navigation Bar.
2. Select a location on the model using the left mouse button to define the corner of the bounding box zoom area.

3. Drag the mouse to draw a box over the area to zoom.
4. Press or release the left mouse button when the box has been drawn.

Refit the Model

Click (Zoom All) in the *View* tab>Navigate panel or in the Navigation Bar. The view returns to its default zoom level and the model is centered in the graphics window.

Look At

To orient a face parallel to the screen, click (Look At) in the *View* tab>Navigate panel or in the Navigation Bar, and select the face. The model reorients and displays the selected face parallel to the screen. In the example shown in Figure 1–23, a face was selected and was reoriented using this command.

Select this surface to be parallel to the screen.

Figure 1–23

ViewCube

*To display the ViewCube settings, right-click on it and select **Options**. The ViewCube Options dialog box enables you to control the location, size, default ViewCube orientation, etc. The orientation enables you to select two parallel Origin planes to define the orientation.*

As an alternative to the **Look At** command, you can use ViewCube functionality to orient a model face parallel to the screen. By default the ViewCube displays in the top-right corner of the graphics window, as shown in Figure 1–24.

Figure 1–24

The ViewCube enables the following:

- Select any of the sides of the cube to display the parallel view that is associated with it (**Front**, **Right**, **Bottom**, etc.). Edges can also be selected on the ViewCube to reorient the model.

- Set the type of view to **Orthographic**, **Perspective**, or **Perspective with Ortho Faces** by right-clicking on the ViewCube and selecting the required option.

- Return to a Home View by clicking 🏠 , which displays at the top-left of the ViewCube when you hover the cursor over it. Initially the Home View is the default isometric orientation.

- Set a new Home View for your model by right-clicking on the ViewCube and selecting **Select Current View as Home**.

- Select and drag a surface on the ViewCube to rotate.

Full Navigation Wheel

The Full Navigation Wheel (shown in Figure 1–25) provides an alternative to the *View* tab and Navigation Bar commands for zooming, panning, and rotating. The **Rewind** command on the wheel enables you to navigate through previous views.

Figure 1–25

The Full Navigation Wheel moves with the cursor to provide access to the navigation tools.

How To: Use the Navigation Tool

*In addition to the **Zoom**, **Orbit**, **Pan**, and **Rewind** commands, other more advanced tools are available in the Full Navigation Wheel that are not covered in this student guide.*

1. Enable the tool by clicking 🛞 (Full Navigation Wheel) in the *View* tab>Navigate panel or in the Navigation Bar. The Full Navigation Wheel displays attached to the mouse.
2. Press and hold the mouse on a command (e.g., **Zoom**).
3. Move the cursor to change the view as required.
4. Release the mouse button to end the navigation command.

5. Click 🛞 or the **x** in the top right corner of the tool to close the Full Navigation Wheel.

Model Display

By default, new models created using the default templates are displayed as **Shaded with Edges**. However, other visual styles can be assigned. All visual styles are available in the *View* tab> Appearance panel as shown in Figure 1–26. The ability to use many of the styles depends on your computer's graphics hardware.

The **Realistic** setting is dependent on the color and lighting settings that are applied in the model.

When using the Realistic style you can also incorporate Ray Tracing to further enhance model display.

The watercolor and illustration settings provide artistic, hand-painted, and drawn representations of the model.

Figure 1–26

Figure 1–27 shows some examples of the available visual styles.

Shaded

Shaded with Edges

Shaded with Hidden Edges

Wireframe

Wireframe with Hidden Edges

Wireframe with Visible Edges OnlyEdges

Monochrome

Figure 1–27

Object Selection

In the default color scheme, unselected objects are displayed in dark blue, pre-highlighted objects are displayed in white, and selected objects in light blue.

There are several ways to select sketched entities for editing. Consider using any of the following:

- To select an individual object in a sketch, select it using the left mouse button.

- To add additional objects to the selection set, hold <Ctrl> or <Shift> and left-click additional objects.

- Select and drag a boundary box from left to right around objects (as shown in Figure 1–28) to select them. Only objects that are entirely enclosed in the window are selected. This is called the Window Selection technique.

Window: 1st point on left side.

Window: 2nd point on right side.

All enclosed entities are selected.

Figure 1–28

If you drag a boundary box in the wrong direction (i.e., start a window instead of a crossing) select a second point so that the sketched area is empty, and start again.

- Select and drag a boundary box from right to left around objects (as shown in Figure 1–29) to select them. Objects are selected if they are entirely enclosed in the window, or if any part of the object crosses the sketched border. This technique is called the Crossing Selection technique.

Crossing: 1st point on right

Crossing: 2nd point on left side.

All enclosed and crossing entities are selected.

Figure 1–29

- To clear objects you can hold <Ctrl> or <Shift> and individually select entities, or use the window or crossing techniques to select entities. To clear all of the objects, click in a blank space in the graphics window.

Entity Selection

- To quickly select tangent entities in a model, right-click on an entity and select **Select Tangencies**. This option can be used to select both edges and faces, as shown Figure 1–30. As an alternative to using the context menu to access the command, you can also double-click on the entity to quickly select all tangent entities.

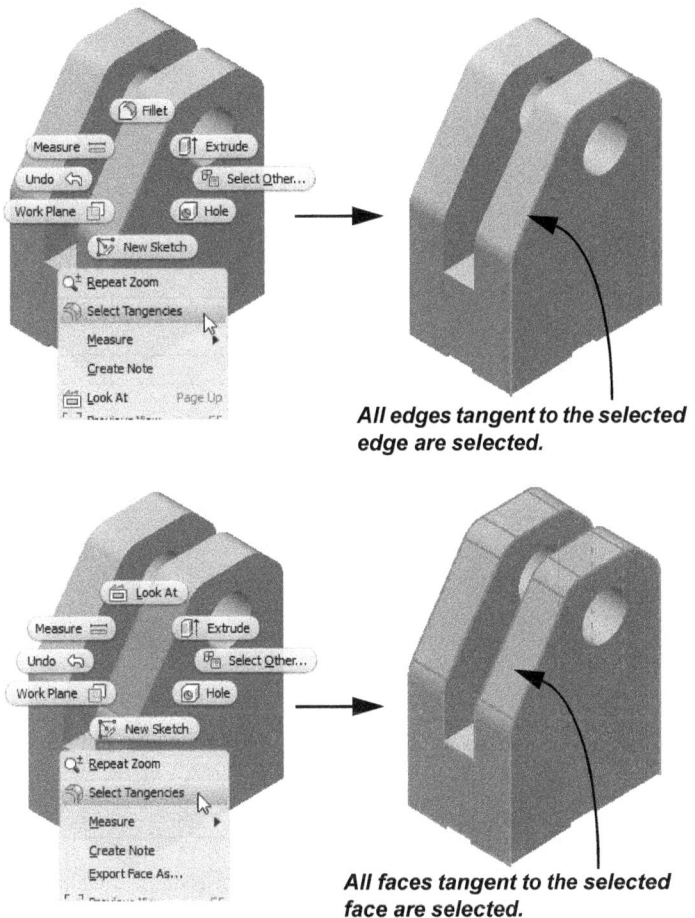

All edges tangent to the selected edge are selected.

All faces tangent to the selected face are selected.

Figure 1–30

- To select hidden features, hover the cursor over an object until a drop-down list displays. The drop-down list displays all of the shown and hidden features based on the current cursor location, as shown in Figure 1–31. Scroll through the drop-down list and select the required entity when it is highlighted.

You can also use the middle mouse button to scroll through the shown and hidden features.

Figure 1–31

Practice 1a | Open and Manipulate a Part

Practice Objectives

- Open part and drawing files and navigate between them using the tabs at the bottom of the graphics window.
- Orient the model using the **Zoom**, **Pan**, **Rotate**, and **Look At** commands available in the ribbon, Navigation bar, and ViewCube.
- Change the visual style of a model for improved visualization.
- Change the visibility status of features in the model.
- Modify dimension values and delete features associated with a model to verify associativity between a part and its drawing file.
- Use the Select Other drop-down list to efficiently select hidden features in a model.

In this practice, you will open and work in part and drawing files to learn the Autodesk Inventor interface. You will also manipulate the orientation of a model, delete, and modify features to learn about associativity of files between environments.

Task 1 - Open a model.

1. If the Autodesk Inventor software is not already open, select **Start>All Programs>Autodesk>Autodesk Inventor 20178>Autodesk Inventor 2018** or double-click on the **Autodesk Inventor 2018** icon on the desktop.

2. Project files identify the folders that contain the required models. Use one of the following methods to open the Projects dialog box to assign the project file:

   - In the *Get Started* tab>Launch panel, click 🗁 (Projects).
   - In the **File** menu, select **Manage>Projects**.

3. Click **Browse**, navigate to *C:\Autodesk Inventor 2018 Intro Practice Files* (or the directory to which you extracted the practice files) and select **Intro to Modeling.ipj**. Click **Open**. The Projects dialog box updates and a checkmark displays next to the new project name, indicating that it is the active project.

4. Click **Done** to return to the Open dialog box.

5. In the *My Home* dashboard, select the *Projects* tab and scroll through the list to verify that the **Intro to Modeling** project has a checkmark adjacent to it to indicate that it is active. Once a project has been added you can use this tab to activate different project files.

*Project files can also be assigned using the New or Open dialog boxes by clicking **Projects**.*

*If the file extensions do not display, open Windows Explorer. Select **Options> Change Folder and search options**, select the View tab, and clear the **Hide extensions for known file types** option.*

6. Use one of the following methods to open a new file:

   - In the *Get Started* tab>Launch panel, click 📂 (Open).

   - In the Quick Access Toolbar, click 📂 (Open).

   - In the **File** menu, select **Open>Open**.

7. Select **Joint.ipt** and click **Open**. The model geometry displays and the Model browser lists all of the features in the model, as shown in Figure 1–32.

Figure 1–32

The model name is displayed in the header of the interface and at the top of the Model browser listing. Both names identify the model as a part (.IPT) file. The model consists of solid geometry and work features that were used as references in creating the solid geometry. In addition to the geometry and work features, there is a Solid Bodies node at the top of the Model browser. This node identifies the solid bodies that are included in the part model.

Task 2 - Zoom in and out on the model using the Zoom command.

1. The *3D Model* tab is the active tab. Select the *View* tab at the top of the ribbon interface. The options in each tab are subdivided into panels to help you quickly find commands. Locate the Navigate panel. It contains all of the commands that you can use to manipulate the location and orientation of the model.

2. In the Navigate panel, click (Zoom), as shown in Figure 1–33. In some situations, similar commands are compressed in a panel and you must expand commands to access them.

Figure 1–33

3. Move the cursor to the graphics window, click and hold the left mouse button, and move the mouse downward to zoom in and upward to zoom out.

4. Click (Zoom) again in the Navigate panel to toggle it off. You can also use the mouse scroll wheel to zoom in or out.

5. As an alternative to the *View* tab>Navigate panel, you can manipulate the model display using the options in the Navigation Bar on the right side of the graphics window. Similar to the Navigate panel, you need to expand the zoom options. Expand $^{Q^{\pm}}$ (Zoom) in the Navigation Bar and click ^{Q} (Zoom All), as shown in Figure 1–34. The **Zoom All** command is now active and the model is refit in the center of the screen.

Figure 1–34

Task 3 - Zoom in on an area of the model and zoom out on the model.

---

1. Expand the zoom commands in the Navigation Bar and select **Zoom Window**.

2. Select a location on the model using the left mouse button to define a corner of the bounding box zoom area.

3. Drag the mouse to draw a box over the area to zoom.

4. Click or release the left mouse button again when the box is the required size. The model zooms in on the sketched bounding box.

5. Expand the zoom commands in the Navigation Bar and **Zoom All** to refit the model in the center of the screen.

6. You can also zoom to a selected feature, face, or edge. Ensure that **Select Faces and Edges** is selected in the Filter drop-down list in the Quick Access Toolbar, as shown in Figure 1–35.

Figure 1–35

To zoom in on a face, you can also select the face first and then click 🔍 *(Zoom Selected).*

7. Expand the zoom commands in the Navigation Bar and select **Zoom Selected** to zoom in on a selected element. Select the face shown in Figure 1–36. The model is zoomed to the selected face.

Select this face

Figure 1–36

8. Expand the zoom commands in the Navigation Bar and select **Zoom All** to refit the model in the center of the screen. Alternatively, double-click on the scroll wheel to zoom all.

When zooming in on an edge, the order in which you select the entity and the command is important.

9. Expand the zoom commands in the Navigation Bar, select **Zoom Selected**, and select anywhere on the edge, as shown in Figure 1–37. When selected in this order, the selection point on the edge is positioned in the center of the screen and the current zoom is maintained.

Select this edge

Figure 1–37

10. Expand the zoom commands in the Navigation Bar and select **Zoom All** or double-click on the scroll wheel to refit the model in the center of the screen.

11. Select anywhere on the same edge and select **Zoom Selected** in the Navigation Bar to zoom to the selected entity. This time, the model zooms to the selected edge.

Task 4 - Zoom in and out on the model using the Navigation Wheel.

As an alternative to using **Zoom** (not **Zoom Selected**), you can also use the Full Navigation Wheel:

1. In the Navigate panel or Navigation Bar, click ⬭ (Full Navigation Wheel).

2. Click and hold the left mouse button on the **Zoom** navigation command.

3. Drag the mouse to change the view as required.

4. Release the mouse button to end the navigation command.

5. Click ⬭ (Full Navigation Wheel) in the Navigate panel or Navigation Bar to close the Full Navigation Wheel. Alternatively, click the **X** icon on the Full Navigation Wheel.

6. Refit the model in the center of the screen.

Task 5 - Pan the model using the Pan command.

1. In the Navigate panel or Navigation Bar, click ✋ (Pan).

2. Click and hold the left mouse button.

3. Move the mouse to drag the model.

4. Refit the model in the center of the screen.

Consider trying the various zooming alternatives so that you can decide which works best for you.

Task 6 - Pan the model using the Navigation Wheel.

You can also pan a model using the middle mouse button or the Full Navigation Wheel:

1. Ensure that ✋ (Pan) is toggled off, and press and hold the middle mouse button to drag the model.

2. In the Navigate panel, click ⬤ (Full Navigation Wheel) to enable the Full Navigation Wheel. Click and hold the left mouse button on the **Pan** navigation command. Drag the mouse to pan the view as required.

3. Click ⬤ (Full Navigation Wheel) again to close the Full Navigation Wheel.

Task 7 - Rotate the model using the Orbit command.

*While you are still in the orbit circle you can also disable the **Orbit** command by moving the cursor away from the model until 🔖← displays and then clicking in the graphics window.*

To change the center of the rotation, click inside or outside the circle to set the new center.

1. In the Navigate panel or Navigation Bar, click ⊕ (Orbit). A circle displays on the screen. The appearance of the cursor changes depending on its location relative to the circle.

2. Move the cursor inside the circle. The cursor appearance changes to ⬦.

3. Click and hold the left mouse button and rotate the model freely in any direction.

4. Release the mouse button and move the cursor outside the circle. The cursor appearance changes to ↺.

5. Click and hold the left mouse button to rotate about an axis through the center of the circle symbol (normal to the screen).

6. Move the cursor to the line at the top of the circle. The cursor appearance changes to ◖.

7. Click and hold the left mouse button and rotate the model about the horizontal axis.

8. Move the cursor to the line at the right or left side of the circle. The cursor appearance changes to ⬯.

9. Click and hold the left mouse button and rotate the model about the vertical axis.

10. Move the cursor over the ViewCube and click ⌂ in the top-left corner of the ViewCube (as shown in Figure 1–38), to orient the model into its Isometric Home view (3D). Alternatively, you can right-click and select **Home View** to orient the model in the same way. Note that ⌕ (Zoom All) only refits the model in the center of the screen and maintains the same orientation.

Figure 1–38

Task 8 - Rotate the model using the ViewCube, keyboard, or Navigation Wheel.

As an alternative to using ⟳ (Orbit), you can use the ViewCube, keyboard, or Full Navigation Wheel to rotate a model:

1. Ensure that ⟳ (Orbit) is toggled off, click and hold the left mouse button anywhere on the ViewCube, and drag the mouse. Move the mouse away from the ViewCube to stop rotating.

2. Press and hold <F4>. By keeping <F4> depressed, the cursor behaves as it did when ⟳ (Orbit) was active. Release <F4> to stop rotating.

3. Hold <Shift> and the middle mouse button and drag to rotate the model. Release <Shift> to stop rotating.

4. In the Navigate panel, click ⊕ (Full Navigation Wheel) to enable the Full Navigation Wheel. Click and hold the left mouse button on the **Orbit** navigation command. Drag the mouse to rotate the view as required.

5. Click ⊕ (Full Navigation Wheel) again to close the Full Navigation Wheel. The selection of the method to use to rotate the model is based on user preference.

6. Click 🏠 in the ViewCube to orient the model into its Isometric Home view, or right-click and select **Home View**.

7. Click the **X** icon in the top right corner of the Navigation Bar to toggle off its display.

8. In the *View* tab>Windows panel, expand User Interface. Select the box next to **Navigation Bar** to return it to the display. The remaining options enable you to control the display of the Model browser (Model), ViewCube, Status Bar, Document Tabs, and other interface tools.

Task 9 - Orient the model.

1. In the Navigate panel or Navigation Bar, click 🔲 (Look At) to orient a model face parallel to the screen. Select the face as shown in Figure 1–39. The model orients into a 2D orientation.

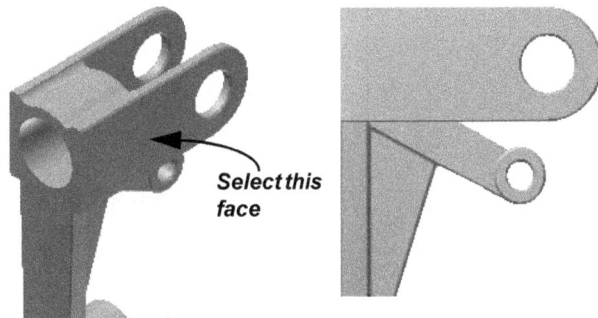

Select this face

Figure 1–39

2. Note that the ViewCube has reoriented and **RIGHT** is displayed. Click 🏠 to orient the model to its Isometric Home view.

The 🔲 (Look At) command can help to orient faces that are not parallel with the Origin Planes. However, the ViewCube is a more efficient option for orienting into views that are parallel with the origin work planes.

3. Select the **RIGHT** face in the ViewCube as shown in Figure 1–40. The model orients as it did previously with one less step.

Select the RIGHT surface

Figure 1–40

4. With the model still in a 2D orientation, move the mouse back over the ViewCube. It displays as shown in Figure 1–41. Select either of the rotating arrows to rotate the model while remaining in the RIGHT view.

Figure 1–41

5. Click any of the four triangular icons in the ViewCube to change to a different orientation.

6. Practice orienting the model into different orientations. You can also select edges of the ViewCube for orienting.

7. Click 🏠 to orient the model into its Isometric Home view.

Task 10 - Manipulate the visual style of the model.

The ability of a software to spin a shaded model and use all of the styles depends on the quality of its graphics hardware.

1. In the *View* tab>Appearance panel, expand Visual Style as shown in Figure 1–42. Note that the model display is set to ⌖ (Shaded) for this model.

*The default Visual Style for models that are started with a default template is **Shaded with Edges**.*

Figure 1–42

2. Click ⌖ (Shaded with Hidden Edges) to set the view display so that it displays hidden edges while shaded.

3. Click ❯ next to **Origin** to expand it in the Model browser.

Planes, axes, center points, and coordinate systems are features that exist in the model by default.

4. Right-click on the YZ plane in the Model browser and select **Visibility**, as shown in Figure 1–43. The YZ plane displays.

Figure 1–43

To temporarily display an origin object, hover the cursor over the feature name.

5. Hold <Ctrl> and select the XZ plane and Y-Axis. Right-click and select **Visibility** to display both the XZ plane and Y-Axis in the model.

6. Return the model to the (Shaded) display. The model displays as shown in Figure 1–44.

Figure 1–44

7. Toggle off the visibility for the three origin objects by selecting them all again and disabling the **Visibility** option. Press and hold <Ctrl> while selecting the option to select all of the objects as one selection set.

Task 11 - Open a drawing of the model.

1. Use one of the following methods to open **Joint.idw**. The header in the graphics window displays the name of the drawing.

   - In the *Get Started* tab>Launch panel, click 📂 (Open).

   - Click 📂 (Open) in the Quick Access Toolbar at the top of the window.

   - In the **File** menu, select **Open>Open**.

2. Note that there are now two tabs along the bottom of the graphics window. The first tab is the model and the second (currently active tab) is the drawing of that model.

3. Select the *Joint.ipt* tab to activate it.

Task 12 - Edit feature dimensions on the model.

To select features directly on the model you must have the selection filter in the Quick Access Toolbar set to 🏠 (Select Features).

1. Right-click on **Fillet9** in the Model browser and select **Show Dimensions**.

2. Double-click on the 0.010 dimension in the graphics window.

3. Enter **0.05** as the new value, as shown in Figure 1–45, and press <Enter>.

Figure 1–45

(Local Update) *recalculates the model geometry. The length of update time depends on the complexity of the change and the model.*

4. In the Quick Access Toolbar, click (Local Update). The radius of the fillet updates.

5. Double-click on **Hole1** in the Model browser or graphics window to open the dialog box and mini-toolbar that was used to create the hole.

6. Change the 0.25 diameter to **0.15** in either the feature's dialog box or the mini-toolbar. Click **OK** in the dialog box or click in the mini-toolbar to complete the feature change. The model displays as shown in Figure 1–46.

Change the diameter of the hole to 0.15.

Figure 1–46

In the Hole diameter example, you edited the feature by opening the Feature dialog box. Alternatively, you can right-click on the feature and select **Show Dimension**. This is faster for editing multiple dimension values because the model is not updated until you explicitly click (Local Update). Using the Feature Creation dialog box, the model is updated when you click **OK**. Therefore, each is updated individually. If you are making a lot of changes, the update can be more time-consuming.

7. Select the *Joint.idw* tab to activate the drawing. Note how the sizes of the fillet and hole update to reflect the changes that were made in the model.

Task 13 - Delete a feature in the model.

1. Select the *Joint.ipt* tab to activate it.

To select features directly on the model you must have the selection filter in the Quick Access Toolbar set to ⬚ (Select Features).

2. In the Model browser, select **Extrusion11**. Right-click and select **Delete**. The Delete Features dialog box opens as shown in Figure 1–47. It prompts you to determine whether the sketch that was used to create Extrusion11 should also be deleted. You might want to delete it or you might want to retain it for use in another feature.

Delete this Extrusion

Figure 1–47

3. Click **OK** to confirm the deletion of the sketches that were created as part of the extrusion (slot cut). To retain the sketch, clear the **consumed sketches and features** option.

4. Select the *Joint.idw* tab to activate the drawing. Note that the extrusion has been removed from all of the views in the drawing. If it does not update, click ⬚ (Local Update).

Task 14 - Edit a hole diameter in the drawing.

---

1. Right-click on the Ø.15 diameter dimension as shown in Figure 1–48 and select **Edit Model Dimension**.

Edit this dimension value

Figure 1–48

---

2. Enter **0.25** as the new dimension value and press <Enter>. The size of the hole updates in the drawing.

3. Activate the window containing the part to verify that the model has changed.

Task 15 - Use the Select Other tool to select hidden features in the model.

---

1. In the part model, select the *View* tab, change the visual style to **Shaded with Hidden Edges**.

2. Hover the cursor over the extruded cut as shown in Figure 1–49. In this orientation you cannot directly select the cut geometry.

— *Hover the cursor over the extruded cut that was created on the back of the model.*

Figure 1–49

3. A drop-down list displays. Expand it as shown in Figure 1–50, and hover the cursor over each of the selections. When **Extrusion10** highlights, click to select it. The cut is highlighted in the Model browser.

As an alternative to expanding the down-drop list to review the other options, use the middle mouse to scroll through the options.

Figure 1–50

4. Right-click and select **Suppress Features**. Note that the Model browser displays **Extrusion10** in gray and is crossed out. Alternatively, you can select **Extrusion10** in the Model browser to suppress it. The previous method is more effective when you have a model with a large number of the features, and it is difficult to identify the features in the Model browser using only names.

5. Activate the window containing the drawing to verify that the drawing has changed.

6. In the Quick Access Toolbar, click 🔲 to save the drawing. The Save dialog box opens indicating that changes were made to both the Model and the drawing. Click **OK** to save both files.

7. Close both the drawing and part file by clicking **X** in the top right corner of the graphics window for both of the files. Alternatively, you can click **X** on the file's tab at the bottom of the graphics window or from the **File** menu.

Chapter Review Questions

1. After editing the dimensions of a part model, you must open all drawings referencing that part to make the same dimension changes.

   a. True

   b. False

2. Match the numbers shown in Figure 1–51 with the interface components listed below.

Figure 1–51

   a. Navigation Bar

   b. Model Browser

   c. Status Bar

   d. Quick Access Toolbar

   e. Ribbon Panel

   f. Graphics Window

   g. ViewCube

3. Which of the following are valid filename extensions for Autodesk Inventor files? (Select all that apply.)

   a. .IPT

   b. .IDW

   c. .IAM

   d. .INV

4. Clicking [icon] enables you to automatically reorient the display of the model to its top view.

   a. True

   b. False

5. Which mouse button do you click and hold to pan the model without activating the **Pan** command?

   a. Left

   b. Middle

   c. Right

6. Which combination of items do you select to quickly orient a model face parallel to the screen without spinning? (Select all that apply.)

   a. A surface and [icon].

   b. A planar surface and [icon].

   c. A surface and [icon].

   d. A planar surface and [icon].

   e. A face on the ViewCube.

7. You can open multiple windows in one session.

   a. True

   b. False

8. What can you control by right-clicking on the ribbon and selecting **Ribbon Appearance**, as shown in Figure 1–52?

Figure 1–52

a. Text descriptions next to buttons in the panel.

b. Menus at the top of the interface.

c. Command prompts at the cursor.

d. Pop-up tooltips on buttons.

9. What is the purpose of the menu shown in Figure 1–53?

Figure 1–53

a. To switch back to a previous view or ahead to a current view.

b. To cycle through different objects for selection.

c. To pan the view left or right.

d. To zoom in or out on the selected object.

Command Summary

Button	Command	Location
	Full Navigation Wheel	• **Ribbon:** *View* tab>Navigate panel • **Navigation Bar**
	Help	• **Quick Access Toolbar** • **Keyboard:** < F1>
	Home View	• **Ribbon:** *View* tab>Navigate panel • **ViewCube** • **Context Menu:** In the graphics window • **Keyboard:** <F6>
	Look At	• **Ribbon:** *View* tab>Navigate panel • **Navigation Bar** • **ViewCube**
	Open	• **Ribbon:** *Get Started* tab>Launch panel • **Quick Access Toolbar** • **File Menu** • **My Home:** Recently Used
	Orbit (rotate)	• **Ribbon:** *View* tab>Navigate panel • **Navigation Bar** • **ViewCube**
	Pan	• **Ribbon:** *View* tab>Navigate panel • **Navigation Bar**
Projects...	**Projects**	• **Ribbon:** *Get Started* tab>Launch panel • **Dialog Box:** Open and New • **My Home:** Projects
	Save	• **Quick Access Toolbar** • **File Menu**
	Visual Style	• **Ribbon:** *View* tab>Appearance panel
	Zoom	• **Ribbon:** *View* tab>Navigate panel • **Navigation Bar** • **Full Navigation Wheel**
	Zoom All	• **Ribbon:** *View* tab>Navigate panel • **Navigation Bar**
	Zoom Selected	• **Ribbon:** *View* tab>Navigate panel • **Navigation Bar**
	Zoom Window	• **Ribbon:** *View* tab>Navigate panel • **Navigation Bar**

Creating the Base Feature

A base feature is the first solid feature that you create in an Autodesk® Inventor® part file. It forms the foundation on which other features are added to the model. The general workflow for creating a base feature is to create a sketch and then use the feature creation controls to create solid geometry.

Learning Objectives in this Chapter

- Create a new part model using a predefined template.
- Create a sketch by appropriately selecting a sketch plane.
- Project references onto a sketch plane for use in locating entities.
- Create, dimension, and constrain 2D entities in a sketch.
- Create a 3D solid base feature.
- Make changes to a sketched feature.

2.1 Creating a New Part File

To create a new part file, you must select a template. Templates enable you to create new parts with standardized configurations and settings. Template files can contain features and settings, such as units, grid settings, origin planes, work features, sketches, geometry, parameters, and properties.

Using the Default Template

The *My Home* dashboard enables you to easily create part, assembly, drawing, and presentation files using default templates. The *My Home* dashboard is shown in Figure 2–1.

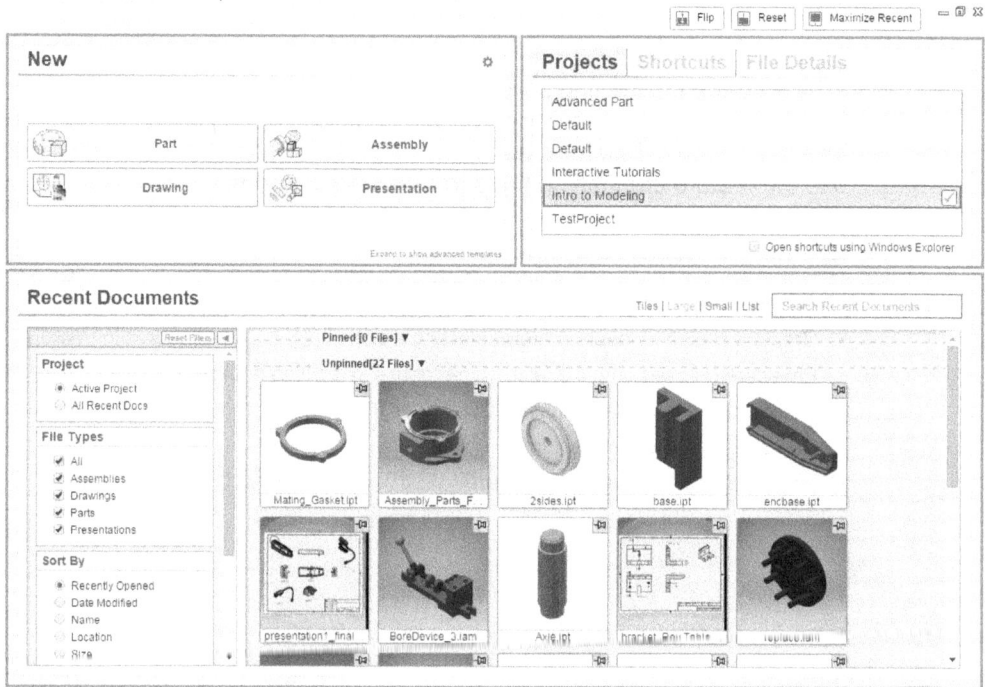

Figure 2–1

To create a new part using the default template, click **Part** in the *New* category in the *My Home* dashboard. A new part file is created and the *3D Model* tab is active.

How To: Set the Default Template

1. In the *My Home* dashboard, in the *New* area, click
   ⚙ (Configure Default Templates).
2. Set the required measurement types in the Configure Default Template dialog box to set the default template, as shown in Figure 2–2.

Figure 2–2

3. Click **OK** to assign the template.

Selecting a Template

To select a template for use as the basis for a new file you can use the *My Home* dashboard or the Create New File dialog box.

How To: Create a New File using the My Home Dashboard

1. In the *New* area, expand the Advanced options.
2. Navigate to the required template in the directory (as shown in Figure 2–3).
3. Double-click on the template name to create the new file.

New

Advanced Templates(C:\Users\Public\Documents\Autodesk\Inventor 2018\Templates\)

- Sheet Metal (mm).ipt
- Standard (DIN).iam
- Standard (DIN).ipn
- Standard (DIN).ipt
- Standard (mm).iam
- Standard (mm).ipn
- Standard (mm).ipt
- Weldment (ANSI - mm).iam
- Weldment (BSI).iam

No Template/Folder Selected.

Figure 2–3

How To: Create a New File using the Create New File Dialog Box

*You can save a custom template using **Save Copy as Template** in the **File** menu.*

1. Use one of the following techniques to open the Create New File dialog box:

    - In the *Get Started* tab>Launch panel, click ⬜ (New).
    - Click ⬜ (New) in the Quick Access Toolbar at the top of the window.
    - In the **File** menu, select **New**.

    The Create New File dialog box opens as shown in Figure 2–4.

2. Select a template folder in the left column to select the required template units.
3. Select a specific template in one of the sections in the right column.
4. Click **Create** to create the new file.

Select the template units in this area of the dialog box.

Select the template name in this area of the dialog box.

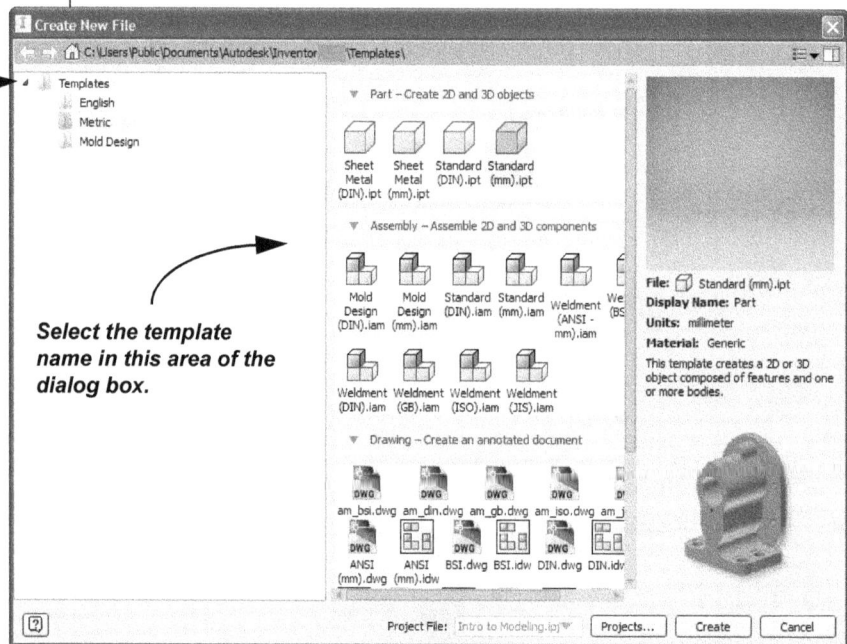

Figure 2–4

Origin Features

Origin Planes are non-solid features that only exist in space. They do not have a thickness or mass.

The default part templates contain the following Origin features:

- Three orthogonal planes: YZ Plane, XZ Plane, and XY Plane.

- Three axes: X Axis, Y Axis, and Z Axis.

- A Center Point at the default (0,0,0) point.

These Origin features can never be moved or deleted. Figure 2–5 shows the default Origin features.

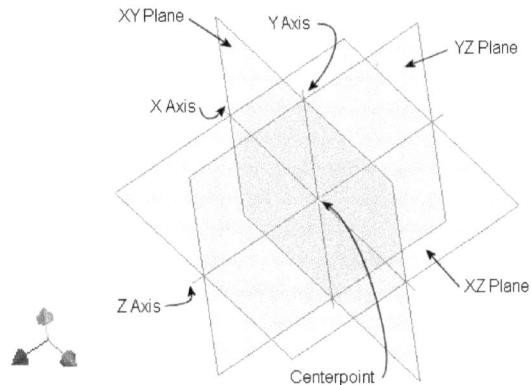

Figure 2–5

When you create a new part, the Origin features are not displayed. They can be displayed in any of the following ways:

- To toggle on origin feature visibility, expand the **Origin** node in the Model browser, right-click on the feature (e.g., YZ plane), and select **Visibility**.

- To temporarily display an Origin feature, hover the cursor over the feature in the Model browser to display it in the graphics window.

2.2 Sketched Base Features

The base feature is the first solid feature in a new part. It is
created by locating new geometry using references to the Origin
features. The base feature is often a solid extrusion with a
sketched cross-section. This section discusses the workflow that
creates and modifies a sketched base feature.

An example of a base feature is shown in Figure 2–6.

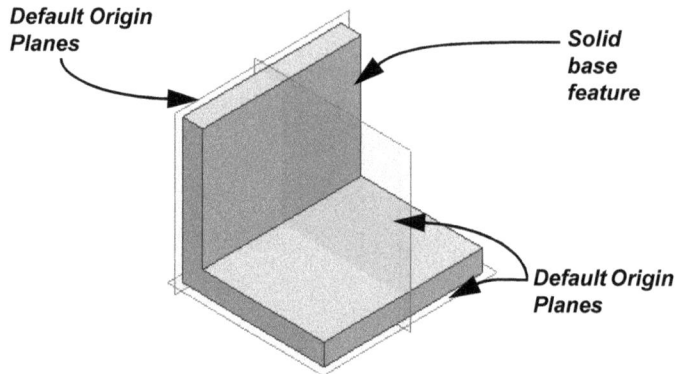

Figure 2–6

General Steps

Use the following general steps to create a sketched base
feature:

1. Start the creation of the sketch.
2. Define the sketch plane.
3. Project reference entities, if required.
4. Create a 2D sketch of the base feature.
5. Select the base feature type.
6. Define the depth and direction.
7. Complete the feature.

Step 1 - Start the creation of the sketch.

To create a sketched base feature, you must start with a sketch.
A sketch is a 2D representation of the section that is used to
create the solid geometry in the model. To start the creation of a
sketch in the model, use one of the following methods:

• In the *3D Model* tab>Sketch panel, click ⬚ (Start 2D
  Sketch).

• Right-click in the graphics window and select **New Sketch**.

Step 2 - Define the sketch plane.

Before sketching you must define the 2D plane on which to sketch the entities. During base feature creation, any one of the default origin planes (YZ, XZ, and XY) can be selected. Once the new sketch command has been initiated, the origin planes are temporarily displayed in the graphics window and can be selected, as shown in Figure 2–7. You can hover the cursor over any of the displayed planes to display the plane's name. Select any of the planes to define the plane on which the sketch is going to be created.

As you create geometry in your models, refer to the Origin indicator

(⋅⁺⋅) in the bottom left corner of the graphics window to ensure that you understand the X-, Y-, and Z-orientations when selecting origin planes.

Alternatively, in the Model browser, next to the Origin, click ❯ to expand it and select any of the origin planes, as shown in Figure 2–7.

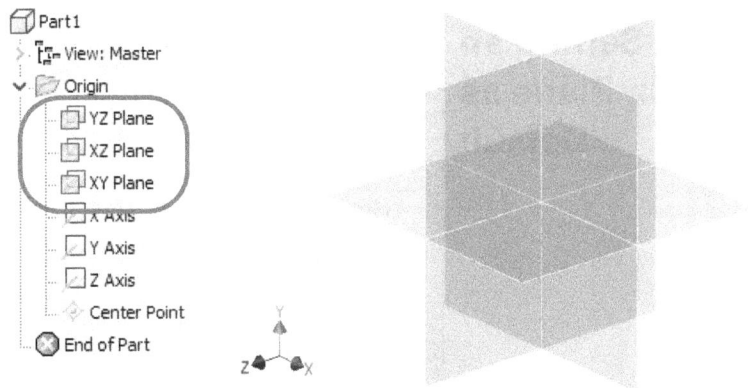

Figure 2–7

Once the sketch plane has been selected, it is reoriented parallel to the screen. The origin (0,0,0) of the sketch is positioned at the center of the graphics window. You are now in the Sketch environment and the *Sketch* tab is active.

Hint: Creating the Sketch

As an alternative to initiating a new sketch command and then selecting the sketch plane, you can select the sketch plane first and then initiate the command, using any of the following methods:

- Right-click on the origin plane name in the Model browser and select **New Sketch**.

- Select the origin plane name in the Model browser, and in the *3D Model* tab>Sketch panel, click (Start 2D Sketch).

- Select the origin plane name in the Model browser and click (Create Sketch) in the graphics window.

Setting an Origin Plane as Default

When you consistently create base features on the same Origin plane, you can set an option so that when a new part is created you are immediately placed in the Sketch environment, ready to sketch on a specified Origin plane.

How To: Set an Application Option

1. In the *Tools* tab>Options panel, select **Application Options**.
2. In the Application Options dialog box, in the *Part* tab, select a sketch plane in the *Sketch on new part creation* area.
3. Click **OK**. All of the new parts are launched and sketch creation is started on the specified plane.

Step 3 - Project reference entities, if required.

While a part can be created without referencing Origin features, using them is strongly recommended to create a robust model that is easy to modify.

Sketched geometry should be located with respect to existing reference entities. Reference entities provide a reference for dimensioning and constraining sketched entities so that their location is fully defined in the model.

For a base feature, the Origin features that exist in the template can be used. By default, the Origin Center Point is projected onto the sketch plane. You must explicitly project any of the origin planes (or axes) as further references.

How To: Project a Reference Entity

As you progress in a design, previously sketched or solid entities can also be selected and projected as reference entities for new sketches.

1. In the Create panel, click ☐ (Project Geometry) or right-click and select **Project Geometry**.
2. Select any of the origin planes or axes to be projected onto the sketch plane. The references are represented as yellow lines on the sketch plane.
3. Right-click and select **OK** to complete the reference selection or press <Esc> to cancel the command.

Step 4 - Create a 2D sketch of the base feature.

The Sketch tab contains options for sketching and editing the 2D geometry for a feature.

Once the reference entities have been projected, you can begin to create the 2D sketched entities using the remaining options in the *Sketch* tab. The *Sketch* tab is shown in Figure 2–8.

— **Sketch tab**

Figure 2–8

Grid and Axis Display

By default, grid lines are not displayed in a sketch. You can control the display of the grid lines in the *Sketch* tab in the Application Options dialog box (*Tools* tab>Options panel, click

☐ (Application Options)). The *Display* area in the *Sketch* tab displays as shown in Figure 2–9. You can also toggle the coordinate system indicator on and off.

The Application options are global and affect all files that you open. For individual files, snap and grid spacing can be set in Document Settings.

Display
- ☐ Grid lines
- ☑ Minor grid lines
- ☑ Axes
- ☐ Coordinate system indicator

Figure 2–9

You can also toggle on the **Snap to grid** option on the *Sketch* tab, which causes the cursor to move in increments.

Sketch Entities

To create a solid base feature, the sketched entities must form a closed section. If the sketch's section is not closed, you can only create surface geometry. The available sketch entities are all located on the *Sketch* tab>Create panel. Only a sub-set of the available entity types are covered in this section. Additional types are covered later in the student guide.

Line

In the Create panel, click ✏ (Line), or right-click and select **Create Line**, to sketch a geometry line. Move the crosshairs to the start point of the line and click the left mouse button (do not press and drag). Move the crosshairs to the end point and click the left mouse button to locate the line. Continue selecting points to add more lines. To finish sketching, use any one of the following:

- Press <Esc>.

- Right-click and select **OK**.

- Press <Enter>. (The **Create** Line command remains active.)

- Activate a new sketcher tool.

Line Close

After two or more line segments have been drawn consecutively, you can right-click and select **Close** to automatically add a final line segment between the first and last points entered.

*To delete a sketch entity, select the entity and press <Delete>. You can also right-click on the entity and select **Delete**.*

Rectangle

In the Create panel, click ▭ (Rectangle) or right-click and select **Two Point Rectangle** to sketch a rectangle. Move the crosshairs to the point at which the rectangle begins and click the left mouse button. Move the crosshairs to the point at which the rectangle ends and click the left mouse button. Use any of the methods listed above to finish sketching.

To undo or redo sketching actions, click

⤺ *and* ⤻ *in the Quick Access Toolbar, respectively. The **Undo** command is also available in the marking menu.*

Circle

In the Create panel, click ⊘ (Circle) or right-click and select **Center Point Circle** to sketch a circle. Select the center point and a point on the outer extent of the circle.

Slot

*The marking menu does not contain a **Slot** option.*

In the Create panel, expand Rectangle, and click 🖾 (Slot Center to Center) to sketch a slot. Move the crosshairs to the start point of the arc-center on one end of the slot and click the left mouse button. Move the crosshairs to locate the arc-center on the other end of the slot and click the left mouse button to locate the center-line. Move the cursor away from the center-line to the required size of the slot and click the left mouse button. Other **Slot** options are available in the drop-down list. The selections required to create each type vary slightly. Refer to the Status Bar for guidance with entity placement.

Sketching Revolved Sections

Only half of the cross-section of a revolved feature needs to be sketched. It is then revolved about the axis of revolution at a specified angle. The sketch of a revolved feature must:

- Contain a straight entity to define the axis of revolution if an existing axis in the model cannot be used (i.e., lines, projected edges, projected work planes, and construction lines).

- Have all entities on one side of the axis of revolution.

Examples of a sketch and its revolved features are as follows:

Sketch	Revolve Geometry	Description
		In this sketch, entities are revolved about the line that is part of the sketch.
		In this sketch, the center line is offset from the section. The result is a hole in the revolve.
	Invalid	This is a sketch with the center line intersecting the section. A Revolve feature cannot have sketched geometry on both sides of the axis of rotation because the geometry would overlap.

Dynamic Input & Dimensioning for Sketching

When creating a **Line**, **Rectangle**, **Circle**, **Arc**, or **Slot** entity, a dynamic input line displays when you move the cursor in the graphics window. This line provides you with a heads-up display of the input fields. These fields enable you to enter explicit values for the start location of an entity, values to extend the entity, and angular values to position the entity, as shown in Figure 2–10. The field highlighted in blue is the active value, indicating that you can enter a value in the field.

X -37.788 mm   Y 21.321 mm

14.745 mm

12.15 deg

4.304 mm

10.410 mm

Figure 2–10

When sketching entities using dynamic input, the dimensions default to using polar coordinates while measuring relative. To change the coordinate type, right-click and expand the Coordinate Type options.

After entering a value in a dynamic input field, press <Tab> to toggle to the next field and enter its value. Only press <Enter> to finalize the entity after all of the values have been entered. A dimension is automatically created when a dynamic input field is used to define a value. Note that any entities located with the cursor must be explicitly dimensioned.

To disable dynamic input using the heads-up display, clear the **Enable Heads-Up Display (HUD)** option in the *Sketch* tab in the Application Options dialog box (*Tools* tab>Options panel, click

(Application Options)).

> **Hint: Preventing Dimension Creation on Dynamic Input**
>
> To disable the automatic creation of dimensions when entities are created using the heads-up display, open the Constraints Settings dialog box (in the Sketch panel>Constraints panel, and
>
> click (Constraint Settings)) and clear the **Create dimensions from input values** option.

Dimensioning

Dimensions define the size and locations of the objects in the sketch.

A sketch does not need to be dimensioned or constrained to create 3D geometry. However, it is recommended to verify the correct design intent in your model.

How To: Create a Dimension

1. In the Constrain panel, click (Dimension) or right-click and select **General Dimension**.
2. Select the entity or entities with your left mouse button.
3. Move the cursor to the dimension's placement location and press the left mouse button to place the dimension.

The number of dimensions required to fully constrain a sketch is displayed in a field in the bottom right corner of the main window.

The dimension type created depends on whether you select an entity or its endpoints. For example, selecting two non-parallel lines creates an angular dimension, while selecting two end points creates a linear dimension. A constrained sketch is shown in Figure 2–11.

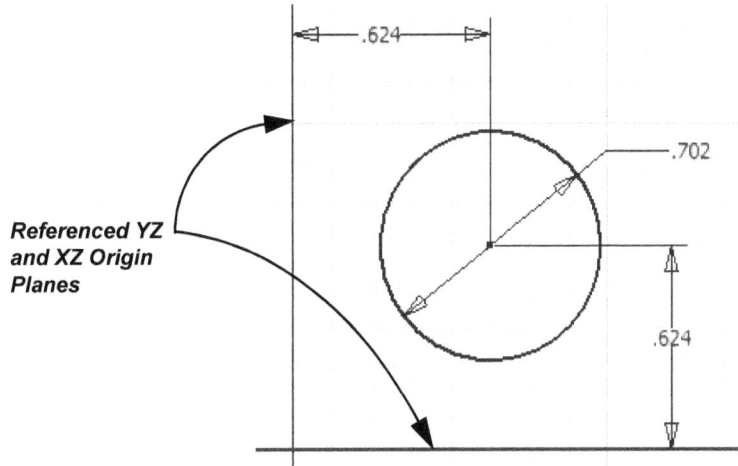

Referenced YZ and XZ Origin Planes

.624

.702

.624

Figure 2–11

When dimensioning the cross-section of a revolved feature, you can create a diameter dimension. To dimension, select the center of the revolved cross-section, then select the geometry, right-click and select **Linear Diameter**, and place the dimension, as shown in Figure 2–12.

This type of dimensioning scheme can also be used to dimension symmetrical entities.

Linear Diameter
Edit Dimension
Previous View   F5
Home View   F6
How To...

Center of section

$\emptyset d11$

$\emptyset d12$

Figure 2–12

The first General dimension (not automatic) that is added to a sketch and then subsequently modified, determines the sketch's scale. All of the other sketch entities scale to reflect the value used. As soon as a second dimension is added, the automatic scaling no longer functions.

Modifying Dimensions

Sketch dimensions control the size of the geometry and therefore are parametric.

By default, a dimension is immediately modifiable as soon as it is placed in the sketch. To disable this functionality so that you can first place all of the dimensions and then modify them later, right-click in the graphics window and clear the **Edit Dimension** option before placing the dimension.

How To: Edit a Value of a Dimension

1. Double-click on the dimension. If the **Dimension** command is already active only a single-click is required.
2. Enter a new value in the Edit Dimension dialog box.
3. Click ☑ or press <Enter>.

Deleting Dimensions

To delete a dimension, select the dimension, right-click, and select **Delete** or press <Delete>.

Automatic Dimensions

The **Automatic Dimensions and Constraints** command automatically assigns dimensions. However, it might not create them to suit your design intent.

In the Constrain panel, click ⊢ (Automatic Dimensions and Constraints) to place all of the dimensions and/or constraints required to fully constrain the sketch. This command dimensions to existing sketched or projected geometry. The Auto Dimension dialog box is shown in Figure 2–13.

⊢ (Automatic Dimensions and Constraints) is useful for determining how many additional dimensions and constraints are required.

Figure 2–13

Consider using **Remove** in the Auto Dimension dialog box to quickly remove dimensions and constraints from selected objects.

The options in the Auto Dimension dialog box are described as follows:

Curves	Enables you to select the objects to be dimensioned.
Dimensions Required	Lists the number of dimensions and constraints required to fully dimension the sketch.
Dimensions	Enables you to apply dimensions to the selected objects.
Constraints	Enables you to apply constraints to the selected objects.

Driven Dimensions

An error message opens when you try to add a dimension that over-constrains a sketch. You can cancel the command or place a driven dimension. A driven dimension is a dimension that changes as the result of a change to another dimension. The dimension shown in Figure 2–14 is a driven dimension and acts as a reference. A driven dimension cannot be modified, but updates if changes are made.

Figure 2–14

Constraining

Constraints are relationships between:

* Two entities,

* An entity and the coordinate system, or

* An entity and projected reference entities.

Constraints can be implied in a sketch or they can be explicitly assigned.

By default, the software automatically infers Horizontal, Vertical, Parallel, and Perpendicular constraints as entities are sketched. Constraint indicators are displayed as you sketch an entity that is horizontal/vertical, or parallel/perpendicular with a reference. Once located, the constraint is applied.

A sketch does not need to be dimensioned or constrained to create 3D geometry. However, it is recommended that you ensure the correct design intent.

> **Hint: Changing the Inferred Constraint Reference**
>
> The software automatically determines which existing reference and inferred constraint type is assigned to an entity as it is being sketched. If the inferred constraint is not as required, hover the cursor over a different entity in the sketch to infer a different constraint type and then place the entity.

*The **Show Constraints** and **Show All Constraints** settings remain active while sketching, or until they are disabled.*

- To view constraints that are assigned, in the Constrain panel, click ⬚ (Show Constraints) and select the entities to display their constraint indicators, as shown in Figure 2–15.

- Alternatively, you can click ⬚ (Show All Constraints) in the Status Bar to toggle the display of the constraint indicators on and off. You can select the entities individually or by drawing a bounding box around them.

Figure 2–15

The sketched geometry colors depend on the assigned Color scheme, which is set in the Colors tab in the Application Options dialog box.

The default sketched geometry colors (based on the default color scheme) are described as follows:

Green	Sketched geometry that is unconstrained.
Dark Blue	Sketched geometry that is fully constrained and dimensioned.
White	Sketched geometry (e.g., lines) is white when you hover the cursor over it.
Light Blue	Sketched geometry (e.g., lines) is light blue when selected.
Yellow	Projected geometry or origin features.

Constraints are automatically assumed and created as you sketch. However, you can also apply your own constraints to further capture your design intent. Assigning constraints is discussed later in this student guide.

Once the sketch is fully constrained, in the Exit panel, click ✔ (Finish Sketch) or right-click and select **Finish 2D Sketch.** To ensure that the sketch is fully constrained, review its status in the lower right corner of the graphics window, as shown in Figure 2–16.

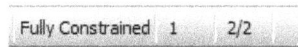

Fully Constrained   1   2/2

Figure 2–16

Step 5 - Select the base feature type.

*A solid base feature cannot be created without a sketched section. If initiated without a sketch, a dialog box opens indicating that you need to create a 2D sketch to proceed. Click **Create 2D Sketch** to start a new sketch.*

Once the sketch has been drawn and constrained, the next step in creating a 3D object is to add thickness or depth to the sketch.

The simplest way to add depth is to extrude the sketch so that it is perpendicular to the sketch plane. However, there are other feature form types that can be used to create the solid base feature. The available feature forms are described as follows:

Form	2D Cross-Section	3D Base Feature
Extrude		
Revolve		
Loft		
Sweep		

Use any of the following methods to create a solid base feature extruded from a sketch:

- In the *3D Model* tab>Create panel, click ⬚ (Extrude).

- Right-click in the graphics window and select **Extrude**.

- In the Model browser, left-click on the Sketch name and click ⬚ in the graphics window's Heads-up display.

- Press <E>.

The option to create a Revolve feature is found in the same locations as those listed above, or by pressing <R>.

*By default, the display of the Mini-Toolbar is toggled off. To display it, in the View tab, expand **User Interface** and enable the **Mini-Toolbar** option. To collapse a dialog box, click the up arrow at the bottom of the dialog box.*

Once a feature command is selected (i.e., Extrude or Revolve), its dialog box and a mini-toolbar open, as shown in Figure 2–17. All of the settings available in the dialog box are also available in the mini-toolbar. The use of one over the other is personal preference. If a single sketch exists in the model, it is automatically selected as the profile for the feature. In the case of an Extrude, a preview of the model is displayed. If multiple sketches exist, you need to select the profile and in the case of a revolve feature the axis of revolution must be selected before a preview is displayed.

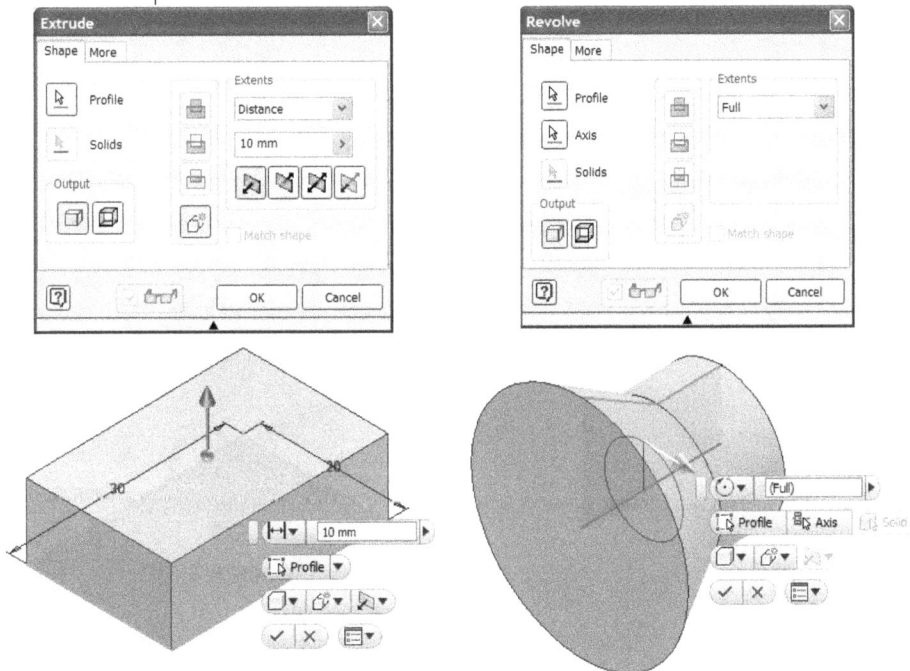

Figure 2–17

Step 6 - Define the depth and direction.

Depth

There are several options for defining the depth. Many of these options enable you to reference other geometry to control depth. For an extruded base feature, the depth is commonly defined with a dimension value that can be easily modified. The Extrude dialog box and the mini-toolbar both contain an entry field to enter a value.

Direction

Direction icons (⊠, ⊠, ⊠, and ⊠) set the direction the sketch is to extrude/revolve from the sketch plane or how it extrudes on both sides of the sketch plane. Extrude directions are shown in Figure 2–18. You can select the direction using the icons in the dialog box or select an option in the drop-down list in the mini-toolbar.

Figure 2–18

Step 7 - Complete the feature.

Once the values for the depth and direction have been defined, you can complete the feature using any of the following methods:

- In the mini-toolbar, click .

- Right-click in the graphics window and click **OK**.

- In the Extrude dialog box, click **OK**.

- Press <Enter>.

The Model browser updates to list the feature. It displays in the Model browser below the default Origin features.

2.3 Editing Sketched Features

To make modifications to a feature, right-click on the feature in the Model browser and select the required option, as shown in Figure 2–19.

You can rename the default feature by selecting the feature in the Model browser twice (do not double-click) and entering a new name. Assigning custom names to features can help you to locate and identify features in the Model browser.

Figure 2–19

Alternatively, you can click ⬜ (Edit Feature) or ⬜ (Edit Sketch) in the graphics window when the feature is selected. The feature can be selected in the Model browser or in the graphics window.

Show Dimensions

If you are only making changes to dimension values for a feature or its sketch, right-click and select **Show Dimensions** to display the dimensions for the selected feature. This enables you to change the values by double-clicking on the value of the dimension and entering a new value in the field that displays, as shown in Figure 2–20. The dimensional changes are not automatically reflected until you click ⬜ (Local Update) in the Quick Access Toolbar to update the model.

*Feature dimensions that are displayed using **Show Dimensions** are displayed only until another feature is selected in the Model browser or in the graphics window.*

Figure 2–20

Sketch Visibility

By default, a sketch used to create a feature is not visible on the model. To make the sketch visible, right-click on it in the Model browser and select **Visibility**. The sketch and its dimensions display on the part, as shown in Figure 2–21. Double-click on any dimension to edit its value.

Figure 2–21

- If the screen becomes too cluttered after displaying a number of sections, you can hide the dimensions of a selected sketch by right-clicking on the sketch in the Model browser and selecting **Dimension Visibility**.

- You can clear the display of dimensions from all sketches in the model at once by selecting the **Sketch Dimensions** Object visibility setting (View tab>Visibility panel),

Edit Sketch

To make changes to the sketch, use one of the following methods to activate the Sketch environment:

- Double-click on the sketch in the Model browser.

- In the Model browser or the graphics window, select the sketch, right-click, and select **Edit Sketch**.

- Select an entity in the sketch or in the solid feature, and click

   in the heads-up display on the sketch.

Edit Feature

To make changes to the options and elements that were available when a feature (e.g., extrusion) was originally created. use one of the following methods:

- Double-click on the feature in the Model browser.

- In the Model browser or the graphics window, select the feature, right-click, and select **Edit Feature**.

- Select a face on the feature and click in the heads-up display on the model.

- Double-click on the feature in the graphics window.

Show Input

To display the source sketch plane for a sketch, right-click on the sketch and select **Show Input**.

Change the Sketch Plane

The sketch plane for a base feature is defined when the sketch is created and the base feature becomes a child of that plane.

How To: Change the Sketch Plane

1. In the Model browser, right-click on the sketch and select **Redefine**. If the sketch is consumed by a solid feature, expand the solid feature name and then select the sketch plane.
2. Select another sketch plane (e.g., YZ plane) in the Model browser.

Practice 2a | Extruded Base Features I

Practice Objectives

- Create two new part models using predefined templates.
- Create extruded and revolved base features on origin planes using a provided dimension and constraint scheme.

In this practice, you will create new models using the default template. The geometry in the model will be created using either rectangular or circular sketches to create the extrusions shown in Figure 2–22.

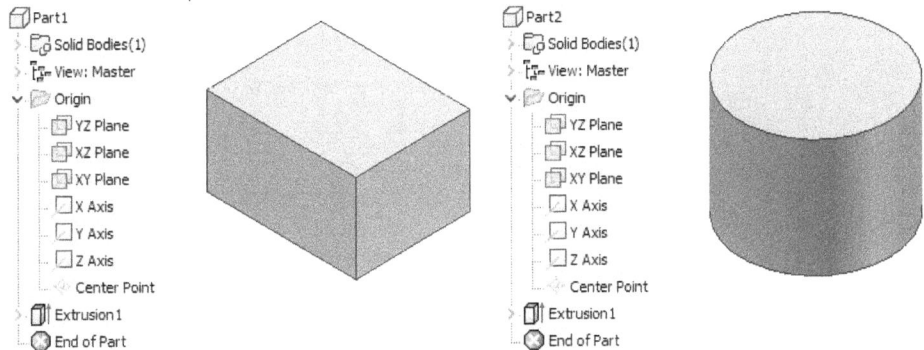

Figure 2–22

Task 1 - Create a new model using the default part template.

1. In the *Get Started* tab>My Home panel, click (Home) to toggle on the display of the *My Home* dashboard, if not already displayed.

2. In the *My Home* dashboard, in the *New* category, click

    (Configure Default Templates). Select **Millimeters** in the Configure Default Template dialog box and click **OK** and **Overwrite** to assign the standard metric templates as the defaults.

3. Click (Part) to create a new part with the default template. A part file is created and the *3D Model* tab is active.

- Alternatively, to select a template using the *My Home* dashboard, expand the Advanced options, navigate to the required template in the directory, and double-click its name to create the new file. You might need to drag and increase the size of the *New* area to access the Advanced options.

Hint: Creating New Files

As an alternative to using the *My Home* dashboard you can use the following techniques to select a new template as the basis of a new file:

- In the *Get Started* tab>Launch panel, click [ ] (New).
- In the Quick Access Toolbar, click [ ] (New).
- In the **File** menu, select **New**.

Task 2 - Create a sketch.

In the Model browser, next to the Origin, click ▷ to expand it and review the Origin Planes. Rolling the cursor over any of the plane names temporarily highlights them in the graphics window.

1. In the *3D Model* tab>Sketch panel, click [ ] (Start 2D Sketch). The Origin planes are temporarily displayed in the graphics window, as shown in Figure 2–23, so that you can select the sketch plane.

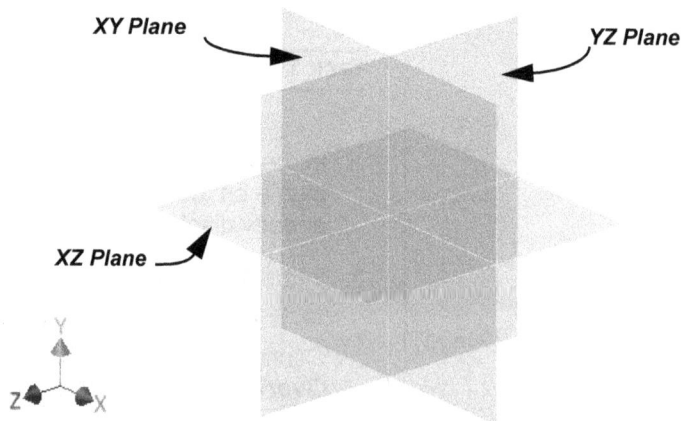

XY Plane   **YZ Plane**

XZ Plane

Figure 2–23

*Alternatively, you can right-click on the plane name in the Model browser or in the graphics window, right-click and select **New Sketch**.*

2. Hover the cursor over the origin planes in the model until you locate the XY Plane. Select the XY Plane in the graphics window to start a new sketch. You are placed in the Sketch environment, the XY Plane is the current sketch plane, and the *Sketch* tab is active.

By default, the Origin Center Point is projected onto the XY sketch plane. It can be used as the dimensioning reference when adding geometry. By referencing the projected Center Point, you are directly locating the sketch relative to the Origin Center Point of the entire model. In the next task, you will project two of the Origin Planes and use them as references for locating geometry in the sketch. The decision to use the projected Center Point or Planes is based on the required design intent.

By projecting Planes as references, you are providing references that can be used to ensure symmetry or create revolved features. Referencing a Center Point is acceptable for cylindrical base features.

As you gain more experience, you will learn which reference is the most appropriate to use as a reference.

Task 3 - Define sketch references.

It is recommended that sketched geometry be located with respect to existing features in the part. Therefore, projected sketch reference entities are required.

1. In the Create panel, click ▱ (Project Geometry) or right-click and select **Project Geometry**. Select the YZ and XZ planes, in the **Origin** node of the Model browser as references to locate the sketched geometry. The references are represented as yellow lines that are projected onto the sketch plane.

2. Right-click and select **OK** to complete the reference selection or press <Esc>.

Task 4 - Sketch the rectangular section.

When placed in the Sketch environment, the sketch should automatically be in a 2D orientation. If not, select a face on the ViewCube to return to a 2D view parallel to the XY plane. Alternatively, you can click ▱ in the Navigation Bar and select the XY Plane in the Model browser.

1. In the Create panel, click ▭ (Two Point Rectangle) or right-click and select **Two Point Rectangle** to sketch the base feature as a rectangular section.

2. Start the sketch by moving the cursor to the point at which the rectangle begins (as shown in Figure 2–24), and click.

3. Move the cursor to the point at which the rectangle ends (opposite corner), as shown in Figure 2–24, and click to complete the rectangle.

Figure 2–24

*To delete a sketch entity, right-click on the entity in the graphics window and select **Delete** or select the entity and press <Delete>.*

4. To complete the command you can select a new option, right-click and select **OK**, or press <Esc>.

The bottom right corner of the main window indicates that four dimensions are required to fully locate the sketch. Two dimensions are required to fully define the size of the rectangle and two are required to locate it relative to the projected Planes.

Automatically dimensioning a sketch is helpful when determining a missing dimension. However, it is not recommended for use in dimensioning a full sketch, because it cannot assume the design intent of the sketch.

5. In the Constrain panel, click ^{⊢⊣} (Automatic Dimensions and Constraints) to locate and dimension the rectangle. The Auto Dimension dialog box opens as shown in Figure 2–25. Four dimensions are required.

Figure 2–25

6. Click **Apply** to display the dimensions, similar to Figure 2–26.

Your dimensions might be different in size and location from the dimensions shown.

Figure 2–26

7. Click **Done** to close the dialog box.

8. Delete the two dimensions shown in Figure 2–27. To delete a dimension, right-click on it and select **Delete**.

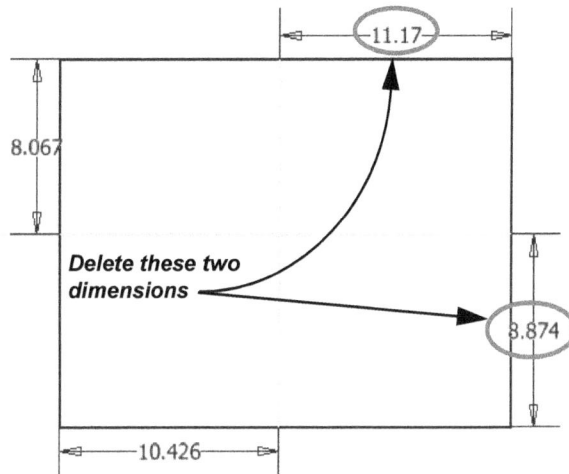

Figure 2–27

9. In the Constrain panel, click ⊓ (Dimension) or right-click in the graphics window and select **General Dimension**. Select the two sketched entities shown in Figure 2–28.

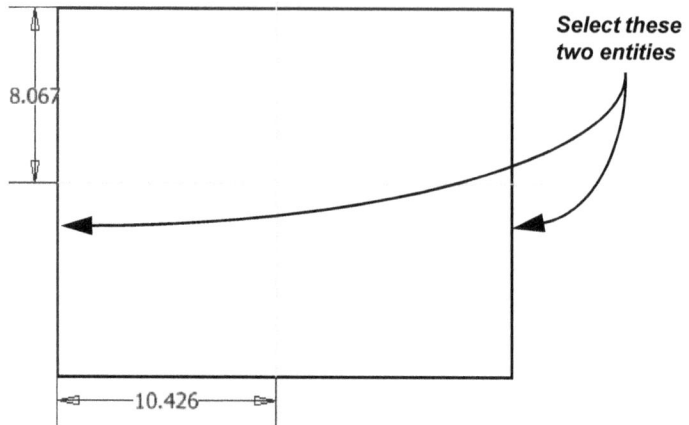

Select these two entities

8.067

10.426

Figure 2–28

10. Move the cursor between the two selected lines and click to place the dimension in the location shown in Figure 2–29.

11. Click ☑ in the Edit Dimension dialog box to accept the default dimension value. The dimension displays as shown in Figure 2–29.

New dimension

21.596

8.067

10.426

Figure 2–29

12. Create a second dimension, as shown in Figure 2–30.

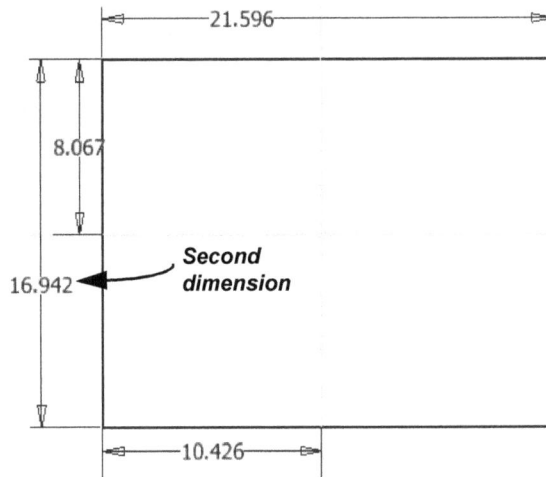

Figure 2–30

13. Modify the dimensions so that the sketch displays as shown in Figure 2–31. If ⌐⌐ (Dimension) is still toggled on, you can modify dimensions by single-clicking on them and entering the new value. If the dimensioning command is not active, double-click on a dimension to modify it. Once dimensioning has been toggled off, you can select and drag dimensions to place them as required.

Figure 2–31

14. The base feature geometry is sketched and fully constrained.

In the Exit panel, click ✔ (Finish Sketch), or right-click and select **Finish 2D Sketch**.

The sketch is now dimensioned relative to Origin Planes and is therefore anchored. Depending on the design intent, another method is to add Symmetry constraints between the sketched lines and the Origin Planes. Using Symmetry constraints would remove two dimension values, ensuring that the rectangle remains symmetric to the Origin Planes, regardless of the size of the rectangle. Constraints are discussed later in this student guide.

Task 5 - Select the type of feature.

1. Use any of the following methods to activate the **Extrude** option:

- In the *3D Model* tab>Create panel, click ▣⭱ (Extrude).
- Right-click in the graphics window and select **Extrude**.
- In the Model browser, left-click on the Sketch name and click ▣⭱ in the graphics window's Heads-up display.
- Press <E>.

The Extrude dialog box, mini-toolbar, and a model preview are displayed, as shown in Figure 2–32.

By Default, the display of the Mini-Toolbar is toggled off. To toggle on its display, in the *View* tab, expand **User Interface** and enable the **Mini-Toolbar** option on the list of interface items.

Figure 2–32

The rectangular section is identified as the *Profile* and has been extruded to a default depth. It was preselected because it is the only section in the model. You can work in the dialog box or in the mini-toolbar to define the feature. The mini-toolbar enables you to work while remaining focused on the model.

Task 6 - Define the depth of the extrusion.

Do not press <Enter> after typing the depth value. After typing the value, pause for a few seconds and the model updates with your changes.

1. A default depth value and direction is set by default. You can accept or change these defaults. Enter **15** as the depth. This can be entered in the Extrude dialog box or in the mini-toolbar on the model, or by using the drag handle on the model. Once a value has been entered, right-click and click

   OK (Enter) or click ✓ in the mini-toolbar. Alternatively, click **OK** in the feature's dialog box.

2. Hover the cursor over the ViewCube in the upper right corner of the graphics window and click 🏠, to rotate the model to its default orientation. The model displays in its default view, as shown in Figure 2–33.

Figure 2–33

Task 7 - Save the model and close the file.

1. In the Quick Access Toolbar, click 🖫 (Save) to save the model. The Save As dialog box opens.

2. Enter **rectangle** in the *File name* field.

3. Click **Save** to save the rectangle.

4. Close the rectangle file.

Task 8 - Create a new part using the default part template.

1. Use one of the techniques in Task 1 to create a new part model using the metric (mm) standard template file. The *3D Model* tab is the active tab.

Task 9 - Create the sketch.

To create the previous sketch, you first selected the command and then selected the sketch plane. In this task, you will first select the sketch plane and then initiate the command.

1. In the Model browser, next to the Origin, click ⟩ to expand it.

2. Select the XY Plane in the Model browser. In the *3D Model* tab>Sketch panel, click 🗒 (Start 2D Sketch), Alternatively, click 🗒 (Create Sketch) in the graphics window to start a new sketch. You are placed in the Sketch environment, the XY Plane is the current sketch plane, and the *Sketch* tab is active.

*Alternatively, you can right-click on the plane name in the Model browser or in the graphics window (if visible), right-click and select **New Sketch**.*

Task 10 - Sketch a circular section.

By default, the Origin Center Point is automatically projected, so you do not need to project it. In this task, you will reference cylindrical geometry to the Center Point.

1. In the Create panel, click ⊘ (Circle) or right-click and select **Center Point Circle** to sketch the base feature as a circular section.

2. Start the sketch by pressing the left mouse button at the projected Center Point. Drag the mouse away from the center point. Press the left mouse button again to define the diameter of the circle, as shown in Figure 2–34.

A green dot displays, indicating that the referenced center point has been selected.

To undo or redo sketching actions, click ⬅ *and* ➡ *in the Quick Access Toolbar, respectively.*

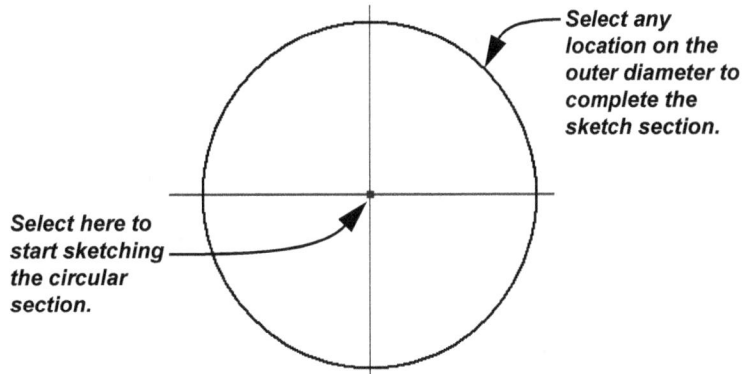

Figure 2–34

*You can also press <D> to start the **General Dimension** command.*

3. In the Constrain panel, click ⊏⊐ (Dimension) or right-click and select **General Dimension** to dimension the circle.

4. Select the circle in the graphics window. Move the cursor away from the circle. The dimension is attached to it. Select a location outside the circle to place the dimension. The sketch displays similar to the one shown in Figure 2–35.

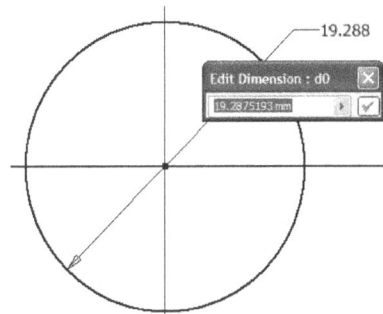

Figure 2–35

5. Enter **20.00** in the *Edit Dimension* field and press <Enter> to update the sketch.

6. In the graphics window, right-click and select **OK** to finish dimensioning.

7. The base feature geometry is sketched and fully constrained.

   In the Exit panel, click ✓ (Finish Sketch), or right-click and select **Finish 2D Sketch**.

8. Hover the cursor over the ViewCube and click 🏠 (Home) to return the model to its default 3D orientation, if it does not automatically return to its default orientation.

Task 11 - Select the feature type and define the depth.

1. Use any of the following methods to activate the **Extrude** option:

   - In the *3D Model* tab>Create panel, click ⬜↑ (Extrude).
   - Right-click in the graphics window and select **Extrude**.
   - In the Model browser, left-click on the Sketch name and click ⬜↑ in the graphics window's Heads-up display.
   - Press <E>.

   The Extrude dialog box, mini-toolbar, and a preview of the extruded model are displayed. The circular section was automatically selected as the *Profile* and has been extruded to a default depth.

2. Enter **15** as the *Extents* value (depth). This can be entered in the Extrude dialog box or mini-toolbar.

3. Once a value has been entered, right-click and click **OK (Enter)** or click ✓ in the mini-toolbar. Alternatively, click **OK** in the feature dialog box. The model and Model browser display as shown in Figure 2–36.

Figure 2–36

Task 12 - Save the model and close the file.

1. In the Quick Access Toolbar, click 🖫 (Save) to save the model. The Save As dialog box opens.

2. Enter **cylinder** in the *File name* field.

3. Click **Save** to save the cylinder, then close the file.

You can work in the dialog box or mini-toolbar to define the feature. Remember that the mini-toolbar enables you to work while remaining focused on the model.

Practice 2b

Extruded Base Features II

Practice Objectives

- Create a new part model using a predefined template.
- Create an extruded base feature on an origin plane, using a provided dimension and constraint scheme.
- Modify the extruded base feature to incorporate dimensional and feature direction changes.

In this practice, you will create a new model using a standard template file. The geometry is an extruded base feature, as shown in Figure 2–37. It is created by referencing the projected Center Point to dimension and constrain sketched line entities.

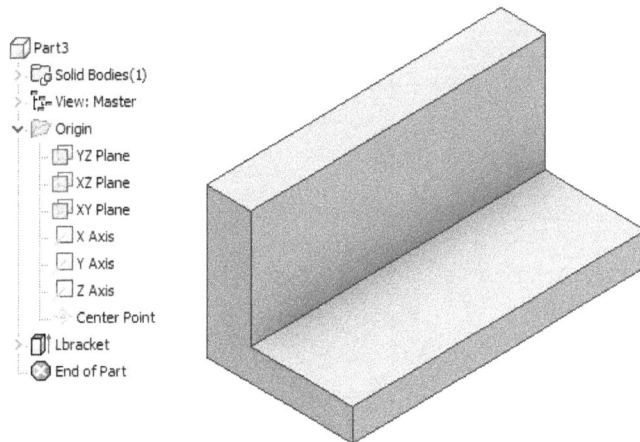

Figure 2–37

Task 1 - Create a new part model and sketch its geometry.

1. Create a new part file using the standard metric (mm) template.

2. In the Model browser, next to the Origin, click ⟩ to expand it.

3. In the Model browser, select the XZ Plane. In the *3D Model* tab>Sketch panel, click ⟲ (Start 2D Sketch) or click ⟲ (Create Sketch) in the graphics window to start a new sketch.

Note that you could also have initiated the command first and then selected the XZ Plane as the sketching plane.

*Alternatively, you can right-click on the plane name in the Model browser or in the graphics window (if displayed), right-click and select **New Sketch**.*

Task 2 - Sketch the base feature section.

1. In the Create panel, click ╱ (Line) or right-click and select **Create Line**.

2. Hover the cursor over the projected Center Point at the center of the sketch. The cursor should snap to this reference. Start the sketch by pressing the left mouse button at the projected Center Point, as shown in Figure 2–38.

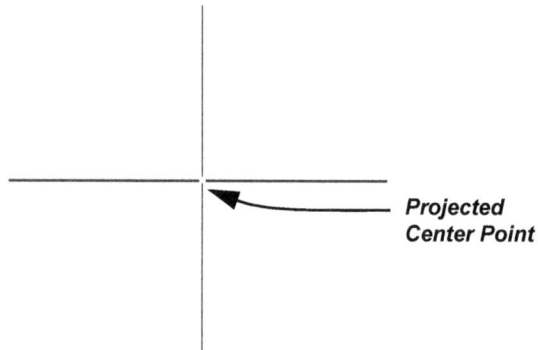

Projected Center Point

Figure 2–38

If required, you can quickly restart a command by pressing <Spacebar> or <Enter>, or by right-clicking and selecting the command again from the top of the list.

3. Sketch the six lines shown in Figure 2–39. Use the left mouse button to start and end each line segment. When drawing the last line segment, which returns to the projected Center Point, ensure that the cursor snaps to this reference before selecting.

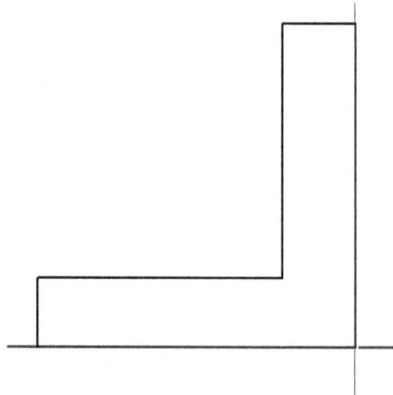

Figure 2–39

The bottom right corner of the main window also indicates that four dimensions are required.

4. In the Constrain panel, click ↤ (Automatic Dimensions and Constraints) to reveal the number of required dimensions, as shown in Figure 2–40.

Four dimensions are required ⟶

Auto Dimension	☒
▶ Curves	☑ Dimensions
	☑ Constraints
4 Dimensions Required	
⟨?⟩ Apply Remove Done	

Figure 2–40

5. Click **Apply** to apply the dimensions automatically.

6. Click **Done** to close the Auto Dimension dialog box.

7. If required, delete, recreate, and modify the dimensions to match those shown in Figure 2–41.

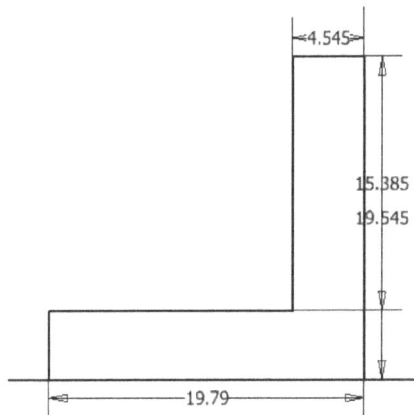

⊣4.545⊳

15.385
19.545

⊢19.79⊣

Figure 2–41

Automatically dimensioning a sketch is helpful when determining a missing dimension. However, it is not recommended for use in dimensioning a full sketch, as it does not assume the design intent of the sketch.

8. In the Exit panel, click ✓ (Finish Sketch), or right-click and select **Finish 2D Sketch**.

9. Hover the cursor over the ViewCube and click ⌂ (Home) to return to the model to its default 3D orientation, if it does not automatically return to its default orientation.

Task 3 - Select the feature type and define the depth.

1. Use any of the following methods to activate the **Extrude** option:

   - In the *3D Model* tab>Create panel, click ⬛↑ (Extrude).
   - Right-click in the graphics window and select **Extrude**.
   - In the Model browser, left-click on the Sketch name and click ⬛↑ in the graphics window's Heads-up display.
   - Press <E>.

   The section is identified as the *Profile* and has been extruded to a default depth.

Do not press <Enter> after typing the depth value. After typing the value, pause for a few seconds and the model updates with your changes.

2. Enter **30** as the *Extents* value (depth) in the Extrude dialog box or in the mini-toolbar. Once a value has been entered, right-click and click **OK (Enter)** or click ✓ in the mini-toolbar. Alternatively, click **OK** in the feature dialog box. The model displays as shown in Figure 2–42.

*By Default, the display of the Mini-Toolbar is toggled off. To toggle on its display, on the View tab, expand **User Interface** and enable the **Mini-Toolbar** option on the list of interface items.*

Figure 2–42

Task 4 - Modify dimension values associated with the extrusion.

*If you double-click on **Extrusion1** in the Model browser, the Extrude dialog box opens, enabling you to modify the extrusion details.*

1. Right-click on **Extrusion1** in the Model browser and select **Show Dimensions**. The extrusion dimensions display on the model.

2. Double-click on the dimension that represents the thickness of the feature (in Figure 2–43, this is the dimension with the value of 4.545). Enter **6** as the new dimension value and press <Enter>.

3. Double-click on the dimension that represents the depth of the feature (in Figure 2–43, this is the dimension with the value of 30). Enter **40** as the new dimension value and press <Enter>. Figure 2–43 is shown in Wireframe to clearly display all of the dimension values.

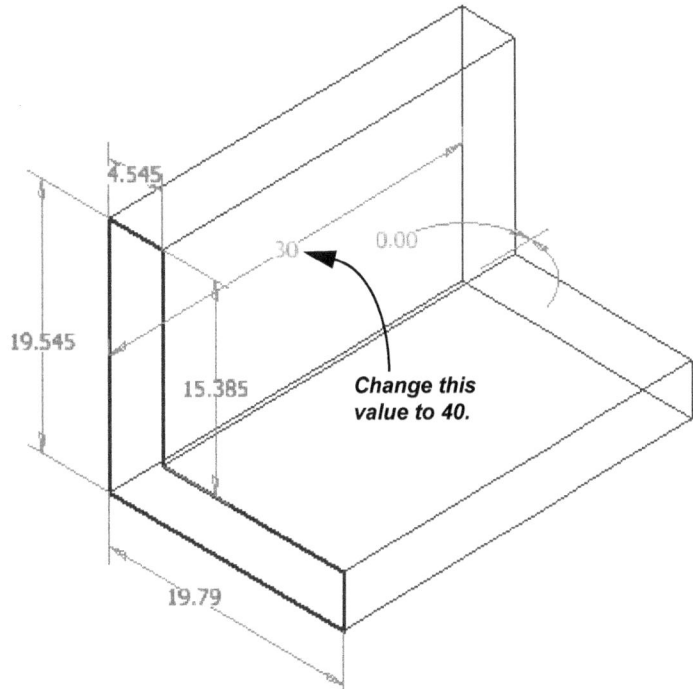

4.545

30

0.00

19.545

15.385

Change this value to 40.

19.79

Figure 2–43

4. In the Quick Access Toolbar, click [icon] (Local Update) to update the feature.

Task 5 - Redefine the extrusion direction.

*Alternatively, you can right-click on **Extrusion1** in the Model browser and select **Edit Feature** to open the Extrude dialog box.*

1. Double-click on **Extrusion1** in the Model browser. The Extrude dialog box and the mini-toolbar are displayed.

2. Click [icon] (Flip Direction) to flip the direction of the extrusion. You can click the icon in the dialog box or select it in the drop-down list in the mini-toolbar. Note that the preview of the extrusion flips to the opposite side of the sketch plane.

3. Click [image] (Asymmetric) as the extent direction. The Extrude dialog box updates for you to specify extent settings on both sides of the sketch plane. To use the mini-toolbar, select the direction arrow on each side of the sketch plane to activate its side and enter a unique value. Note the preview of the extrusion.

4. Click [image] (Symmetric) to extrude the feature equidistant from the sketch plane. Note the preview of the extrusion.

5. Click **OK** or [image].

6. Change the name of the base feature. Select **Extrusion1** in the Model browser and select it again (do not double-click). Enter **Lbracket** as the new name and press <Enter>. The model and Model browser display as shown in Figure 2–44.

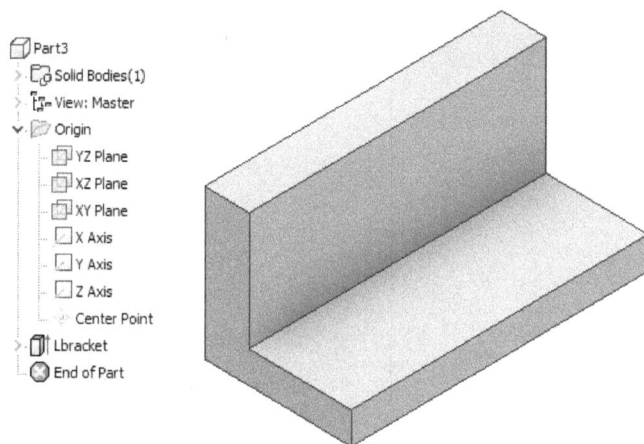

Figure 2–44

Task 6 - Save the model and close the file.

1. In the Quick Access Toolbar, click [image] (Save) to save the model.

2. Enter **L_shape** in the *File name* field and click **Save**.

3. Close the L_shape file.

Practice 2c

Revolved Base Feature

Practice Objectives

- Create a new part model using a predefined template.
- Create a revolved base feature on an origin plane using a provided dimension and constraint scheme.

In this practice, you will create a new model using a default template. Linear geometry will be used in the model to create the revolve feature shown in Figure 2–45.

Figure 2–45

Task 1 - Create a new part model and start a sketch.

1. Create a new part file using the standard metric (mm) template.

2. Using one of the techniques discussed in the previous practices, start a sketch on the XY Plane.

Task 2 - Define sketch references.

1. In the Create panel, click ▱ (Project Geometry) or right-click and select **Project Geometry**. Select the YZ and XZ planes as references to locate the sketched geometry. The references are represented as yellow lines that are projected onto the sketch plane.

2. Right-click and click **OK** to complete the reference selection or press <Esc>.

Task 3 - Sketch the section.

1. In the Create panel, click ✎ (Line) or right-click and select **Create Line** to sketch the base feature.

2. Start the sketch by moving the cursor to the left of the projected Center Point, as shown in Figure 2–46, and clicking the left mouse button to start the line.

3. Move the cursor vertically upwards and click again to place another vertex. Continue to sketch the four remaining entities in the sketch, as shown in Figure 2–46.

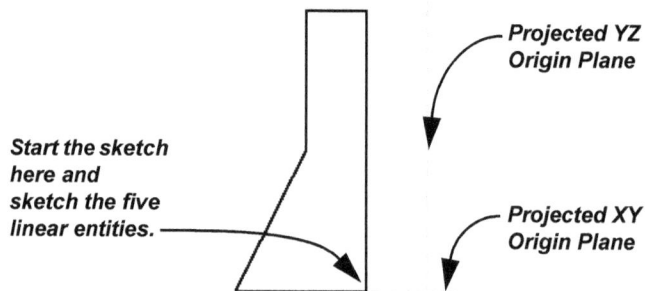

Projected YZ Origin Plane

Start the sketch here and sketch the five linear entities.

Projected XY Origin Plane

Figure 2–46

*To delete a sketched entity, right-click on the entity in the graphics window and select **Delete**, or select the entity and press <Delete>.*

4. To complete the command you can select a new option, right-click and click **OK**, or press <Esc>.

The bottom right corner of the main window indicates that five dimensions are required to fully locate the sketch.

5. In the Constrain panel, click ⊢⊣ (Dimension) or right-click and select **General Dimension**. Place the vertical dimension value by selecting the upper and lower horizontal entities by clicking them. Move the cursor to the dimension's placement location and click to place the dimension. When prompted, enter **12** as the value (as shown in Figure 2–47) and press <Enter>. All of the sketch entities scale based on the modification of the first dimension in the sketch. When you add a second dimension the scaling will not work.

Figure 2–47

6. Place the remaining four dimensions, shown in Figure 2–48 to fully dimension the sketch. To place dimensions, select the entity or entities by clicking them. Move the cursor to the dimension's placement location and click to place the dimension.

Figure 2–48

7. To complete the command you can select a new option, right-click and select **OK**, or press <Esc>. This sketch is now dimensioned relative to the Origin Planes, and the base feature geometry is sketched and fully constrained.

8. In the Exit panel, click ✓ (Finish Sketch), or right-click and select **Finish 2D Sketch**.

9. Hover the cursor over the ViewCube and click 🏠 (Home) to return to the model to its default 3D orientation, if it does not automatically return to its default orientation.

Task 4 - Create a Revolve feature.

1. Use any of the following methods to activate the **Revolve** option:

   - In the *3D Model* tab>Create panel, click 🍞 (Revolve).
   - Right-click in the graphics window and select **Revolve**.
   - In the Model browser, left-click on the Sketch name and click 🖼 in the graphics window's Heads-up display.
   - Press <R>.

   The sketched section is identified as the *Profile,* as shown in Figure 2–49. However, the *Axis* has not been defined so a preview of the model cannot be provided. The axis is required to determine how the features revolve. The profile has been preselected because it is the only section in the model. The axis must be selected manually.

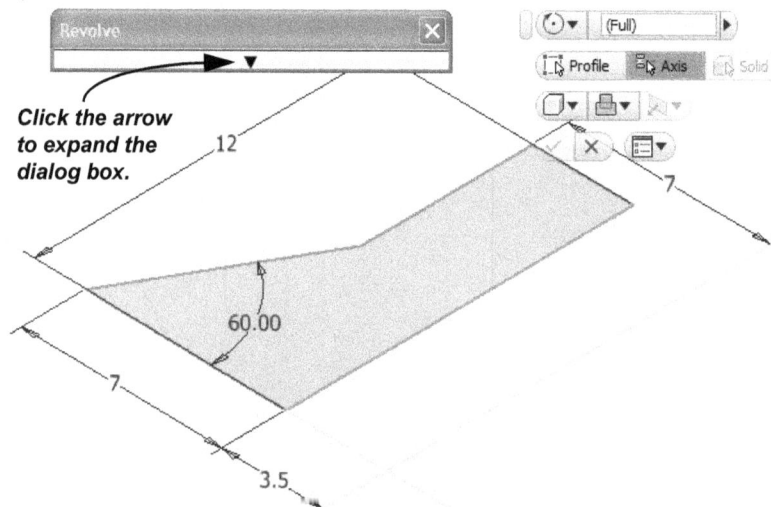

Click the arrow to expand the dialog box.

Figure 2–49

2. Select the **Y Axis** in the Model browser as the *Axis.* The section is fully revolved (360 degrees) about the selected axis. You can accept or change this. In this practice, you will maintain the full revolve.

3. Right-click and select **OK (Enter)** or click ✓ in the mini-toolbar. Alternatively, click **OK** in the feature's dialog box. The model and the Model browser display as shown in Figure 2–50.

Figure 2–50

Task 5 - Save the model and close the file.

1. In the Quick Access Toolbar, click 🖫 (Save). The Save As dialog box opens.

2. Enter **revolve** in the *File name* field and click **Save** to save the revolve.

3. Close the revolve file.

Practice 2d

Additional Parts

Practice Objective

- Create base features in new part models that represent the geometry and default orientation provided.

In this practice, you will create base features as the first solid features in new models.

Task 1 - Create new parts.

1. Create each of the new parts shown in Figure 2–51. As you begin each part, carefully consider your sketching plane and references (Origin Planes or Center Point).

Figure 2–51

Chapter Review Questions

1. What template would you use to create a new standard Part file?

    a. **Standard.ipn**

    b. **Standard.idw**

    c. **Standard.ipt**

    d. **Standard.iam**

2. Which of the following should be defined before sketching geometry? (Select all that apply.)

    a. Sketch Plane

    b. Sketch References

    c. Constraints

    d. Dimensions

3. An Origin Plane cannot be selected as a sketch plane.

    a. True

    b. False

4. Match the command in the left column to its interface icon in the right column.

    Answer

    a. Dimension

    _____

    b. Automatic Dimensions and Constraints

    _____

    c. Extrude

    _____

    d. Show Constraints

    _____

    e. Project Geometry

    _____

5. The **Automatic Dimensions and Constraints** option controls whether all of the dimensions and/or constraints required to constrain a sketch are automatically added. Additionally, it controls how the dimensions are positioned in the sketch.

   a. True

   b. False

6. The sketched entities shown on the left in Figure 2–52 are fully constrained. Which of the following statements best describes the (113. 91) dimension value, as shown on the right in Figure 2–52?

Figure 2–52

   a. The (113.91) dimension is a Driven Angular Dimension and cannot be modified to change the size of the sketch.

   b. The (113.91) dimension is a General Angular Dimension and cannot be modified to change the size of the sketch.

   c. The (113.91) dimension is a Driven Angular Dimension and can be modified to change the size of the sketch.

   d. The (113.91) dimension is a General Angular Dimension and can be modified to change the size of the sketch.

7. Match the feature form name in the left column with the geometry that would be created using this type of feature.

Answer

a. Revolve _____

b. Sweep _____

c. Loft _____

d. Extrude _____

8. Which option do you use to open the Feature dialog box, which would enable you to make a change to the feature (such as, flipping the extrusion direction)?

  a. **Edit Sketch**

  b. **Show Dimensions**

  c. **Edit Feature**

  d. **Properties**

9. What option enables you to change the sketch plane of a feature?

  a. **Show Dimension**

  b. **Edit Feature**

  c. **Edit Sketch**

  d. **Redefine**

10. What option enables you to make changes to a sketch so that you could delete entities?

a. **Show Dimension**

b. **Edit Feature**

c. **Edit Sketch**

d. **Redefine**

Command Summary

Button	Command	Location
	Application Options	• **Ribbon:** *Tools* tab>Options panel • **File Menu**
	Automatic Dimensions	• **Ribbon:** *Sketch* tab>Constrain panel
	Circle	• **Ribbon:** *Sketch* tab>Create panel • **Context Menu:** In the graphics window
	Create 2D Sketch	• **Ribbon:** *3D Model* tab>Sketch panel • **Context Menu:** In the graphics window • **Heads-up Display:** In the graphics window with a face selected
	Dimension	• **Ribbon:** *Sketch* tab>Constrain panel • **Context Menu:** In the graphics window
	Document Settings	• **Ribbon:** *Tools* tab>Options panel
	Extrude	• **Ribbon:** *3D Model* tab>Create panel • **Heads-up Display:** In the graphics window with a sketch selected • **Context Menu:** In the graphics window • **Keyboard:** <E>
	Finish Sketch	• **Ribbon:** *Sketch* tab>Exit panel • **Context Menu:** In the graphics window
	Line	• **Ribbon:** *Sketch* tab>Create panel • **Context Menu:** In the graphics window
	New	• **Ribbon:** *Get Started* tab>Launch panel • **My Home Dashboard** • **Quick Access Toolbar** • **File Menu**
	Project Geometry	• **Ribbon:** *Sketch* tab>Create panel • **Context Menu:** In the graphics window
	Rectangle	• **Ribbon:** *Sketch* tab>Create panel • **Context Menu:** In the graphics window
	Revolve	• **Ribbon:** *3D Model* tab>Create panel • **Heads-up Display:** In the graphics window with a sketch selected • **Keyboard:** <R>
	Show All Constraints	• **Context Menu:** In the graphics window • **Status Bar**

	Show Selected Constraints	• **Ribbon:** *Sketch* tab>Constrain panel
	Slot	• **Ribbon:** *Sketch* tab>Create panel

Additional Sketching Tools

When creating a sketch, knowledge of all of the available sketched entity types, editing tools, and dimensioning and constraining techniques enables you to create sketches that can be used to create the required solid geometry.

Learning Objectives in this Chapter

- Create, dimension, and constrain 2D sketch entities so that they capture design intent.
- Edit existing 2D sketches.

3.1 Additional Entity Types

In the previous chapter you learned about lines and the basic rectangle, circle, and slot commands. This topic focuses on the additional sketching commands that are available. Figure 3–1 shows the drop-down lists for each entity in the Create panel.

Figure 3–1

Line, Circle, Arc, and Rectangle are the default entity options that are displayed in the Create panel. These defaults are replaced by the most recently selected entity from each drop-down list as they are used.

Line Drop-Down List

- **(Spline (Control Vertex)):** Enables you to sketch a free-form curve. Select multiple points to create the spline. Each point that is placed defines the vertices of the control frame.

- **(Spline (Interpolation)):** Enables you to sketch a free-form curve. Select multiple points to create the spline. The spline is drawn through each point.

- **(Equation Curve):** Draws a curve based on the entry of an equation.

- **(Bridge Curve):** Draws a smooth (G2) continuous curve between two curves.

Circle Drop-Down List

- (**Tangent Circle**): Draws a circle tangent to three selected lines.

- (**Ellipse**): Creates an ellipse. Select the first point to define the center. Select the second point to define its major or minor axes. Select the third point to finalize the size of the ellipse.

Arc Drop-Down List

- (**Tangent Arc**): Draws an arc tangent to an existing line or arc. Select the end of the line or arc as the first point and move the cursor to define the end of the arc.

- (**Three Point Arc**): Draws an arc at three selected points. Select the two end points, and then select a point on the arc. The last point determines the center and radius.

- (**Center Point Arc**): Draws an arc at three selected points. The first point determines the center of the arc and the other two determine the ends of the arc.

Rectangle Drop-Down List

- (**Three Point Rectangle**): Draws a rectangle at any angle. Select three points to create the rectangle. The first two points define one side and the third point locates the opposite side.

- (**Two Point Center**): Draws a rectangle along the X- and Y-axes. Select two points to create the rectangle. The first point defines the center of the rectangle and the second point defines an outer corner.

- (**Three Point Center**): Draws a rectangle at any angle. Select three points to create the rectangle. The first point defines the center of the rectangle, the second defines the first side, and the third point defines the second side.

- ⬭ **(Overall):** Draws a slot by selecting three points. The first two points define the entire length of the slot and the third selection defines the slot's thickness.

- ⬭ **(Center Point):** Draws a slot by selecting three points. Select the center point of the slot, followed by the center point of one arc and finally select a point to define the slot's thickness.

- ⬭ **(Three Point Arc):** Draws a slot by selecting four points. The first three points define the arc length and radius of the slot and the fourth selection defines the slot's thickness.

- ⬭ **(Center Point Arc):** Draws a slot by selecting four points. The first three points define the center point of the arc, its arc length, and the radius of the slot. The fourth selection defines the slot's thickness.

- ⬠ **(Polygon):** As with rectangles, polygons can be drawn with a series of lines. However, it is easier to use this command so that all of the sides and angles are equal. You can the draw polygons as:

  - ⬠ **(Inscribed):** Uses the vertex between two edges to determine size and orientation.

  - ⬠ **(Circumscribed):** Uses the midpoint of an edge to determine the size and orientation.

The following additional sketching tools are also useful when creating a sketch.

Tangent Arc Using a Line

The **Line** command also enables you to sketch tangent or perpendicular arcs. These types of arcs must start at the end of an existing line or arc.

How To: Draw an Arc Tangent to or Perpendicular to a Line

The yellow dot at the center of the crosshairs displays in green if you are drawing a new object or gray if you are continuing an object.

1. With ✐ (Line) enabled, place the cursor at the end point of the line/arc.
2. Press and hold the left mouse button and drag in the required direction (i.e., tangent or perpendicular).
3. Release the left mouse button to select the end point for the arc.

Tangent Line Between Two Circles/Arcs

As of the release of this training guide (March 2017), the tangency to the second circular/arc entity is not being automatically assigned. If required, ensure that you manually assign the tangent constraint.

How To: Sketch a Line that is Tangent to Two Circles/Arcs

1. Start the **Line** command.
2. Select and hold the cursor over one of the two circles.
3. While continuing to hold the left mouse button, drag it to the next circle and position the cursor so that the Tangent constraint is visible.
4. Release the mouse button to locate the tangent line, as shown in Figure 3–2.

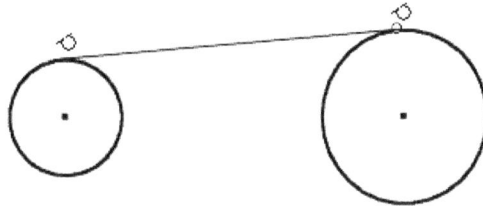

Figure 3–2

Fillets and Chamfers

The **Fillet** and **Chamfer** commands enable you to modify the intersection of two lines in a 2D sketch, as shown in Figure 3–3.

- The fillet rounds corners in a sketch by placing an arc at the intersection of two lines. The fillet arc is always tangent to the intersecting entities.

- A chamfer is an angled corner. Its size is determined by distances along each line from their intersection, or by a distance and an angle.

Figure 3–3

How To: Create a Fillet

1. In the Create panel, click ⬚ (Fillet).
2. Enter a dimension value in the 2D Fillet dialog box, but do not press <Enter>.
3. Select the intersected entities or directly at the intersection point to create the fillet. The dimension is added to the fillet arc.

   • By default, the first fillet added includes a dimension value. Any additional fillets are driven by this value and no dimension is added. To place a fillet that has independent dimensions for each fillet, click = prior to creating the fillet.

4. Continue to select entities to add additional fillets.

5. Press <Esc> or close the 2D Fillet dialog box to end the command.

How To: Create a Chamfer

1. In the Create panel, click ◻ (Chamfer). The 2D Chamfer dialog box opens, as shown in Figure 3–4.

Figure 3–4

2. Select the chamfer option and dimensioning scheme.
3. Enter a dimension value(s) in the 2D Chamfer dialog box. Do not press <Enter>.
4. Select the intersected entities to create a chamfer. The dimension is added to the chamfer.

The options in the 2D Chamfer dialog box are described as follows:

▧ (Create dimension)	Enable this option to create a chamfer without any dimensions.
= (Linked values)	Links the values for second and subsequent chamfers to the first chamfer.
▨ (Equal distances)	Creates a line at equal distances from the corner on each side. Enter the distance in the *Distance* field.
▨ (Two distance)	Creates a line at Distance1 along the first selected line and at Distance2 along the second selected line.
▨ (Distance & angle)	The line created is defined by a distance and an angle. The angle is between the first line you select and the new line that you create.

Part Features versus 2D Sketched Entities

When designing a model, you can include fillets and chamfers in your 2D sketches or create them as separate fillet and chamfer part features. Consider the following:

- Chamfer and fillet features can be deleted, modified, and suppressed without needing to access the original sketch.

- If you need to change the edges selected for fillets or chamfers, you can easily edit the feature and select the edges you want to add or remove from the feature.

- The model is more robust and easier to modify if fillets and chamfers are created as features, rather than in the sketch.

Point Snaps

When sketching entities, consider right-clicking and using the **Point Snaps** options in the context menu. Snaps enable you to locate the entity points by snapping to the following points of existing entities in a sketch:

- Endpoints
- Midpoints
- Intersections
- Centers
- Quadrants

- Tangencies
- Apparent intersection points of existing entities
- The middle of two selected points

Construction Entities

Construction entities are used as references and aids in sketching. They do not create solid geometry. It is common to use construction lines when sketching to indicate that arcs or circles lie along the same line or to indicate the midpoint of a line.

In the Format panel, click ⟋ (Construction) to sketch a construction entity (e.g., line, arc, etc.). Construction entities display as dashed lines and you can add dimensions and constraints to them. An example of construction entities is shown in Figure 3–5.

To change a construction entity to solid geometry, select the entity and click

⟋ *(Construction) in the Format panel. The reverse is also true.*

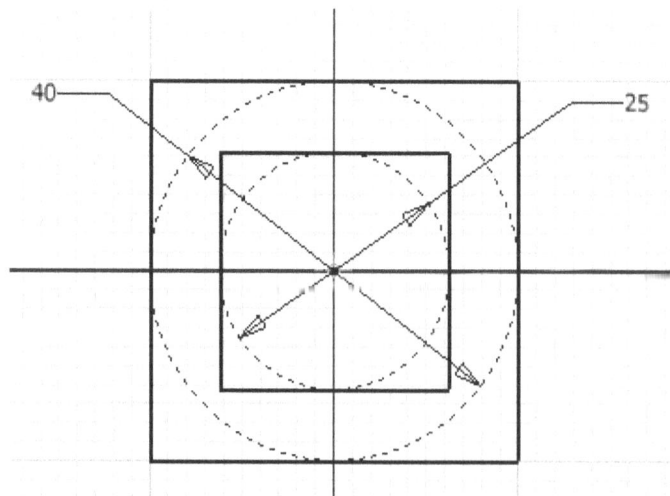

The circular construction entities are used to create squares centered about the center point. The dimensions of each square are driven by the diameter of the construction circle.

Figure 3–5

3.2 Basic Editing Tools

The **Trim**, **Extend**, and **Mirror** editing tools that are available on the Sketch tab provide basic editing tools that can be used to modify sketch entities.

Trim

Trim removes the segment of the entity to the nearest intersection in each direction from the selected point. The selected portion of an object (e.g., lines or arcs) is removed, as shown in Figure 3–6. Selecting an object without an intersection deletes the object.

If the intersections contain multiple possibilities for trimming, move the cursor over each segment. If it can be trimmed it displays as a red dashed entity.

Selected portion of the line

Figure 3–6

How To: Trim Sketched Entities

1. In the Modify panel, click (Trim) or right-click and select **Trim.**
2. Move the cursor over the portion of the entity that you want to trim. A preview of the trim displays.
3. Click the left mouse button to remove the portion.

*To toggle between **Trim** and **Extend** (or vice-versa) when a command is active, press and hold <Shift>.*

- Trimming can also be done dynamically once the command is initiated. Drag the freehand line over the required entities that are to be removed. Release the mouse button to remove the entities from the sketch.

Extend

Extend continues an entity to meet the next entity in its path or to close an open sketch, as shown in Figure 3–7.

Select these lines to extend

Figure 3–7

*To toggle between **Trim** and **Extend** (or vice-versa) when a command is active, press and hold <Shift>.*

How To: Extend Sketched Entities

1. In the Modify panel, click ⌐⁻¹ (Extend) or if the **Trim** command is already active, right-click and select **Extend**.
2. Move the cursor over the portion of the entity that you want to extend. A preview of the extend displays.
3. Click the left mouse button to extend the entity.

- Extending can also be done dynamically once the command is initiated. Drag the freehand line over the required entities that are to be extended. Release the mouse button to extend the entities from the sketch.

Mirror

How To: Mirror a Selected Object about a Mirror Line

1. In the Pattern panel, click ◧◧ (Mirror). The Mirror dialog box displays.
2. Select the sketch entities that you want to mirror.

3. In the Mirror dialog box, click ⊾ (Mirror line).
4. Select a mirror line, and click **Apply**.

The mirror line can be:

- Part of the geometry that is selected to mirror

- Projected Origin feature

- Projected model edge

- Straight sketched or construction lines

The sketch shown in Figure 3–8 is created using the **Mirror** sketch tool and a construction line as the mirror line.

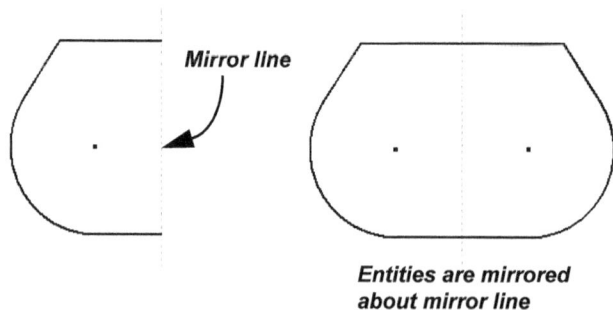

Figure 3–8

3.3 Additional Constraint Tools

Constraints control how the sketched entities behave. As you sketch the geometry, constraints are assumed and applied when the cursor drags within a specific tolerance of other entities. Symbols display on the entity that is being sketched indicating which constraint is applied. If the assumed constraints do not fully capture the required design intent or fully constrain the sketch, additional constraints can be added manually.

Reviewing Existing Constraints

To display the constraints applied to your sketch, use one of the following techniques:

- Select the entity in the sketch to temporarily display the constraint.

- To display of the all constraints in the sketch, in the Status Bar, click (Show All Constraints), or press <F8>.

- To only display the constraints applied to the selected entities, click (Show Constraints) in the Constrain panel. Showing the constraint using this method keeps the constraint on the screen until it is cleared.

When a constraint is displayed, you can select and drag it as required. Consider the following:

- Hover the cursor over a constraint symbol to highlight the entities affected.

- To hide all of the constraints from the sketch, in the Status Bar, click (Show All Constraints) to toggle their display off or press <F9>.

The icon that identifies the Sketch in the Model browser is displayed as when the sketch is partially constrained and changes to when fully constrained.

Reviewing Degrees of Freedom

Reviewing the remaining degrees of freedom can help you to determine where additional constraints and dimensions are required. To display the degrees of freedom in a sketch, click (Show Degrees of Freedom) in the Status Bar.

Assigning Constraints

Once entities have been sketched, you can manually add additional constraints using the Constrain panel, shown in Figure 3–9. Select the required constraint icon and select the entities that you want to constrain.

Figure 3–9

When assigning constraints, the order in which they are selected does not determine how they update. The driving entity is the first drawn in the sketch, unless there are other constraints or dimensions assigned that prevent updating.

Parallel and Perpendicular

(Parallel) and (Perpendicular) ensure that lines are parallel or perpendicular, respectively. The lines shown in Figure 3–10 are constrained to be parallel and perpendicular.

Figure 3–10

Tangent

(Tangent) ensures that the selected items are tangent. The objects do not need to touch to be tangent. The arc shown in Figure 3–11 is constrained to be tangent to the geometry lines at its end point.

Figure 3–11

Smooth (G2)

(Smooth) ensures that the selected entities continue the same curvature values between the entities (curvature continuous). The spline shown in Figure 3–12 is constrained to be curvature continuous to the geometry line at its end point.

Figure 3–12

Collinear

(Collinear) ensures that selected objects lie on the same line. The constraints can be applied between lines and ellipse axes. The lines shown on the right in Figure 3–13 are constrained to be collinear.

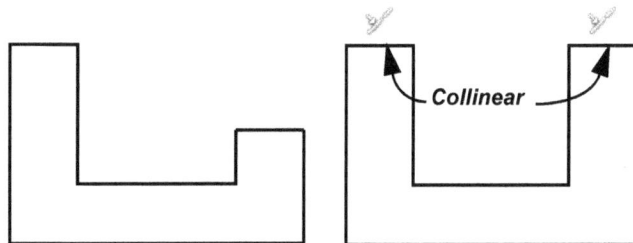

Figure 3–13

Coincident

▫— (Coincident) ensures that two selected points are coincident. If a point and an entity are selected, the point lies on the entity or along the extension of the entity. As shown in Figure 3–14, two Coincident constraints were automatically created when the arc was sketched. They indicate that the end points of the arc lie on the horizontal line. One additional Coincident constraint was added manually (as shown on the right), so that the center of the circle lies on the center of the horizontal line. With Coincident constraints, only small yellow boxes display in a sketch when **Show Constraints** is used.

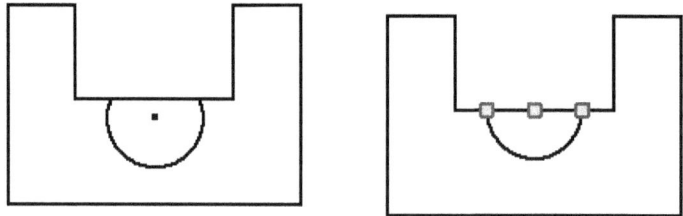

Figure 3–14

Concentric

◎ (Concentric) ensures that the selected arcs, circles, or ellipses have the same center point. The circles shown on the right in Figure 3–15 are constrained to be concentric with one another.

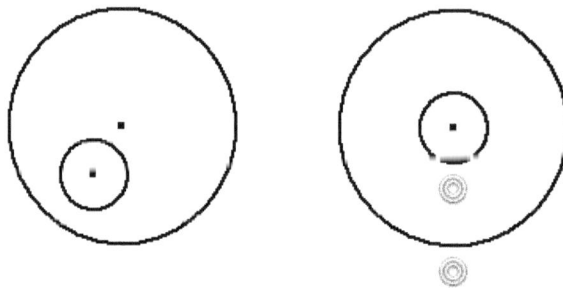

Figure 3–15

Equal

(Equal) ensures that all selected lines have the same length or that all selected circles and arcs have the same radius. The lines shown on the right in Figure 3–16 are constrained to be equal in length.

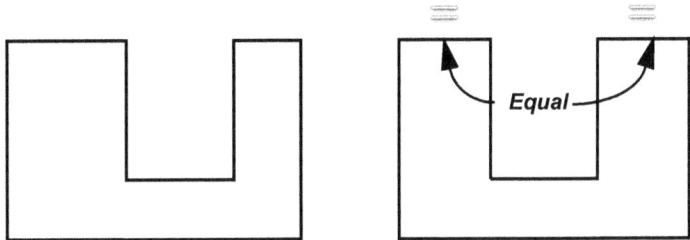

Figure 3–16

When assigning the Equal constraint, the result depends on if dimensions are present on the entities:

If...	Then...
No dimensions are present on either selected entity	The resulting entities are resized as the average size.
One dimension is present	The values of the resulting constrained entities are those of the dimension.
Dimensions are present on both entities	A prompt displays noting that the sketch is over-constrained.

Horizontal and Vertical

(Horizontal) and (Vertical) ensure that a line is horizontal or vertical, respectively. The lines shown on the right in Figure 3–17 are constrained to be horizontal and vertical.

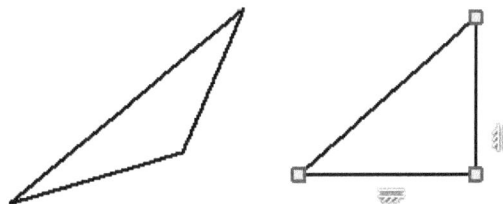

Figure 3–17

Horizontal can also be used to align two circle center points horizontally and Vertical can be used to align two circle center points vertically. The circle center points shown on the left in Figure 3–18 are constrained to line up horizontally and vertically, as shown on the right.

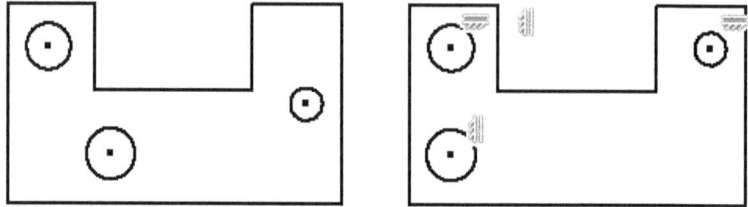

Figure 3–18

Fix

(Fix) fixes a selected point or object relative to the default coordinate system (Sketch environment 0,0,0). The vertex shown in Figure 3–19 is fixed relative to the default coordinate system.

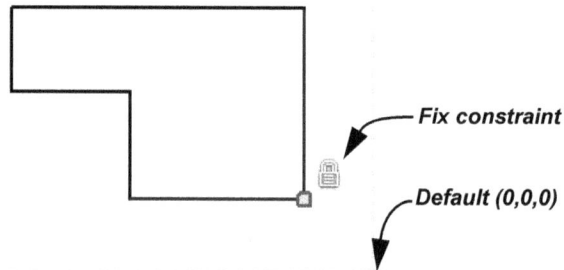

Fix constraint

Default (0,0,0)

Figure 3–19

Symmetric

(Symmetric) ensures that the selected lines or points are symmetric about a selected line. To apply this constraint, select the first line or point, select the second line or point, and then select the line of symmetry. The vertical lines in Figure 3–20 are constrained to be symmetric about the center line.

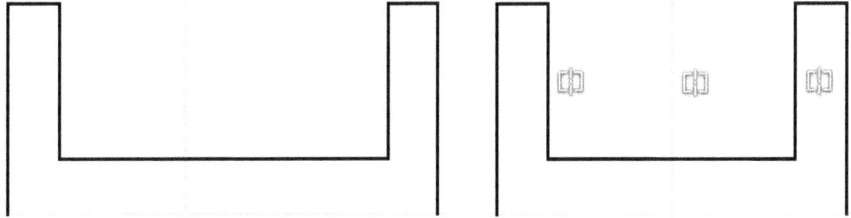

Figure 3–20

Reference

A Reference constraint is automatically added to sketches when you use the **Project Geometry** option, as shown in Figure 3–21. This constraint cannot be explicitly set using a constraint in the Constrain panel.

Projected origin planes

Figure 3–21

Over Constraining Entities

If you try to place a constraint that over-constrains the sketch, an Error dialog box opens, as shown in Figure 3–22. You must click **Cancel** to continue. It is not possible to over constrain a sketch.

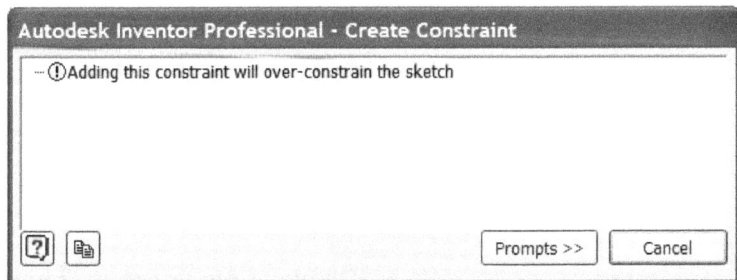

Autodesk Inventor Professional - Create Constraint

Adding this constraint will over-constrain the sketch

Prompts >>   Cancel

Figure 3–22

If you encounter an over-constrained sketch, keep the dimension that best suits the design intent.

Constraint Settings

Using constraint settings enables you to customize how constraints are inferred and displayed in a sketch. To open the Constraint Settings dialog box, in the *Sketch* tab>Constrain panel, click 🔲 (Constraint Settings). The Constraint Setting dialog box is shown in Figure 3–23.

Figure 3–23

Using the *General* and *Inference* tabs in the Constraint Settings dialog box you can do the following:

Control Constraint Display

In the *General* tab you can use the following constraint options to control how constraints are displayed when creating a sketch.

- **Display constraints on creation:** Enables you to display the constraint symbols for the constraints that are being assumed as you sketch.

- **Show constraints for selected objects:** Enables you to display the constraints associated with a selected entity. If disabled, the only way to display an entity's constraint symbols is to click 🔲 (Show All Constraints) in the Status Bar.

- **Display Coincident constraints in Sketch:** Enables you to control whether the coincident constraint symbol is displayed when entities are sketched.

Control Constraint Inference

The *Inference* tab (shown in Figure 3–24) in the Constraint Settings dialog box controls how the software assumes constraints as entities are sketched.

Figure 3–24

- The automatic assignment of constraints is called *constraint inference*. By default, constraint inference is enabled in a sketch. To disable it, clear the **Infer constraints** option.

- With **Infer constraints** toggled on, the additional **Persist constraints** option is also available. It controls whether the inferred constraint is permanently assigned once the entity has been placed. By default, this option is enabled in a new sketch.

- If **Infer constraints** is disabled, **Persist constraints** is automatically disabled. When enabling **Infer constraints**, ensure that **Persist constraints** is set as required.

*Toggling off **Infer constraints** or **Persist constraints** does not affect the creation of the Coincident constraint. This helps in preventing open profile sketches.*

> **Hint: Temporarily Controlling Constraint Inference and Persistence**
>
> When sketching geometry, you can manually enable and disable the inference and persistence options in the Constraint Settings dialog box. However, you can also press and hold <Ctrl> to disable them during the sketching process.

Although a constraint inference might be disabled for a specific constraint, you can still apply it manually if required.

- The *Selection for Constraint Inference* area enables you to select the constraints that the software can infer during sketch creation. Select the constraint options as required.

- The *Constraint Inference Priority* area enables you to determine the priority of whether the Parallel/Perpendicular or Horizontal/Vertical constraints are inferred over one another when the sketch is created.

Deleting Constraints

To delete constraints, use one of the following:

- Display the constraint symbol that is to be deleted, select it, right-click, and select **Delete**, as shown in Figure 3–25. To display a coincident constraint symbol, hover over its yellow square icon.

- Select the required constraint symbol, and press <Delete>.

- Select entities in the sketch, right-click and select **Delete Constraints**. To delete coincident constraints, select the entities, right-click and select **Delete Coincident Constraints**. The delete options in the context menu are shown in Figure 3–25.

Constraint being deleted

Figure 3–25

Relax Mode

Constraints can prevent entities from moving when changes are required. When enabled, Relax Mode enables you to make changes to the geometry and to apply new constraints that would otherwise not be possible without deleting constraints.
Figure 3–26 shows an example of Relax Mode. Once a sketched entity has been moved constraints are assigned based on the new placement location of the entity.

Constraints prevent the movement of this vertex ———

With Relax Mode enabled the vertex can be moved ———

Figure 3–26

By default, Relax Mode is disabled. To enable it, use one of the following techniques:

- In the Status Bar, click ⬚ (Relax Mode) to toggle it on/off.

- In the *Sketch* tab>Constraint panel, click ⬚ (Constraint Settings), and select the *Relax Mode* tab. Select **Enable Relax Mode** to toggle it on.

The Constraint Settings dialog box contains added configuration options for Relax Mode. Once enabled, the *Constraints to remove in relax dragging* area becomes available, as shown in Figure 3–27. You can enable or disable specific constraints to define which constraint types are to be relaxed during dragging.

Figure 3–27

3.4 Additional Dimension Tools

You can also press <D> to start dimensioning.

In the previous chapter you learned that Linear dimensions can be placed by activating the ⊓ (Dimension) command and selecting entities and placing the dimensions using the left mouse button. The type of dimension created depends on whether you select an entity or the points related to the entity. The following are types of additional dimensions that can be placed on a sketch once the dimensioning command is active.

Center Dimensions

To create center dimensions, select the two entities to dimension the distance between circles and arcs. Move the cursor to the required location and place the dimension using the left mouse button. The different methods for dimensioning the linear entities shown in Figure 3–28 are as follows:

Figure 3–28

To place dimension d0	Select the centers of the arcs. Position the cursor in the location in which you want to place the dimension, right-click, and select **Aligned**. Alternatively, place the dimension at a point along a line that joins the two centers. When it displays, click the left mouse button. Move the cursor to the required location and click to locate the dimension.
To place dimensions d1 and d2	Select the centers of the circles or circular entities. Position the cursor in the location at which you want to place the dimension and click the left mouse button.

Radius/ Diameter Dimensions

To create radius or diameter dimensions, select an arc or circle to create a radius dimension. Position the cursor at the location in which you want to place the dimension and press the left mouse button. By default, the dimension type for arcs is radius and the dimension type for circles is diameter, as shown in Figure 3–29.

To delete a dimension, right-click on the dimension and select **Delete**.

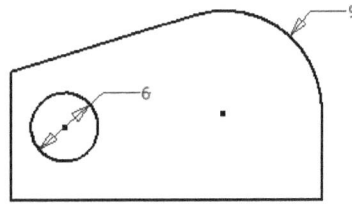

Figure 3–29

To change the type of dimensions, right-click and select **Radius** or **Diameter** before placing the dimension. Position the cursor at the location at which you want to place the dimension and click the left mouse button.

Angular Dimensions

To create angular dimensions, select lines A and B and place the angular dimension using the left mouse button. The resulting angle is dependent on the placement location of the dimension, as shown in Figure 3–30. Alternatively, you can create an angular dimension by selecting three points.

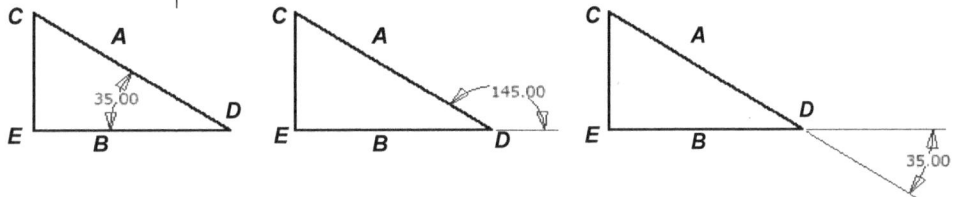

Figure 3–30

Tangent Dimensions

To create a tangent dimension, select the first arc, and move the cursor over the second arc. When $\overline{\sigma^{\mathcal{I}}}$ is displayed, select the second arc and place the dimension, as shown in Figure 3–31.

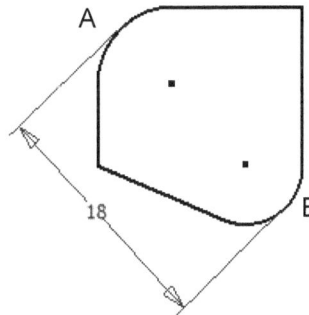

Figure 3–31

Revolved Sketch Dimensions

When sketching a cross-section of a revolved feature, only half of the section needs to be sketched. The cross-section is then revolved about the center line at a specified angle.

This dimensioning scheme can also be used to dimension symmetrical entities.

To create a diameter dimension on the section of a revolved feature, select the center line of the revolved cross-section and then the geometry, right-click and select **Linear Diameter**. Figure 3–32 shows a revolved diameter dimension.

Figure 3–32

Arc Length Dimensions

To create an Arc Length dimension, select the arc, right-click, and select **Dimension Type>Arc Length** and then place the dimension, as shown in Figure 3–33.

Figure 3–33

Dimension Types

When you are working in an Imperial template, you have the flexibility to change the dimension style from **Decimal** to **Fractional** or **Architectural**. This is done by editing the dimension value, expanding the menu in the *Dimension* field, and selecting a new option, as shown in Figure 3–34.

Figure 3–34

Over Dimensioned Entities

If you try to apply a dimension that is going to over-dimension the sketch, the dialog box shown in Figure 3–35 displays. You can cancel the command or place as a driven dimension. Driven dimensions are displayed in parentheses, as shown in Figure 3–35. You cannot modify them, but they update if other dimensions are changed.

Figure 3–35

If you encounter an over-dimensioned sketch, keep the dimension that best suits the design intent.

Practice 3a

Apply Constraints

Practice Objectives

- Open an existing part model and edit its sketch.
- Show existing constraints in a sketch.
- Add constraints to the sketch.
- Automatically add dimensions to ensure that the sketch is fully constrained.

In this practice, you will apply constraints to define the shape of the sketched geometry shown in Figure 3–36. You will also use automatic dimensions to fully place the geometry with respect to the sketch references.

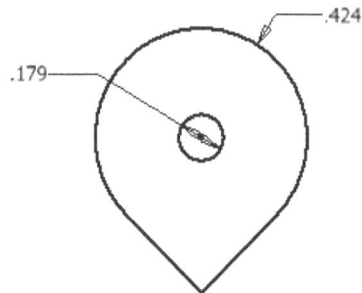

Figure 3–36

Task 1 - Open a part file.

1. Open **constraints_1.ipt**. The sketch displays as shown in Figure 3–37.

Figure 3–37

2. Double-click on **Sketch1** in the Model browser to activate the sketch. Note the number of dimensions required to fully constrain the sketch.

You can also press <F8> to display all of the constraints.

3. In the Status Bar, click (Show All Constraints) to display the constraints applied in the sketch. The sketch displays as shown in Figure 3–38. Review the constraints.

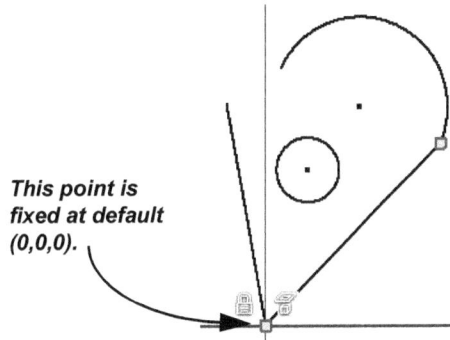

This point is fixed at default (0,0,0).

Figure 3–38

You can also press <F9> to hide all of the constraints.

4. In the Status Bar, click (Show All Constraints) again to hide the constraints.

Task 2 - Apply constraints.

1. In the Constrain panel, review each of the twelve constraints that can be used to constrain geometry in a sketch by hovering over them with the cursor to display their tooltip.

2. In the Constrain panel, click (Vertical Constraint) and select the center point of the arc followed by the projected Center Point, as shown on the left in Figure 3–39. The sketch displays as shown on the right.

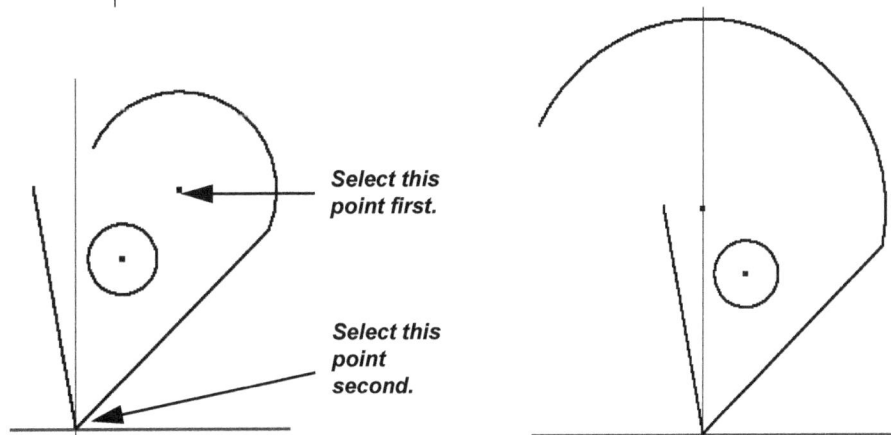

Select this point first.

Select this point second.

Figure 3–39

3. In the Constrain panel, click ⊥ (Coincident Constraint) and select the end points of the arc and line, as shown on the left in Figure 3–40. The sketch displays as shown on the right.

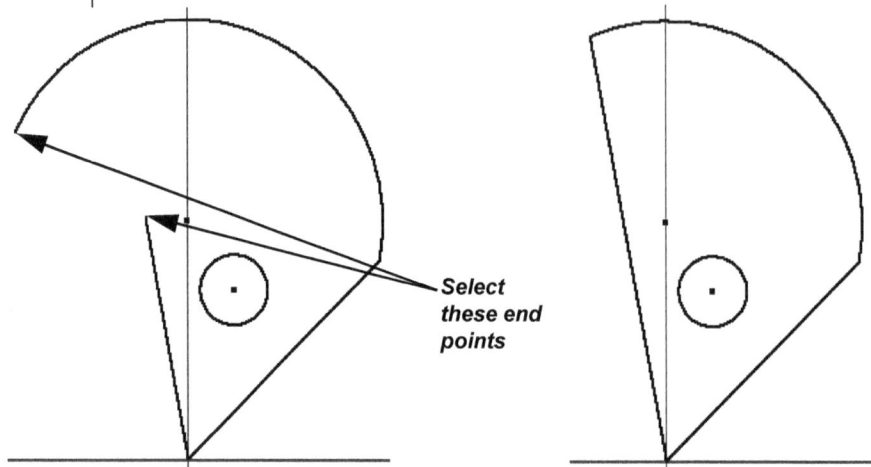

Select these end points

Figure 3–40

4. In the Constrain panel, click ✓ (Perpendicular Constraint) and select the two lines shown on the left in Figure 3–41. The sketch displays as shown on the right.

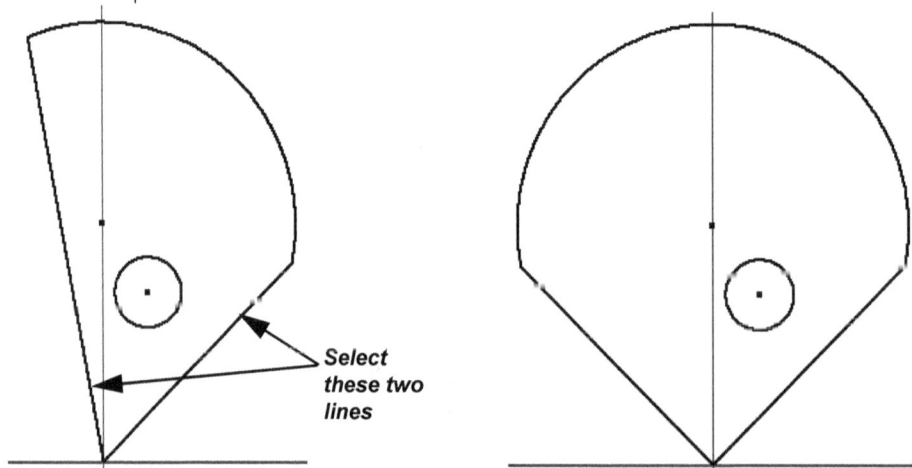

Select these two lines

Figure 3–41

5. In the Constrain panel, click ◌ (Tangent Constraint) and select the arc and line shown on the left in Figure 3–42. The entities on the opposite side update automatically based on the Perpendicular constraint. However, a Tangent constraint is not added automatically.

6. With the Tangent constraint still active, apply another Tangent constraint to the opposite geometry. The sketch displays as shown on the right in Figure 3–42.

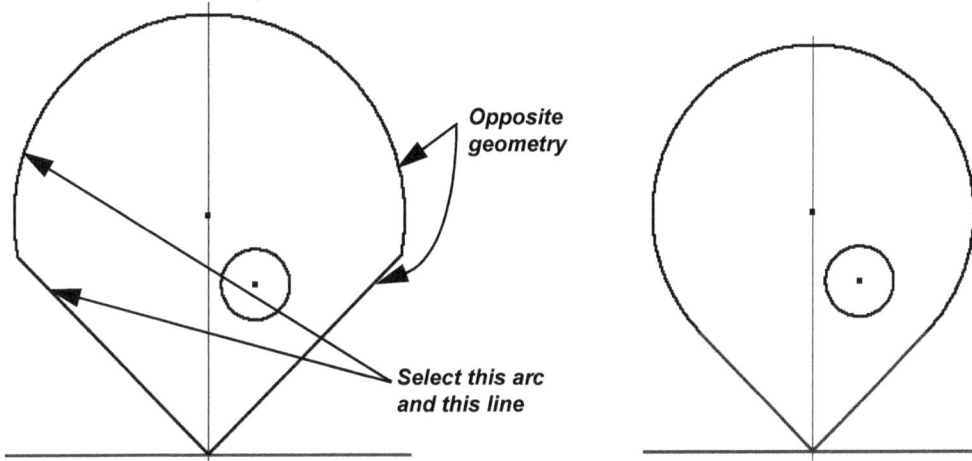

Opposite geometry

Select this arc and this line

Figure 3–42

7. In the Constrain panel, click ⌐ (Coincident Constraint) and apply a Coincident constraint to the center points of the circle and arc, as shown on the left in Figure 3–43. The sketch displays as shown on the right.

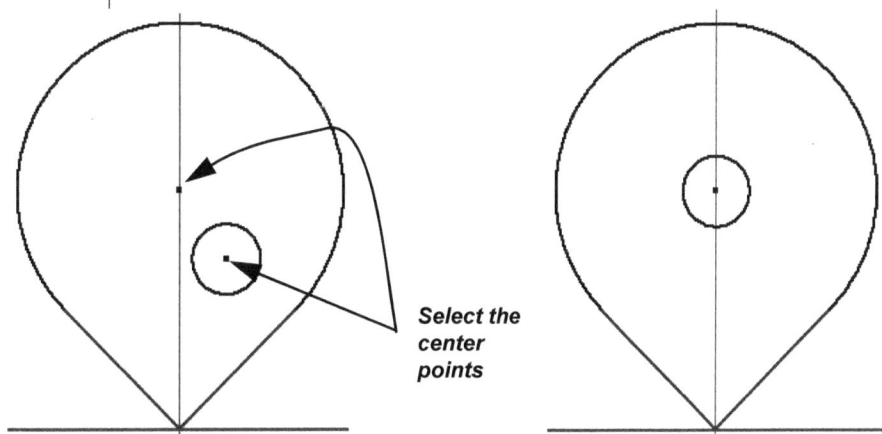

Select the center points

Figure 3–43

Task 3 - Dimension the sketch.

The shape of the sketched geometry is defined, but some of the geometry is still not fully constrained, as indicated in the lower right corner of the Status Bar.

1. In the Constrain panel, click ⌐ (Automatic Dimensions and Constraints). The Auto Dimension dialog box opens as shown in Figure 3–44.

Note the required dimensions in the dialog box.

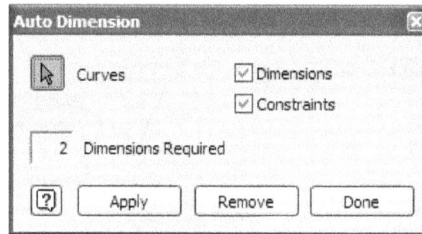

Figure 3–44

2. Click **Apply** to apply the required dimensions.

3. Click **Done** to close the dialog box.

4. Select each dimension and drag them to the locations shown in Figure 3–45.

Figure 3–45

5. In the Exit panel, click ✓ (Finish Sketch) or right-click and select **Finish 2D Sketch** to finish the sketch.

6. Save the file and close the window.

Practice 3b

Create Sketched Geometry I

Practice Objectives

- Sketch, dimension, and constrain entities to fully constrain a sketch.
- Use Relax mode to temporarily suspend constraints and dimensions to move constrained sketched entities.

In this practice, you will create sketch geometry in a new part model. The sketched geometry that you will create is shown in Figure 3–46.

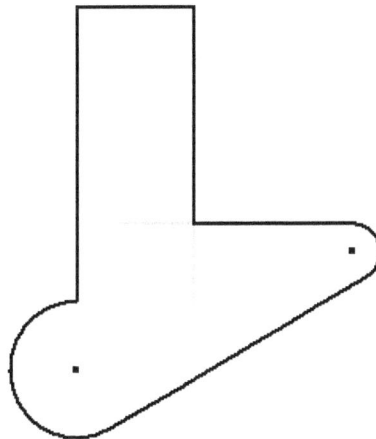

Figure 3–46

Task 1 - Create a new part and create a sketch.

1. Create a new part file using the standard metric (mm) template. The *3D Model* tab is active.

2. In the Sketch panel, click (Start 2D Sketch) and select the XY Plane as the sketch plane.

To project geometry, in the Create panel, click

(Project Geometry), *or right-click and select Project Geometry.*

3. Project the YZ and XZ planes in the sketch so that you can select them as references when locating the sketched geometry. Note that the Origin Center Point has been projected automatically.

4. Right-click and select **OK**, or press <Esc> to complete the operation.

Task 2 - Sketch the section.

1. In the *Sketch* tab>Create panel, click ✎ (Line) to sketch the line geometry.

2. Sketch the five linear entities as shown in Figure 3–47, beginning at the projected origin point so that the beginning of the line is coincident with the projected Center Point. Sketch the first vertical line (shown in Figure 3–47) so that it is approximately 40 mm to determine the overall scale of the sketch.

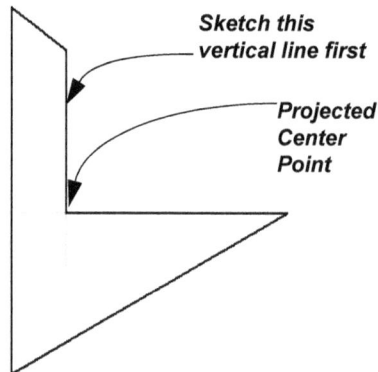

Sketch this
vertical line first

Projected
Center
Point

Figure 3–47

3. In the Create panel, click ⬜ (Fillet) to sketch a fillet arc.

4. In the *2D Fillet* field, enter **5.00**. Do not press <Enter>.

5. Select the two lines shown in Figure 3–48. A fillet arc is created and the two lines are automatically trimmed.

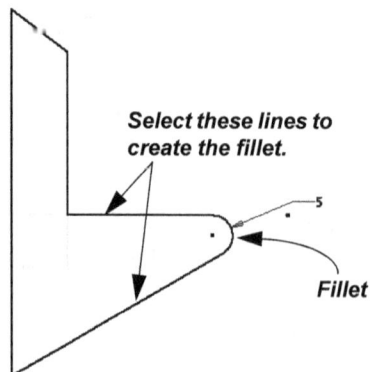

Select these lines to
create the fillet.

Fillet

Figure 3–48

6. In the Create panel, click ✑ (Three Point Arc) to sketch a three-point arc.

7. Select the vertex and edge shown in Figure 3–49 to locate the arc, and drag the edge of the arc to the location shown to define the size of the arc.

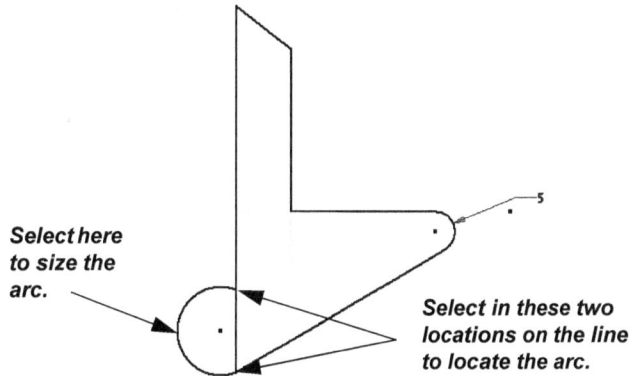

Select here to size the arc.

Select in these two locations on the line to locate the arc.

Figure 3–49

8. In the Constrain panel, click ⊥ (Coincident Constraint) to apply a Coincident constraint to the center of the arc and the left vertical line, as shown in Figure 3–50.

When sketching the Arc, if tangency is assumed with the vertex, assigning the Coincident constraint changes the shape of the geometry to maintain both constraint requirements. Show the constraint, delete the Tangent constraint, and assign the Coincident constraint.

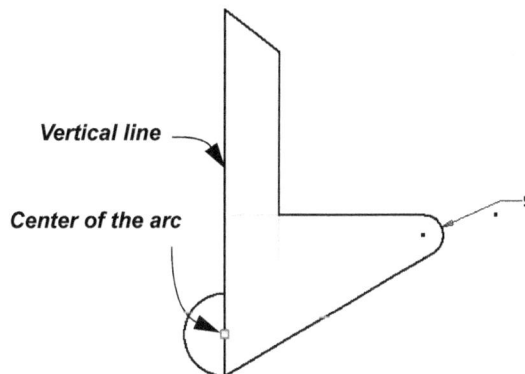

Vertical line

Center of the arc

Figure 3–50

9. In the Modify panel, click ✂ (Trim).

10. Trim the inner intersection of the arc with the left vertical line by selecting it. The sketch displays as shown in Figure 3–51.

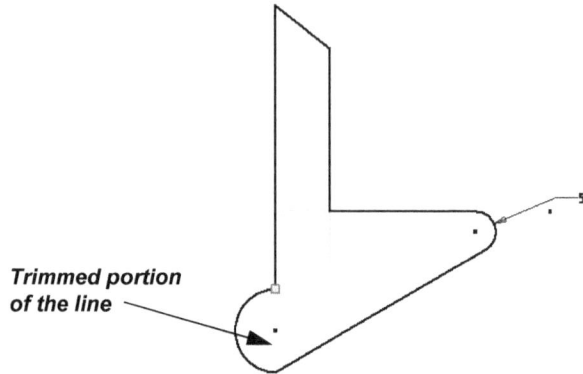

Trimmed portion of the line

Figure 3–51

11. In the Constrain panel, click ∂ (Tangent Constraint) and select the arc and line shown in Figure 3–52.

If coincidence is assumed between the arc and the vertical line, assigning the Tangent constraint changes the shape of the geometry to maintain both constraint requirements. Delete the Coincident constraint before assigning the Tangent constraint.

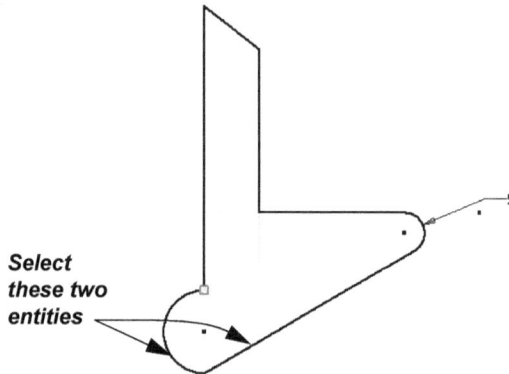

Select these two entities

Figure 3–52

12. In the Constrain panel, click ⊓ (Dimension) or right-click and select **General Dimension**.

13. Add and modify the dimensions, as shown in Figure 3–53.

*To apply the 25 unit dimension, select the entity. Before placement, right-click and select **Aligned**. Place the dimension by clicking at that point.*

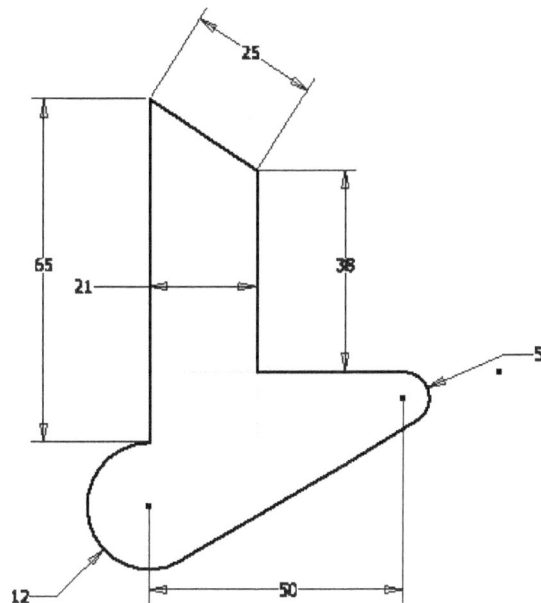

Figure 3–53

14. To finish dimensioning, right-click and select **OK**.

15. In the Status Bar, note that the sketch is Fully Constrained. Select any of the entities and try to drag them to reposition them. This is not possible because the sketch is fully defined with dimensions and constraints.

To make changes to constrained entities without using Relax Mode you would have to delete dimensions and constraints, make the change, and then constrain the entities again.

16. In the Status Bar, click (Relax Mode) to temporarily disable the constraints and dimensions so that changes can be made to the sketch.

17. Select the entity shown in Figure 3–54 and drag it downwards so that it is horizontal. Note that the dimensions and constraints reflect the change and the sketch remains Fully Constrained.

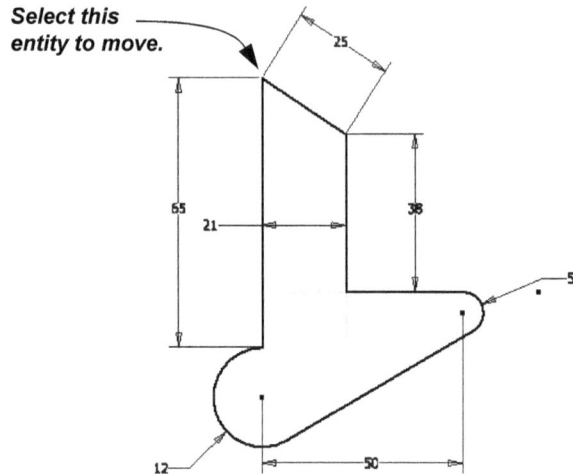

Select this entity to move.

Figure 3–54

18. In the Status Bar, click (Relax Mode) to disable Relax Mode. Note that the sketched entity remains in its moved location.

*To control the display of sketch dimensions in a model, right-click on the sketch in the Model browser and enable or disable the **Dimension Visibility** options, as required.*

19. In the Exit panel, click (Finish Sketch) or right-click and select **Finish 2D Sketch** to finish the sketch. The Front view of the model is shown in Figure 3–55.

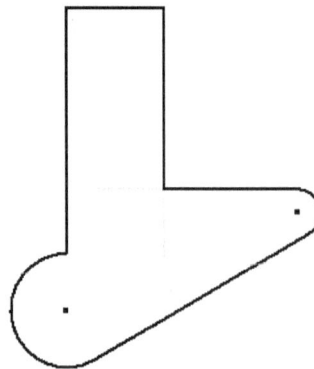

Figure 3–55

20. Save the part and close the window.

Practice 3c

Create Sketched Geometry II

Practice Objectives

- Create a new sketch on an origin plane.
- Sketch and mirror entities to create the required shape.
- Apply dimensions and constraints so that the sketch captures the design intent and is fully constrained.

In this practice, you will create sketched geometry in a new part, as shown on the left in Figure 3–56. This geometry can be used to create the solid geometry shown on the right.

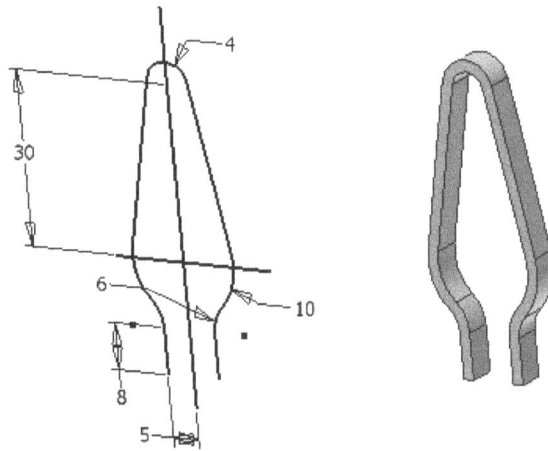

Figure 3–56

Task 1 - Create a new part and create a sketch.

1. Create a new part file using the standard metric (mm) template. The *3D Model* tab is active.

2. Start the creation of a new sketch on the XY Plane.

3. Project the YZ and XZ planes in the sketch so that you can select them as references when locating the sketched geometry. Note that the Origin Center Point has been projected automatically.

4. Right-click and select **OK** or press <Esc> to complete the operation.

To project geometry, in the Create panel, click

(Project Geometry) or right-click and select **Project Geometry**.

Task 2 - Create the sketch geometry.

*To sketch a line that is tangent to two circles, start the **Line** command, and then select and hold the cursor over one of the two circles. While continuing to hold, drag the cursor to the next circle and position it so that the Tangent constraint is visible. Release the mouse button to locate the tangent line. The same procedure can be used for tangent lines between arcs.*

As of the release of this training guide (March 2017), the tangency to the second circular/arc entity is not being automatically assigned. If required, ensure that you manually assign the tangent constraint.

1. Start the sketch by sketching two circles, two tangent lines, and a vertical attached line, as shown in Figure 3–57. Position the circles relative to the reference entities. You might have to manually add the Tangent constraint between the lines and circles after you sketch the entities.

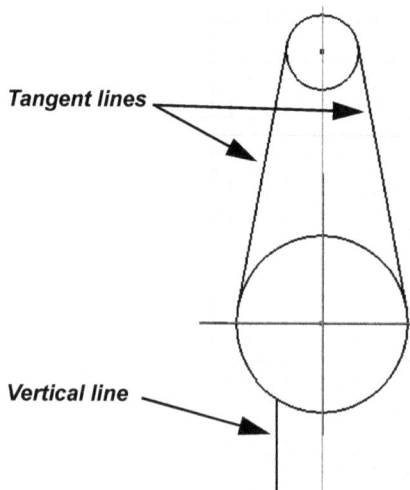

Figure 3–57

2. In the Pattern panel, click (Mirror) to mirror the vertical line about the YZ plane. The Mirror dialog box opens as shown in Figure 3–58.

Figure 3–58

3. Select the vertical line.

4. Click ⬚ (Mirror Line) in the Mirror dialog box and select the projected YZ plane, as shown in Figure 3–59. Click **Apply**.

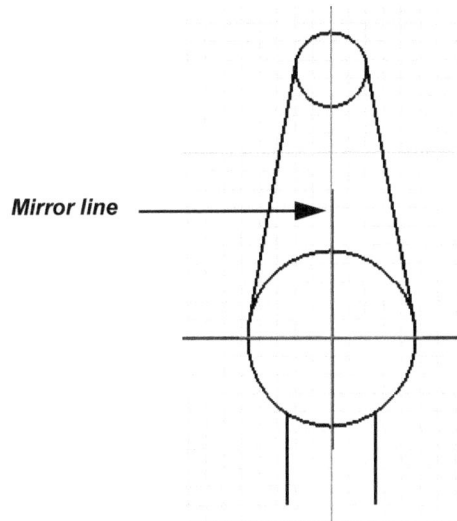

Mirror line ⟶

Figure 3–59

5. Click **Done**.

6. In the Modify panel, click ✂ (Trim) or right-click and select **Trim**. Select the unwanted segments of the circles so that the sketch displays as shown in Figure 3–60.

*To dynamically trim entities, initiate the **Trim** command, press and hold the left mouse button and drag the trim line over the entities to be removed. Release the mouse button to remove the entities from the sketch.*

Figure 3–60

7. In the Create panel, click ⬚ (Fillet).

8. In the *2D Fillet* field, enter **6.00**, and create fillets between the vertical lines and the arc segments, as shown in Figure 3–61.

Figure 3–61

9. In the lower right corner of the Status Bar, note that five dimensions are required to fully constrain the sketch.

10. Click [icon] (Show All Degrees of Freedom) in the Status Bar to display the degrees of freedom in a sketch, as shown in Figure 3–62.

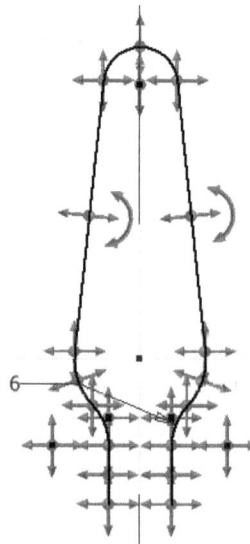

Figure 3–62

11. In the Constrain panel, click [icon] (Dimension) or right-click and select **General Dimension**.

Note that the icon that identifies the Sketch in the Model browser is displayed as 🖊 *while the sketch remains partially constrained and changes to* 🖊 *when it is fully constrained.*

12. Add and modify the dimensions, as shown in Figure 3–63. Add additional constraints, if required. Note that as each degree of freedom is constrained, its symbol is removed from the sketch.

Figure 3–63

13. In the Exit panel, click ✔ (Finish Sketch) or right-click and select **Finish 2D Sketch** to finish the sketch.

14. Hover the cursor over the ViewCube and click 🏠 (Home) to return the model to its default isometric Home View, as shown in Figure 3–64.

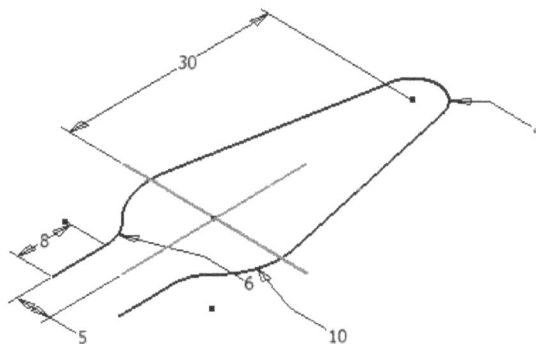

Figure 3–64

15. Save the model and enter **clip** as the name of the file.

16. Close the window.

Practice 3d

Create Sketched Geometry III

Practice Objective

- Sketch, dimension, and constrain entities to fully constrain a sketch.

In this practice, you will create the sketch shown in Figure 3–65. To successfully create this sketch you will be required to sketch linear, arc, and circular entities and ensure that they are fully dimensioned and constrained.

Figure 3–65

Task 1 - Create a new part file and start the creation of a sketch.

1. Use the standard metric (mm) template to create a new part file. The *3D Model* tab is active.

2. Start the creation of a new sketch on the XY Plane.

To project geometry, in the Create panel, click

(Project Geometry) or right-click and select ***Project Geometry.***

3. Project the YZ and XZ planes in the sketch so that you can select them as references when locating the sketched geometry. Note that the Origin Center Point has been projected automatically.

4. Right-click and select **OK** or press <Esc> to complete the operation.

Task 2 - Sketch the section.

1. In the *Sketch* tab>Create panel, click ✏ (Line) to sketch the line geometry. Begin by sketching the top horizontal line above the projected XZ plane, as shown in Figure 3–66.

2. Continue to sketch the additional arc and line entities to create the final sketch, similar to that shown in Figure 3–66.

   • When sketching the tangent arcs from the horizontal linear entities continue using the **Line** command by pressing and holding the left mouse button and dragging in the required direction. Release the left mouse button to select the end point for the arc.

   • In the Create panel, click ⌒ (Three Point Arc) to sketch the three-point arcs. Select the start point followed by the endpoint and drag the arc as required.

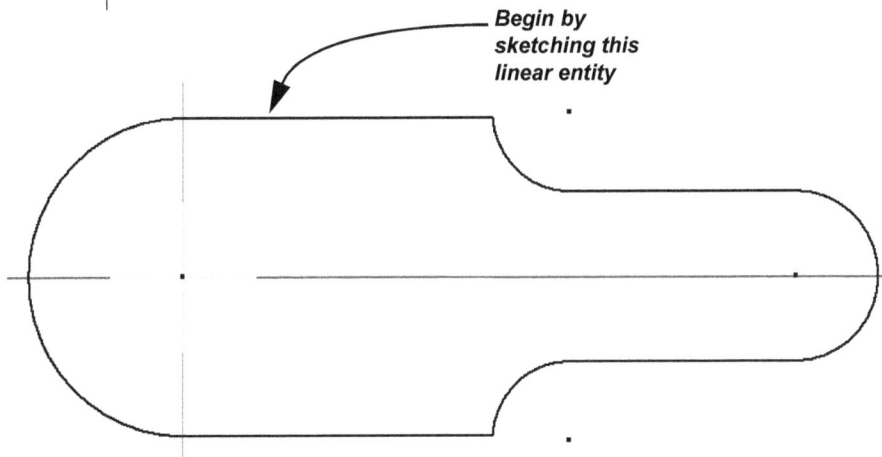

Begin by sketching this linear entity

Figure 3–66

Task 3 - Dimension and Constrain the sketch.

1. In the constrain panel, use the Horizontal, Vertical, or Coincident constraint options, as required, to ensure that the centers of the arcs on both ends of the sketch lie on the projected XZ plane. Also ensure that the two equal arcs are aligned vertically.

2. In the Constrain panel, click ⊢⊣ (Dimension) or right-click and select **General Dimension**.

3. Add and modify the dimensions shown in Figure 3–67.

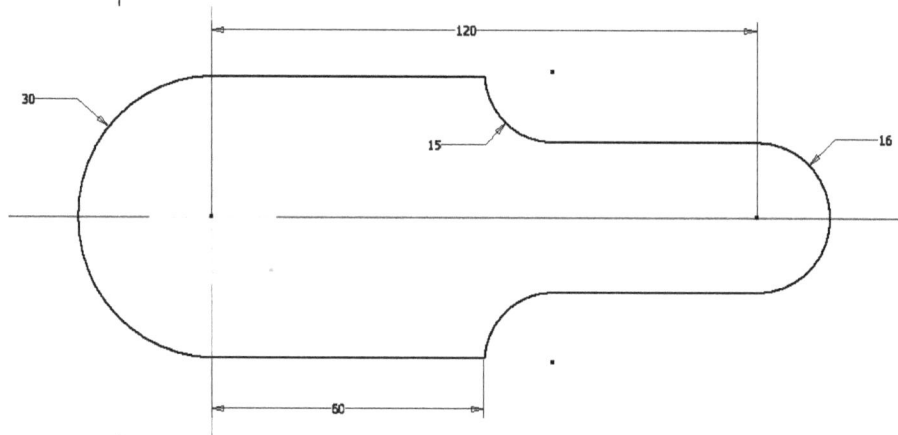

Figure 3–67

4. To finish dimensioning, right-click and select **OK**.

5. In the Constrain panel, click ▦ (Show Constraints) and select all of the sketched entities. All of the constraints that were implied when sketching are shown in the sketch,

6. Verify the existing constraints and review the Status Bar to see how many dimensions/constraints are required to fully constrain the sketch.

7. In the Status Bar, click ⬚ (Hide All Constraints) to clear the display of the constraints from the sketch.

Constraints display in light gray in a model. In Figure 3–68, the constraints are selected and displayed in red for clarity.

8. Assign additional constraints (similar to those shown in Figure 3–68) to fully constrain the sketch. The final list of constraints that you use to complete the sketch might vary, however, consider the following:

   • The four linear entities should be horizontal.

   • Tangency should be assigned between the linear entities and the arcs (4 locations).

   • The center of the large arc should be located on the projects Center Point origin.

   • The entities above and below the projected XZ plane should be symmetric. This can be achieved using the Symmetric constraint or other constraints.

   • Endpoints should be aligned between the top and bottom of the sketch.

   • Small arcs should be equal in size.

Figure 3–68

9. In the Status Bar, verify that the sketch is Fully Constrained.

10. Add the four sketch circles shown in Figure 3–69 and dimension and constrain them so that the sketch remains fully constrained. Consider the following:

- The circles all lie on the projected horizontal XZ plane.
- The two smaller circles are equal in diameter. One is dimensioned from the projected Center Point, and the other is concentric with the right-hand arc.
- The two circles on the left are concentric with the large arc and the dimension scheme shows one diameter and an offset distance.

Figure 3–69

11. Finish the sketch.

12. Save the part and close the window.

Practice 3e | Manipulating Entities (Optional)

Practice Objectives

- Open an existing part model and edit an existing sketch in the model.
- Modify the existing entities into a alternate sketch.

In this practice, you will open a model and use only the editing tools available in the sketch to obtain the required final geometry. You can use **Trim**, **Extend**, and **Mirror**, but cannot create any new entities.

Task 1 - Open a part file and edit a sketch.

1. Open **manipulating_entities.ipt**. The part only contains one sketch.

2. Right-click on **Sketch1** in the Model browser and select **Edit Sketch**. Alternatively, select the Sketch in the Model browser and click [icon] in the graphics window or double-click the sketch's name in the Model browser.

3. Using only the **Trim**, **Extend**, and **Mirror** commands, edit the sketch so that it displays as shown on the right in Figure 3–70.

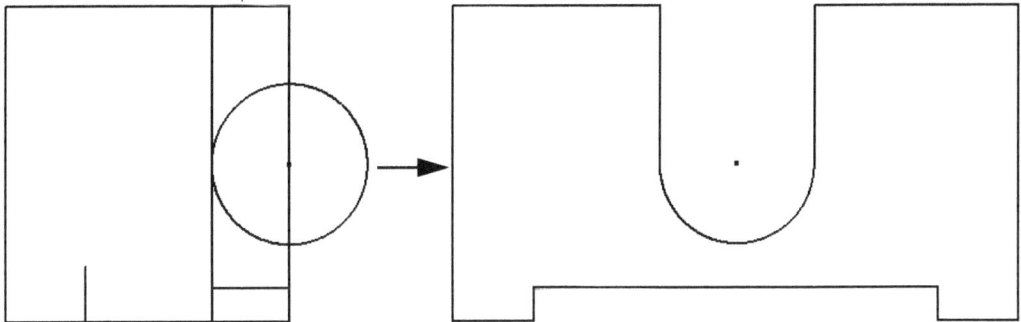

Figure 3–70

4. Save the part and close the window.

Chapter Review Questions

1. Construction entities can be used directly to create solid geometry.

    a. True

    b. False

2. Which of the following statements describes Trimming sketch entities?

    a. Continues an entity to meet the next entity in its path or to close an open sketch.

    b. Removes the segment of the entity to the nearest intersection in each direction from the point selected.

    c. Duplicates a source entity to one or more locations in the sketch or to another sketch.

    d. Provides a specific tool for stretching sketched entities versus simply selecting and dragging them in the sketch.

3. Which of the following statements describes Extending sketch entities?

    a. Continues an entity to meet the next entity in its path or to close an open sketch.

    b. Enables you to relocate original 2D sketch geometry.

    c. Duplicates a source entity to one or more locations in the sketch or to another sketch.

    d. Provides a specific tool for stretching sketched entities versus simply selecting and dragging them in the sketch.

4. How was the profile, shown in Figure 3–71, created in sketch mode?

Figure 3–71

    a. **Mirror**

    b. **Revolve**

    c. **Extend**

    d. **Trim**

5. Which of the following can be made equal using $=$ (Equal Constraint)? (Select all that apply.)

   a. Angles between lines

   b. Line Lengths

   c. Arc Radii

   d. Circle Diameters

6. Which constraints enable you to create two circles with the same center? (Select all that apply.)

   a. Concentric

   b. Colinear

   c. Coincident

   d. Tangent

7. How can you remove a visible constraint symbol from the graphics window display? (Select all that apply.)

   a. To show or hide all of the constraints on a sketch, toggle

   ![icon] (Show All Constraints) in the Status Bar.

   b. Select the entity to which it is associated.

   c. Use <F8> to show all of the constraints and <F9> to hide them.

   d. Select the symbol and press <Delete>.

8. What is the purpose of the Fix constraint, as shown in Figure 3–72?

Figure 3–72

   a. To position one point exactly on another.

   b. To edit an existing constraint.

   c. To resolve conflicts among other constraints.

   d. To fix a point relative to the default coordinate system of the sketch.

9. All constraints must be manually assigned to the sketched geometry.

   a. True

   b. False

10. Which of the following sets of constraints is used to manipulate the geometry on the left to that on the right in Figure 3–73?

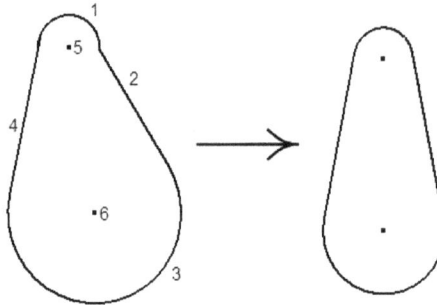

Figure 3–73

   a. 1 tangent with 2, 1 tangent with 4, 5 coincident with 6.

   b. 1 tangent with 2, 1 tangent with 4, 5 concentric with 6.

   c. 1 tangent with 2, 1 tangent with 4, 5 collinear with 6.

   d. 1 tangent with 2, 1 tangent with 4, 5 vertical with 6.

11. Based on the constraint symbols shown in Figure 3–74, which constraint types are applied to the bottom horizontal entity? (Select all that apply.)

Figure 3–74

   a. Symmetric

   b. Parallel

   c. Perpendicular

   d. Tangent

   e. Collinear

   f. Coincident

12. Fillets and chamfers that are added in the sketch become separate Fillet and Chamfer features in the Model browser once the sketch has been completed. They can be selected and deleted independent of the sketch.

    a. True

    b. False

13. What types of sketch entities can you use as the mirror line when mirroring geometry? (Select all that apply.)

    a. Construction line

    b. Solid line

    c. Projected part edge

    d. Projected work plane

Command Summary

Button	Command	Location
	Bridge Curve	• **Ribbon:** *Sketch* tab>Create panel
	Center Point Arc	• **Ribbon:** *Sketch* tab>Create panel
	Center Point Arc Slot	• **Ribbon:** *Sketch* tab>Create panel
	Center Point Slot	• **Ribbon:** *Sketch* tab>Create panel
	Chamfer (sketch)	• **Ribbon:** *Sketch* tab>Create panel
	Coincident	• **Ribbon:** *Sketch* tab>Constrain panel
	Collinear	• **Ribbon:** *Sketch* tab>Constrain panel
	Concentric	• **Ribbon:** *Sketch* tab>Constrain panel
	Constraint Settings	• **Ribbon:** *Sketch* tab>Constrain panel
	Construction	• **Ribbon:** *Sketch* tab>Format panel
	Ellipse	• **Ribbon:** *Sketch* tab>Create panel
	Equal	• **Ribbon:** *Sketch* tab>Constrain panel
	Equation Curve	• **Ribbon:** *Sketch* tab>Create panel
	Extend	• **Ribbon:** *Sketch* tab>Modify panel • (*toggle between* **Trim** *and* **Extend** *using* <Shift>)
	Fillet *(sketch)*	• **Ribbon:** *Sketch* tab>Create panel
	Fix	• **Ribbon:** *Sketch* tab>Constrain panel
	Horizontal	• **Ribbon:** *Sketch* tab>Constrain panel
	Mirror	• **Ribbon:** *Sketch* tab>Pattern panel
	Overall Slot	• **Ribbon:** *Sketch* tab>Create panel
	Parallel	• **Ribbon:** *Sketch* tab>Constrain panel
	Perpendicular	• **Ribbon:** *Sketch* tab>Constrain panel
	Polygon	• **Ribbon:** *Sketch* tab>Create panel

	Reference	• **Ribbon:** *Sketch* tab>Constrain panel
	Smooth (G2)	• **Ribbon:** *Sketch* tab>Constrain panel
	Symmetric	• **Ribbon:** *Sketch* tab>Constrain panel
	Tangent	• **Ribbon:** *Sketch* tab>Constrain panel
	Tangent Arc	• **Ribbon:** *Sketch* tab>Create panel
	Tangent Circle	• **Ribbon:** *Sketch* tab>Create panel
	Three Point Arc	• **Ribbon:** *Sketch* tab>Create panel
	Three Point Arc Slot	• **Ribbon:** *Sketch* tab>Create panel
	Three Point Center Rectangle	• **Ribbon:** *Sketch* tab>Create panel
	Three Point Rectangle	• **Ribbon:** *Sketch* tab>Create panel
	Trim	• **Ribbon:** *Sketch* tab>Modify panel • **Context Menu:** In the graphics window • (*toggle between* **Trim** *and* **Extend** *using* <Shift>)
	Two Point Center Rectangle	• **Ribbon:** *Sketch* tab>Create panel
	Vertical	• **Ribbon:** *Sketch* tab>Constrain panel

Advanced Sketch Editing Tools

The Sketch environment provides you with a variety of sketch functions and settings that enable you to efficiently create and edit sketch entities. The effective use of these tools saves time when designing and making changes to models.

Learning Objectives in this Chapter

- Relocate existing entities in a sketch by moving and rotating them.
- Resize existing sketched entities by scaling and stretching them.
- Split single entities into multiple entities.
- Copy sketched entities into the same or a different sketch.
- Create a circular or rectangular pattern of sketched entities.
- Customize sketching preferences using the Application and Document Setting options.

4.1 Advanced Editing Tools

Move, Copy, Rotate, Scale, and Stretch

The following describes some of the more advanced tools that can be used to edit a sketch. All of the editing tools described are located in the *Sketch* tab>Modify panel.

⊹	(Move)	Moves original 2D sketch geometry or copies and moves it.
⊙	(Copy)	Copies the source entities to one or more locations in the sketch or to another sketch. No relationship is established between the new and source entities. Copying entities can also be done using **Move** and **Rotate**. However, **Copy** enables you to create multiple instances at once.
↻	(Rotate)	Rotates sketch entities about a center point.
▢	(Scale)	Enlarges or reduces the size of sketched entities by entering a scale factor.
⬚	(Stretch)	Stretches entities versus simply selecting and dragging them. Unlike using the select-and-drag technique, which does not enable you to manipulate constrained geometry, the **Stretch** command enables you to stretch constrained geometry while maintaining its constraints.

The workflow for these modification commands are similar.

How To: Edit Sketched Geometry using these Tools

1. Select the required editing command. The associated dialog box opens, as shown in Figure 4–1.

Figure 4–1

To quickly select all of the entities in the sketch, right-click and select **Select All**.

2. Select the entities to edit using ⬚ (Select). To select multiple entities, press and hold <Ctrl>, or use one of the two window selection techniques shown in Figure 4–2.

Start dragging the selection window here (includes only enclosed entities).

Start dragging the selection window here (includes intersected and enclosed entities).

End dragging here.

End dragging here.

Figure 4–2

The **Optimize for Single Selection** option can be used to automatically advance to ⬚ (Base/Center Point) selection once a single entity has been selected for editing.

Hint: Selection Tools

• For the **Copy** command, once entities are selected, you can use **Clipboard** to place the entities on the clipboard for pasting into the same or another sketch.

• For the **Stretch** command, entity selection (lines, points, arcs) is important, otherwise the command functions similar to the **Move** command.

---

3. For the **Move** and **Rotate** editing commands, you can select **Copy** in the dialog box to make a copy of the entities as you move or rotate them.

4. For the **Move**, **Copy**, **Scale**, and **Stretch**, click ⬚ (Base Point) and for **Rotate**, click ⬚ (Center Point). In both situations, select a point on the original geometry as the reference/pivot point for the operation. Alternatively, you can select **Precise Input** to enter a location for the reference.

5. Select a point to which to move, copy, scale, rotate, or stretch. As you drag the cursor, the edited sketch displays. When rotating or scaling, you can also manually enter a rotation or scale value.

6. Click **Done** to complete the operation.

You can also click **Prompts** *to set how the software handles dimension/constraint conflicts in the future.*

Depending on the dimensional and geometric constraints, the dialog box shown in Figure 4–3 (or a similar dialog box) might open, prompting you to remove constraints or relax dimensions. Click **Yes** to remove any existing constraints; however, consider that you might want to add them again later to ensure that the design intent is maintained.

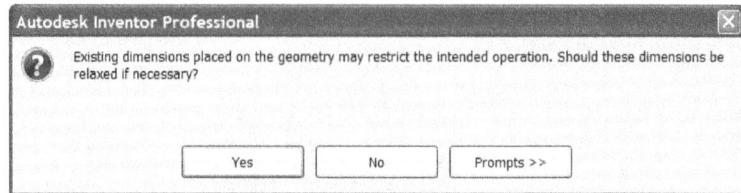

Figure 4–3

Split

The **Split** command enables you to split an entity (e.g., line, arc, or spline) based on an intersecting entity (e.g., entity, workplane, or surface). To split an entity, click $-|-$ (Split) in the Modify panel and select the entity to split. Before selecting the entity to split, hover the cursor over the entity to preview a cross mark that indicates the split location. In cases where multiple solutions are possible, the nearest one is assigned. Once split, the segments maintain all constraints, except for **Equal** and **Symmetric**, if they apply. Dimensions are also maintained when entities are split.

Copy and Paste

As an alternative to using the **Copy** command in the Modify panel, you can use the standard keyboard driven **Copy** (right-click and select **Copy** or <Ctrl>+<C>) and **Paste** (right-click and select **Paste** or <Ctrl>+<V>) functionality in a sketch. You can copy in the same sketch, to another sketch in the same model, or a sketch in a different model. Regardless of the target location, select the source entities and initiate the copy functionality. Once the entities are saved to the clipboard you can paste using any of the following techniques.

Use the right-click **Paste** *option on a Model browser* **Sketch** *node or in the graphics window if the sketch is active.*

- Right-click and select **Paste** in the same sketch.

- Finish the current sketch, in the Model browser locate the target sketch in the same model, right-click and select **Paste**.

- Open a new part to copy into, locate the target sketch in the Model browser, right-click, and select **Paste**. If the sketch does not exist, create it, right-click in the graphics window, and select **Paste** while in the Sketch environment.

4.2 Rectangular Sketch Patterns

Sketched patterns should only be used when absolutely required. Where possible it is better to create a feature pattern. Sketched patterns are less robust and harder to modify. They can also make sketches very large and hard to work with.

Patterning in a sketch enables you to quickly create identical entities in your sketch. The geometry shown in Figure 4–4 is patterned horizontally and vertically using a rectangular sketch pattern.

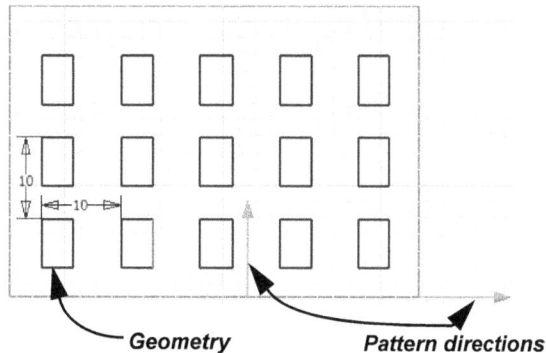

Figure 4–4

How To: Create a Rectangular Sketch Pattern

1. In the *Sketch* tab>Pattern panel, click ⬚⬚ (Rectangular Pattern) to open the Rectangular Pattern dialog box.

2. With ▨ (Geometry) selected, select the geometry to pattern.

3. To define the first pattern direction, click ▨ in the *Direction 1* area and select existing linear geometry, including lines and part edges, to define the pattern direction.

4. Enter the number of occurrences (including selected) in the ⠶⠶ *(Count)* field, and the distance between each occurrence in the ◇ *(Spacing)* field, as shown in Figure 4–5. To change the direction of the pattern, click ⬚ in the *Direction 1* area.

Drag a boundary box around sketched entities to select multiple entities at once. To clear entities, press and hold <Ctrl> and reselect the entities.

Figure 4–5

5. To define the second pattern direction, click [cursor icon] in the *Direction 2* area and select an edge or line.

6. Enter values in the ••• *(Count)* and ◇ *(Spacing)* fields in the *Direction 2* area to define the second direction pattern.

7. Click [>>] to display the additional rectangular pattern options, shown in Figure 4–6 and described as follows.

[☐ Suppress]   ☑ Associative
                ☐ Fitted

Figure 4–6

Suppress	Suppresses selected instances. Activate the option and select the element(s) to suppress. To unsuppress, activate the option again and select again. The line style of a suppressed element is dashed.
Associative	Maintains constant size and spacing for the pattern instances (default), even if changes are made to the original instance. If not selected, each pattern instance remains independent of the original.
Fitted	Defines the pattern instances such that pattern spacing measures the overall distance for the pattern. If this option is not selected (default), the pattern spacing measures the distance between instanced.

8. Click **OK** to complete the pattern.

The geometry shown in Figure 4–7 is patterned in two directions using the values shown in the Rectangular Pattern dialog box.

Figure 4–7

Once a pattern is completed, you can edit the spacing values directly on the sketch by changing their dimension value. To change the number of occurrences or spacing, right-click on any of the patterned entities and select **Edit Pattern** to access the Rectangular Pattern dialog box.

4.3 Circular Sketch Patterns

Sketched patterns should only be used when absolutely required. Where possible, it is better to create a feature pattern. Sketched patterns are less robust and harder to modify. They can also make sketches very large and difficult to work with.

Patterning in a sketch enables you to quickly create identical entities in your sketch. The geometry shown in Figure 4–8 is patterned using a circular pattern.

Figure 4–8

How To: Create a Circular Sketch Pattern

1. In the *Sketch* tab>Pattern panel, click 🔁 (Circular Pattern). to open the Circular Pattern dialog box.

2. With 🔍 (Geometry) selected, select the geometry to pattern.

3. Click 🔍 (Axis) and select the axis about which to create the pattern. You can select the center of a circle or point, the end of a line, or the end point of a projected edge as the pattern axis reference.

Drag a boundary box around sketched entities to select multiple entities at once. To clear entities, press and hold <Ctrl> and reselect the entities.

4. Enter the number of occurrences (including selected) in the ⠿ (*Count*) field, as shown in Figure 4–9. To change the direction of the pattern, click ⤴.

5. Define the angle between the occurrences in the ♡ (*Angle*) field, as shown in Figure 4–9.

Figure 4–9

6. To display the additional options in the Circular Pattern dialog box, click [>>]. The expanded options display in Figure 4–10.

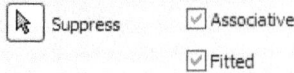

Figure 4–10

The additional options are described as follows.

Suppress	Suppresses selected instances. Activate the option and select the element(s) to suppress. To unsuppress, activate the option again and select again. The line style of a suppressed element is dashed.
Associative	Maintains constant size and spacing for the pattern instances (default), even if changes are made to the original instance. If not selected, each pattern instance remains independent of the original.
Fitted	Evenly spaces the occurrences by setting the total angle between the first and last occurrence of the pattern. If this option is not selected, the angle defines the value between each adjacent instance.

7. Click **OK** to complete the pattern.

The geometry shown in Figure 4–11 is patterned about the projected center point of the arc (pattern axis) using the values shown in the Circular Pattern dialog box.

Figure 4–11

Once a pattern is completed, you can edit the pattern by right-clicking on the pattern geometry while editing the sketch and selecting **Edit Pattern**. Change the count or angle, as required, in the Circular Pattern dialog box and click **OK**.

4.4 Sketch Preferences

Sketch settings can be set to improve usage while in the sketch environment.

Application Options

Sketch settings can be set for the software using the *Sketch* and *Part* tabs (shown in Figure 4–12) in the Application Options dialog box (*Tools* tab>Options panel, click ▦ (Application Options)). The tabs are shown in Figure 4–12.

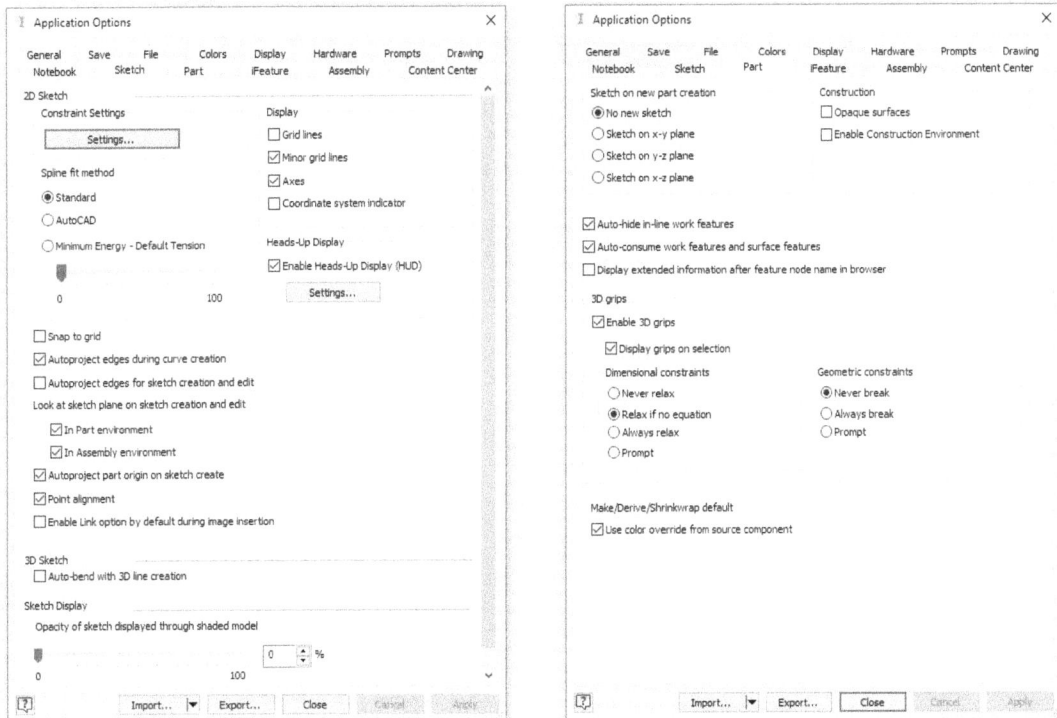

Figure 4–12

The most commonly used options in the *Sketch* tab include:

- Use the Constraint Settings dialog box to customize general constraint settings, such as editing and displaying constraints on creation, constraint inference, and Relax Mode settings.

- Set the display of **Grid lines**, **Axes**, and the **Coordinate system indicator**.

- Enable the **Snap to grid** option for sketch creation.

The size of dimensions on the screen can be adjusted using the Annotation scale field in the General tab in the Application dialog box.

- Select the **Autoproject edges for sketch creation and edit** option to automatically project existing model edges that exist on a planar face that is selected as a sketch plane.

- Enable the **Look at sketch plane on sketch creation** (in the part and assembly environments) options to orient the sketch parallel to the screen by default.

- Select the **Enable Heads-Up Display** option to control how sketched entities are located in a sketch. Clearing this option enables you to place entities using the mouse only. Activating this option enables you to place entities using the mouse or by entering values dynamically as you are sketching.

The most commonly used options in the *Part* tab include:

- Start a new part in the Sketch environment on a specific origin plane (**Sketch on x-y plane**, **Sketch on y-z plane**, or **Sketch on x-z plane**).

- Select **Auto-consume work features and surface features** to have the work features and surface features automatically consumed when they are used in the creation of a feature.

Document Settings

Sketch grid settings for the active part can be modified in the *Sketch* tab in the Document Settings dialog box (*Tools* tab> Options panel, click ⬛ (Document Settings)), as shown in Figure 4–13.

Figure 4–13

The *Sketch* tab settings include the following:

- **Snap Spacing:** Sets the snap distance in the X and Y.

- **Snaps per minor:** Sets the distance between minor grid lines relative to the defined snap distance. For example, if you set the X snap distance to 1.5mm and specify two snaps per minor, the minor lines are spaced 3mm apart.

- **Minor lines:** Sets the number of minor lines to display between major lines. Major lines display heavier in the grid display.

- **Line Weight Display Options:** Controls the display of line weights. This does not affect the line weights in printed sketches.

- **Auto-Bend Radius:** Sets the radius for the corner bends that are automatically placed on 3D lines as you sketch them.

Practice 4a | Sketch Editing Tools

Practice Objective

- Use sketch commands to copy, scale, and split sketched entities.

In this practice, you will create a sketch and use the **Copy**, **Scale**, and **Split** commands to complete the sketch. The basic sketch that you will create is shown in Figure 4–14. Using this geometry you will create solid geometry.

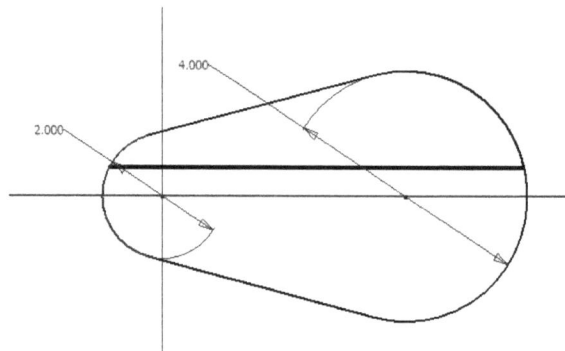

Figure 4–14

Task 1 - Create a new file.

1. Create a new part file using the Standard Imperial (in) template. If your template is set as Metric in the *My Home* dashboard, click ⬜ (New) in the Quick Access Toolbar to open the Create New File dialog box and select the Imperial template.

Task 2 - Start a new sketch and use the Copy command.

1. Create a sketch on the XY plane.

2. Sketch a circle with its center on the projected origin point.

3. Add a **2.00** inch diameter dimension to the circle.

4. In the Modify panel, click ⬚ (Copy). The Copy dialog box opens.

5. Select the circle.

6. Click ⬚ (Base Point) and select the center of the circle as the Base Point.

7. Drag the copied circle to the right of the existing one and click to place.

8. Click **Done** to end the command.

9. In the Constrain panel, click ⊢⊣ (Dimension).

10. Add the 4 inch dimension, as shown in Figure 4–15. Add a horizontal constraint to ensure that the centers of both circles remain horizontal with one another.

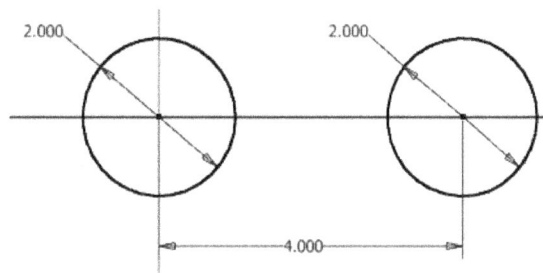

Figure 4–15

Task 3 - Use the Scale command.

1. In the Modify panel, click ⬚ (Scale). The Scale dialog box opens.

2. Select the circle that was created using the **Copy** command.

3. Click ⬚ (Base Point) and select the center of the circle.

4. When prompted to relax existing dimensions and constraints, click **Yes** for both prompts. Note that the diameter dimension is temporarily set as a reference dimension.

5. Move the cursor to see how the scale is affected. In the Scale dialog box, in the *Scale Factor* field, enter **2**. Press <Enter>.

6. Click **Done** to end the command.

*To sketch the tangent lines between the circles, start the **Line** command, and select and hold the cursor over one of the two circles. While continuing to hold, drag the cursor to the next circle and position the cursor so that the Tangent constraint is visible and release the mouse button. If you do not use this technique, you must assign the Tangency constraint to the sketch.*

As of the release of this training guide (March 2017), the tangency to the second circular/arc entity is not being automatically assigned. If required, ensure that you manually assign the tangent constraint.

7. Draw two lines tangent to the circles at the top and bottom.

8. Trim the sketch as shown in Figure 4–16.

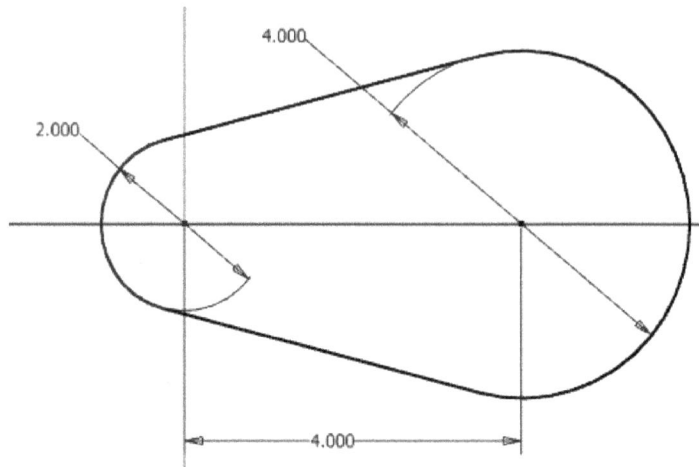

Figure 4–16

Task 4 - Use the Split command.

1. Draw a horizontal line with its end point on both arcs, as shown in Figure 4–17. The exact distance above the origin point is not important.

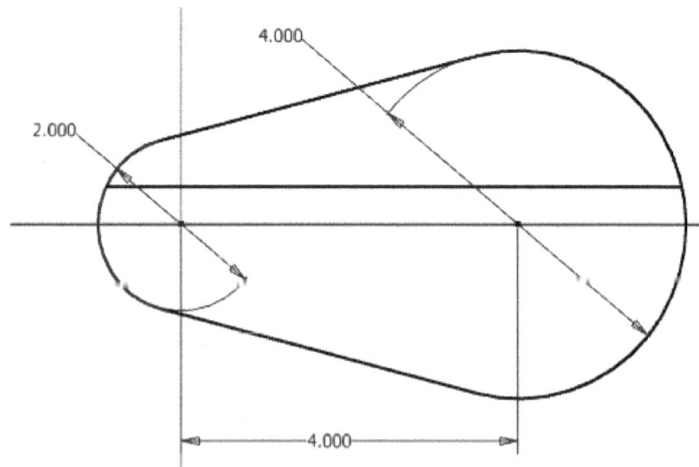

Figure 4–17

2. In the Modify panel, click $-|-$ (Split). Hover the cursor over the arc on the left side. Note that the **X** marks where the arc is split, as shown in Figure 4–18. Click on the arc to split it where it intersects the line. The design intent for the part requires that both sections of the arc remain in the sketch, so trimming is not appropriate.

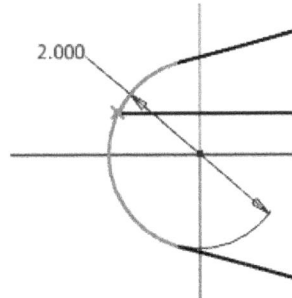

Figure 4–18

3. Repeat for the arc on the right side.

4. Right-click and select **OK** to end the command.

5. Finish the sketch.

6. Right-click on the sketch in the Model browser and clear **Dimension Visibility** to hide the dimensions in the sketch. Hiding the dimensions is not required to create an extrude, but it can help to simplify the view of the 3D geometry.

Task 5 - Extrude the geometry.

1. Create an extrude feature. The section is not automatically selected because there are two closed loops in Sketch1.

2. Select the lower half of the sketch to extrude it.

3. Extrude the feature **1** inch away from the sketch plane (behind the model when it is in the Home view).

4. Complete the feature. The model displays as shown in Figure 4–19.

Figure 4–19

5. Edit **Extrusion1**.

6. Select the *Profile* field in either the Extrude dialog box or in the mini-toolbar and select the top half of the sketch to add it to the selection set. The Split Tool can be used to divide a single sketch so that different closed areas can be extruded to different depths. In this case you are adding to the existing Extrusion.

7. Complete the feature. The model displays as shown in Figure 4–20.

Figure 4–20

8. Save the part as **practice_sketch_tools** and close the window.

Practice 4b

Copy and Paste a Sketch

Practice Objectives

- Use the keyboard driven **Copy** and **Paste** commands to duplicate entities between different sketches.
- Move entities in a sketch.
- Apply dimensions and constraints to fully constrain a sketch.

In this practice, you will create the sketch shown on the left of Figure 4–21 by copying and pasting existing sketch geometry, and modifying it. Using this method, you can reuse a sketch in multiple models. This sketch geometry can be used to create the revolved extrusion shown on the right in Figure 4–21.

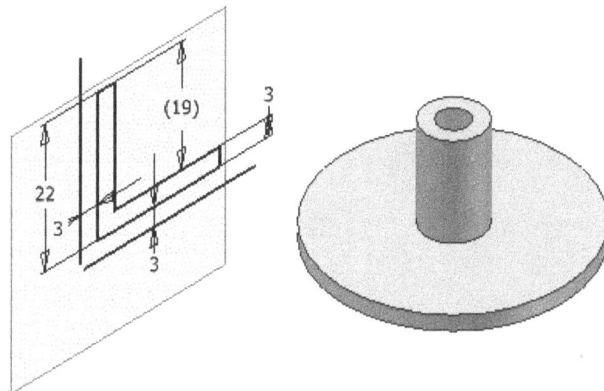

Figure 4–21

Task 1 - Open a part file and copy the sketch.

1. Open **solid_base_feature.ipt**.

2. Expand **Extrusion1** in the Model browser.

3. Right-click on **Sketch1** and select **Copy**.

Task 2 - Create a new part and paste the sketch.

1. Create a new part file using the standard metric (mm) template.

2. Create a new sketch on the YZ Plane.

3. Right-click in the graphics window and select **Paste**.

(Copy) (Tools tab> Clipboard panel) could have also been used. An alternate method has been shown that does not require the dialog box.

4. The sketch is pasted into a new sketch. You might need to reorient the sketch to the Left view to display the orientation shown in Figure 4–22. Note that the projected reference lines from the original sketch have been copied as well. Delete the reference lines shown in Figure 4–22.

Delete these lines

Figure 4–22

5. Project the XZ and XY planes as a reference to locate the copied sketched geometry.

Task 3 - Move the sketch.

---

1. Hold <Ctrl> and select all of the lines of a sketch.

2. Place the cursor on one of the lines, press and hold the left mouse button and move the sketch to the location shown in Figure 4–23.

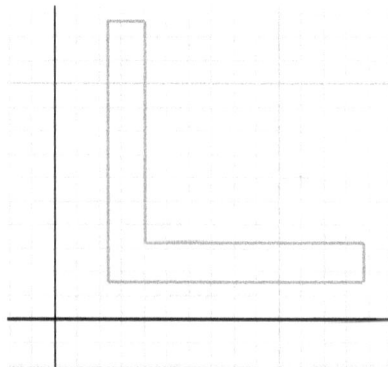

Figure 4–23

3. Click away from the entities to clear the selection.

Task 4 - Apply constraints.

1. Apply Equal constraints to the lines shown in Figure 4–24.

Apply Equal constraints to these lines.

Apply Equal constraints to these lines.

Figure 4–24

Alternatively, you can toggle the display of constraints on using <F8> and off using <F9>.

2. In the Status Bar, click ⬚ to show all of the constraints. Ensure that the equal constraints were applied.

3. In the Status Bar, click ⬚ to hide all of the constraints.

Task 5 - Dimension the sketch.

1. Dimension the sketch and locate it with respect to the reference lines, as shown in Figure 4–25. Modify the dimensions as shown.

Figure 4–25

2. Finish the sketch.

Task 6 - Create a solid base feature using the sketch.

1. Create a fully revolved base feature using the copied sketch. The final model should display as shown in Figure 4–26.

Figure 4–26

2. Save the part, enter **rev_flange** as the new part name, and close the window.

3. Close the **solid_base_feature** window without saving.

Practice 4c | Pattern Sketched Entities

Practice Objectives

- Create a circular pattern of sketched entities that rotate about a selected point in a sketch.
- Create a rectangular pattern of sketched entities that translate along a first and second direction in a sketch.

In this practice, you will pattern the circular and rectangular sketched entities shown in Figure 4–27.

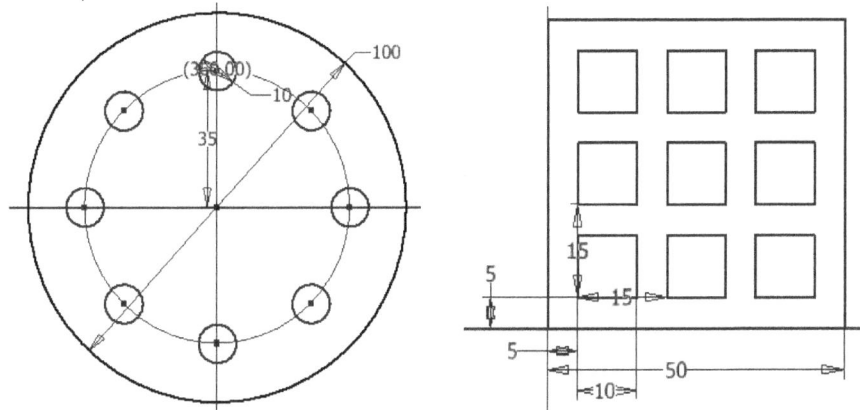

Figure 4–27

Task 1 - Create a circular pattern of entities.

1. Open **pattern_circular.ipt**.

2. Edit the sketch that was provided for you in the model.

3. In the Pattern panel, click ⬡ (Circular Pattern). The Circular Pattern dialog box opens as shown in Figure 4–28.

Figure 4–28

4. With ⬚ (Geometry) selected, select the small circle as shown in Figure 4–29.

5. Click ⬚ (Axis) and select the vertex at the center of the large circle, as shown in Figure 4–29.

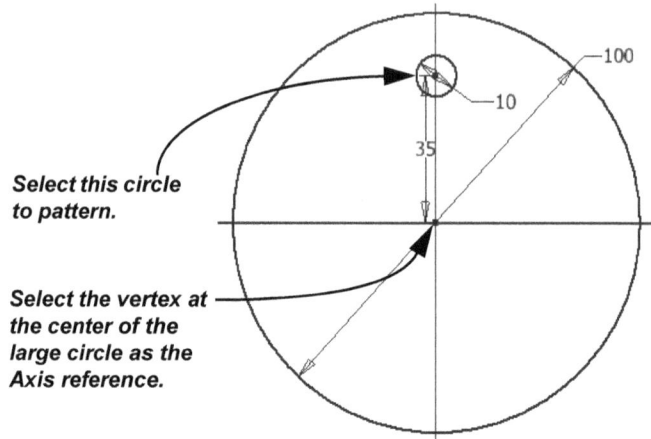

Select this circle to pattern.

Select the vertex at the center of the large circle as the Axis reference.

Figure 4–29

6. In the ⬚ (Count) field, enter **8** and maintain the **360 deg** angular value.

7. Click **OK** to complete the pattern. The sketch displays as shown in Figure 4–30.

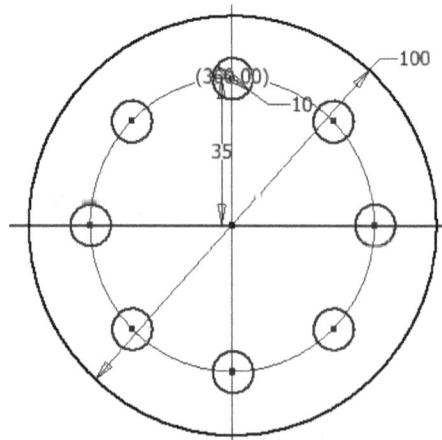

Figure 4–30

8. Finish the sketch. Save and close the model.

Task 2 - Create a rectangular pattern of entities.

1. Open **pattern_rectangular.ipt**.

2. Edit the Sketch that was provided for you in the model.

3. In the Pattern panel, click ▯▫ (Rectangular Pattern). The Rectangular Pattern dialog box opens as shown in Figure 4–31.

Figure 4–31

4. With [▯] (Geometry) selected, select the four entities of the rectangle, as shown in Figure 4–32.

5. Click [▯] (Direction1) and select the horizontal line entity, as shown in Figure 4–32.

Figure 4–32

6. In the ⸱⸱⸱ (Count) field, enter **3**, and in the ◇ (Spacing) field, enter **15** as the distance between each occurrence. The pattern previews as shown in Figure 4–33.

Figure 4–33

7. Click [cursor icon] (Direction2) and select a vertical line entity that is perpendicular to **Direction1**.

8. In the ⸱⸱⸱ (Count) field, enter **2**, and in the ◇ (Spacing) field, enter **15** as the distance between each occurrence.

9. In the *Direction2* area, click [flip direction icon] to change the direction of the pattern.

10. Click **OK** to complete the pattern. The sketch displays as shown in Figure 4–34.

Figure 4–34

11. Double-click on the **20** dimension and enter **5**. Note how the entire pattern updates to reflect the change, as shown in Figure 4–35. This is because all of the occurrences are located with respect to the initial entities that were selected for patterning.

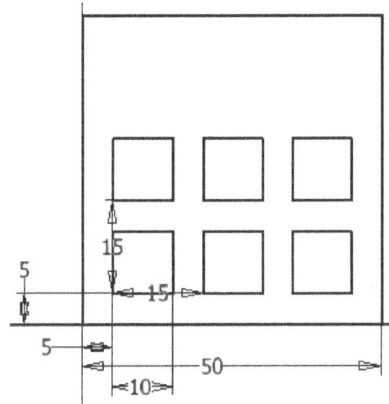

Figure 4–35

12. Right-click on any one of the patterned entities and select **Edit Pattern** in the marking menu. The Rectangular Pattern dialog box opens.

13. Change the value in the *Count* field for *Direction 2* to **3**. Click **OK** to complete the pattern.

14. Finish the sketch. The completed sketch displays as shown in Figure 4–36.

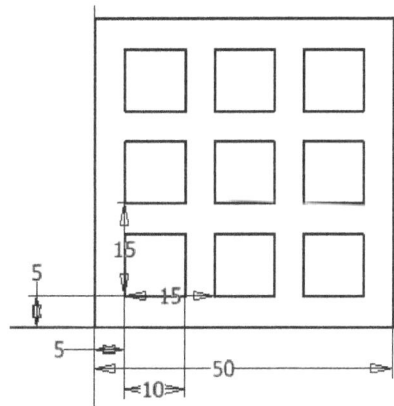

Figure 4–36

15. Save the model and close the window.

Chapter Review Questions

1. Which commands can be used to copy sketched entities? (Select all that apply.)

    a. **Copy**

    b. **Trim**

    c. **Move**

    d. **Extend**

2. Which of the following statements describes the **Move** command for sketch entities?

    a. Continues an entity to meet the next entity in its path or to close an open sketch.

    b. Enables you to relocate original 2D sketch geometry.

    c. Removes the segment of the entity to the nearest intersection in each direction from the point selected.

    d. Provides a specific tool for stretching sketched entities versus simply selecting and dragging them in the sketch.

3. You can rotate and make a copy of the entities at the same time.

    a. True

    b. False

4. Which of the following statements best describe the difference between the **Stretch** command and the select and drag technique for manipulating constrained geometry?

    a. The **Stretch** command enables you to stretch constrained geometry, maintaining established constraints, whereas, the select and drag technique cannot be used to manipulate constrained geometry.

    b. The select and drag technique enables you to stretch constrained geometry, maintaining established constraints, whereas, the **Stretch** command cannot be used to manipulate constrained geometry.

5. What is the purpose of defining the Base Point for the **Move**, **Copy**, **Scale**, and **Stretch** sketching tools?

    a. The Base Point defines a point on the original geometry as the reference point for the operation.

    b. The Base Point defines the location to which you are copying the selected entities.

6. You can copy a sketch from one part into another part.

   a. True

   b. False

7. Which of the following are required when creating a rectangular pattern in two directions, as shown in Figure 4–37? (Select all that apply.)

Figure 4–37

   a. Geometry to pattern (i.e., circular sketch)

   b. First pattern direction

   c. Second pattern direction

   d. Angle between occurrences

   e. Pattern axis

   f. Count and Space in the first direction

   g. Count and Space in the second direction

8. Which of the following tools enables you to customize the sizing of the grid display for a sketch?

   a. Application Options

   b. Document Settings

Command Summary

Button	Command	Location
	Application Options	• **Ribbon:** *Tools* tab>Options panel • **File Menu:** Options
	Circular Pattern (sketch)	• **Ribbon:** *Sketch* tab>Pattern panel
	Copy	• **Ribbon:** *Sketch* tab>Modify panel • **Context Menu:** In the graphics window with an entity selected • **Keyboard:** <Ctrl>+<C> (*to copy and* <Ctrl>+<V> *to paste*
	Document Settings	• **Ribbon:** *Tools* tab>Options panel
	Move	• **Ribbon:** *Sketch* tab>Modify panel
	Rectangular Pattern (sketch)	• **Ribbon:** *Sketch* tab>Pattern panel
	Rotate	• **Ribbon:** *Sketch* tab>Modify panel
	Scale	• **Ribbon:** *Sketch* tab>Modify panel
	Split	• **Ribbon:** *Sketch* tab>Modify panel
	Stretch	• **Ribbon:** *Sketch* tab>Modify panel

Chapter 5

Sketched Secondary Features

Sketched secondary features, such as extrusions, add or remove material from a model. As features and design intent become more complex, additional options are available to help you create more advanced secondary features.

Learning Objectives in this Chapter

- Create an extruded and revolved secondary feature.
- Create offset entities that reference existing features.
- Project Geometry to create references between sketched entities and existing features.
- Create a shared version of an existing sketch so that it can be used again to create model geometry.

5.1 Sketched Secondary Features

A secondary feature is any geometry that is added after base feature creation. It can be created as a sketch or a pick and place feature.

- Sketched features require the selection of an existing sketch to create additional geometry.

- A pick and place feature is a feature in which the shape is implied. You are not required to sketch the section (e.g., chamfer, fillets, holes).

The workflow for creating a sketched secondary feature is the same as that for base feature creation. The following differences and available tools should be noted:

- As an alternative to selecting an Origin Plane as the sketching plane, you can also select planar faces.

- Reference projection is done the same way as for base feature creation. However, because they now exist, you can project part edges to be used as constraint and dimension references. Additionally, as you reference model edges while sketching (i.e., dimensioning or offsetting), these edges or vertices are automatically projected.

This chapter covers sketched secondary features. Pick and place features are covered later in this student guide.

> **Hint: Projecting Geometry**
>
> It is strongly recommended to use Origin features as references for sketched geometry. Origin features are more stable than feature edges and the result is a robust model that is easy to modify.

- When the sketch plane is located in or behind other geometry, you can temporarily remove the portion of the model that is in front of the sketch plane using the **Slice Graphics** option. To use this option:

  1. Orient the model so that the portion you want to remove is in front of the sketching plane.

  2. Right-click on the graphics window and select **Slice Graphics**, as shown in Figure 5–1. Alternatively, you can click (Slice Graphics) in the Status Bar.

Figure 5–1

- The 🖉 (New Solid) option creates the new feature as a new solid body. This is required when modeling using the multi-body modeling technique. This is discussed in advanced level student guides.

*When creating a base feature only the **Join** option is available.*

- When creating a secondary extrude or revolve feature, the

  🗖 (Join), 🗖 (Cut), and 🗖 (Intersect) options all become available. These options enable you to specify whether the feature will add material (Join), remove material (Cut), or create the feature as an intersection (Intersect), as shown in Figure 5–2. The **Intersect** option creates geometry from the shared volume of the new and existing features and removes material outside the shared volume.

Adds material

Removes material

Intersects material (adds and removes)

Figure 5–2

Hover the cursor over the icon to display its tooltip information.

- When creating a secondary extrude or revolve feature, a number of additional options are provided for defining the depth and direction. Many of these options enable you to reference other geometry to control the depth. The Extents drop-down lists in the mini-toolbar are shown in Figure 5–3.

Two additional Depth options are available for secondary extrusions.

One additional Depth option is available for secondary revolves.

Figure 5–3

The additional extent options that are available when creating secondary sketched features are defined as follows:

To next face/body	Creates an extruded or revolved feature so that it extends to the next possible face or plane that it fully encounters. The sketch that is being extruded or revolved must fully intersect the face or body that it encounters for the feature to be created. This option is called **To Next** in either of the dialog boxes.
Through All	Creates an extruded or revolved feature through all of the features in a defined direction.

Alternate Solution Option

This option only displays for the **To**, **Between**, and **Distance from face/plane** options in the Extents drop down list, and is applicable if an irregular surface or a cylinder is selected as a termination surface. In these situations the extend location on the face might not be clear (e.g., it could be on either side of the cylinder), or there might be multiple intersection locations.

To specify the direction of the extrusion, select the *More* tab in the Extrude dialog box. You can extrude the feature to the face nearest to the profile by selecting **Minimum Solution**.

Figure 5–4 shows how the **Minimum Solution** option can be used when the extrude reference has two possible solutions. With the option enabled (as shown on the left), the extrusion extrudes to the cylindrical face nearest the sketch. With the option disabled (as shown on the right), it extrudes to the further cylindrical face.

Minimum Solution enabled   *Minimum Solution disabled*

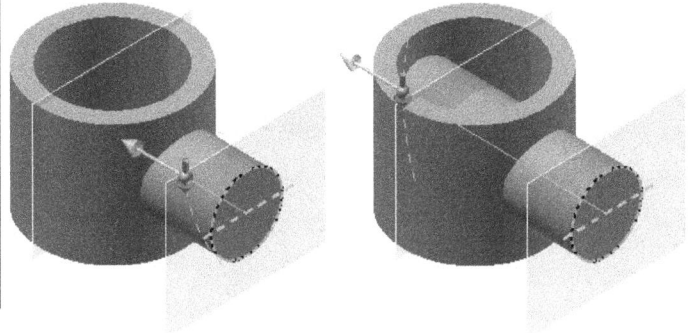

Figure 5–4

You can toggle between the taper angle value input and the extent value input by selecting inside the value input box of the mini-toolbar and pressing <Tab>.

Taper

Tapering enables you to specify an angle for an extruded feature. This is available for all but the **Distance from face/plane** extent option. A positive taper angle increases the cross-section, while a negative taper angle decreases the cross-section. To taper, select the *More* tab in the dialog box and enter a taper angle, as shown in Figure 5–5.

Taper = -15

Taper = 0

Figure 5–5

5.2 Using Existing Geometry

Once a base feature exists in a model, additional geometry is created by referencing it. The following sketching tools enable you to create new entities based on existing geometry.

Offset

The **Offset** command enables you to create new entities by offsetting existing feature edges. Rather than sketching each set of entities separately, offsetting enables you to create a copy of the projected geometry and positions it at an offset distance from the original. An example of a sketch created by offsetting feature edges is shown in Figure 5–6.

Projected geometry can be offset as well as sketch geometry.

Offset geometry ← → **Existing geometry** (2.886)

Figure 5–6

How To: Offset Entities

The option settings are maintained the next time the Offset command is used.

1. Sketch or project the geometry that is to be offset.

2. In the Modify panel, click ⬚ (Offset).
3. Right-click in the graphics window and select one of the options shown in Figure 5–7.

Loop Select: *Enables you to select one or more entities to offset loops or continuous curves. To offset individual edges, clear this option.*

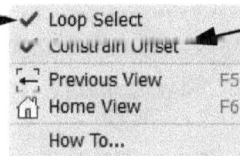

✓ Loop Select
✓ Constrain Offset
← Previous View   F5
🏠 Home View   F6
How To...

Constrain Offset: *Applies an Equal constraint to the distance between the offset geometry and the original geometry, requiring only a single dimension. To control each offset entity with its own dimension, clear this option.*

Figure 5–7

4. Select the entities or projected geometry to offset.
5. Drag the entities to the offset location and click to place them. As the entities are dragged and reach zero length, they are removed from the offset geometry set.

6. To complete the offset, right-click and select **OK,** press <Esc>, or select a new command.

7. Dimension and constrain the offset geometry as required to fully locate it in the sketch. Offset geometry only needs one offset dimension to fully locate it relative to its parent entities.

Projected Geometry

Incorporating the use of projected geometry into a sketch enables you to build relationships between features. For example, the extrusion shown on the right in Figure 5–8 was built from the projected silhouette edges of the hole shown on the left.

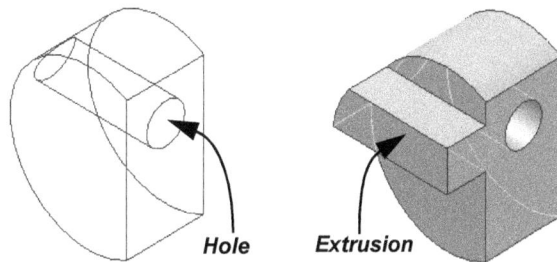

Hole   *Extrusion*

Figure 5–8

Consider the following when incorporating projected geometry into a sketch:

- To project an edge onto a sketch plane, in the Create panel, click (Project Geometry) and select the entity to project onto the sketch plane.

- Existing geometry or origin/work features can be selected for projection.

- Constraining and dimensioning sketch geometry to a part edge automatically projects the part edge onto the sketch plane.

- To project all of the edges that are intersected by the sketch plane, click (Project Cut Edges). If all of the edges are not required, select an edge and change it to construction or delete it.

- When using projected geometry, if the source changes the projected geometry also updates. To break the link between the referenced geometry and the projected geometry, right-click on the projected geometry in the sketch and select **Break Link**.

Share Sketch

A single sketch can be used to create multiple features, as shown in Figure 5–9.

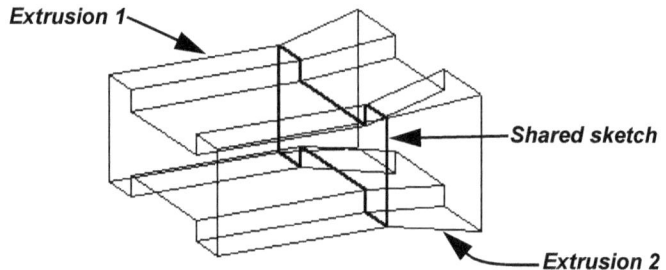

Figure 5–9

As soon as a sketch is used as a profile it is consumed in that parent feature. To reuse it, you must share it. Right-click on the sketch in the Model browser and select **Share Sketch**. Alternatively, you can select the consumed sketch and drag it to the top-level of the Model browser to share it. When you share a sketch, it is listed with the same name in the Model browser before the original feature or where ever it was placed when dragging, as shown in Figure 5–10.

A sketch is also automatically shared if it is visible and it is selected for use in creating a new solid feature.

Figure 5–10

By default, the shared sketch and all of its dimensions are displayed. To control the visibility of the sketch and/or its dimensions, right-click on the shared sketch and select or clear the **Visibility** or **Dimension Visibility** respectively. In order to use a Shared Sketch, its visibility must be toggled on, but its dimension visibility can be either on or off.

Using AutoCAD Data in Inventor

There are two workflows that can be used to incorporate AutoCAD® .DWG data into the Autodesk® Inventor® software for use in creating 3D geometry. The choice of whether to use either workflow is dependent on whether you require an associative link to be maintained with the AutoCAD .DWG data.

- When creating a sketch, the 🖼 (Insert ACAD File) option on the Insert panel, enables you to select and import an AutoCAD .DWG file into a sketch to create 3D geometry.

  - During import you can select which layers and selectively choose entities that are to be imported onto the active sketch. The data is imported as native Autodesk Inventor data and no associative link is maintained to the DWG file.
  - You can add dimensions and/or constraints as required to capture your design intent and use the sketch to create solid geometry.

- An AutoCAD .DWG file can also be inserted directly into a part file and used to create 3D geometry or placed in an assembly file and used to constrain geometry. This option enables you to maintain an associative link between the AutoCAD DWG and the part file, so that any changes to the DWG data updates in the part file.

More information on this workflow is covered in the advanced student guide, or you can search on Associative DWG or DWG Underlay in the help documentation.

  - The general workflow for inserting an AutoCAD part file includes inserting the file (*Manage* tab>Insert panel, click 🖼 (Insert)) on a selected planar face or work plane and then projecting the data onto a sketch using the **Project DWG Geometry** option in the sketch.
  - The general workflow for placing an AutoCAD part file in an assembly involves using the **Place** option, selecting the file, and selecting a reference plane and point to locate the .DWG file. The **Place** option can be used to create or locate geometry in an assembly.
  - Multiple AutoCAD DWG files can be inserted on different planes to create the required 3D geometry.

Practice 5a

Create a Sketched Revolve

Practice Objectives

- Create a revolved base feature using a provided sketch.
- Create a secondary extrude feature that references a face and entities in the base feature to fully constrain it.

In this practice, you will create a revolved base feature from an existing sketch and create an extruded cut on a face of the base feature, as shown in Figure 5–11.

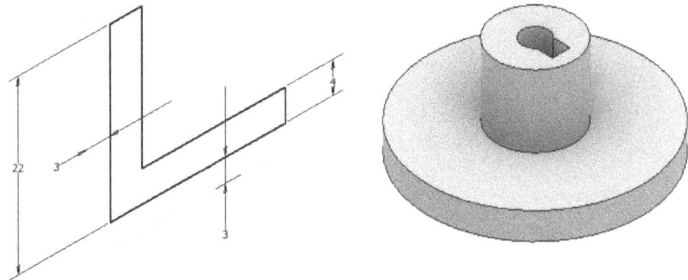

Figure 5–11

Task 1 - Open a part file and create a revolved base feature.

1. Open **rev_flange_1.ipt**.

2. In the Create panel, click 🍞 (Revolve).

3. The sketch is automatically selected as the Profile. Select the line (projected XZ Plane) shown in Figure 5–12 as the axis of rotation.

Select this line as the axis of rotation

Figure 5–12

4. The revolved feature is automatically revolved 360 degrees (**Full**), as shown in Figure 5–13.

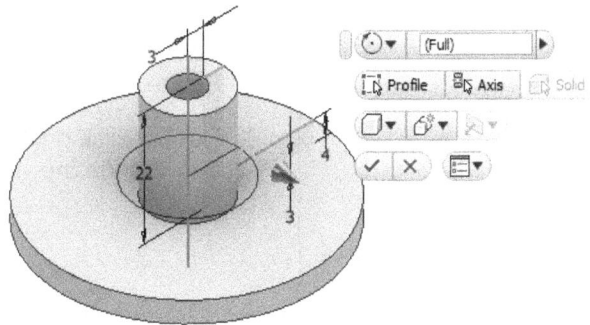

Figure 5–13

5. To change the value of the revolved angle, select **Angle** in the Extents drop-down list and enter **220** in the field. This can be done in the Revolve dialog box or directly in the mini-toolbar.

6. Click to change the direction of the feature creation. The revolved feature displays as shown in Figure 5–14.

Select Angle in the drop-down list.

Select Direction 2 in the drop-down list.

Figure 5–14

7. Complete the feature.

Task 2 - Modify the feature.

1. Right-click on **Revolution1** in the Model browser and select **Show Dimensions**.

2. Double-click on the 220 degrees dimension as shown in Figure 5–15 and change the angle value to **360** degrees.

3. Double-click on the 4 dimension as shown in Figure 5–15 and change the value to **6**.

Modify these dimensions

Figure 5–15

4. In the Quick Access Toolbar, click ![icon] (Local Update) to update the model.

Task 3 - Create an extruded cut by sketching the section.

1. Select the top circular face of the model and click ![icon] to create a new sketch on the selected plane, as shown in Figure 5–16.

Alternatively, you can right-click on the top circular face of the model and select New Sketch to create a new sketch on the plane.

Top circular face

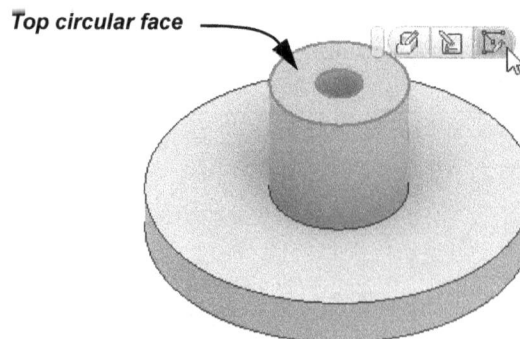

Figure 5–16

2. Sketch and dimension three lines with respect to the center point of the circular edge, as shown in Figure 5–17. Project the XZ Plane and apply the Symmetric constraint to the two parallel horizontal lines to fully constrain the sketch.

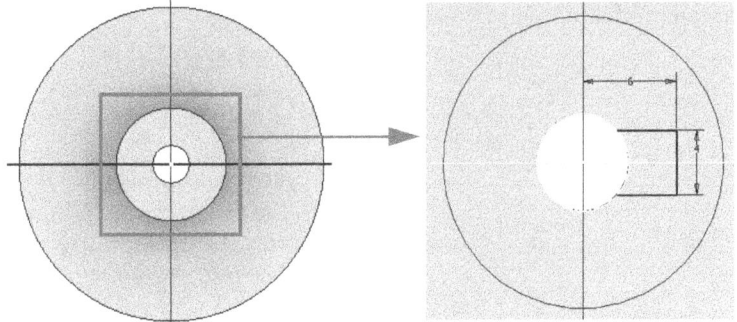

Figure 5–17

3. Finish the sketch.

4. In the *3D Model* tab>Create panel, click (Extrude) to create a cut using this sketch.

5. Select the new sketched profile. It is not automatically selected because there are now two closed sections in the part. Both of the sections exist in the newly created sketch.

6. Click (Cut) to remove material, if not already set.

7. Enter **16** in the *Extents distance* field.

8. Ensure that the cut is extruded inside the part. If required, change its direction.

9. Complete the feature. Display the model as shaded, as shown in Figure 5–18.

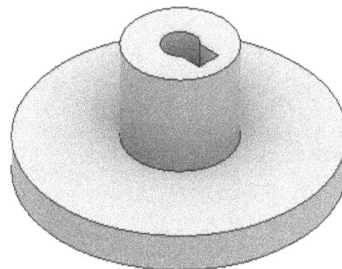

Figure 5–18

10. Save the part and close the window.

Practice 5b

Create Sketched Extrusions

Practice Objectives

- Create features that add and remove material to a model.
- Use the **Offset** command to create entities that reference other features so that the design intent is built into the model.
- Modify features in the model to ensure that the new features update based on the references that were established.

In this practice, you will create two extruded features using geometry that exists in a model that is provided for you. The new geometry will be created using the **Offset** command. The initial and final models are shown in Figure 5–19.

Initial Model   *Final Model*

Figure 5–19

Task 1 - Open a part file.

1. Open **Offset.ipt**.

2. In the Sketch panel, click ▱ (Start 2D Sketch) and select the top face of the bracket, as shown in Figure 5–20, as the sketching plane.

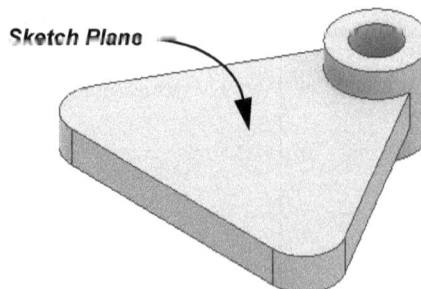

Sketch Plane

Figure 5–20

If a model is not automatically oriented into 2D on sketch creation, you can select a face and click

▱ (Look at) in the Navigation bar to look at the plane, or you can select a face on the ViewCube. If the orientation is not as expected, spin the model into the approximate location using the arrows around the outer extent of the ViewCube.

Task 2 - Offset geometry.

1. In the Create panel, click ⬟ (Project Geometry) or right-click and select **Project Geometry**. Select the face shown in Figure 5–21 to project the six edges that bound the face onto the sketch plane.

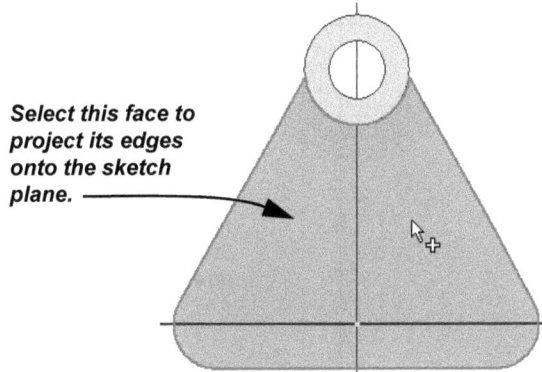

Select this face to project its edges onto the sketch plane. —————

Figure 5–21

2. In the *Sketch* tab>Modify panel, click ⬟ (Offset).

3. Select a location on any of the projected entities. Drag the cursor towards the center of the model. Note that the loop of projected entities are automatically being offset, as shown in Figure 5–22.

Offset entities

3.114 mm

Figure 5–22

4. Right-click and select **Cancel** to cancel the command or press <Esc>.

5. In the Modify panel, click ⬚ (Offset) again.

6. Right-click in the graphics window and toggle off **Loop Select**. This enables you to individually select entities to offset.

7. Select the three entities shown in Figure 5–23 to be offset.

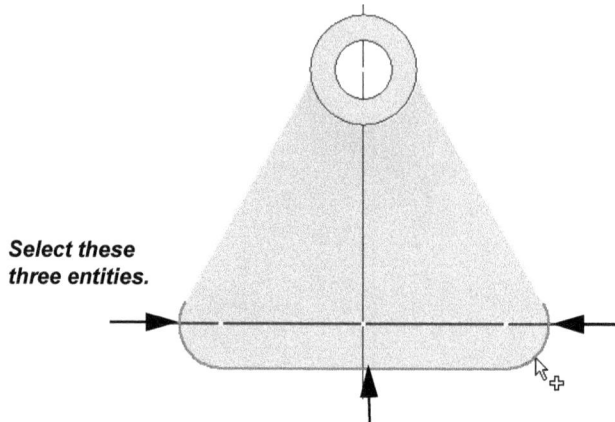

Select these three entities.

Figure 5–23

8. Right-click and select **Continue**. Drag the entities to the location shown in Figure 5–24 and select to place them.

2.297 mm

Figure 5–24

Task 3 - Sketch line and apply a Tangent constraint.

1. Sketch a horizontal line shown in Figure 5–25.

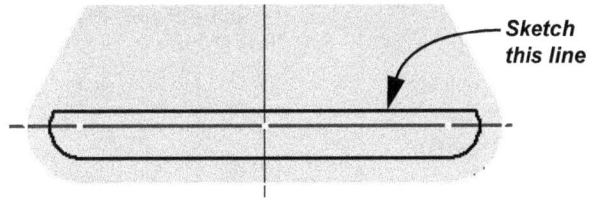

Sketch this line

Figure 5–25

2. At the bottom of the screen, the Status Bar indicates that dimensions are required to fully constrain the sketch. Click

    (Show all degrees of Freedom) in the Status Bar. The arrows that display on the screen indicate the degrees of freedom remaining in the sketch. Select the option again to clear their display.

3. Apply Tangent constraints to the line and arcs, as required.

4. Apply and modify a vertical linear dimension to the lines shown in Figure 5–26 to fully locate the geometry.

Depending on how the horizontal line was sketched, you might require an additional Coincident constraint at the right end.

3.15

Figure 5–26

5. Review the degrees of freedom remaining in the sketch. Note that there are no remaining degrees of freedom symbols in the sketch.

6. Finish the sketch.

Task 4 - Extrude the sketch.

Because the face was selected as the Project Geometry reference, there are two closed sections in the sketch. This means that the required closed section is not automatically selected to be extruded. Consider changing the projected entities to construction lines if the edges are not required.

1. In the Create panel, click ⬚ (Extrude) to create an extrusion. Select the profile such that the extrusion displays similar to that shown in Figure 5–27.

Figure 5–27

This extrusion is created to add material.

2. Set the depth extent to 10mm and complete the extrusion.

Task 5 - Offset projected edges.

1. Select the top face you have just created and click ⬚ to create a new sketch on this face, as shown in Figure 5–28.

*To select a face on the model, the **Select Face and Edges** filter option in the Quick Access Toolbar must be active.*

Select this
top face

Figure 5–28

2. In the Create panel, click ⬚ (Project Geometry). Select the face used as the sketch plane to project its edges.

3. In the *Sketch* tab, in the Modify panel, click ⚏ (Offset).

4. Right-click and select **Loop Select**. Because the option was cleared in the previous task it must be enabled again.

5. Select one of the edges of the extrusion, as shown in Figure 5–29.

Select this edge

Figure 5–29

6. Offset (to the inside), enter **1** in the entry field, and press <Enter>. The entities are offset and the dimension is automatically added to the sketch, as shown in Figure 5–30.

Offset entities

Figure 5–30

7. Finish the sketch.

8. In the *3D Model* tab>Create panel, click ▱ (Extrude) to remove material using the sketch you have just created.

9. Select the sketch that was just created as the profile for the feature.

10. Using either the Extrude dialog box or the mini-toolbar, click ⊟ (Cut) to remove material from the model, if not already set.

11. Accept the defaults and complete the cut. The model displays as shown in Figure 5–31.

Figure 5–31

Task 6 - Edit the model.

1. Right-click on the last extrusion that you have created (cut) in the Model browser and select **Edit Feature**. You can also double-click the feature in the Model browser, or select a surface that makes up the feature and click [icon]. The Extrude dialog box and mini-toolbar for the feature display.

2. Select **Through All** (**All** if selecting in the dialog box) in the Extents drop-down list to extrude the cut through the entire part.

3. Complete the feature.

Sketch1 is a shared sketch that was used to create multiple features in the model.

4. Double-click on **Sketch1** (below the **Origin** node in the Model browser). Change the fillet from 6 units to **10**. Finish the sketch. The model displays as shown in Figure 5–32. Both of the extrusions that you created update based on the change to Sketch1 because of the established relationships.

Figure 5–32

5. Save the model and close the window.

Practice 5c

Share Sketch

Practice Objectives

- Appropriately reuse a shared sketch to create required geometry in the model.
- Control the visibility of sketched entities and dimensions.

In this practice, you will use a single sketch to create four extrusions to create the geometry shown in Figure 5–33. To use the same sketch for multiple features you will use the **Share Sketch** command to add it as an independent node in the model so that it can be reused.

Figure 5–33

Task 1 - Open the part and create the base feature.

1. Open **Shared Sketch.ipt**.

2. Create the extrusion shown in Figure 5–34 using the sketch provided. The depth of the extrusion should be 6. You must select multiple closed sections to obtain geometry. To select multiple closed sections at one time, you can manually select them or drag a crossing-window around all the closed sections.

Figure 5–34

Task 2 - Share the sketch.

1. Expand **Extrusion1** in the Model browser.

A shared sketch is not consumed by the extruded features which are created from it. It can be found in the Model browser under any features that use it, and in the tree on its own.

2. In the Model browser, right-click on the **Sketch1** and select **Share Sketch**. The sketch is shared and is now listed as an independent node, as shown in Figure 5–35. The shared sketch can now be used for additional features without having to create a new sketch.

Figure 5–35

A sketch must remain visible if it is to be used to create geometry. However, dimension visibility is not required.

3. When a sketch is shared, its sketched entities and dimensions are set as visible. To clear the dimensions (not entities) from the display, right-click **Sketch1** in the Model browser and select **Dimension Visibility** to clear it.

Task 3 - Create additional features.

1. Create the extrusion shown in Figure 5–36 using the shared sketch. Both of the cuts are created as a single extruded feature and they are to remove all material through the entire model.

Figure 5–36

2. Create the extrusion shown in Figure 5–37 using the shared sketch. The depth of the extrusion should be **20**. Note that the extrusion adds material to the model. The extrusion cannot cut through the base feature and add material at the same time.

Figure 5–37

3. Create another extrusion that removes the material shown in Figure 5–38.

Create an extruded cut that removes this material.

Figure 5–38

Task 4 - Modify the sketch.

---

*Dimension Visibility can be controlled through either the **Sketch1 Shared Sketch** node or the **Sketch1** node in **Extrusion1**.*

1. Right-click on **Sketch1** and select **Dimension Visibility** to toggle on the display of dimensions.

2. Double-click on the **120** dimension and enter **160**.

3. Double-click on the **30** diameter dimension and enter **40**.

4. In the Quick Access Toolbar, click (Local Update) to update the model. Note how all of the features that referenced the sketch update.

5. Right-click on *Offset* (to the inside), enter **1** in the entry field, and press <Enter>. Select **Visibility** to remove the sketch from the display.

6. Save the model and close the window.

Chapter Review Questions

1. The **Offset** option is commonly used to create sketched entities offset from projected geometry. In the sketch shown in Figure 5–39, how many dimensions are required to fully constrain the sketch? Assume **Constrain Offset** and **Loop Select** are toggled on.

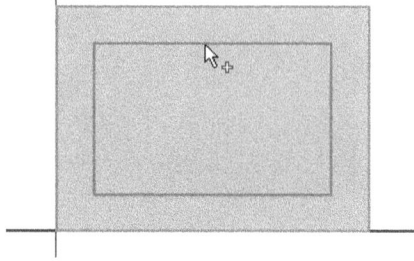

Figure 5–39

   a. 1

   b. 2

   c. 3

   d. 4

   e. More than 4

2. To create a new feature in the model, you are required to reuse a Sketch that was created for **Extrusion2**, as shown in Figure 5–40. Is this possible? If so, which option would you use?

Figure 5–40

   a. You cannot reuse an existing sketch, you must recreate it using projected geometry.

   b. It is possible using the **Visibility** option.

   c. It is possible using the **Edit Sketch** option.

   d. It is possible using the **Share Sketch** option.

3. Sketch1 was used to create **Extrusion1**, as shown in Figure 5–41. Has **Sketch1** been shared?

Figure 5–41

   a. Yes

   b. No

4. Which of the following is true regarding Projected Geometry in a sketch?

   a. You can only project edges into a sketch that lie in the same plane as the sketching plane.

   b. When selecting a Work Plane as a sketching plane, the edges that lie in the plane are automatically projected into the sketch.

   c. When selecting an existing edge as a constraint or dimension reference it is automatically projected into the sketch.

   d. When you use a projected edge as a dimension reference, no relationship between the sketch and the projected edge's parent feature is established.

5. Which command is used to create an extrusion that adds material to existing solid geometry?

   a. ⬚ (Join)

   b. ⬚ (Intersect)

   c. ⬚ (Cut)

   d. ⬚ (Solid)

6. The **Alternate Solution** option displays in the *More* tab in the Extrude dialog box if the termination face is not clear. Which of the following extent options is being used if this option displays? (Select all that apply.)

   a. **Distance**

   b. **To Next**

   c. **To**

   d. **Between**

   e. **All**

   f. **Distance From Face**

7. Which tool temporarily hides the portion of a part that is above the sketch plane to display the plane more clearly for sketching, as shown in Figure 5–42?

Figure 5–42

   a. **Slice Graphics**

   b. **Relax Mode**

   c. **Look At**

   d. **Hidden Edge Display**

Command Summary

Button	Command	Location
	Insert ACAD File (into sketch)	• **Ribbon:** *Sketch* tab>Insert panel
	Insert ACAD File (into model)	• **Ribbon:** *Manage* tab>Insert panel
	Offset	• **Ribbon:** *Sketch* tab>Modify panel
	Project Cut Edges	• **Ribbon:** *Sketch* tab>Create panel, expanded Project Geometry drop-down list
	Project Geometry	• **Ribbon:** *Sketch* tab>Create panel • **Context Menu:** In the graphics window
N/A	**Share Sketch**	• **Context Menu:** In Model browser with sketch selected
	Slice Graphics	• **Status Bar** • **Context Menu:** In the graphics window

Creating Pick and Place Features

Chamfers, fillets, and holes are known as pick and place features. This means that the shape of the feature is implied; therefore, you are not required to sketch the section. Pick and place features can be added once the model's base feature has been created.

Learning Objectives in this Chapter

- Create a chamfer by defining its dimension scheme and placement references.
- Create constant and variable fillets by defining placement references, dimensions, and shape settings.
- Create a face fillet between faces that do not share an edge.
- Create a full round fillet between three adjacent face.
- Create a hole by defining its type, placement reference, dimensions, and depth options.
- Create a thread on a cylindrical face.

6.1 Edge Chamfer

A chamfer adds a beveled edge between two adjacent surfaces, as shown in Figure 6–1. An edge chamfer can add or remove material.

Edge chamfer (material added)

Edge chamfer (material removed)

Figure 6–1

General Steps

Use the following general steps to create an edge chamfer along the entire length of an edge:

1. Start the creation of the feature.
2. Define the dimensioning scheme.
3. Select the placement references and enter distances.
4. Select additional options, as required.
5. Select references to create a partial chamfer, as required.
6. Complete the feature.

Step 1 - Start the creation of the feature.

Use one of the following methods to create an edge chamfer:

- Select the edge(s) to be chamfered and click ⬦ in the heads-up display on the model.

- In the *3D Model* tab>Modify panel, click ⬦ (Chamfer) to start the creation of an edge chamfer.

*By Default, the display of the Mini-Toolbar is toggled off. On the View tab, expand **User Interface** and enable the **Mini-Toolbar** option to display it. To collapse a dialog box, click the up arrow at the bottom of the dialog box.*

Step 2 - Define the dimensioning scheme.

Edge chamfers have three alternative dimension types that can be used. Select the type from the lists shown in Figure 6–2.

Select a dimension type
using the icons in the
Chamfer dialog box.

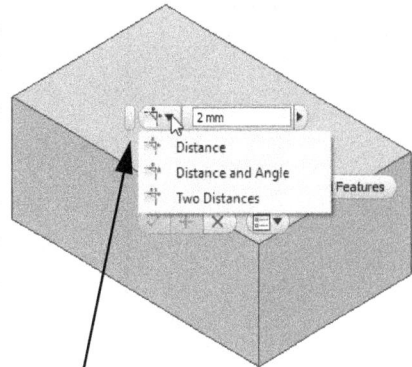

Expand the Dimension type
drop-down list in the mini-toolbar
to select a dimension type.

Figure 6–2

Changing dimension types clears the reference edge selection. It is recommended that you define the dimension type before selecting a placement reference.

The dimension types are described as follows:

(Distance)	The chamfer is created at the same distance from the edge on each face.	
(Distance and Angle)	The chamfer is created at a distance from the edge on one face and at an angle to that face.	
(Two Distances)	The chamfer is created at one distance from the edge of one face and a different distance from the edge of another.	

Step 3 - Select the placement references and enter distances.

Alternatively, you can select the reference before clicking

(Chamfer).

The references and dimensions required to locate a chamfer depend on the dimension type that is used.

- For a (Distance) chamfer, select the edge(s) to chamfer and enter a distance value from the edge to be removed.

To toggle between the fields in the mini-toolbar, press <Tab> or select the field to activate it.

- For a ⬚ (Distance and Angle) chamfer, select the face and then select the edge(s) from the face that contains the chamfer. Enter a distance value from the edge to be removed and an angular value.

- For a ⬚ (Two Distances) chamfer, select the edge and click

  ⬚ or ⬚ to toggle between the two surfaces that touch the edge. Enter a distance value to be removed from the highlighted surface. With this method, you can only chamfer one edge at a time.

If you select multiple edges, a single dimension is applied to all of the edges. This method enables you to control changes to all edges with a single value. To clear the selection of an edge, press <Ctrl> or <Shift> and reselect the edge.

Step 4 - Select additional options, as required.

Additional options (shown in Figure 6–3) enable you to further define the edges of the chamfer.

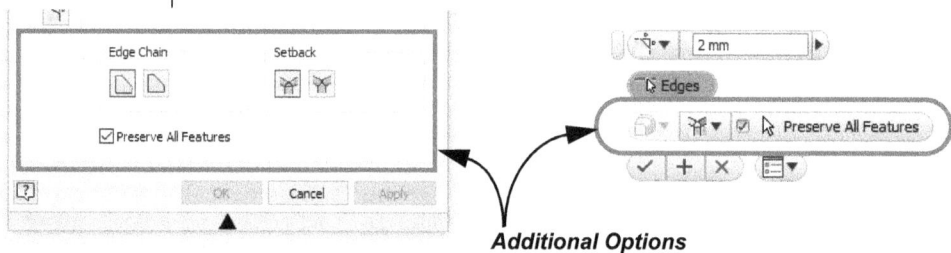

Additional Options

Figure 6–3

The additional options are described as follows:

- The **Edge Chain** options determine how edges with curves are selected.

  - Click ⬚ (All tangentially connected edges) to select all of the tangent edges.

  - Click ⬚ (Single edge) to select each edge individually.
  - In the mini-toolbar, the options are available as shown in Figure 6–4.

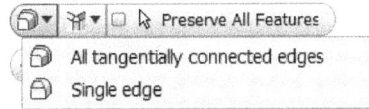

Figure 6–4

*The **Setback** icons are only available when using ▦ (Distance).*

- Setback options control how chamfers meet at corners, as shown in Figure 6–5.

Figure 6–5

- The **Preserve All Features** option retains the existing features affected by the chamfer (e.g., a hole near the chamfered edge).

Step 5 - Select references to create a partial chamfer, as required.

New in 2018

To create a chamfer that does not fully extend the length of a selected reference edge, you can use the options on the *Partial* tab of the Chamfer dialog box. A partial chamfer cannot be defined using the Mini-Toolbar options. To define a partial chamfer on a selected reference, complete the following:

1. Select the *Partial* tab.
2. Select a point on the edge to define the end vertex. The start point is automatically set on the edge and is identified with a black dot. Once selected, the partial chamfer previews in the model and values populate in the dialog box.
3. The *Set Driven Dimension* option is set to **To End** by default. This sets the *To End* field as driven and prevents you from editing it. All changes to the size of the chamfer are made using the *To Start* and *Chamfer* fields. To adjust which fields are modifiable, you can change the option in the *Set Driven Dimension* option to **To Start** or **Chamfer**.
   - The **Chamfer** option enables you to enter distances from the start and end of the line to define the extent of the partial chamfer.

- The **To Start** option enables you to enter a distance to the end and the chamfer length to define the extent of the partial chamfer on the edge.

4. Modify the values in the columns as required to define the extent of the partial chamfer. As changes are made, a preview of the feature displays in the graphics window, as shown in Figure 6–6.

Figure 6–6

Step 6 - Complete the feature.

Once the edge chamfer is defined, you can complete the feature using any of the following options:

- Click ☑ in the mini-toolbar.

- Right-click in the graphics window and select **OK (Enter)**.

- Click **OK** in the Chamfer dialog box.

- Press <Enter>.

⚠ displays in the mini-toolbar for a Chamfer when the feature cannot be created.

6.2 Constant Fillets

Fillets can add or remove material, as shown in Figure 6–7. A constant edge fillet has a constant radius along its entire reference edge.

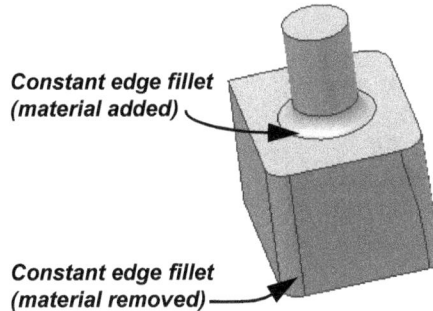

Constant edge fillet (material added)

Constant edge fillet (material removed)

Figure 6–7

General Steps

Use the following general steps to create a constant fillet:

1. Start the creation of the feature.
2. Select placement references by selecting edges.
3. Define the fillet size and shape.
4. Define the setbacks, as required.
5. Complete the feature.

Step 1 - Start the creation of the feature.

Use one of the following methods to create a fillet:

- Select the edge(s) to be filleted and click ⬡ in the heads-up display on the model.

- In the *3D Model* tab>Modify panel, click ⬡ (Fillet).

- Right-click anywhere in the graphics window and select **Fillet**.

*By Default, the display of the Mini-Toolbar is toggled off. On the View tab, expand **User Interface** and enable the **Mini-Toolbar** option to display it. To collapse a dialog box, click the up arrow at the bottom of the dialog box.*

Step 2 - Select placement references by selecting edges.

To clear the selection of an edge, hold <Ctrl> or <Shift> and reselect the edge.

*To fillet all concave and convex edges and corners, use the **All Fillets** and **All Rounds** option in the dialog box respectively.*

Select edges on the model to fillet them. You can select one of the methods listed in the *Select mode* area in the dialog box, or in the drop-down list in the mini-toolbar to refine the selection of the edges, as shown in Figure 6–8 and described below.

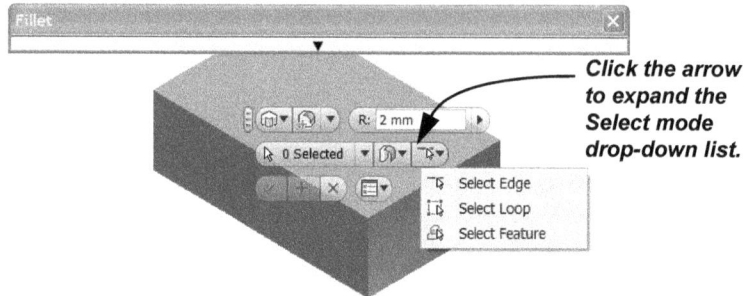

Click the arrow to expand the Select mode drop-down list.

Figure 6–8

Edge	Selects one edge at a time. To select multiple edges to fillet, select each one independently.
Loop	Selects all of the edges on the selected face.
Feature	Select all of the edges on a selected feature.

By default, all selected edges are included in one set and are controlled by a single radius. To add edges with unique radius values in the same feature, you must add additional sets. To add a set, select **Add Constant Radius Fillet Set** in the mini-toolbar drop-down list or select **Click to add** in the *Edges* area of the dialog box, as shown in Figure 6–9. Once the set is active, select new edges.

Edge set 1
Edge set 2

Add a new fillet set using these options.

Figure 6–9

Step 3 - Define the fillet size and shape.

To modify the radius of the fillet, enter the new value in the *Radius* column in the Fillet dialog box, or use the *Radius value* field in the mini-toolbar, as shown in Figure 6–10.

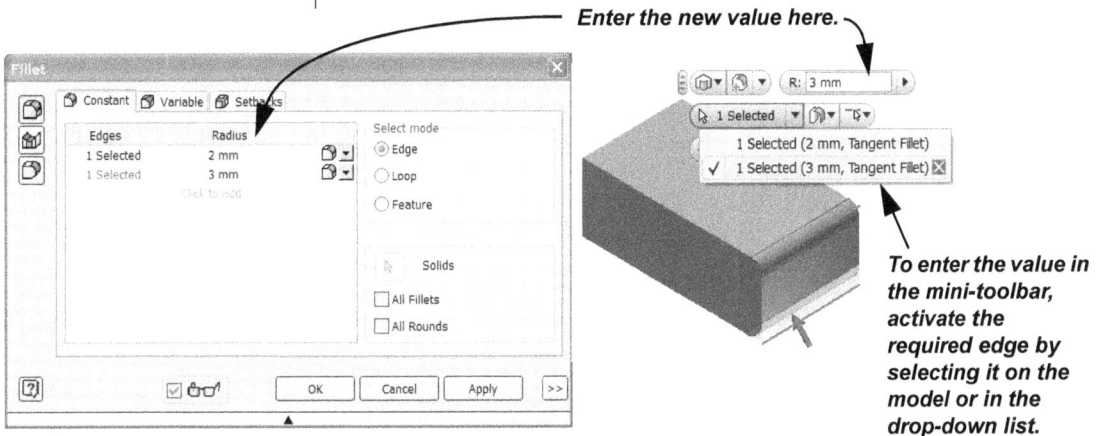

Enter the new value here.

To enter the value in the mini-toolbar, activate the required edge by selecting it on the model or in the drop-down list.

Figure 6–10

Continuity

Edge fillets can be created with Tangent or G2 continuity. Tangent is the default continuity.

- Tangent continuity (□) means that the transition between the fillet and the adjacent surfaces is tangent.

- G2 continuous (□) means the transition between the fillet and the adjacent surfaces is tangent and has a common curvature, producing a smooth connection between the fillet and adjacent surfaces.

To switch between the two continuity settings, use the drop-down lists shown in Figure 6–11.

Figure 6–11

Additional Fillet Options

To display additional fillet options, click >> in the Fillet dialog box, as shown in Figure 6–12. These options are not available in the mini-toolbar.

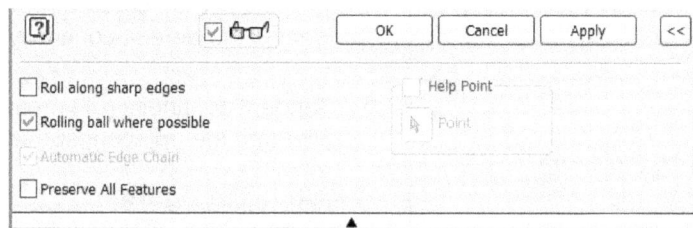

Figure 6–12

The options in the expanded area are described as follows:

Roll along sharp edges	Varies the radius of the fillet, if required, to preserve the edges of the adjacent faces.
Rolling ball where possible	Sets the corner style for fillets. If selected, the shape of surfaces that contain adjacent edges to which fillets are applied, is maintained. The corner is not rounded.
Automatic Edge Chain	Determines how edges that contain curves are selected. When selecting an edge, any edge that is tangent to it is also selected.
Preserve All Features	All edges that intersect a fillet are calculated when a fillet is applied. When this option is cleared, only edges that are part of the fillet are calculated.

Step 4 - Define the setbacks, as required.

When three or more fillets intersect, you can define tangent continuous transitions between them using setbacks. Examples with and without setback distances are shown in Figure 6–13.

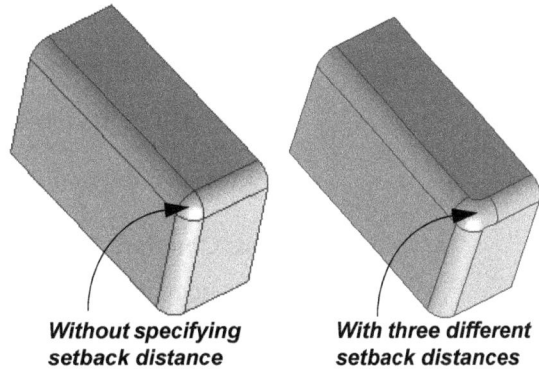

Without specifying setback distance   **With three different setback distances**

Figure 6–13

*The **Minimal** option enables you to define the setback values as the minimum allowable for that vertex.*

How To: Add a Setback

1. Select **Add Setback** in the mini-toolbar drop-down list or select the *Setbacks* tab in the dialog box, as shown in Figure 6–14.
2. Select a vertex where the fillets intersect. The intersecting edges are automatically listed, as shown in Figure 6–14.
3. Select an edge in the list and adjust the setback distance by entering a value in the *Setback value* field in the mini-toolbar or in the *Setback* column in the dialog box.

Setback

Once a vertex is selected its edges are listed.

Figure 6–14

Step 5 - Complete the feature.

Once the references are defined, you can complete the feature using any of the following options:

displays in the mini-toolbar for a Fillet when the feature cannot be created.

- Click ✓ in the mini-toolbar.

- Right-click in the graphics window and select **OK (Enter)**.

- Click **OK** in the Fillet dialog box.

- Press <Enter>.

Hint: Constant Fillet Failures

If any edge in a fillet set cannot be blended due to the fillet size, you are prompted with a dialog box. You can select whether to accept that only the successful fillets will be added or you can cancel the entire operation.

6.3 Variable Fillets

A variable fillet's radius changes along the length of the edge. Radii values are applied to the ends of the edge and at intermediate points, if required. Each value can be independent. Two examples of variable fillets are shown in Figure 6–15.

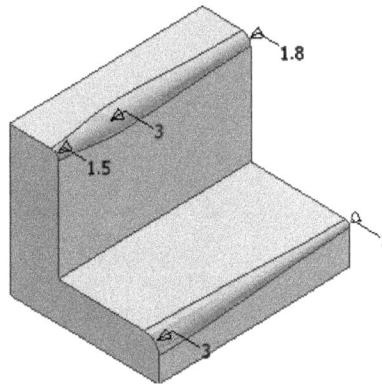

Figure 6–15

General Steps

Use the following general steps to create a variable fillet:

1. Start the creation of the feature.
2. Select the placement references.
3. Define the dimensions of the feature.
4. Define additional options, as required.
5. Complete the feature.

Step 1 - Start the creation of the feature.

Use one of the following methods to create a variable fillet:

• In the *3D Model* tab>Modify panel, click (Fillet).

• Right-click in the graphics window and select **Fillet**.

*By Default, the display of the Mini-Toolbar is toggled off. On the View tab, expand **User Interface** and enable the **Mini-Toolbar** option to display it. To collapse a dialog box, click the up arrow at the bottom of the dialog box.*

*If you preselect the edge and click ⬡ in the heads-up display, you create a constant fillet. To change to a variable fillet, you must clear the edge selection, use the **Add Variable Radius Fillet Set** option, and reselect the edge.*

By default, fillets are created as constant radius. To create a variable fillet, select **Add Variable Radius Fillet Set** in the mini-toolbar drop-down list (shown in Figure 6–16) or select the *Variable* tab in the dialog box.

Figure 6–16

Step 2 - Select the placement references.

To clear the selection of an edge, press and hold <Ctrl> or <Shift> and reselect the edge.

Select an edge to fillet. By default, radius values can be entered at the end points of the selected edge. To vary the radius between the ends, add intermediate point(s) using **Click to add**, as shown in Figure 6–17. As intermediate points are selected, they display on the edge and the position and radius values can be edited, as shown in Figure 6–17.

Intermediate point.

Select to add an intermediate point.

Intermediate point.

Figure 6–17

*The **Smooth radius transition** option is not available in the mini-toolbar.*

- The **Smooth radius transition** option defines how the fillet transitions between points. When enabled, the transition between adjacent points is a complex curve. This produces a fillet surface that is tangent to its adjacent surfaces. When disabled, the transition between the points is a straight line and is not necessarily tangent to its adjacent surfaces.

Step 3 - Define the dimensions of the feature.

Use one of the following methods to enter the radius for each point along the edge:

- In the Fillet dialog box, select the point in the *Point* column and enter the value in the *Radius* field, as shown in Figure 6–18.

Figure 6–18

- In the mini-toolbar, select the point in the drop-down list and enter the value in the *Radius value* field, as shown in Figure 6–19.

Figure 6–19

Step 4 - Define additional options, as required.

Consider using the following options to further control the fillet:

- Similar to constant edge fillets, variable edge fillets are created with Tangent continuity by default. The continuity of a variable edge fillet can be changed to **Smooth (G2)**. Defining continuity for a variable edge fillet is the same process as for a constant fillet.

- Similar to creating a Constant Fillet, you can access the same additional options to control the fillet's shape. This is done by clicking ⌊>>⌋ in the dialog box (not available in the mini-toolbar).

- When fillets intersect, you can define tangent continuous transitions between them in the *Setbacks* tab in the dialog box or by selecting **Add Setback** in the drop-down list in the mini-toolbar. Defining a setback for a Variable Fillet is the same as for a Constant Fillet.

Step 5 - Complete the feature.

Once the references are defined, you can complete the feature using any of the following options:

⚠ displays in the mini-toolbar for a Fillet when the feature cannot be created.

- Click ☑ in the mini-toolbar.

- Right-click in the graphics window and select **OK (Enter)**.

- Click **OK** in the Fillet dialog box.

- Press <Enter>.

6.4 Face Fillets

Use a face fillet when traditional edge-based filleting is not suitable for your geometry. It creates fillets between two sets of faces that do not share an edge. An example of a face fillet is shown in Figure 6–20.

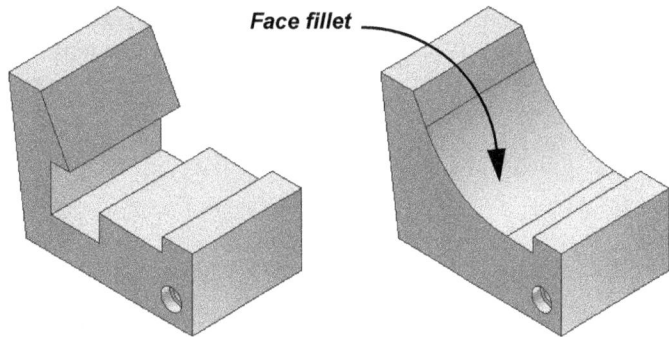

Face fillet

Figure 6–20

How To: Create a Face Fillet

*By Default, the display of the Mini-Toolbar is toggled off. On the View tab, expand **User Interface** and enable the **Mini-Toolbar** option to display it. To collapse a dialog box, click the up arrow at the bottom of the dialog box.*

1. In the *3D Model* tab>Modify panel, click ⬡ (Fillet) or right-click anywhere in the graphics window and select **Fillet**.
2. Select **Face Fillet** in the drop-down list in the mini-toolbar, or click 🏠 (Face Fillet) in the dialog box, as shown in Figure 6–21.
    *   Note that you cannot create a face fillet by preselecting the faces and then selecting **Fillet**.

Select this option to create a Face Fillet.

Select Face Fillet in the drop-down list.

Fillet

Face

Face Set 1

Face Set 2

Radius

0.125 in

☑ Include Tangent Faces
☑ Optimize for Single Selection

OK   Cancel   Apply   >>

R: 2 mm

🏠 Edge Fillet
🔴 Face Fillet
🔵 Full Round Fillet

Figure 6–21

*The **Optimize for Single Selection** option enables a single selection before automatically prompting for the next reference. Clear this option to select more than one reference at a time.*

3. The ⬚ (Face Set 1) field should be automatically active, if not, then select it. Select a face in the model to include as the first face set.

4. The ⬚ (Face Set 2) field should be automatically active, if not, then select it. Select a second face in the model to include as the second face set.

   • To manually change reference selection in the mini-toolbar, click the appropriate option in the drop-down list, as shown in Figure 6–22.

Figure 6–22

*The **Include Tangent Faces** option is only available in the dialog box.*

   • Select **Include Tangent Faces** to automatically fillet adjacent faces.

5. Enter a value in the *Radius* field, as shown in Figure 6–23.

Enter radius value in these fields.

Figure 6–23

6. Complete the feature using any of the following options:

   • Click ✓ in the mini-toolbar.
   • Right-click in the graphics window and select **OK (Enter)**.
   • Click **OK** in the Fillet dialog box.
   • Press <Enter>.

⚠ displays in the mini-toolbar for a Fillet when the feature cannot be created.

Hint: Face Fillet Failures

Face fillets fail if the radius value is not large enough to span between the faces, or if the specified radius is so large that it extends beyond the two faces.

6.5 Full Round Fillets

Full round fillets can be used for rounding ribs and other geometry that might be difficult or impossible to fillet using edge-based fillets. A full round fillet enables you to create a variable radius fillet between three adjacent faces. An example of a full round fillet is shown in Figure 6–24.

Full round fillet

Figure 6–24

How To: Create a Full Round Fillet

*By Default, the display of the Mini-Toolbar is toggled off. On the View tab, expand **User Interface** and enable the **Mini-Toolbar** option to display it. To collapse a dialog box, click the up arrow at the bottom of the dialog box.*

1. In the *3D Model* tab>Modify panel, click 🪨 (Fillet) or right-click anywhere in the graphics window and select **Fillet**.

2. Select **Full Round Fillet** in the mini-toolbar drop-down list, or click 🪨 (Full Round Fillet) in the dialog box, as shown in Figure 6–25.

Select this option to create a Full Round Fillet.

Select Full Round Fillet in the drop-down list.

Figure 6–25

Note that you cannot initiate the creation of a full round fillet by preselecting the faces and then selecting **Fillet**.

The **Optimize for Single Selection** *option enables a single selection before automatically prompting for the next reference. Clear this option to select more than one reference at a time.*

The **Include Tangent Faces** *option is only available in the dialog box.*

⚠ *displays in the mini-toolbar for a Fillet when the feature cannot be created.*

3. The 🔲 *(Side Face Set 1)* field should be automatically active, if not, then select it. Select a face in the model to include as the first side face set.

4. The 🔲 *(Center Face Set)* field should be automatically active, if not, then select it. Select the center face reference

5. The 🔲 *(Side Face Set 2)* field should be automatically active, if not, then select it. Select the final face reference to define the full round fillet.

- To manually change reference selection in the mini-toolbar, click the appropriate option in the drop-down list, as shown in Figure 6–26.

Figure 6–26

- Select **Include Tangent Faces** to automatically fillet tangent adjacent faces.

6. Complete the feature using any of the following options:

- Click ✓ in the mini-toolbar.
- Right-click in the graphics window and select **OK (Enter)**.
- Click **OK** in the Fillet dialog box.
- Press <Enter>.

6.6 Straight Holes

Holes remove material from the model. You can create the following types of holes: drilled, counterbore, spotface, or countersink holes. An example of each hole type is shown in Figure 6–27.

A Spotface hole is similar in geometry to a Counterbore hole, However, its purpose is to create a shallow flat area in an irregular surface, from which you can create a hole. On planar geometry, the difference is not obvious.

(Drilled Hole)   (Counterbore Hole)

(Spotface Hole)   (Countersink Hole)

Figure 6–27

General Steps

Use the following general steps to create a simple hole:

1. Start the creation of the feature.
2. Define the type of hole.
3. Select the placement references.
4. Define the dimensions of the feature.
5. Define the depth of the feature.
6. Complete the feature.

Step 1 - Start the creation of the feature.

The following methods can be used to create a new hole in a model:

- In the *3D Model* tab>Modify panel, click [icon] (Hole).

- Right-click anywhere in the graphics window and select **Hole**.

- Preselect a sketched point and click ⬚ in the heads-up display on the model.

The Hole dialog box opens, as shown in Figure 6–28.

*A complete mini-toolbar is not available for hole creation. Applicable mini-toolbars display, as required, if the **Mini-Toolbar** option has been set to display on the View tab>User Interface drop-down list.*

Figure 6–28

Step 2 - Define the type of hole.

There are four types of hole available to choose from:

- ⬚ (Drilled)

- ⬚ (Counterbore)

- ⬚ (Spotface)

- ⬚ (Countersink)

The Drilled hole type is the default when creating a new hole.

The following additional drill point and property settings can be used to define the new hole:

* You can create a hole with a flat or angled drill point. If you select angled, you must specify the angle of the point, as shown in Figure 6–29. A flat drill point is useful if the hole is molded instead of machined.

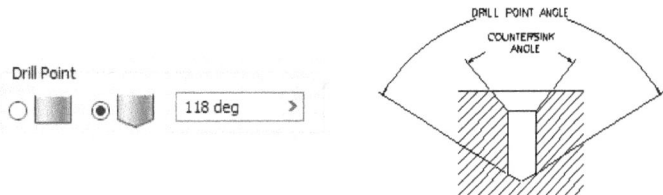

Figure 6–29

* To create a Simple hole, click ▮▮ (Simple Hole). There are no additional options to be defined for Simple Holes.

* To create a Clearance hole that fits a selected fastener, click ▮▮ (Clearance Hole). Select the standard, fastener type, fastener size, and fastener fit from the options that display.

* To create a Tapped hole, click ▤ (Tapped Hole). Select from the additional hole options available for a Tapped hole.

* To create a Taper Tapped hole, click ▨ (Taper Tapped Hole). Select from the additional hole options available for a Taper Tapped hole.

Step 3 - Select the placement references.

Holes are placed by referencing existing features. Any one of the following four placement schemes can be used:

* **Linear**

* **Concentric**

* **From Sketch**

* **On Point**

These schemes are selected in the Placement drop-down list, as shown in Figure 6–30. Once selected, the placement options update in the dialog box.

Placement

⬚ Linear	⌄

- ⬚ From Sketch
- ⬚ Linear
- ◎ Concentric
- ⊙ On Point

Figure 6–30

Linear Placement

How To: Locate a Linear Hole

1. Expand the Placement drop-down list and select **Linear**, to place a linear hole.

2. Click ⬚ (Face) and select a planar face or work plane as the placement plane for the hole, as shown in Figure 6–31. Once selected, the mini-toolbar opens and a preview of the hole displays on the model. You can select the circular ball on the previewed hole feature to move its location on the selected face.

3. The ⬚ (Reference 1) field should be automatically active, if not, then select it. Select the first linear edge to locate the hole on the model, as shown in Figure 6–31. Enter the offset distance from *Reference 1* in the mini-toolbar entry field.

4. The ⬚ (Reference 2) field should be automatically active, if not, select it. Select the second linear edge to locate the hole on the model, as shown in Figure 6–31. Enter the offset distance from *Reference 2* in the mini-toolbar entry field.

To place the hole, first select the placement plane.

Select the first linear reference.

Select the second linear reference.

Figure 6–31

Concentric Placement

How To: Locate a Concentric Hole

1. Expand the Placement drop-down list and select **Concentric** to place a concentric hole.

2. The [⌖] *(Plane)* field should be automatically active, if not, select it. Select a planar face or work plane as the placement plane for the hole. Once selected, a preview of the hole is automatically placed, as shown in Figure 6–32.

3. The [⌖] *(Concentric Reference)* field should be automatically active, if not, select it. Select the circular edge or a cylindrical face to reference the concentric hole center on the placement plane. Once selected, the hole preview is repositioned, as shown in Figure 6–32.

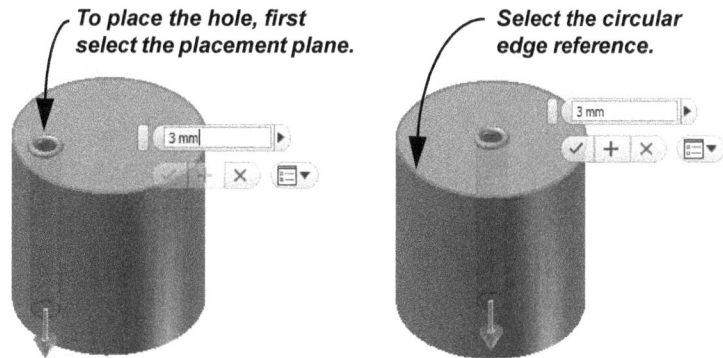

To place the hole, first select the placement plane.

Select the circular edge reference.

Figure 6–32

From Sketch Placement

How To: Locate a Hole on a Sketch

1. Expand the Placement drop-down list and select **From Sketch**.

2. The [cursor icon] *(Centers)* field should be automatically active, if not, select it. Select the location for the centers of the holes by selecting entities in an existing sketch, as shown in Figure 6–33. The entities can be points, endpoints of sketched entities, or centers of arcs and circles.

- By default, holes are automatically placed on sketched points if a single sketch is listed in the Model browser. If multiple sketches exist, you must manually select references or drag a bounding box around the points.

This method of placing holes is commonly used to place a first hole and then pattern it or to place a hole on an irregular surface. Placing too many holes with point centers can limit some higher level uses for Assembly purposes.

A sketch is required to indicate hole placement.   **Sketched Points are selected by default.**   **Select additional reference entities.**

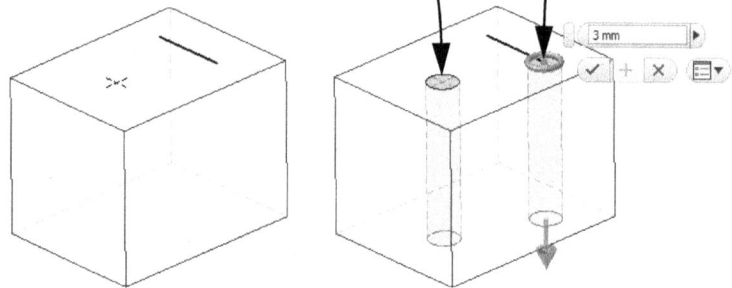

Figure 6–33

On Point Placement

How To: Locate a Hole on a Point

1. Expand the Placement drop-down list and select **On Point** to place a hole based on an existing point.

2. The [cursor icon] *(Point)* field should be automatically active, if not, select it. Select an existing work point to define the center of the hole, as shown in Figure 6–34.

This type of hole is also used for complex hole placement based on Work features.

3. The [cursor icon] *(Direction)* field should be automatically active, if not, select it. To set the direction of the hole axis, select a planar face, a work plane, an edge, or axis. The hole axis is created parallel to the direction reference, as shown in Figure 6–34.

Select a work point as the reference for the hole.   **Select a directional reference to define the axis of the hole.**

Figure 6–34

Step 4 - Define the dimensions of the feature.

To set the dimensions of the hole, enter values as shown in Figure 6–35. The values available depend on the type of hole. The mini-toolbar entry fields for holes show one entry field at a time. To toggle between them, you must select entities in the previewed hole.

Select the ring on the hole diameter to activate its entry field.

Select a dimension value to activate its entry field.

Enter dimension values in the Hole dialog box to define the hole.

Select the ring on the countersink diameter to activate its entry field.

Figure 6–35

Step 5 - Define the depth of the feature.

To specify the depth of the hole, select a *Termination* option, as shown in Figure 6–36.

Select a Termination option in the Hole dialog box or use the mini-toolbar.

Select the depth arrow to activate its entry field. All (Through All) is the default option, enter a value to assign a depth value or select the menu to change the Termination option.

Figure 6–36

Enhanced
in **2018**

The termination options are as follows:

Distance	Creates a blind hole of a specified depth. Using the direction buttons you can define the direction of the hole.
Through All	Creates a hole through the entire model. Using the direction buttons you can define the direction of the hole. For drilled simple holes, the direction can also be defined as symmetric.
To	Creates a blind hole that terminates at a selected plane or at the extension of the selected plane. Use the **Extended Face** option when the selected termination plane does not completely intersect the hole.

New
in **2018**

Hint: Extend Start

You can enable the **Extend Start** option in the *Termination* area to extend the start plane to remove fragments, similar to the example shown in Figure 6–37. In this example, a hole and a fillet are intersecting and you can remove the material on the fillet using the **Extend Start** option. This option is only available to extend the start face within a single body.

Extend Start disabled   *Extend Start enabled*

Figure 6–37

Step 6 - Complete the feature.

Once the references are defined, you can complete the feature using any of the following options:

- Click [✓] in the mini-toolbar.

- Right-click in the graphics window and select **OK (Enter)**.

- Click **OK** in the Hole dialog box.

- Press <Enter>.

6.7 Threads

You can use the **Thread** tool to add a cosmetic image of a thread to holes, shafts, bolts, and pins, as shown in Figure 6–38. Thread information can also be assigned or read from a spreadsheet so that it can be used when detailing the model.

*You can also use the **Hole** tool to create threaded holes.*

Figure 6–38

How To: Create a Thread Feature

1. In the *3D Model* tab>Modify panel, click 🗐 (Thread) to create a thread. The Thread Feature dialog box opens, as shown in Figure 6–39.

Figure 6–39

The mini-toolbar is not available for creating threads.

2. Click 🔖 (Face) and select a cylindrical or conical face on which to create the thread. A thread can only be created on one face at a time.

3. Define the thread using the following options:
   - Select **Display in Model** to display the thread in the model.
   - Select **Full Length** to set the thread length to cover the entire length of the selected face. Clear the **Full Length** option to set the thread length. A non-full length thread starts from the placement face of the parent feature or at the required *Offset* value. Enter a *Length* value to define the thread depth.
   - Toggle [icon] to change the direction of the thread.
4. Select the *Specification* tab (shown in Figure 6–40) to define the thread specifications.

Figure 6–40

The options are described as follows:

Thread Type	Sets the series of threads to apply.
Size	Sets the diameter size of the selected thread type.
Designation	Sets the number of threads based on the unit of length and bolt size.
Class	Sets the class of threads.
Right/Left Hand	Sets the direction the threads should be applied.

5. Click **OK** in the dialog box or right-click and select **OK (Enter)** to complete the thread and close the Thread dialog box. Alternatively, you can press <Enter> to complete the feature.

6.8 Editing Pick and Place Features

Once you have created a pick and place feature, you might need to modify it. The available options are described as follows:

Show Dimensions	Displays the dimensions associated with the feature. You can double-click on the values to make dimensional changes.
(Edit Sketch)	Accesses the Feature Sketch to redefine any of the elements used to define the sketch. For pick and place features this applies to the hole features created using the **From Sketch** option.
(Edit Feature)	Opens the dialog box to redefine any of the elements used to define the feature. To clear the references for fillets and chamfers, press and hold <Ctrl> or <Shift> and select the referenced edge.

To access any of these options, use one of the following methods to open the feature dialog box.

- Double-click on the feature in the Model browser.

- Right-click on the feature in the Model browser and select an option in the menu, as shown on the left in Figure 6–41.

- Select any face that is generated by the feature and click
  , as shown on the right in Figure 6–41.

Figure 6–41

6.9 Creation Sequence

Feature-based modeling involves creating features, one by one, on a base feature until the model is complete. By this point in this student guide you have learned to create sketched and pick and place based features. These are the main components in the modeling process. The flowchart in Figure 6–42 shows the paths available when creating these features.

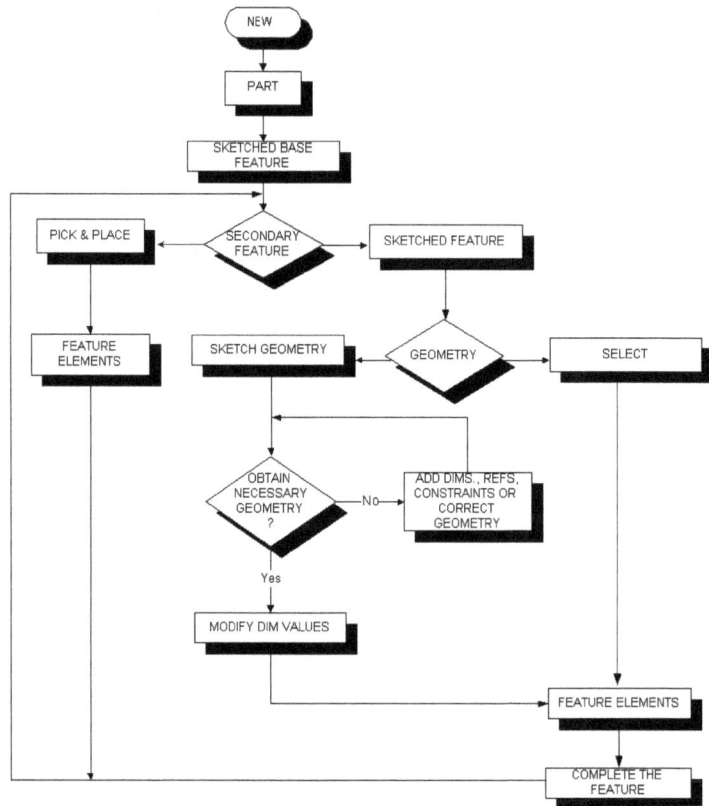

Figure 6–42

When creating features, it is important to consider your design intent. Every aspect of feature creation, such as specifying the references, dimensioning, and constraining the model, affect design intent and the design sequence.

Practice 6a

Add Pick and Place Features

Practice Objectives

- Create constant and variable edge fillets along specific edges in the model.
- Create a From Sketch and Linear hole based on specific criteria.
- Create an edge chamfer along a specific edge in the model.

In this practice, you will add pick and place features to a model. The resulting model displays as shown in Figure 6–43.

Figure 6–43

Task 1 - Open a part file and create fillets.

1. Open **rectangle_1.ipt**.

2. In the *3D Model* tab>Modify panel, click ⬭ (Fillet) to create a constant fillet.

*Set the selection filter to **Select Face and Edges** to pick edges in the model.*

3. To create the fillet, select the edges of the model as shown in Figure 6–44. Selecting multiple edges ensures that the fillets are all the same radius and are driven by one dimension value. A default fillet automatically displays on the model.

To clear the edges selected for fillets, press and hold <Ctrl> or <Shift> and select the referenced edge a second time.

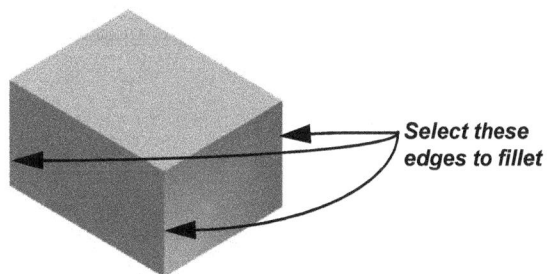

Select these edges to fillet

Figure 6–44

4. In the *Radius* field, enter **2.54** as the radial dimension for the fillets in the mini-toolbar as shown in Figure 6–45. All three fillets act as one and update dynamically.

Radius

Figure 6–45

5. Click ✓ to complete the simple fillet. The model is shown in Figure 6–46. Note how the Model browser updates to display the single fillet feature.

Figure 6–46

Task 2 - Create the variable fillet.

1. Switch the model to Wireframe. The Wireframe visual style is being used for clarity in the upcoming images. You do not need to work in Wireframe to create a variable fillet.

2. In the graphics window, right-click and select **Fillet**.

3. In the mini-toolbar, select **Add Variable Radius Fillet Set** in the drop-down list, as shown in Figure 6–47.

Figure 6–47

4. Select the vertical edge shown in Figure 6–48 on which to create the variable fillet.

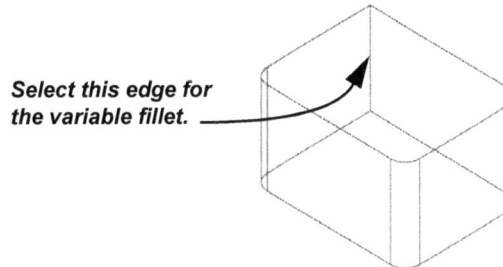

Select this edge for the variable fillet.

Figure 6–48

5. A variable fillet with the same radius at both ends is created by default.

6. Modify the radius of the start point. Enter **3.81** in the *Radius* field in the mini-toolbar.

7. Modify the radius of the end point. Select **End** in the drop-down list in the mini-toolbar, as shown in Figure 6–49. Enter enter **3.81** in the *Radius* field.

R: 3.81 mm   P: 1.0

1 Selected   End

✓ + ×

Start (R: 3.81 mm, P: 0.0)
✓ End (R: 3.81 mm, P: 1.0)
Click to add

Figure 6–49

8. Add an intermediate point on the same edge. In the mini-toolbar, select **Click to add** in the drop-down list and select a point approximately in the middle of the edge, as shown in Figure 6–50.

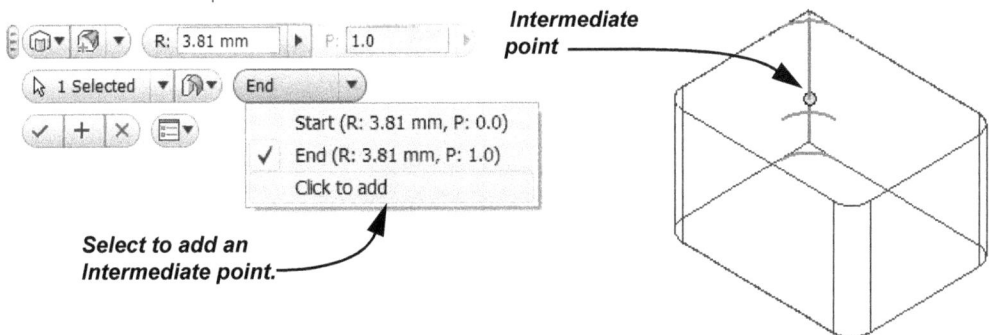

R: 3.81 mm   P: 1.0

1 Selected   End

✓ + ×

Start (R: 3.81 mm, P: 0.0)
✓ End (R: 3.81 mm, P: 1.0)
Click to add

Intermediate point

Select to add an Intermediate point.

Figure 6–50

9. In the mini-toolbar, enter **0.5** in the *Position* field (if it didn't snap to the midpoint when placing the intermediate point) and **7.62** in the *Radius* field, as shown in Figure 6–51.

Enter Radius   **Enter Position**

Figure 6–51

10. Click ✓ to complete the variable fillet. The model displays as shown in Figure 6–52. Note how the Model browser updates with a second fillet feature added.

Variable fillet

Figure 6–52

Task 3 - Sketch the center point of the hole.

1. Create a sketch on the rectangular top surface of the model.

2. In the Create panel, click ⊣⊢ (Point) and place a point on the sketch plane, as shown in Figure 6–53.

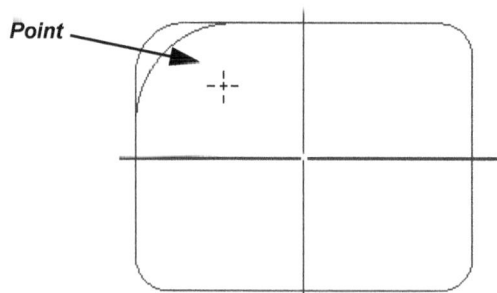

Point

Figure 6–53

3. Dimension the point as shown in Figure 6–54.

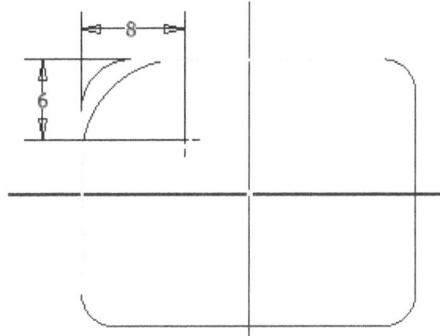

Figure 6–54

4. Finish the sketch.

Task 4 - Create the hole with the From Sketch option.

---

1. Select the point and click in the heads-up display on the model. Select **From Sketch** in the Placement drop-down list, if not already active. The Hole dialog box opens and the sketched point is automatically selected for hole placement, as shown in Figure 6–55.

Figure 6–55

2. Enter **7.5** as the diameter of the hole in the Hole dialog box or in the mini-toolbar.

3. Select **Through All** in the Termination drop-down list in the Hole dialog box, if not already set. Accept the default direction cutting into the model.

4. Click **OK** or click ✓ in the mini-toolbar to complete the hole. The model displays as shown in Figure 6–56.

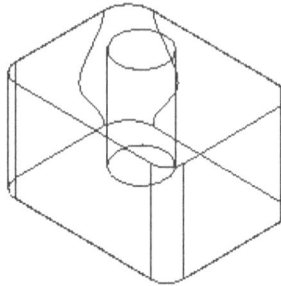

Figure 6–56

Task 5 - Create a hole with the Linear option.

---

1. In the Modify panel, click 🔘 (Hole). The Hole dialog box opens with the **Linear** option as the default in the Placement drop-down list.

2. Click 🔲 (Face), if it is not already selected, and select the face shown in Figure 6–57 as the placement plane for the hole. Once selected, the hole is automatically placed.

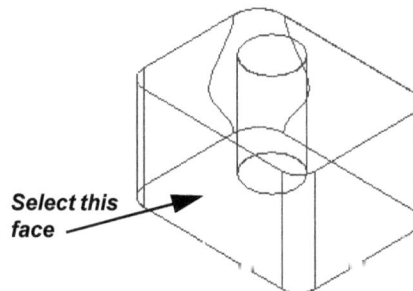

Select this face

Figure 6–57

3. 🔲 (Reference 1) is active. Select the first linear edge as shown in Figure 6–58 to locate the hole.

4. Modify the first edge reference dimension to **5**. Do not press <Enter>.

5. 🔲 (Reference 2) is active. Select the second linear edge as shown in Figure 6–58 to locate the hole. The references place the hole relative to the existing geometry.

Remember to consider your design intent when dimensioning to fillet and chamfer edges.

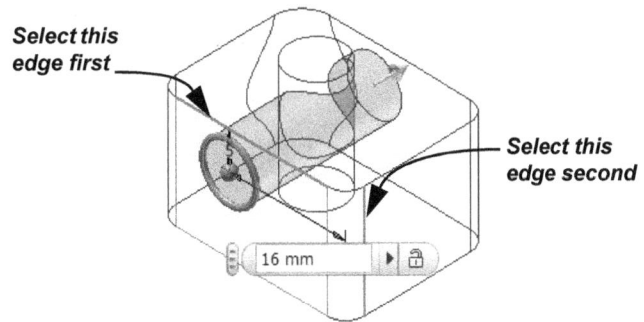

Figure 6–58

6. Modify the second edge reference dimension to **16**. Do not press <Enter>.

7. Select **Through All** in the Termination drop-down list, if not already set. Accept the default direction cutting into the model.

8. Select the diameter of the hole in the graphics window and enter **4.50** or enter the diameter in the Hole dialog box.

9. Click **OK** or click [✓] in the mini-toolbar to complete the hole.

Task 6 - Create an edge chamfer.

---

1. Select the edge shown in Figure 6–59, and click [🔖] in the heads-up display on the model. The edge chamfer automatically displays encompassing all four edges. This is because the fillets made the edges tangent to one another and all tangent edges are included.

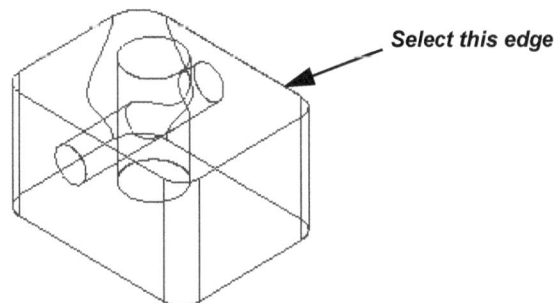

Figure 6–59

2. In the mini-toolbar, enter **1.20** in the *Distance* field, as shown in Figure 6–60.

Figure 6–60

3. Click ✓ to complete the chamfer. The model displays as shown in Figure 6–61.

Figure 6–61

4. Save the model and close the window.

Practice 6b

Create a Coaxial Hole

Practice Objectives

- Create a Coaxial hole based on specific criteria.
- Make modifications and redefine the type of hole to achieve a required result.

In this practice, you will add a coaxial hole to the cylinder. The resulting model displays as shown in Figure 6–62.

Figure 6–62

Task 1 - Open a part file and create a Concentric hole.

1. Open **cylinder_1.ipt**.

2. Right-click in the graphics window, and select **Hole**. The Hole dialog box opens with the **Linear** option as the default in the Placement drop-down list.

3. Select **Concentric** in the Placement drop-down list.

4. Select the top surface as a placement plane. The model displays as shown in Figure 6–63. The initial placement of the hole on the selected face depends on where you select on the face.

Placement plane

Figure 6–63

5. ⬚ (Concentric Reference) is active. Select a circular edge or a cylindrical face. The hole is placed at the center of the face.

6. Select **Distance** in the Termination drop-down list.

7. Enter **7.5** for the diameter of the hole in the mini-toolbar or in the Hole dialog box. Note that the hole diameter is the active field in the mini-toolbar if the diameter of the hole is highlighted in the graphics window.

8. Select the arrow representing the depth of the hole in the graphics window. Enter **13.5** for the depth of the hole in the mini-toolbar or in the Hole dialog box.

9. Click ⬚ (Flat) in the *Drill Point* area, as shown in Figure 6–64.

10. Click **OK** or click ✓ to complete the hole. The model displays as shown in Figure 6–64.

Figure 6–64

Task 2 - Change the diameter of the coaxial hole.
---

1. Right-click on the hole in the Model browser and select **Show Dimensions**.

2. Double-click on the diameter dimension in the graphics window.

3. Enter **9.00** in the *Hole Diameter* field in the Hole Dimensions dialog box.

4. Click **OK** to close the dialog box.

5. In the Quick Access Toolbar, click (Local Update). The updated model displays as shown in Figure 6–65.

Figure 6–65

*Alternatively, you can double-click on the hole in the Model browser and simply edit the value in the feature dialog box. Using this technique you do not have to update the model because it is automatically regenerated when you click **OK**.*

Task 3 - Redefine the type of hole.

1. Right-click on the hole in the Model browser and select **Edit Feature**, or select any surface on the hole and click . The Hole dialog box opens.

2. Click (Countersink), as shown in Figure 6–66.

3. Enter **15.25** for the diameter of the countersink in the mini-toolbar or in the Hole dialog box, as shown in Figure 6–66.

4. Click **OK** to complete the feature. The model displays as shown in Figure 6–66.

Countersink hole

Countersink diameter

Figure 6–66

5. Save the model and close the window.

Practice 6c

Add Fillets

Practice Objectives

- Create constant and full round fillets in the model.
- Describe how the order of fillet creation can affect the resulting geometry.

In this practice, you will create fillets. The order in which these fillets are added is important because it can affect the resulting geometry. The completed model displays as shown in Figure 6–67.

Figure 6–67

Task 1 - Open a part file and create a fillet.

1. Open **fillet.ipt**.

2. In the Modify panel, click (Fillet). The Fillet dialog box displays.

3. Select all four outside edges of **Extrusion7**, as shown in Figure 6–68. The fillet automatically previews on the model.

Figure 6–68

4. In the mini-toolbar, modify the fillet radius to **6.35**.

Alternatively, you can preselect the edges to be filleted and click in the heads-up display on the model.

5. Click ✓ to complete the feature. The model displays as shown in Figure 6–69.

The Shaded with Edges visual style (View tab> Appearance panel) has been used for the following images for clarity.

Figure 6–69

Task 2 - Create a second fillet.

1. Select the edge shown on the left in Figure 6–70.

2. Activate the **Fillet** command in the ribbon or shortcut menu, or by preselecting the four edges of **Extrusion7** (as shown in Figure 6–70) and activating the command in the heads-up display. All of the tangent edges are automatically selected and a preview of the fillet is applied to the edges.

Alternatively, you can click 🗀 (Fillet) in the Modify panel before or after selecting an edge reference to create a fillet.

3. Modify the fillet radius to **9.00**.

4. Click ✓ to complete the feature. The model displays as shown on the right in Figure 6–70.

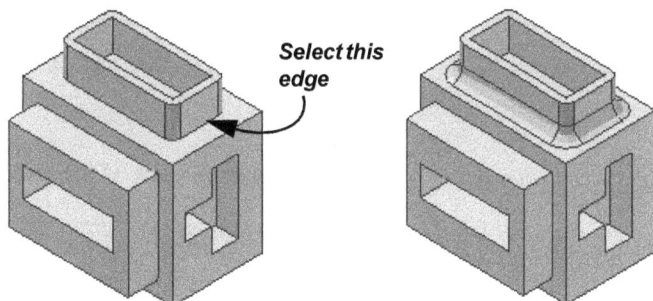

Select this edge

Figure 6–70

Task 3 - Create a third fillet.

1. Activate the **Fillet** command in the ribbon or shortcut menu, or by preselecting the four outside edges of **Extrusion4** and activating the command in the heads-up display. The reference edges are shown on the left in Figure 6–71.

2. Modify the radius to **5.50** and complete the feature. The model displays as shown on the right side of Figure 6–71.

Select these four edges (2 hidden)

Figure 6–71

Task 4 - Create a fourth fillet.

1. Activate the **Fillet** command and select the four edges shown on the left in Figure 6–72. When you select the edges, all of the tangent edges highlight automatically.

2. Modify the radius to **3.80** and complete the feature. The model displays as shown on the right in Figure 6–72. Note the difference in the fillets that were created on this feature and previously on **Extrusion7**. This is because the order in which the edges were selected were different.

Select these four edges (1 hidden)

Figure 6–72

Task 5 - Create a fifth fillet.

1. Activate the **Fillet** command.

2. Select **Select Feature** in the Select mode drop-down list in the mini-toolbar, as shown in Figure 6–73, to quickly select all of the edges of a feature.

Figure 6–73

3. Select **Extrusion1** in the Model browser.

4. Enter **12.5** as the radius. You are not able to complete the feature. The model and its mini-toolbar display as shown in

   Figure 6–74. ⚠ indicates that there is a problem with the geometry and the feature cannot be created.

Figure 6–74

5. Click ⚠ to display a descriptive message. Read the message and click **Close** to close the message window.

6. Return to the mini-toolbar or fillet dialog box and enter **7.0** as the radius.

7. Complete the feature. The initial radius was too large. The model displays as shown in Figure 6–75.

Figure 6–75

Task 6 - Create a sixth fillet.

1. Activate the **Fillet** command and select the four inside edges of **Extrusion7**, as shown on the left in Figure 6–76.

2. Modify the fillet radius to **6.35**.

3. Complete the feature. The model displays as shown on the right in Figure 6–76.

Create these fillets

Figure 6–76

Task 7 - Create a full round fillet.

1. Activate the **Fillet** command in the ribbon.

2. Select **Full Round Fillet** in the drop-down list in the mini-toolbar, as shown in Figure 6–77, to display its options.

Figure 6–77

3. Select the references, as shown on the left in Figure 6–78.

4. Complete the feature. The model displays as shown on the right in Figure 6–78.

Select the opposite side of this face for Side Face Set 2.

Center Face Set

Side Face Set 1

Figure 6–78

5. Save the model and close the window.

Practice 6d	# Adding Pick and Place Features (Optional)

Practice Objective

- Create appropriate hole, chamfer, and fillet features to create the required geometry.

In this practice, you will continue to practice placing pick and place features on the model. The completed model displays as shown in Figure 6–79. Minimal instruction is provided for this practice.

Figure 6–79

Task 1 - Open a part and add features.

1. Open **placed_features.ipt**.

2. Add a **.5** chamfer to edge **A** and a **.25** chamfer to the three edges meeting at corner **B**.

3. Add a **1.0** radius fillet at edge **C**.

4. Create a **.5 dia.** hole through the part, concentric to fillet **C**.

5. Add a through all hole with a **.5** diameter and a **.75** countersink in the center of the surface **D** that is 2in by 2in.

6. Fillet the loop on surface **D**. Use a radius of **0.25**.

7. Save the model and close the window.

Chapter Review Questions

1. Which chamfer type (shown in Figure 6–80) requires you to select a reference surface?

Figure 6–80

   a. Distance

   b. Distance and Angle

   c. Two Distances

2. In the Fillet mini-toolbar, as shown in Figure 6–81, which option enables you to fillet all of the edges of a feature?

Figure 6–81

   a. **Select Edge**

   b. **Select Loop**

   c. **Select Feature**

3. Chamfer features always remove material.

   a. True

   b. False

4. Fillet features can add or remove material.

   a. True

   b. False

5. Which keys on the keyboard can be used to clear the edges selected for a fillet or chamfer feature? (Select all that apply.)

   a. <Tab>

   b. <Ctrl>

   c. <Shift>

   d. <Alt>

6. Fillets on multiple edges can be controlled by one dimension.

   a. True

   b. False

7. How many separate fillet features are listed in the Model browser, if you click **OK** to create the features shown in the Fillet dialog box (Figure 6–82)?

Figure 6–82

   a. 1

   b. 2

   c. 4

   d. 6

8. You can add threads to both cylindrical faces and conical faces.

   a. True

   b. False

9. Without creating a sketch or work geometry, which placement method enables you to place a hole that is centered on a cylindrical feature, as shown in Figure 6–83?

Figure 6–83

   a. Linear

   b. Concentric

   c. From Sketch

   d. On Point

10. How can you modify an existing placed feature, such as a fillet or chamfer?

   a. Return to the sketch mode and change the sketch profile.

   b. Double-click on the feature in the model or in the Model browser.

   c. Select the same tool used to create the feature to edit it.

11. Which option do you select to change the reference edges for a chamfer?

   a. **Show Dimensions**

   b. **Edit Feature**

   c. **Edit Sketch**

   d. **Suppress Features**

Command Summary

Button	Command	Location
	Chamfer (feature)	• **Ribbon:** *3D Model* tab>Modify panel • **Heads-up Display:** In the graphics window with an entity selected
	Fillet (Edge, Face, Full Round, and Variable)	• **Ribbon:** *3D Model* tab>Modify panel • **Context Menu:** In the graphics window • **Heads-up Display** In the graphics window with an entity selected
	Hole	• **Ribbon:** *3D Model* tab>Modify panel • **Context Menu:** In the graphics window
	Thread	• **Ribbon:** *3D Model* tab>Modify panel

Work Features

During the design process, the features that currently exist in the model might not provide the references required to place a new feature. In these situations, you can use work features to create the required references.

Learning Objectives in this Chapter

- Use the work plane creation types to create new work planes in a model.
- Use the work axes creation types to create new work axes in a model.
- Use the work point creation types to create new work points in a model.
- Describe how using work planes, work axes, and work points in a model can assist you in creating geometry that cannot otherwise be created using existing planes or geometry.

7.1 Work Planes

Work planes are non-solid features. They do not have thickness or mass and are used as references when creating other features in a model. When creating a part, three Origin Work Planes are automatically created in the default templates.

Additional work planes can be created if a feature's sketching plane is not satisfied by any of the three Origin Work Planes or existing geometry. Multiple work planes might be required to create a required work plane.To create the extrusions shown in Figure 7–1, additional work planes were required.

An additional work plane was required as a sketching plane.

Figure 7–1

How To: Create a Work Plane

1. Start the creation of a work plane using one of the following techniques:
   - In the *3D Model* tab>Work Features panel, click (Plane).
   - In the *3D Model* tab>Work Features panel, expand (Plane) and select a plane placement type.
   - In the graphics window, right-click and select **Work Plane**.

2. Once you have started the creation of a work plane, you must select references to locate it. References can include Origin features, Work features (plane, axis, point), edges, construction lines, vertices, or faces (planar or cylindrical). The reference type required depends on the work plane being created. Once the selected references fully define the work plane's placement, it is displayed.

The end result of any of these methods is the same. However, by selecting a plane placement type you are guided as to which references to select.

Alternatively, you can select the reference before clicking (Plane).

Some of the methods for creating work planes are not available in Assembly mode.

The different work plane placement types are described as follows:

Type	Example
Offset from Plane: Creates a work plane parallel to an existing plane. Place the cursor over a reference plane or face, hold the left mouse button, and drag away from the face. Enter the required offset distance.	
Parallel to Plane through Point: Creates a work plane that is parallel to another plane or face and passes through an edge, axis, or point. Select the reference plane and then select a point.	Point — Face —
Midplane between Two Planes: Creates a work plane in the middle of two planes (parallel or non-parallel). Select two planes to create a work plane evenly spaced between them.	
Midplane of Torus: Creates a work plane through the center or mid-plane of a torus. Select the torus to place the plane at its mid-plane.	
Angle to Plane around Edge: Creates a work plane at an angle to an existing plane or face. Select the plane to which the work plane is referenced. Select the edge or axis through which the work plane passes. Enter the required angle in the mini-toolbar to create a plane perpendicular to another plane.	Reference face, Edge
Three Points: Creates a work plane through three selected points (midpoints, end points, and/or work points). Select three point references to place the plane.	Three points
Two Coplanar Edges: Creates a work plane by selecting two coplanar straight edges or work axes. Select the two linear references to place the plane.	

Tangent to Surface through Edge: Creates a work plane that lies on the curved surface or its projection and passes through an edge or axis. To create the work plane, select the edge and the curved face.

Curved face

Edge

Tangent to Surface through Point: Creates a work plane that is tangent to a cylindrical face at a point defined by a construction line. The construction line should be drawn on a plane perpendicular to the cylindrical surface and from the center line of the cylinder to a point on the cylinder

Tangent to Surface and Parallel to Plane: Creates a work plane that is tangent to a cylindrical face and parallel to a planar surface. To create the work plane, select the cylindrical face and the planar surface.

Planar surface

Normal to Axis through Point: Creates a work plane that is perpendicular to an axis and passes through a selected point. To create the work plane, select the axis or edge to which it is perpendicular and select the point (i.e., end point, midpoint, or work point).

Point

Axis

Normal to a Curve at Point: Creates a work plane that is perpendicular to a non-linear sketch curve at a work point, sketch point, vertex, or the midpoint of an edge. To create the work plane, select the edge or sketch curve and select the point.

Non-linear curve

Point

Normal plane

Consider the following when working with work planes:

- There are often situations in which you have started to define the sketch and realized that the required plane does not exist. For these situations, you can quit and create the required plane, or, if an offset work plane is appropriate, you can create one on-the-fly. To create an offset work plane while ◫ (Start 2D Sketch) is active, select and drag the plane from a reference plane, and enter an offset value.

- Work axes and work points can be created during work plane creation and used as references. To do so, start the creation of the work plane (using either the **Plane** option or a specific work plane placement type), right-click, and select **Create Point** or **Create Axis**, as shown in Figure 7–2. Once the references have been selected, the work plane is created.

Figure 7–2

- To change the name of the work plane, select it in the Model browser and select it again (do not double-click). Enter a new name.

- To redefine the references of a work plane, right-click on the work plane, select **Redefine Feature**, and select new references.

- To modify the dimension values associated with work planes, double-click on the work plane in the graphics window or Model browser or right-click the work plane in the graphics window or Model browser and select **Edit Dimension**. Once the dimension value displays, enter a new value.

- Work planes are infinite in size, but on screen they are sized to fit the geometry. To change its size, select its corner, wait until ⬚ displays, and drag. To automatically resize to fit the model, right-click on the work plane and select **Auto-Resize** to automatically resize the work plane. To manually change size, **Auto-Resize** must be toggled off.

The work plane's normal color depends on the color scheme defined in the Application Options dialog box.

- The two sides of a work plane are different colors. The normal side is a lighter color than the non-normal side. The normal side of the work plane can be reversed by right-clicking on the work plane and selecting **Flip Normal**. When entering offset values, the positive direction is always taken from the normal side of the plane.

- To toggle a work plane's visibility, right-click on the work plane and select **Visibility**. You can also globally control their display using the ⬚ (Object Visibility) options (*View* tab> Visibility panel).

7.2 Work Axes

A work axis is a type of feature that can be used to help create work planes, revolved features, or any other feature in the model. For example, a construction line can be sketched to serve as the axis of rotation for rotational features. However, creating a permanent work axis in the model is more efficient if the axial location is referenced by subsequent features (e.g., work plane). The plane shown in Figure 7–3 passes through the center of the rotational feature (work axis) and at an angle to the vertical face.

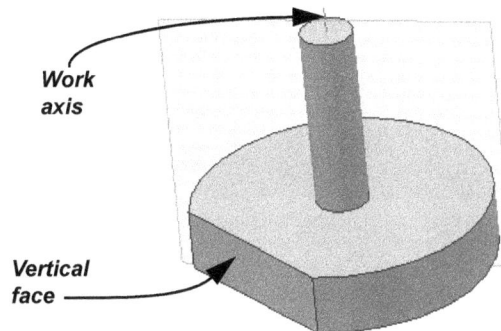

Figure 7–3

How To: Create a Work Axis

The end result of either method is the same. However, by selecting an axis placement type option, you are guided as to which references to select. Alternatively, you can select the reference before

clicking ▨ (Axis).

1. Start the creation of a work axis using one of the following methods:
   - In the *3D Model* tab>Work Features panel, click
     ▨ (Axis).
   - In the *3D Model* tab>Work Features panel, expand
     ▨ (Axis) and select an axis placement type.

2. Once you have started the creation of a work axis, you must select references to locate it. References can include edges/curves, planar faces, work planes, cylindrical surfaces, work points, vertices, or sketched lines. The reference type required depends on the work axis being created. Once the selected references fully define the work axis' placement, the work axis is displayed.

The different work axis placement types are described as follows:

Type	Example
On Line or Edge: Select a line or linear edge. The resulting axis is along that line or edge.	
Parallel to Line through Point: Select a point and then an edge, work axis, or sketched line. The resulting axis is parallel to the edge, work axis, or sketched line and goes through the point.	 *Reference Edge* *Axis*
Through Two Points: Select two end points, center points, or work points. The resulting axis passes through those points.	*Points*
Intersection of Two Planes: Select two work planes or planar faces. The resulting axis is located along the intersection of the two planes.	*Axis*
Normal to Plane through Point: Select a point and a surface. The resulting axis is normal to the surface and goes through the point.	*Point* ➤ *Axis*
Through Center of Circular or Elliptical Edge: Select an edge of a circular or elliptical feature. The resulting axis passes through the center line of the edge.	

Through Revolved Face or Feature: Select a face or feature of a revolved feature to create an axis that passes through the feature's center line.

Consider the following when working with work axis:

- Work planes and work points can be created during work axis creation and used as references. To do so, start the creation of the work axis (using either the **Axis** option or a specific work axis placement type), right-click, and select **Create Plane** or **Create Point**, as shown in Figure 7–4.

Cancel (ESC) ✕   ✓ OK (Enter)

⌂ Home View

Create Point
Create Plane
Repeat command
↵ Previous View   F5
How To...

Figure 7–4

- To change the name of the work axis, select it in the Model browser and select it again (do not double-click). Enter a name.

- To redefine the references of a work axis, right-click on the work axis, select **Redefine Feature**, and select new references.

- Work axes are infinite in length, but on screen they are sized to fit the overall geometry. To change the display size, select one of its ends and drag it. To automatically resize the work axis to fit the model, right-click on it and select **Auto-Resize**. Once toggled on, the work axis automatically resizes. To manually change the size, **Auto-Resize** needs to be toggled off.

- To change a work axis' visibility, right-click on the work axis and select **Visibility**. You can also globally control their display using the ▢ (Object Visibility) options (*View* tab> Visibility panel).

7.3 Work Points

Work points can be used as references when creating work planes, work axes, or other features in the model. In the example shown in Figure 7–5, various methods are used to create work points.

Consider using the **Center Point of Loop of Edges** *point type to create a point. Use the point to create an On Point hole that always remains centered on a selected loop of edges, regardless of how the geometry changes.*

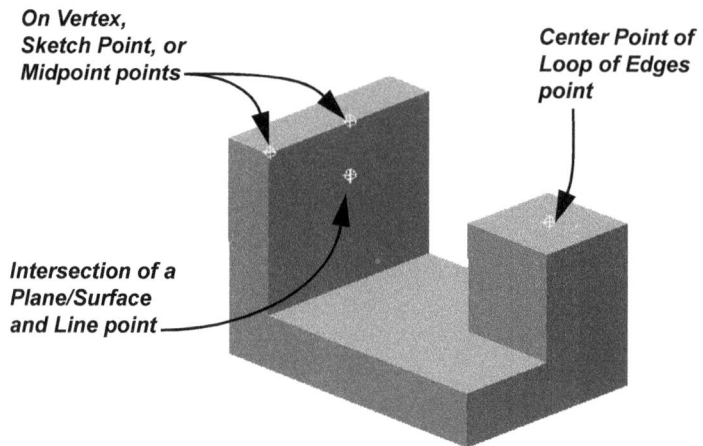

On Vertex, Sketch Point, or Midpoint points

Center Point of Loop of Edges point

Intersection of a Plane/Surface and Line point

Figure 7–5

How To: Create a Work Point

1. Start the creation of a work point using one of the following methods:
   - In the *3D Model* tab>Work Features panel, click

     ◈ (Point).
   - In the *3D Model* tab>Work Features panel, expand

     ◈ (Point) and select a point placement type.

The end result of either method is the same. However, by selecting a point placement type you are guided as to which references to select. Alternatively, you can select the reference before clicking

◈ *(Point).*

2. Once you have started the creation of a work point, you must select references to locate it. References can include work points, vertices, sketched points, midpoints, work planes, edges, work axes, or solid geometry. The reference type required depends on the work point being created. Once the selected references fully define the work point's placement, it is displayed.

The different work point placement types are described as follows:

Type	Example
Grounded Point: Select an existing point and convert it to a grounded point. Grounded work points have all degrees of freedom removed and are fixed in space.	
On Vertex, Sketch point, or Midpoint: Select the end point or midpoint.	
Intersection of Three Planes: Select three work planes or planar faces. The work point is located at their intersection.	
Intersection of Two Lines: Select the two edges, work axes, or lines. The work point is located at their intersection.	
Intersection of a Plane / Surface and Line: Select a plane and sketch line, curve, edge, or axis. The work point is located at their intersection.	

Center Point of Loop of Edges: Toggle on Loop Select Mode in the shortcut menu and select a circle, arc, or edge. A point is created at the center of the loop whether it is circular or not.	
Center of Torus: Select the torus surface. A point is created at the center of the selected surface.	*Point*
Center of Sphere: Select the sphere surface. A point is created at the center of the selected surface.	*Sphere* *Point*

Consider the following when working with work points:

- Work planes and work axes can be created during work point creation and used as references. To do so, start the creation of the work point (using either the **Point** option or a specific work point placement type), right-click and select **Create Axis** or **Create Plane**, as shown in Figure 7–6.

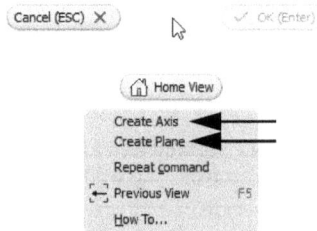

Figure 7–6

- To change the name of the work point (feature) select it in the Model browser and select it again (do not double-click). Enter a new name.

- To redefine the references of a work point, right-click on the work axis, select **Redefine Feature**, and select new references.

- To change a work point's visibility, right-click on the work point and select **Visibility**. You can also globally control their display using the ☐ (Object Visibility) options (*View* tab>Visibility panel).

Practice 7a

Using Work Features to Create Geometry I

Practice Objective

• Create work planes that can be used as references in the creation of a solid geometry feature.

In this practice, you will create the post/handle for the model shown in Figure 7–7. To create the geometry for this model, you need to create two additional work planes.

Figure 7–7

Task 1 - Open a part file.

1. Open **fork.ipt**.

2. Display the XZ Plane in the model.

Task 2 - Create the post for the fork.

1. In the Work Features panel, expand (Plane) and select **Tangent to Surface and Parallel to Plane** to create a work plane.

*Alternatively, you can click ⬜ (Plane) and select the tangent and parallel references without enabling **Tangent to Surface and Parallel to Plane**. Based on the selected references, the software knows the type of plane that should be placed.*

2. Select the bottom circular surface of **Extrusion1** as the reference for the work plane to be tangent to, as shown in Figure 7–8.

3. Select the XZ Plane as the plane to be parallel to. A new work plane displays, as shown in Figure 7–8.

4. In the Model browser, select the new work plane once and then again. Enter **Post Tangent Ref** as the new name of the work plane and press <Enter>.

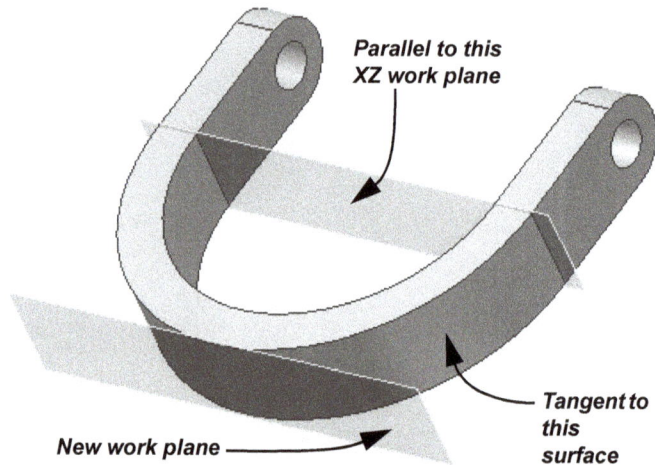

Parallel to this XZ work plane

Tangent to this surface

New work plane

Figure 7–8

The next steps create the post portion of the fork. There are many different ways that this can be accomplished. These steps take into account that the post must be exactly 7.5 in length. To meet this design requirement and create a robust model if changes are required, you will create an additional work plane offset 7.5 from the Post Tangent Ref work plane. A circular section will be placed on this work plane and extruded back to the fork portion of the model. Completing the model like this ensures that if dimensional changes are required, there is an easy and efficient way to make changes to the model.

Alternatively, you can click ⬜ (Plane), hover the cursor over the reference work plane, hold the left mouse button, and drag to position the new offset plane.

5. In the Work Features panel, expand ⬜ (Plane) and select **Offset from Plane** to create a work plane.

6. Select the **Post Tangent Ref** work plane.

7. Enter **-7.5 in** when prompted and click ✓ in the mini-toolbar. The work plane is created as shown in Figure 7–9.

New work plane

Offset from this work plane

Figure 7–9

8. In the Model browser, select the new work plane once and then again. Enter **Post Depth** as the new name of the work plane and press <Enter>.

9. Select the new Post Depth work plane, right-click and select **New Sketch**, or click 📐 in the heads-up display on the model.

10. Sketch a circular entity centered on the projected origin point and dimension, as shown in Figure 7–10. **Hint:** You might need to enable 🔲 (Slice Graphics) in the Status Bar to see the projected origin point and the sketch once it has been created.

—1.500—

Figure 7–10

11. Finish the sketch.

12. In the *3D Model* tab>Create panel, click ⬛↑ (Extrude) to create an extruded feature.

13. The circular section is automatically selected as the profile. Extrude the section using the **To Next** extent option. Complete the feature. The model displays as shown in Figure 7–11. By using the **To Next** extent option you ensure that the post extends as required to lie against the entire circular section of the fork.

Figure 7–11

14. Change the length of the post to 9 inches by editing the offset dimension on the Post Depth work plane to **-9 in**. Update the model.

15. Right-click on **Extrusion1** and select **Show Dimensions**. Edit the current 4 radius to **.5 in**. Update the model. Did the model react correctly?

16. Save the model and close the window.

Practice 7b

Using Work Features to Create Geometry II

Practice Objective

- Create a work plane that can be used as a reference in the creation of a solid geometry feature.

In this practice, you will create the Spotface hole as shown in Figure 7–12. To create the geometry for this model, you need to create additional work planes.

Spotface
hole

Figure 7–12

Task 1 - Open a part file and create work features required to create a hole.

1. Open **cylindrical_surf.ipt**.

2. In the Work Features panel, expand (Plane) and select **Angle to Plane around Edge** to create a work plane.

*Alternatively, you can click ▭ (Plane) and select the references without enabling **Angle to Plane around Edge**. Based on the selected references, the software knows the type of plane that should be placed.*

3. Select the XY Plane as the angular reference for the work plane. The model is shown in Figure 7–13.

4. Select the **Y-axis** in the **Origin** node of the Model browser as the linear reference to measure the angle about, as shown in Figure 7–13.

Select the XY origin work plane

Select the Y-axis as the linear reference

Figure 7–13

5. Enter **45** and click ☑ in the mini-toolbar. The work plane displays, as shown in Figure 7–14.

This new work plane is created

Figure 7–14

6. In the Model browser, select the new work plane once and then again. Enter **Angular Ref** as the new name of the work plane and press <Enter>.

Alternatively, you can click ⬜ *(Plane) and select the tangent and parallel references without enabling* **Tangent to Surface and Parallel to Plane**. *Based on the selected references, the software knows the type of plane that should be placed.*

7. In the Work Features panel, expand ⬜ (Plane) and select **Tangent to Surface and Parallel to Plane** to create a work plane.

8. Select the Angular Ref work plane and select the cylindrical surface, as shown on the left in Figure 7–15. The work plane is created as shown on the right.

Select this Angular Ref work plane

Select this cylindrical surface

Figure 7–15

9. In the Model browser, select the new work plane once and then again. Enter **Hole Sketch Plane** as the new name of the work plane and press <Enter>.

Task 2 - Create the sketch required to create the hole.

In this task you will use Hole Sketch Plane (work plane) as the sketch plane for a point. In the next task you will then use this point to create a hole.

1. Select the new Hole Sketch Plane work plane, right-click, and select **New Sketch**, or click 🖉 in the heads-up display on the model.

2. Project the Y-axis.

3. Project the top edge of the cylinder to use as a dimension reference for the Sketch Point. This dimension reference will control the position of the hole from the top of the cylinder.

4. In the Create panel, click ╌╬╌ (Point). Place and dimension the point, as shown in Figure 7–16.

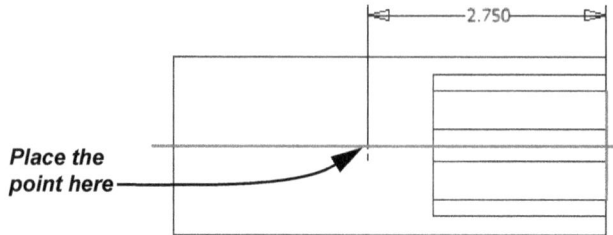

Place the point here

-2.750-

Figure 7–16

5. Finish the sketch.

Task 3 - Create the hole.

In this task you will use the sketch previously created as the placement reference for a Spotface hole.

1. Select the sketch of the point in the Model browser and click

   ▣ in the heads-up display on the model. The **From Sketch** placement option should be selected automatically because you just created a sketch. If not, select it. Create the **Spotface** hole using the values shown in Figure 7–17. Enter the values in the Hole dialog box or in the mini-toolbar.

Figure 7–17

2. Complete the feature. The model displays as shown in Figure 7–18.

Spotface hole

Figure 7–18

Task 4 - Edit the position of the hole (Optional).

1. In this optional task, you will be required to use your previous knowledge to change the position of the Spotface hole, similar to that shown in Figure 7–19. To do so you will have to edit the linear dimension from the top of the cylinder. This dimension was established in the sketch. To edit the angular position of the hole you will have to edit the angle on the Angular Ref work plane.

Figure 7–19

2. Save the model and close the window.

Practice 7c

Using Work Features to Create Geometry III (Optional)

Practice Objective

- Create a work plane and work axis that can be used as references in the creation of a solid geometry feature.

In this practice, you will create the model shown in Figure 7–20. To create the geometry for this model, you need to create an additional work plane and axis.

Figure 7–20

Task 1 - Create a new part and create a sketch.

1. Create a new part using the standard metric (mm) template.

2. Create a sketch on the XY plane.

3. Project the YZ and XZ work planes as references to locate the sketched geometry.

4. Sketch and dimension the section, as shown in Figure 7–21.

Figure 7–21

5. Finish the sketch.

6. In the *3D Model* tab>Create panel, click ⬛ (Extrude).

7. Enter **20.00** in the *Depth* field and complete the feature. The model displays as shown in Figure 7–22.

Depending on the orientation of the sketch plane, the default view of the model might vary. Spin as required, to reorient the model.

Figure 7–22

Task 2 - Create a fillet.

1. In the Modify panel, click 🗇 (Fillet) to create a fillet.

2. Use the **Feature** Select mode option and select **Extrusion1**.

3. Enter **7.00** as the radius.

4. Complete the feature. The model displays as shown in Figure 7–23.

Figure 7–23

Task 3 - Create work features.

In the remaining tasks you will create the extrusion shown in Figure 7–24. In this task you will create a work axis at the intersection of two faces on the base feature and a work plane referencing the axis.

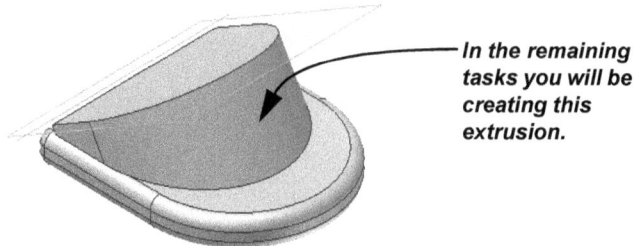

In the remaining tasks you will be creating this extrusion.

Figure 7–24

1. In the Work Features panel, expand ⊿ (Axis) and select **Intersection of Two Planes** to create a work axis.

*Alternatively, you can click ⊿ (Axis) and select the two planes without enabling **Intersection of Two Planes**. Based on the selected references, the software knows the type of plane that should be placed.*

2. Select the two faces shown in Figure 7–25 to create a work axis at their intersection.

Select these faces

Figure 7–25

The work axis is created at the intersection of the faces, as shown in Figure 7–26.

The YZ and XZ Planes are not displayed.

Axis

Figure 7–26

*Alternatively, you can click ⬚ (Plane) and select the references without enabling **Angle to Plane around Edge**. Based on the selected references, the software knows the type of plane that should be placed.*

3. In the Model browser, select the work axis once and then again. Enter **Angular Sketch Plane Axis Ref** as the new name of the work axis and press <Enter>.

4. In the Work Features panel, expand ⬚ (Plane) and select **Angle to Plane around Edge** to create a work plane.

5. Select the **Angular Sketch Plane Axis Ref** (previously Work Axis1) in the Model browser or graphics window.

6. Select the top face of the base feature, as shown in Figure 7–27.

Select this planar face

90.00 deg

Figure 7–27

7. Enter **30** in the *Angle* field and click ✓. The work plane displays as shown in Figure 7–28. Depending on your model, you might need to enter **-30** to obtain the result.

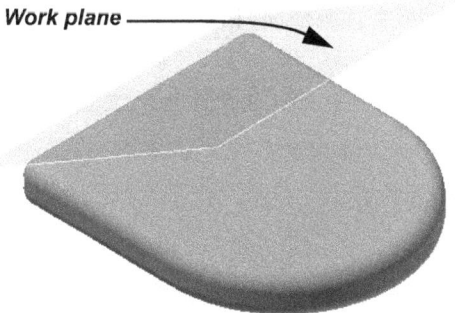

Work plane

Figure 7–28

8. In the Model browser, select the work plane once and then again. Enter **Angular Sketch Plane** as the new name of the work plane and press <Enter>.

Task 4 - Create the angled extrusion.

1. Create a sketch on the new work plane (Angular Sketch Plane).

The Angular Sketch Plane Axis Ref was consumed by Angular Sketch Plane. Expand the branch in the Model browser to select the axis.

2. Project the XZ Plane and the newly created axis (Angular Sketch Plane Axis Ref).

3. Press <Esc> to complete the operation.

4. Sketch the section with the dimensions and constraints shown in Figure 7–29.

Figure 7–29

5. Finish the sketch. The sketch displays as shown in Figure 7–30.

Figure 7–30

6. In the *3D Model* tab>Create panel, click (Extrude) to create an extruded feature.

7. The sketched section is automatically selected. In the Extrude mini-toolbar, expand the Extents drop-down list and select **To selected face/point** (or **To** in the Extrude dialog box) to define the extrusion depth up to a selected face.

8. Select the top face of the base feature to which to extend.

9. Complete the feature. The model displays as shown in Figure 7–31.

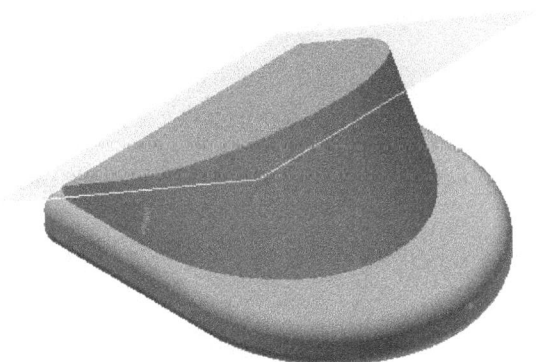

Figure 7–31

Task 5 - Create a hole that remains centered on a face.

In this task you will create a hole that will remain centered on a selected face, regardless of changes to the model that would change the size of the face. To accomplish this, you will create a work point and create the hole based on the point. You will make changes to the model to ensure that the hole placement updates correctly.

1. In the Work Features panel, expand ⊕ (Point) and select **Center Point of Loop Edge** to create a work point.

2. Rotate the model and select the loop of edges, as shown in Figure 7–32.

Select this loop of edges to place the work point.

Figure 7–32

3. A point displays, centered on the face that is bounded by the selected loop.

4. Right-click in the graphics window and select **Hole**.

5. Change the hole placement type to **On Point** and set the options in the Hole dialog box to create a drilled simple hole that cuts through the entire model.

6. Select the new work point that you just created.

7. Select the **Z Axis** as the Direction reference for the hole. Flip the direction of the hole if it is not going into the model.

8. Set the diameter for the hole to **25**.

9. Complete the feature. The model displays as shown in Figure 7–33.

Figure 7–33

10. Show the dimensions for **Extrusion1**.

11. Change the *65* dimension value to **100** and the 85 dimension value to **50**.

12. Update the model. The model displays as shown in Figure 7–34. Note that the hole remains centered on the face after the model is updated.

Figure 7–34

13. Save the model. Set the file name to **work_features**.

14. Close the window.

Chapter Review Questions

1. Origin Planes are the only work planes that can exist in a model.

   a. True

   b. False

2. Which of the following are possible uses for a work plane, as shown in Figure 7–35? (Select all that apply.)

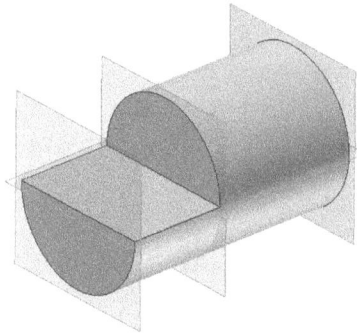

Figure 7–35

   a. To create another work plane.

   b. To define a sketch plane.

   c. To serve as the boundary for the depth of an extrusion.

   d. To set up a drawing sheet.

3. Which of the following are valid options to create a work plane? (Select all that apply.)

   a. **Through a Plane** and **Parallel to an Axis**

   b. **Offset from Plane**

   c. **Tangent to Surface** and **Parallel to Plane**

   d. **Three Points**

4. Which option enables you to create the work plane shown in Figure 7–36?

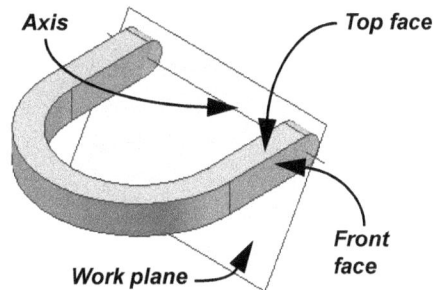

Figure 7–36

a. **Tangent to Surface through Edge**

b. **Tangent to Surface through Point**

c. **Tangent to Surface** and **Parallel to Plane**

d. **Angle to Plane around Edge**

5. Which of the following are valid options for creating a work axis? (Select all that apply.)

a. **Intersection of Two Planes**

b. **Through Two Points**

c. **Parallel to a Line**

d. **On Line or Edge**

6. A work axis can be used as a reference when creating a work plane.

a. True

b. False

7. Which option creates a work point centered on a face and remains centered even after the size of the face changes?

a. **On Vertex**, **Sketch Point**, or **Midpoint**

b. **Center Point of Loop of Edges**

c. **Center of Torus**

d. **Through Center of Circular** or **Elliptical Edge**

8. You can create work planes during work point creation to reference and constrain the work point.

a. True

b. False

Command Summary

Button	Command	Location
	Angle to Plane around Edge	• **Ribbon:** *3D Model* tab>Work Features panel>expand **Plane**
	Axis	• **Ribbon:** *3D Model* tab>Work Features panel
	Center Point of Loop of Edges	• **Ribbon:** *3D Model* tab>Work Features panel>expand **Plane**
	Center Point of Sphere	• **Ribbon:** *3D Model* tab>Work Features panel>expand **Plane**
	Center Point of Torus	• **Ribbon:** *3D Model* tab>Work Features panel>expand **Plane**
	Grounded Point	• **Ribbon:** *3D Model* tab>Work Features panel>expand **Plane**
	Intersection of a Plane/Surface and Line	• **Ribbon:** *3D Model* tab>Work Features panel>expand **Plane**
	Intersection of Three Planes	• **Ribbon:** *3D Model* tab>Work Features panel>expand **Plane**
	Intersection of Two Lines	• **Ribbon:** *3D Model* tab>Work Features panel>expand **Plane**
	Intersection of Two Planes	• **Ribbon:** *3D Model* tab>Work Features panel>expand **Axis**
	Midplane between Two Planes	• **Ribbon:** *3D Model* tab>Work Features panel>expand **Plane**
	Midplane of a Torus	• **Ribbon:** *3D Model* tab>Work Features panel>expand **Plane**
	Normal to a Curve at Point	• **Ribbon:** *3D Model* tab>Work Features panel>expand **Plane**
	Normal to Axis through Point	• **Ribbon:** *3D Model* tab>Work Features panel>expand **Plane**
	Normal to Plane through Point	• **Ribbon:** *3D Model* tab>Work Features panel>expand **Axis**
	Offset from Plane	• **Ribbon:** *3D Model* tab>Work Features panel>expand **Plane**
	On Line or Edge	• **Ribbon:** *3D Model* tab>Work Features panel>expand **Axis**
	On Vertex, Sketch point, or Midpoint	• **Ribbon:** *3D Model* tab>Work Features panel>expand **Plane**
	Parallel to Line through Point	• **Ribbon:** *3D Model* tab>Work Features panel>expand **Axis**

	Parallel to Plane through Point	• **Ribbon:** *3D Model* tab>Work Features panel>expand **Plane**
	Plane	• **Ribbon:** *3D Model* tab>Work Features panel • **Context Menu:** In the graphics window
	Point	• **Ribbon:** *3D Model* tab>Work Features panel
	Tangent to Surface and Parallel to Plane	• **Ribbon:** *3D Model* tab>Work Features panel>expand **Plane**
	Tangent to Surface through Edge	• **Ribbon:** *3D Model* tab>Work Features panel>expand **Plane**
	Tangent to Surface through Point	• **Ribbon:** *3D Model* tab>Work Features panel>expand **Plane**
	Three Points	• **Ribbon:** *3D Model* tab>Work Features panel>expand **Plane**
	Through Center of Circular or Elliptical Edge	• **Ribbon:** *3D Model* tab>Work Features panel>expand **Axis**
	Through Revolved Face or Feature	• **Ribbon:** *3D Model* tab>Work Features panel>expand **Axis**
	Through Two Points	• **Ribbon:** *3D Model* tab>Work Features panel>expand **Axis**
	Two Coplanar Edges	• **Ribbon:** *3D Model* tab>Work Features panel>expand **Plane**

Equations

Equations help incorporate design intent into a model, which ensures that the model behaves as intended when changes occur. They are established by creating mathematical relationships between dimensions and/or parameters.

Learning Objectives in this Chapter

- Change the dimension display type to identify dimension values, names, or equations.
- Create equations between dimensions to incorporate design intent into the model.
- Describe the difference between Model parameters and User-Defined parameters.
- Create user-defined parameters in a model.

8.1 Equations

Features and sketches generate dimensions in a model. Each dimension has a unique dimension name. The dimension name starts with the letter "d" followed by a unique number (e.g., d0 or d1).

Relationships can be defined between these dimensions, enabling you to control a dimension value based on a function of another dimension's value. These relationships are called *equations*. Equations can also include user parameters. When one dimension is referencing another, the referenced dimension in the equation is considered the driving dimension. The model in Figure 8–1 shows a hole being located based on an equation.

*When **fx** displays as part of a dimension name, it indicates that the dimension contains an equation.*

The distance from the center of the hole to the edges of the plate can be defined as half the overall dimension of the plate (i.e., d4=d0/2).

Figure 8–1

General Steps

Use the following general steps to add an equation:

1. Display the dimension symbols.
2. Create equations.
3. Flex the model.
4. Edit the equations, as required.

Step 1 - Display the dimension symbols.

To create equations you must use dimension names. To display dimension names, right-click in the graphics window, select **Dimension Display**, and click **Name**, as shown in Figure 8–2. Additional styles are described as follows.

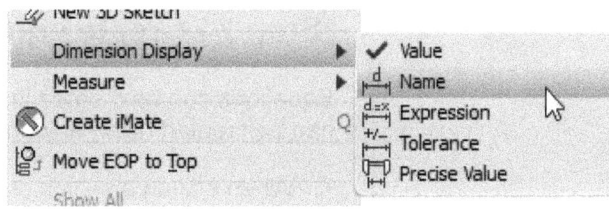

Figure 8–2

To control the display of dimensions in a Sketch, expand

[X⊢⊣ icon] *(Dimension Display) in the Status Bar and select an option. The options are the same as those in the Part environment.*

Value	Displays the numeric values of the dimensions.

Name	Displays the dimension names (e.g., d4 or d5).

Expression	Displays the dimension names with their numeric values or the equations that result in the numeric values (e.g., d2=d0/3 or d4=d5).

Tolerance	Displays the tolerances defined on any dimensions.
Precise value	Displays the precise numeric values of dimensions (not rounded). The **Precise value** option also displays the actual value of a dimension if a tolerance is applied. For example, if the dimension is 2.00 +/- 0.05 and is evaluated at the maximum tolerance, the value is 2.0500000000.

Step 2 - Create equations.

Equations can be created in a sketch or between features. They can be created using any one of the following techniques:

- When editing a sketch or feature dimension you can enter an equation directly in the Edit Dimension dialog box, as shown in the two examples in Figure 8–3. Alternatively, you can also select a dimension to add its dimension name to the Edit Dimension field for use in an equation.

*If **ul** displays next to a value, it indicates that the value is unitless.*

Edit Dimension : d5

d2/3

Dimension d5 is defined as 1/3 of d2 by entering the equation in the Edit Dimension dialog box.

Edit Dimension : d4

d3

Dimension d4 is set equal to d3 by entering the equation in the Edit Dimension dialog box.

Figure 8–3

- During feature creation, you can enter an equation in the entry fields, as shown for the diameter and linear dimension in Figure 8–4.

Figure 8–4

Model parameters can also be renamed in the Parameters dialog box to help recognize what the parameter is controlling.

- Equations can be entered after sketch or feature creation using the Parameters dialog box. This dialog box enables you to review the complete list of all of the parameters (dimension names) and existing equations in the model. To open the Parameters dialog box, in the *Manage* tab>

  Parameters panel, click f_x (Parameters), or in the Quick

  Access Toolbar, click f_x (Parameters). Equations are entered in the *Equation* column, as shown in Figure 8–5.

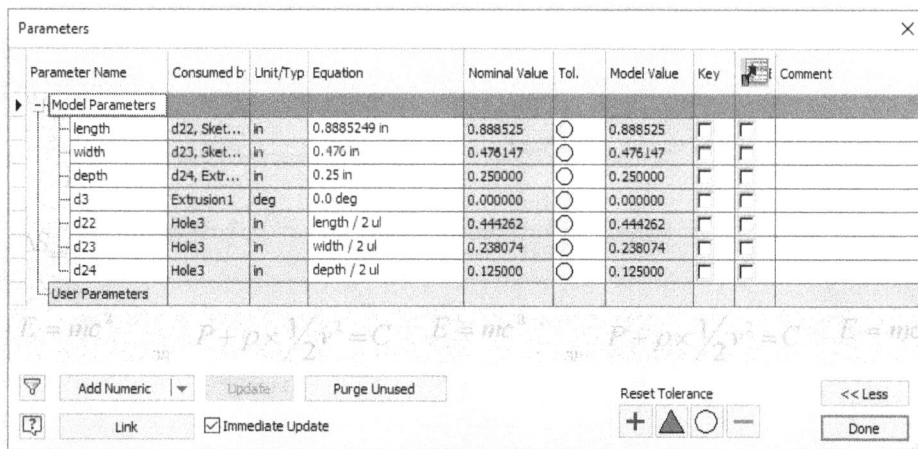

Parameter Name	Consumed b	Unit/Typ	Equation	Nominal Value	Tol.	Model Value	Key		Comment
▶ Model Parameters									
length	d22, Sket...	in	0.8885249 in	0.888525	○	0.888525	□	□	
width	d23, Sket...	in	0.476 in	0.476147	○	0.476147	□	□	
depth	d24, Extr...	in	0.25 in	0.250000	○	0.250000	□	□	
d3	Extrusion1	deg	0.0 deg	0.000000	○	0.000000	□	□	
d22	Hole3	in	length / 2 ul	0.444262	○	0.444262	□	□	
d23	Hole3	in	width / 2 ul	0.238074	○	0.238074	□	□	
d24	Hole3	in	depth / 2 ul	0.125000	○	0.125000	□	□	
User Parameters									

Add Numeric ▼ Update Purge Unused   Reset Tolerance   << Less

Link ☑ Immediate Update   + ▲ ○ −   Done

Figure 8–5

Equations can be written using any of the following operators or functions to capture the intent of the equation.

Mathematical Operators

The following operators can be used in equations:

+	Addition
-	Subtraction
/	Division
*	Multiplication
^	Exponentiation
()	Expression delimiter

Functions

The following functions can be used in equations:

sin( )	tanh( )	sinh( )
cos( )	sqrt( )	cosh( )
tan( )	log( )	ceil( ) converts arbitrary real numbers to close integers. The ceil function of a real number x, ceil(x) returns the next highest integer (e.g., ceil(3.2) =4).
asin( )	ln( )	
acos( )	exp( )	floor( ) converts arbitrary real numbers to close integers. The floor function of a real number x, floor(x) returns the next smallest integer (e.g., floor(3.8) =3).
atan( )	abs( )	

Units

Units are assigned to each value, if you do not assign them first. Some of the symbols used for units of distance are as follows:

Unitless	ul
Inches	in, inch, or "
Feet	ft, foot
Meter	m, meter
Centimeter	cm
Millimeter	mm

*The software can resolve equations that use some operators (+, -, *, /). However, for operators such as exponents, units should be assigned (e.g., 3in^2ul)*

Step 3 - Flex the model.

Once you finish adding an equation, test the model to verify that the equation captures the required design intent. This is called flexing the model and should involve editing the driving dimension values to verify that the model changes as expected.

Step 4 - Edit the equations, as required.

If flexing the model did not result in the required behavior, you can make required changes to the equations. This can be done by editing a dimension or feature, or using the Parameters dialog box.

To help identify which features the model parameters were created by, you can review the Consumed by column in the Parameters dialog box. The column lists the feature that the parameter was created in to help identify it.

8.2 Parameters

As features are created in a model, dimensions are used to define the model's shape. The name and value of the dimension are considered a Model Parameter. Model parameters are listed in the Parameters dialog box.

The Parameters dialog box also enables you to create User-Defined parameters, which can be used in equations to help you control the model. Once created, user-defined parameters are listed under the *User Parameters* area in the Parameters dialog box.

To open the Parameters dialog box, use one of the following methods:

- In the *Manage* tab, on the Parameters panel, click f_x (Parameters).

- In the Quick Access Toolbar, select $\boxed{f_x}$ (Parameters).

Model Parameters

Model parameters are the dimensions that are automatically assigned as you add sketch dimensions and features to the model. They use default dimension names (e.g., d0, d1, d2, etc.), and are listed at the top of the Parameters dialog box, as shown in Figure 8–6.

The sketch and feature dimension are listed in the Model Parameters area.

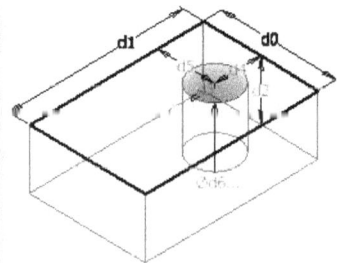

Figure 8–6

Renaming Model parameters enables you to easily identify the parameter in the context of the entire model. To rename a Model parameter enter a new name in the *Parameter Name* column of the Parameters dialog box, as shown in Figure 8–7.

Alternatively, you can enter a new name in the entry fields when creating or modifying dimensions associated with the feature you want to rename.

Model parameter names can assigned in the dialog box, or when creating or editing the model.

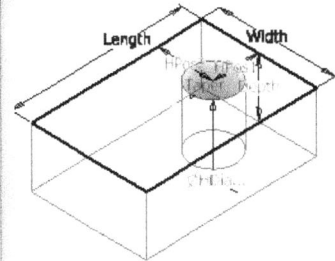

Figure 8–7

User Parameters

User parameters can be added to further capture the model's design intent for use in equations or to add information to the model. User parameters can be any one of three types (i.e., Numeric, Text, or True/False) and are created in the Parameters dialog box.

To create a user parameter, select the Add option that is associated with the required parameter type at the bottom of the Parameters dialog box, as shown in Figure 8–8. Once added, the parameter displays in the *User Parameters* area at the bottom of the Parameters dialog box. Enter a name, unit (if applicable), and value for the new parameter.

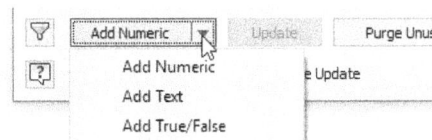

Figure 8–8

- Parameter names must be unique. They are case-sensitive and cannot begin with a numeric digit, nor can they contain spaces or mathematical operators.

- Some names are reserved by the software for specific operations and for mathematical use. If the name is unavailable for use you will be prompted that the parameter cannot be created.

Multi-value parameters can also be assigned for use with model parameters.

- Numeric and text parameters can be either a single-value or a multi-value parameter. To set a parameter as multi-value, right-click on any cell in its row and select **Make Multi-Value**. Using the Value List Editor (shown in Figure 8–9), multiple values can be added. Enter the possible values in the *Add New Items* area in the dialog box and click **Add** to include them in the multi-value list. Multi-value parameters display all of the available values in a drop-down list in the *Equation* row, as shown on the right of in Figure 8–9.

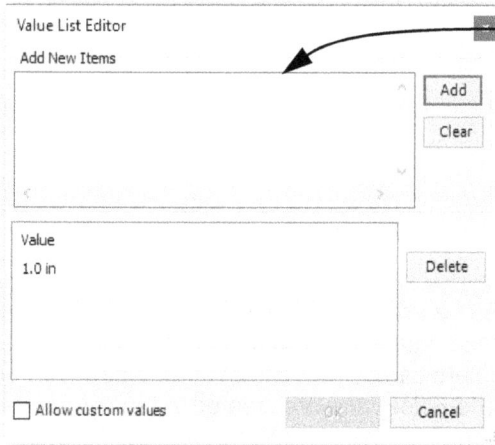

Enter multi-values in the Value List Editor so that they can be displayed in a list in the Parameters dialog box.

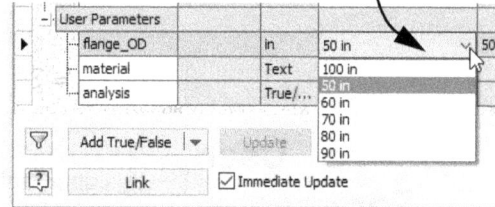

Figure 8–9

- Text parameters provide static text as their value.

- Similar to Multi-Value parameters, True/False parameters also display a drop-down list in the *Equation* row, enabling you to select the True or False value.

- To edit parameter values you can edit the model geometry (in the case of model parameters) or change the Equation cell value in the Parameters dialog box. Editing the value in the *Equation* column has the same effect as editing the dimension value directly on the model. User parameters can only be edited in the Parameters dialog box.

- When editing a dimension value using the *Edit Dimension* field, you can select from the list to efficiently create equations. Click 🔽 when editing and select **List Parameters** to open and directly select from the list of renamed parameters, as shown in Figure 8–10. Only renamed parameters are shown in this list.

Figure 8–10

- Incorporating filters enables you to simplify the list of displayed parameters based on a selected filter type. To filter, click 🔽 (Filter) in the dialog box and select a filter type, as shown in Figure 8–11. The filtering options enable you to show only key parameters (**Key**), non-key parameters (**Non-Key**), renamed parameters (**Renamed**), parameters driven by equations (**Equation**), or parameters for selected features (**By Features**).

Figure 8–11

- To delete individual user-parameters, right-click on the parameter name and select **Delete Parameter**. Alternatively, you can delete multiple unused parameters at once by, clicking **Purge Unused** and selecting the parameters in the Purge Parameters dialog box.

- Some of the other options in the Parameters dialog box are as follows:

Tol column	Displays the evaluated tolerance setting: ⊞ (Upper), ▲ (Median), ◯ (Nominal), or ⊟ (Lower). To change the setting, click an icon and select from the drop-down list.
Consumed by column	Displays the feature or sketch name that contains the parameter. This enables you to identify where the parameter was created.
Model Value column	Displays the actual calculated value for the parameter based on the tolerance setting.
Key column	Identifies existing model and user parameters and flags them as critical (key).
Export Parameter column	Adds the parameter to the custom properties for the model. Custom properties can be used in bill of materials and part lists.
Comment column	Enables you to add a comment about the parameter.
Link	Links a parameter to a spreadsheet or to another file (part, assembly, or sheet metal).
Update and **Immediate Update**	Enables you to specify whether or not the model updates immediately (**Immediate Update**) when a change is made. If the **Immediate Update** option is disabled, you must manually update after closing the Parameters dialog box.
Reset Tolerance	Changes the Tolerance setting for all of the parameters.
Less and **More**	Enables you to customize the display by displaying less or more of the dialog box.

Practice 8a

Add Equations

Practice Objectives

- Show dimensions in a model and obtain their expression value for use in an equation.
- Add equations to a model using the Edit Dimension dialog box and feature creation dialog box.

In this practice, you will modify dimensions in a part using dimension equations. The completed part is shown in Figure 8–12.

Figure 8–12

Task 1 - Open a part file.

1. Open **equation.ipt**.

2. Right-click anywhere in the graphics window and select **Dimension Display>Name**.

3. Right-click on **Extrusion1** and select **Show Dimensions**. The dimensions display as shown in Figure 8–13.

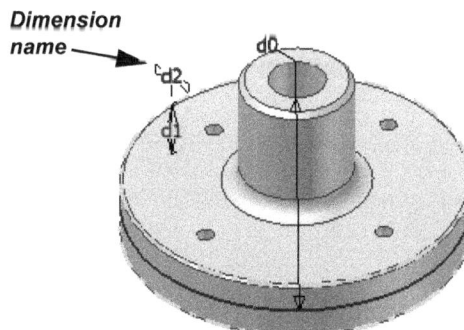

Dimension
name

Figure 8–13

4. Click the left mouse button anywhere in the graphics window to clear the feature selection in the Model browser.

5. Right-click anywhere in the graphics window and select **Dimension Display>Expression**. The dimensions are displayed as equations, as shown in Figure 8–14.

*To display dimensions for multiple features at the same time, select the features using <Shift>, right-click on any of the features in the Model browser, and select **Show Dimensions**.*

Figure 8–14

6. Note the diameter and thickness of the extrusion:

   - *Diameter:* **d0 = 60mm**
   - *Thickness:* **d1 = 10mm**

7. Display the dimensions for **Extrusion3**.

   - *Diameter:* **d6 = 10mm**

Task 2 - Add an equation to control the diameter.

In this task, you will add an equation to control the diameter of **Extrusion3** so that it will be 1/6 of the diameter of **Extrusion1**.

fx indicates that the dimension contains an equation.

1. Double-click on the d6 dimension, and enter **d0/6** in the Edit Dimension dialog box. Press <Enter>. The expression is now **d6=d0/6ul**, as shown in Figure 8–15. The d6 dimension is dependent on the d0 dimension.

Figure 8–15

Task 3 - Add an equation to drive the thickness.

In this task, you will add another equation to drive the thickness of **Extrusion2** so that it is twice as much as the thickness of **Extrusion1**.

1. Press and hold <Shift> and select **Extrusion1** and **Extrusion2**. Right-click on either feature in the Model browser and select **Show Dimensions**.

2. Note the thickness for **Extrusion2**:

    *   **d4 = 20mm**

3. Double-click on the d4 dimension and enter **2*d1** in the Edit Dimension dialog box. Press <Enter>. The expression is now **d4=2ul*d1.** The d4 dimension is controlled by the d1 dimension (the thickness of **Extrusion1**).

4. Modify the thickness of **Extrusion1** from 10mm to **12mm**.

5. In the Quick Access Toolbar, click (Local Update) to update the part.

6. Modify the diameter of **Extrusion1** to **72mm** and then update the part again to review the changes.

Task 4 - Add an equation to control the diameter.

In this task, you will add an equation to control the hole diameters.

1. Right-click on **Hole1** and select **Edit Feature**.

2. The diameter of the hole is 3mm. Change the diameter to **d6/2**. The hole's diameter is now controlled by the d6 dimension (**Extrusion3** diameter). Close the Hole dialog box. The model displays as shown in Figure 8–16.

Figure 8–16

Alternatively, click f_x in the Quick Access Toolbar to open the Parameters dialog box.

3. Select the *Manage* tab. In the Parameters panel, click f_x (Parameters). The Parameters dialog box opens as shown in Figure 8–17.

Parameter Name	Consumed b	Unit/Typ	Equation	Nominal Value	Tol.	Model Value	Key		Comment
– Model Parameters									
d0	d6, Sketch1	mm	72 mm	72.000000	○	72.000000	☐	☐	
d1	d4, Extru...	mm	12 mm	12.000000	○	12.000000	☐	☐	
d2	Extrusion1	deg	0 deg	0.000000	○	0.000000	☐	☐	
d3	Sketch2	mm	20 mm	20.000000	○	20.000000	☐	☐	
d4	Extrusion2	mm	2 ul * d1	24.000000	○	24.000000	☐	☐	
d5	Extrusion2	deg	0 deg	0.000000	○	0.000000	☐	☐	
d6	d18, Sket...	mm	d0 / 6 ul	12.000000	○	12.000000	☐	☐	
d8	Extrusion3	deg	0 deg	0.000000	○	0.000000	☐	☐	
d9	Fillet1	mm	3 mm	3.000000	○	3.000000	☐	☐	
d10	Chamfer1	mm	1 mm	1.000000	○	1.000000	☐	☐	

Add Numeric ▾   Update   Purge Unused   Reset Tolerance   << Less

Link   ☑ Immediate Update   + ▲ ○ —   Done

Figure 8–17

4. Scroll through the list and note the equations that were created. Close the Parameters dialog box.

5. Save the model and close the window.

Practice 8b

Add Parameters

Practice Objectives

- Add equations to a model using the Parameters dialog box and feature dialog boxes.
- Create user-defined parameters for use in equations.

In this practice, you will modify dimensions in a part using model parameters and then add user-defined parameters. The completed model displays as shown in Figure 8–18.

Figure 8–18

Task 1 - Open a part file.

1. Open **parameters.ipt**.

2. Right-click on **Extrusion1** and select **Show Dimensions**.

3. Click the left mouse button to clear the feature selection in the Model browser.

4. Right-click and select **Dimension Display>Expression**. Figure 8–19 shows the model in wireframe, for clarity.

Figure 8–19

Task 2 - Change the model parameter names.

Alternatively, in the Manage tab> Parameters panel, click

f_x *(Parameters).*

1. In the Quick Access Toolbar, select f_x (Parameters) to open the Parameters dialog box.

2. In the *Parameter Name* column in the Parameters dialog box, do the following:
   - Change the name to d0 to **side1**.
   - Change the name of d1 to **side2**.
   - Change the name of d2 to **length**.
   - Change the name of d4 to **dia**.

3. Select the side2 *Equation* column and enter **side1**. The side 2 dimension is now driven by the **side1** value. The Parameters dialog box should be as shown in Figure 8–20.

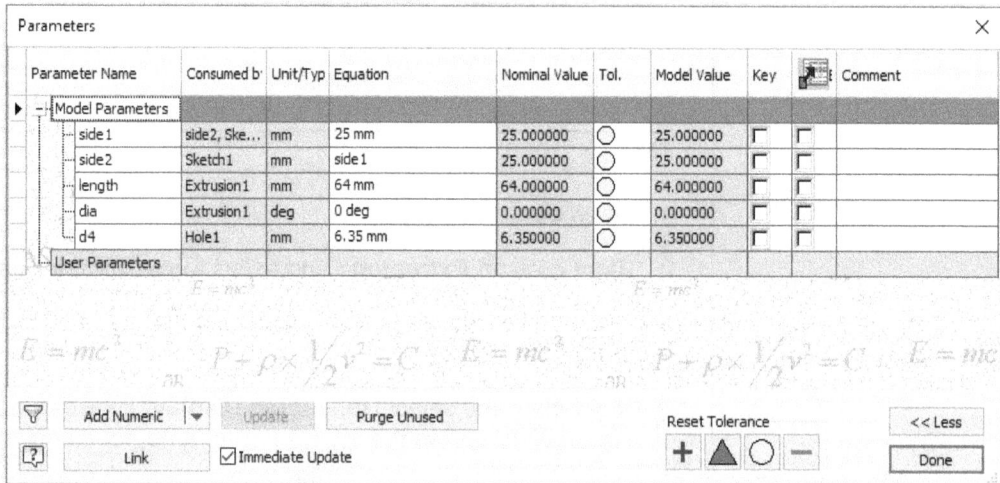

Parameter Name	Consumed b	Unit/Typ	Equation	Nominal Value	Tol.	Model Value	Key		Comment
▶ – Model Parameters									
side1	side2, Ske...	mm	25 mm	25.000000	○	25.000000	☐	☐	
side2	Sketch1	mm	side1	25.000000	○	25.000000	☐	☐	
length	Extrusion1	mm	64 mm	64.000000	○	64.000000	☐	☐	
dia	Extrusion1	deg	0 deg	0.000000	○	0.000000	☐	☐	
d4	Hole1	mm	6.35 mm	6.350000	○	6.350000	☐	☐	
User Parameters									

Add Numeric | Update | Purge Unused | Reset Tolerance | << Less
Link | ☑ Immediate Update | + ▲ ○ − | Done

Figure 8–20

4. Click **Done** to close the Parameters dialog box.

5. Display the **Extrusion1** and **Hole1** dimensions. Note the parameter names that you assigned.

*To display dimensions for multiple features at the same time, select the features using <Shift>, right-click on any of the features in the Model browser, and select **Show Dimensions**.*

6. In the Quick Access Toolbar, select f_x (Parameters) to open the Parameters dialog box again.

7. Select the length *Equation* column, enter **side1*3**, and press <Enter>. The entry in the *Model Value* column changes.

To update the part, click

(Local Update) in
*the Quick Access
Toolbar.*

8. Click **Done** to close the Parameters dialog box.

9. Update the model, if required.

10. Display the **Extrusion1** dimensions. The model displays as shown in Figure 8–21.

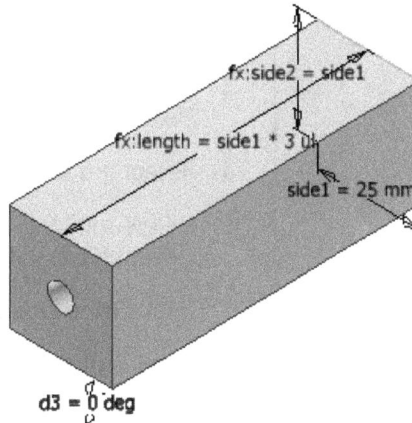

Figure 8–21

11. Edit **Extrusion1** to open its Extrude dialog box and mini-toolbar. Note **side1 * 3 ul** in the *Distance* field, as shown in Figure 8–22.

Figure 8–22

12. Close the Extrude dialog box.

Task 3 - Add a user-defined parameter.

1. In the Quick Access Toolbar, select f_x (Parameters) to open the Parameters dialog box.

2. Click **Add Numeric** in the Parameters dialog box to add a user-defined parameter to the model.

3. Enter **size** in the *Parameter Name* column in the *User Parameters* area.

4. Select the *Unit* column. The Unit Type dialog box opens.

5. Delete mm in the *Unit Specification* field. Expand the **Unitless** branch and select **Unitless (ul)**.

6. Click **OK** to close the Unit Type dialog box.

7. Enter **1 ul** in the *Equation* column and enter **determine overall size** in the *Comment* column in the *User Parameters* area. Press <Enter>. The size parameter should display in the Parameters dialog box as shown in Figure 8–23.

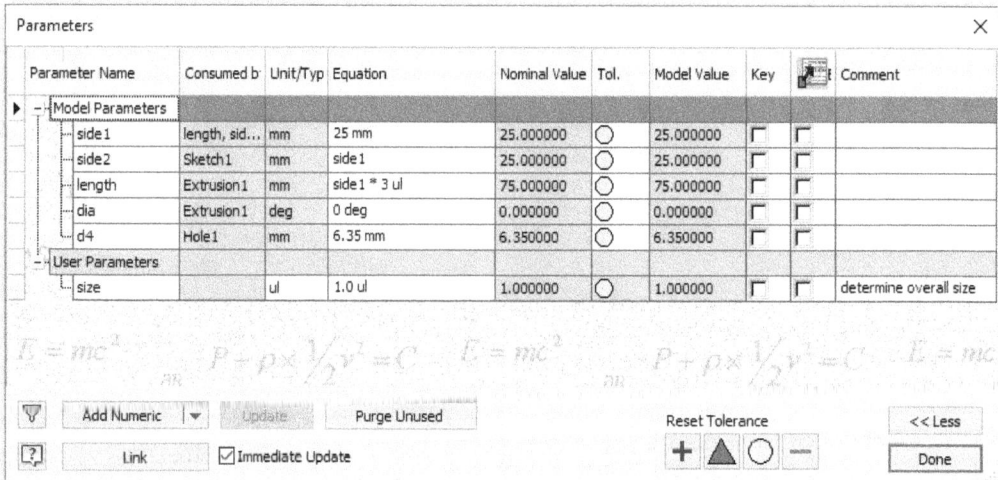

Parameter Name	Consumed b	Unit/Typ	Equation	Nominal Value	Tol.	Model Value	Key		Comment
▶ – Model Parameters									
side1	length, sid...	mm	25 mm	25.000000	○	25.000000	☐	☐	
side2	Sketch1	mm	side1	25.000000	○	25.000000	☐	☐	
length	Extrusion1	mm	side1 * 3 ul	75.000000	○	75.000000	☐	☐	
dia	Extrusion1	deg	0 deg	0.000000	○	0.000000	☐	☐	
d4	Hole1	mm	6.35 mm	6.350000	○	6.350000	☐	☐	
– User Parameters									
size		ul	1.0 ul	1.000000	○	1.000000	☐	☐	determine overall size

Figure 8–23

Task 4 - Add a second user-defined parameter.

1. Click **Add Numeric** to add a second user parameter.

2. Enter **round_1** in the *Parameter Name* column in the second row of the *User Parameters* area.

3. If units are not set to mm, select the *Unit* column, expand the Length branch, and select **millimeter (mm)**.

4. Enter **3.175** in the *Equation* column and **fillet radius** in the *Comment* column in the *User Parameters* area.

5. Select the side1 *Equation* cell and enter **25mm*size**. The Parameters dialog box should be as shown in Figure 8–24. The user-defined size parameter is going to drive the side1 dimension. Since the size parameter is unitless, you must multiply it by a distance to obtain a distance value.

Parameter Name	Consumed b	Unit/Typ	Equation	Nominal Value	Tol.	Model Value	Key		Comment
▶ ─ Model Parameters									
side1	length, sid...	mm	25 mm * size ◀	25.000000	○	25.000000	▢	▢	
side2	Sketch1	mm	side1	25.000000	○	25.000000	▢	▢	
length	Extrusion1	mm	side1 * 3 ul	75.000000	○	75.000000	▢	▢	
dia	Extrusion1	deg	0 deg	0.000000	○	0.000000	▢	▢	
d4	Hole1	mm	6.35 mm	6.350000	○	6.350000	▢	▢	
─ User Parameters									
size	side1	ul	1.0 ul	1.000000 ◀	○	1.000000	▢	▢	determine overall size
round_1		mm	3.175 mm	3.175000 ◀	○	3.175000	▢	▢	fillet radius

$E = mc^2$ $P + \rho \times \frac{1}{2} v^2 = C$ $E = mc^2$ $P + \rho \times \frac{1}{2} v^2 = C$ $E = mc$

| ▽ | Add Numeric | ▼ | Update | Purge Unused | | Reset Tolerance | | << Less |
| [?] | Link | | ☑ Immediate Update | | | + ▲ ○ — | | Done |

Figure 8–24

6. Close the Parameters dialog box.

7. Display the **Extrusion1** dimensions. Note the parameter names and equations that you assigned.

Task 5 - Add fillets.

In this task, you will add fillets to the model and use the parameters you defined to modify the fillets.

1. Start the creation of the fillet.

2. Add fillets to the four long edges of the part.

3. Select the *Radius* field in the dialog box or in the mini-toolbar, and click ▶. The flyout menu displays as shown in Figure 8–25.

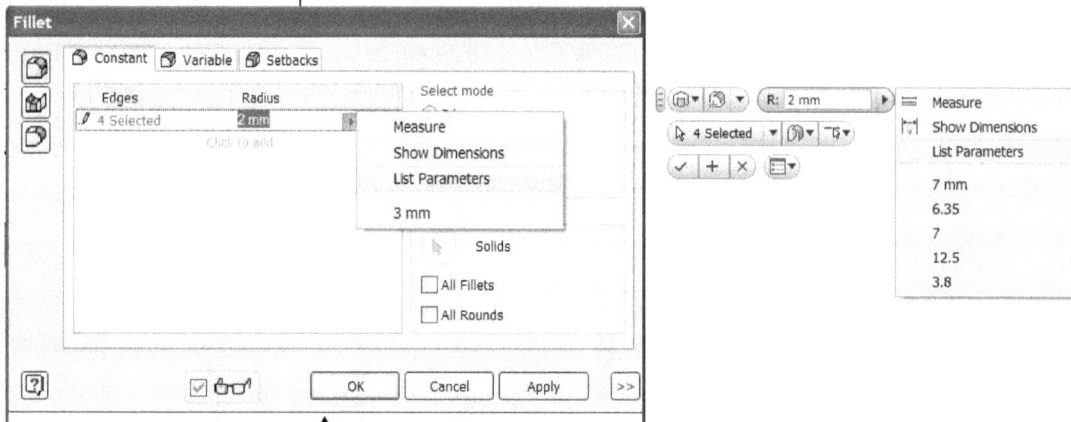

Figure 8–25

4. Select **List Parameters** and select **round_1** in the list that displays. The fillets radii are now controlled by the **round_1** parameter.

5. Complete the Fillet.

6. Change the equation of the **round_1** parameter to **12.5** in the Parameters dialog box.

7. Ensure that **Immediate Update** is selected in the Parameters dialog box. The model displays as shown on the left in Figure 8–26.

8. Change the equation of the size parameter to **2**. The updated model displays as shown on the right in Figure 8–26.

Figure 8–26

9. Save the model and close the window.

Practice 8c

Working with Parameters

Practice Objectives

- Rename parameters using the Edit Dimension and Parameters dialog boxes.
- Use a driven dimension in a model to drive geometry.
- Export a parameter for use in another model.
- Reference a parameter from another model and use it to drive the geometry.

In this practice, you will create a new model. You will rename the default dimension parameters and use a reference parameter to drive the placement of points in the model. In addition, you will export parameters so that they can be linked to other models. Creating and linking reference parameters to other models can reduce rework and redundancy by enabling designs to carry non-part specific values that can be reused in multiple parts. The model that you create is shown in Figure 8–27.

Figure 8–27

Task 1 - Create a new model.

In this task, you will create a sketch of a rectangle and four points, and fully dimension the sketch. You will add one additional dimension to provide a driven dimension. This will be used as a parameter to drive the placement of all points so that they are always equally spaced in the rectangle. To complete the task, you will rename the Reference Parameter and set it so that it can be referenced by other models.

1. Create a new model using the standard imperial (in) template.

Alternatively, you can enable

⌐ *(Construction) before creating the line.*

2. Sketch a rectangle centered about the origin of the sketch, as shown in Figure 8–28.

3. Click ╱ (Line) and draw a line connecting the two midpoints of the vertical edges. Select the line, click

    ⌐ (Construction) to convert it to a construction line, as shown in Figure 8–28.

4. Click ⊢⊣ (Dimension) and place dimensions along the top and the side of the rectangular sketch, as shown in Figure 8–28. Press <Esc> to finish the command. Assign a Symmetric constraint, as required, to ensure that the sketch is fully constrained.

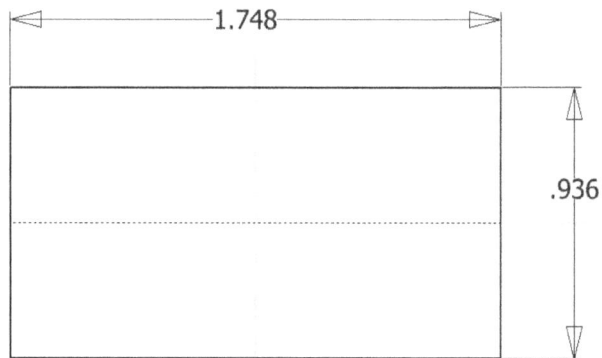

◁────────── 1.748 ──────────▷

.936

Figure 8–28

5. Double-click on the longer dimension value to edit it. Enter **Length = 2.5** in the Edit Dimension dialog box. Edit the width value in the same way. The Edit Dimension dialog boxes are shown in Figure 8–29.

Edit Dimension : d0 ✕	Edit Dimension : d1 ✕
Length = 2.5 ＞ ✓	Width = 1.5 ＞ ✓

Figure 8–29

By entering the parameter name in the dialog box, you are renaming the default d0 and d1 dimension names to *Length* and *Width* without having to rename them in the Parameters dialog box.

6. Click ⁻┆⁻ (Point) and sketch four points on the construction line, as shown in Figure 8–30.

7. Click ⊓ (Dimension) and place dimensions, as shown in Figure 8–30, so that the left-most point is dimensioned from the left vertical edge, and the remaining points are dimensioned from each other. Dimension the last point to the right-most vertical edge. Once this dimension is placed, it will indicate that the sketch is over-dimensioned. Accept this dimension so that it is created as a driven dimension.

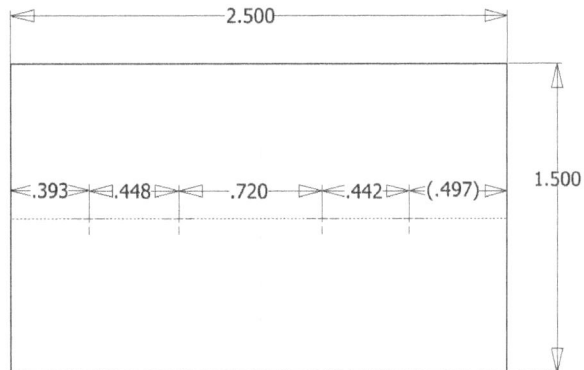

Figure 8–30

8. Expand ⊢ₓ⊣ (Dimension Display) on the Status Bar and select **Name** to display the parameter name for the dimensions. Note that *Length* and *Width* are now the names for the first two dimensions that you created.

9. Double-click on the d2 dimension value and enter **d3** in the Edit Dimension dialog box, as shown in Figure 8–31.

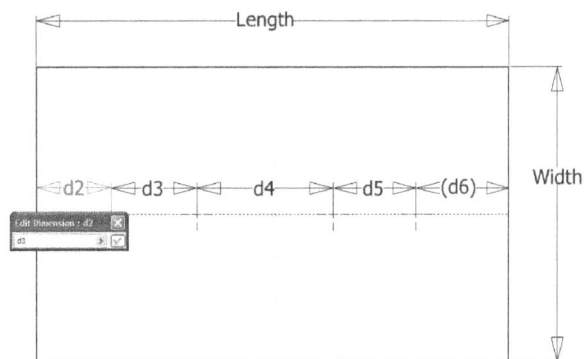

Figure 8–31

10. Continue to edit the remaining dimension values so that **d3 = d4**, **d4 = d5**, and **d5 = d6**. The sketch updates once you have entered all of these values, as shown in Figure 8–32.

By establishing relationships to the driven dimension in the model, you force the points to stay equally spaced based on the overall length of the rectangle.

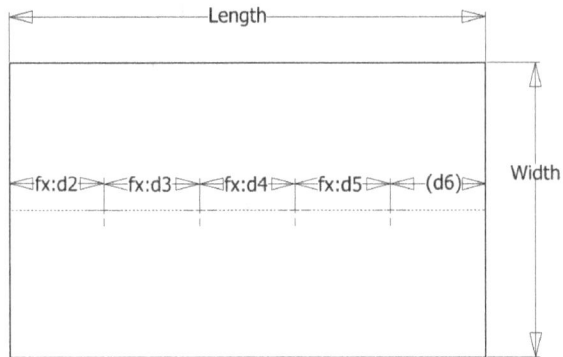

Figure 8–32

11. In the Quick Access Toolbar, select f_x (Parameters) to open the Parameters dialog box. Review all of the parameters and equations that you established in the sketch without using the Parameters dialog box.

12. Rename the Reference Parameter (d6) to **Hole_Spacing** and select it for *Export*, as shown in Figure 8–33. The Reference Parameter has to be renamed in the Parameters dialog box because it is not an editable value; it is a driven value.

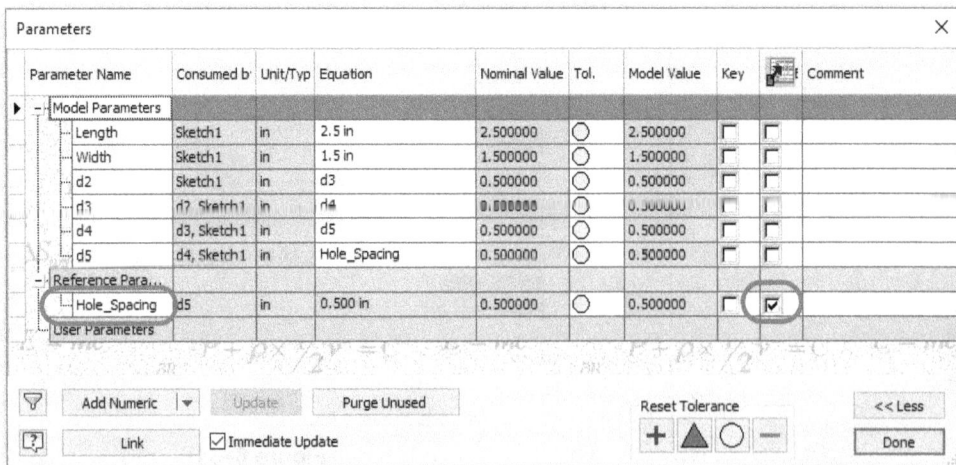

Figure 8–33

13. Click **Done** to close the Parameters dialog box.

14. Finish the sketch.

15. Extrude the sketch as shown in the Figure 8–34.

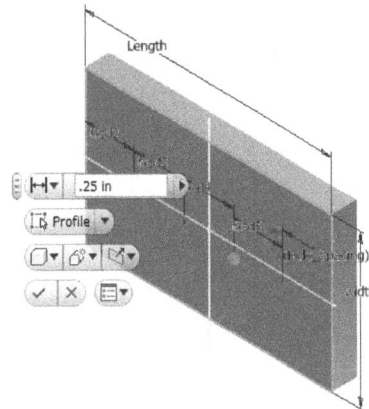

Figure 8–34

16. Expand Extrusion1 in the Model browser. Right-click on **Sketch1** and select **Share Sketch**. Alternatively, you can select and drag it out to the top-level to share it. The sketch that you used to create the extrusion can now be used to create additional features.

17. In the Modify panel, click ⬡ (Hole). Create a hole using the **From Sketch** placement type and the other options shown in Figure 8–35.

Figure 8–35

18. Complete the feature. Because all four points are in the sketch, four holes are created at the same time.

19. Toggle off the visibility of **Sketch1**. The model displays as shown in Figure 8–36.

Figure 8–36

20. Save the file as **DrivenReference.ipt**.

Task 2 - Open a new model and reference the Hole_Spacing parameter in the DrivenReference.ipt model.

In this task, you will open a model that is provided for you and reference parameters from the part model that you just created. By referencing parameters from another part, you will drive the geometry in this provided model.

1. Open **Placement.ipt**.

2. Open the Parameters dialog box.

3. In the Parameters dialog box, click **Link**.

4. Change the Files of type drop-down list option to **Inventor Files (*.ipt, *.iam)**. Browse to the location of the **DrivenReference.ipt** file, select it, and click **Open**.

5. The Link Parameters dialog box opens, listing all of the parameters from the **DrivenReference.ipt**. Click ⬤ next to the **Hole_Spacing** reference parameter. Once selected, it displays as ⊕, indicating it can be referenced. Click **OK**. The Parameters dialog box updates as shown in Figure 8–37.

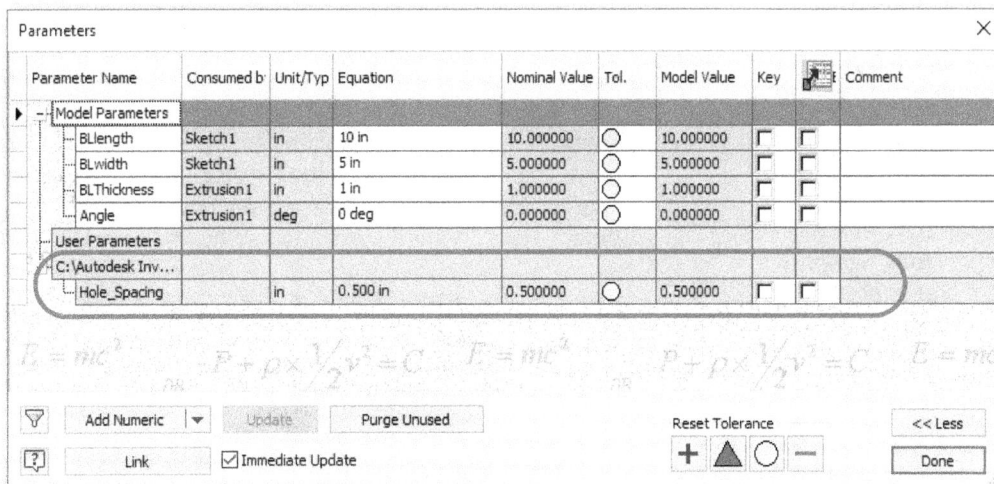

Figure 8–37

A link has been created as a User Parameter to the **DrivenReference.ipt** file. This can be edited or deleted by right-clicking on the row in the Parameters dialog box and selecting the required option on the shortcut menu. Ensure that the file is always maintained in this location and is not deleted. This ensures that the reference is not lost. This is also true if a spreadsheet is used as the reference location for parameters.

6. Close the Parameters dialog box.

7. Edit **Sketch2**.

8. Click ⌐ (Dimension) and place dimensions between all of the points, as shown in Figure 8–38.

Figure 8–38

As an alternative to typing the Hole_Spacing parameter value, when editing, click ▶ and select List Parameters to display the list of available parameters. Select Hole_Spacing in the Parameters dialog box.

9. Edit the values of the four dimensions so that they are equal to the **Hole_Spacing** parameter.

10. Finish the sketch.

11. Select the *3D Model* tab. In the Modify panel, click ⬚ (Hole). Create a simple hole using the **From Sketch** placement type. Enter a diameter of **0.25** and select **Through All** for the *Termination*. The holes display as shown in Figure 8–39.

Figure 8–39

12. Save the model.

Task 3 - Make modifications in the DrivenReference model to test the referenced parameters.

In this task, you will open the **DrivenReference.ipt** model and make changes to it to ensure that the **Placement.ipt** model updates as expected.

1. Activate **DrivenReference.ipt**.

2. In the Parameters dialog box, edit the **Length** parameter from *2.5 in* to **5 in**. Close the dialog box.

3. Return to the **Placement.ipt** model and perform an update. The model updates to reflect the change. This functionality would be useful in an Assembly environment if these two models were assembled.

4. Save and close the models.

Chapter Review Questions

1. You can only add an equation to a model in the Parameters dialog box.

   a. True

   b. False

2. Which of the following statements regarding equations are true? (Select all that apply.)

   a. Dimensions and parameters can be used in an equation to drive a value.

   b. Equations can be manually entered in the Edit Dimension dialog box.

   c. Equations can be created by selecting dimensions directly from the model.

3. Which combination of equations centers the hole, if the length and width are equivalent, as shown in Figure 8–40? (Select all that apply.)

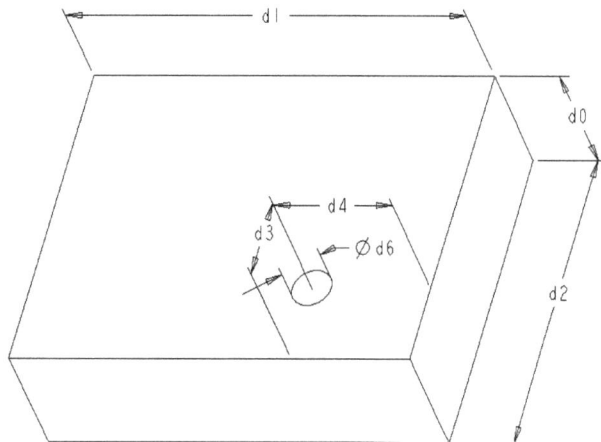

Figure 8–40

   a. d4 = d1 / 2
      d3 = d2 / 2

   b. d1 = d4 / 2
      d2 = d3 / 2

   c. d1 = d2
      d4 = d1 / 2
      d3 = d2 / 2

4. Which dimension display type is set to display the dimensions in the model as shown in Figure 8–41?

Figure 8–41

   a. Value

   b. Name

   c. Expression

   d. Tolerance

   e. Precise Value

5. Which description best describes how the equation shown in Figure 8–42 affects the model?

$$d0 = 3 * d6$$
$$d3 = d4$$

Figure 8–42

   a. The depth of the base extrusion is equal to the diameter of the hole and the hole is centered on the base extrusion.

   b. The depth of the base extrusion is equal to three times the diameter of the hole and the hole is centered on the base extrusion.

   c. The depth of the base extrusion is equal to three times the diameter of the hole, and the values of the horizontal and vertical hole dimensions are equivalent.

   d. The depth of the base extrusion is equal to three times the diameter of the hole, the values of the horizontal and vertical hole dimensions are equivalent, and d1 and d2 are equivalent.

6. Fill in the parameter type: **Model** or **User-Defined**, with the method in which it is created in a model.

   a. _____ parameters are created using the Parameters dialog box where you select the type, name, and enter values.

   b. _____ parameters are automatically assigned each time you add a dimension or feature to a part.

7. Which of the following best describe what **fx** is identifying in the sketch shown in Figure 8–43?

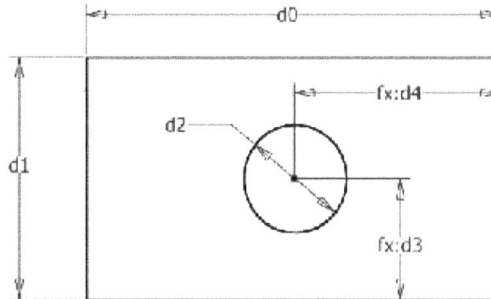

Figure 8–43

   a. d3 and d4 are reference dimensions.

   b. d3 and d4 are equal.

   c. d3 and d4 are generated based on a user-defined equation.

   d. d3 and d4 have a tolerance assigned.

Command Summary

Button	Command	Location
f_x	**Parameters**	• **Ribbon:** *Manage* tab>Parameters panel • **Quick Access Toolbar**

Chapter 9

Additional Features

Numerous combinations of features can be used to build a model. These can include standard sketched features and pick and place features. Drafts, Shells, and Ribs are advanced features that can be incorporated into the model to create geometry.

Learning Objectives in this Chapter

- Create a Face Edge Draft where the draft pull direction is defined along a selected edge.
- Create a Face Edge Draft where the draft pull direction is normal to the selected plane or face.
- Create a Face Edge Draft where the draft is applied above and below a parting line reference.
- Use the Split command to split a face, trim a part, or create two bodies based on a split reference.
- Create a Shell feature that removes faces and assigns uniform or unique wall thickness to the remaining faces in the model.
- Create a Rib feature from a sketched section.
- Create boss and draft geometry in a Rib feature.

9.1 Face Draft

A draft creates sloped surfaces and is often used to remove a part from a mold. You can apply draft over the entire profile, to one face, or apply drafts to different faces, as shown in Figure 9–1.

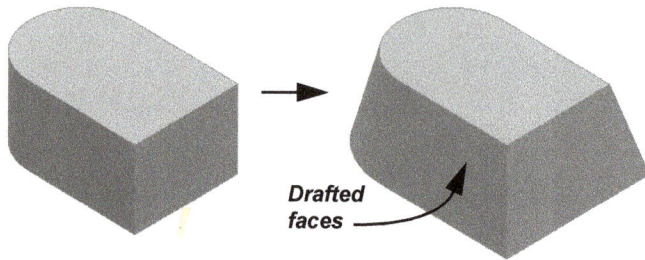

Drafted faces

Figure 9–1

General Steps

Use the following general steps to create a draft:

1. Start the creation of the face draft.
2. Select the draft type.
3. Select the draft references.
4. Select faces to draft.
5. Enter the draft angle.
6. Complete the feature.

Step 1 - Start the creation of the face draft.

In the *3D Model* tab>Modify panel, click (Draft) to create a Face Draft. The Face Draft dialog box and mini-toolbar display.

Step 2 - Select the draft type.

You can create three types of drafts: **Fixed Edge**, **Fixed Plane**, and **Parting Line**. Select the type of draft in the dialog box or in the drop-down list in the mini-toolbar, as shown in Figure 9–2.

Figure 9–2

The three draft types are described as follows:

- A **Fixed Edge Draft** creates a draft about one or multiple tangent fixed edges for a selected face(s), as shown in

  Figure 9–3. To create a fixed edge draft, click in the Face Draft dialog box or select **Fixed Edge** in the drop-down list in the mini-toolbar.

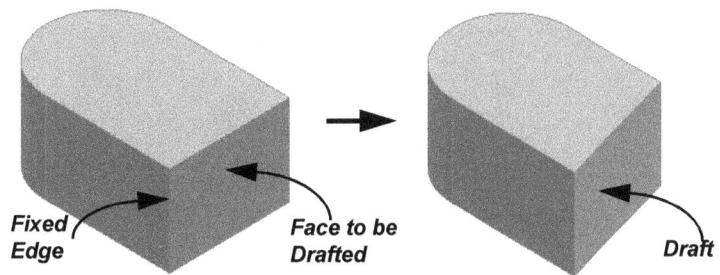

Figure 9–3

- A **Fixed Plane Draft** creates a draft about a fixed plane for a selected face(s), as shown in Figure 9–4. To create a fixed

  plane draft, click in the Face Draft dialog box or select **Fixed Plane** in the drop-down list in the mini-toolbar.

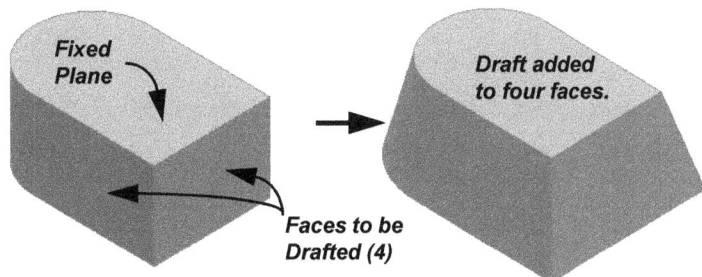

If you apply draft to a face, draft is also applied to all faces that are tangent to it.

Figure 9–4

- A **Parting Line Draft** creates a draft about a parting line (or plane). Draft is applied above and below the parting line for a selected face(s). To create a parting line draft, click [⬚] in the Face Draft dialog box or select **Parting Line** in the drop-down list in the mini-toolbar.

- By default, a Parting Line draft is created using the Fixed Parting Line ([⬚]) option, which ensures that the geometry remains the same size at the parting line and draft is added above or below. Alternatively, the Move Parting Line ([⬚]) option can be selected to add material at the parting line.

- Figure 9–5 shows an example of a work plane being used to define a Fixed Parting Line Draft (top) and a curve being used as the part line for Parting Line Draft that uses the Move Parting Line option (bottom).

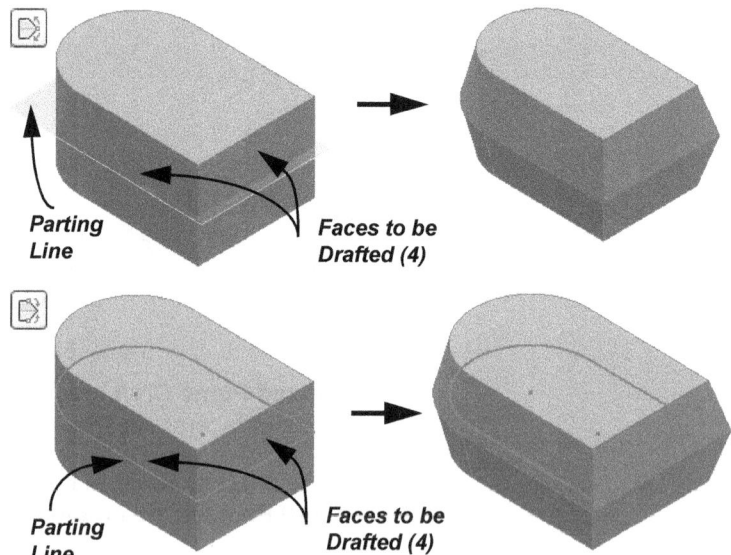

Figure 9–5

Step 3 - Select the draft references.

The references that are required to place a Face Draft depends on the type of draft that is being created. The following summarizes the reference selections that are required and which draft types require them.

Required Reference	Draft Type
Pull Direction	Fixed Edge and Parting Line
Fixed Plane	Fixed Plane
Parting Tool	Parting Line

To select a reference, ensure that its associated reference button

( ) is active in the Face Draft dialog box or that its option is selected in the mini-toolbar drop-down list. The following describes each of the references:

The Pull Direction is the direction in which the mold is pulled from the part.

- When applying a Fixed Edge or a Parting Line Draft, you must specify a Pull Direction, as shown in Figure 9–6. The draft is applied so that the part becomes more narrow toward the pull direction, when positive draft angles are used. Any planar face, edge, work plane, or work axis can be used as the reference for the pull direction and the pull direction is defined as normal to this selected reference. You can flip the

  pull direction by clicking in the mini-toolbar or in the dialog box once the direction arrow is displayed.

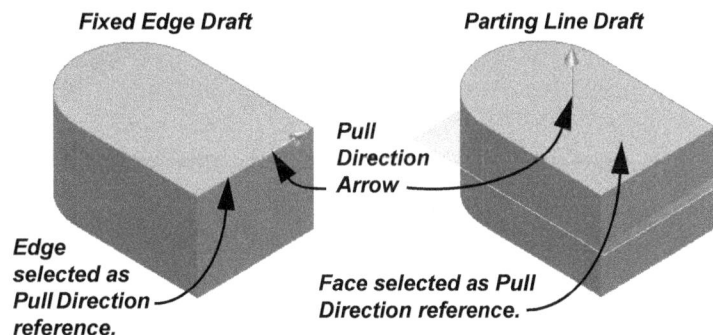

Fixed Edge Draft   *Parting Line Draft*

Pull Direction Arrow

Edge selected as Pull Direction reference.

Face selected as Pull Direction reference.

Figure 9–6

- When creating a Fixed Plane Draft, a fixed plane reference must be defined. The fixed plane defines the plane that remains unchanged (fixed) and defines the pull direction. A work plane or planar face can be used as the reference for a fixed plane. Figure 9–7 shows the fixed plane reference and the resulting pull direction for the Fixed Plane Draft shown previously.

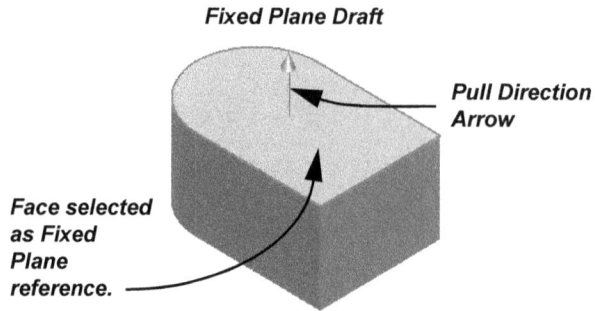

If you apply draft to a face, draft is also applied to all faces that are tangent to it.

Fixed Plane Draft

Pull Direction Arrow

Face selected as Fixed Plane reference.

Figure 9–7

The reference used as the draft pull direction should be normal to the Parting Tool.

- When creating a Parting Line Draft, a Parting Tool reference must be defined. The parting line can be a 2D or 3D sketch, a plane, or a surface and defines where two halves of a mold meet. Figure 9–8 shows the parting line reference for the Parting Line Draft shown previously.

Parting Line Draft

Pull Direction Arrow

Plane selected as Parting Line reference.

Face selected as Pull Direction reference.

Figure 9–8

Step 4 - Select faces to draft.

All three draft types require the selection of face(s) that are to be drafted. To select the face(s) to be drafted, ensure that

▨ (Faces) is active in the Face Draft dialog box or that **Faces** is selected in the mini-toolbar (shown in Figure 9–9), and then select the required faces.

Figure 9–9

- Both face and edge references can be selected to define the geometry that is to be drafted.

- For Fixed Edge Drafts, select the draft face closer to the edge that is to be fixed, as shown in Figure 9–10. The angle preview displays on the fixed edge. If the draft doesn't display as required, clear the face selection by holding <Ctrl> while selecting the reference again.

Fixed Edge Draft

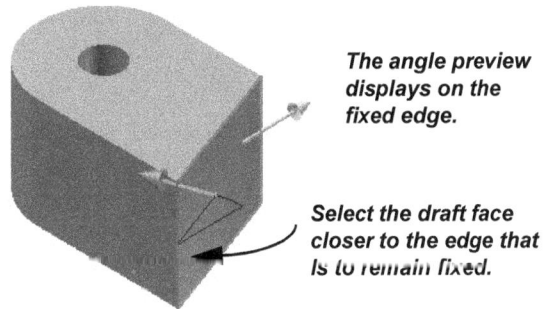

The angle preview displays on the fixed edge.

Select the draft face closer to the edge that is to remain fixed.

Figure 9–10

- Multiple faces or edges can be selected for drafting; however, their draft angles are controlled by one value. Create separate face drafts to individually control the draft angles of individual faces.

- Select **Automatic Face Chain** to automatically include any faces that are tangent to the selected face. This option is available for all three types of drafts.

- Select **Automatic Blending** to blend the resulting draft with adjacent filleted faces. This option is available for all three types of drafts. Figure 9–11 shows that a single face has been selected for drafting (**Automatic Face Chain** was cleared) and the **Automatic Blending** option is on or off.

Automatic ➝   *Automatic* ➝
Blending is Off.   *Blending is On.*

Figure 9–11

- When creating a Parting Line Draft that uses the 🗗 (Move Parting Line) option, you can further customize the draft by setting static edges on the draft geometry. To do so, enable 🖰 (Fixed Edges) once draft faces have been selected and select the individual edges that will not change.

  - Alternatively, click 🗗 (Select Boundary) to select multiple edges automatically.

  - To clear all selected fixed edges, click 🗗 (Clear All). The selection of fixed edges can only be customized in the Face Draft dialog box and not the mini toolbar.

Step 5 - Enter the draft angle.

A default *Draft Angle* value is automatically assigned once all references have been selected. The draft is displayed in preview mode with this value. To change the value, enter a new value in the *Draft Angle* field in the mini-toolbar or Face Draft dialog box, as shown in Figure 9–12. Draft values can be between 0 and 89 degrees.

Figure 9–12

A negative angle value reverses the pull direction.

- For Fixed Edge Drafts, the draft value is measured from the fixed edge.

- For Fixed Plane and Parting Line Drafts that use the Fixed Parting Line (⬚) option, the draft value is measured from the fixed plane or parting line reference.

   - The symmetric (⬚) and asymmetric (⬚) side options can be used to further define the draft angles on either side of the reference plane. For an Asymmetric draft, the draft angle can be different above and below the parting line/fixed plane. To toggle between the draft angles on the model, press <Tab>. Alternatively, enter the draft angle values using the dialog box. Figure 9–13 shows how the symmetric and asymmetric options can be accessed in the mini-toolbar.

One way is not available for parting line drafts.

Figure 9–13

- For Parting Line Drafts that use the Move Parting Line (![icon]) option, the draft value can be specified so that it is on both sides using the Angle for Both (![icon]), Angle for Top (![icon]), or Angle for Bottom (![icon]). Once any of these are activated, enter a value in the *Min. Draft Angle* field. Figure 9–14 shows how to access these options in the Face Draft dialog box and mini-toolbar.

Figure 9–14

Step 6 - Complete the feature.

Click **OK** or ![checkmark icon] to complete the face draft and close the Face Draft dialog box and mini-toolbar. Alternatively, right-click and select **OK (Enter)** or press <Enter>.

9.2 Splitting a Face or Part

You can split a face to manipulate each portion of the face separately. For example, a face that is required to be drafted can be split so that the resulting drafted faces can have different draft angles. Figure 9–15 is an example of a face split using a sketched line as the Split Tool.

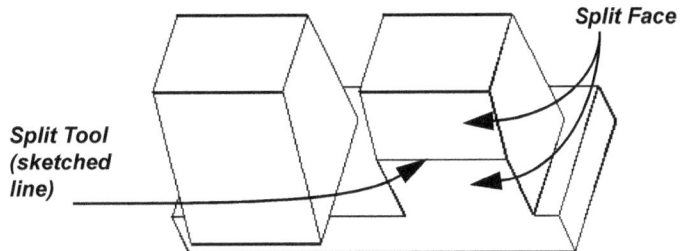

Figure 9–15

How To: Split a Face or Part

The mini-toolbar is not available for creating splits.

1. In the *3D Model* tab>Modify panel, click ⬜ (Split) to split a face. The Split dialog box opens as shown in Figure 9–16.

Figure 9–16

*If a 3D curve is selected as the Split Tool reference, the **Trim Solid** and **Split Solid** options are disabled.*

2. Define the method and face options, as follows:

    *   Click ⬜ (Split Face) to split faces. The entire part remains as one object, but the faces can be manipulated separately.

    *   Click ⬜ (Trim Solid) to trim a part. A portion of the part is removed using the toggle direction icons.

    *   Click ⬜ (Split Solid) to split a part into two bodies along the split reference.

- Click 🏛 (Select) to individually select the faces that are split.

- Click 🏛 (All) to select all part faces that intersect the Split Tool (a work plane, construction surface, or sketch).

The Split Tool reference must completely intersect the entire face being split.

3. Ensure that the ⬚ (Split Tool) option is active and select the Split Tool reference that defines where the split is to occur. This reference can be a work plane, surface, or sketch geometry.

4. Ensure that the ⬚ (Faces) option is active and select the face(s) to split, as shown in Figure 9–17.

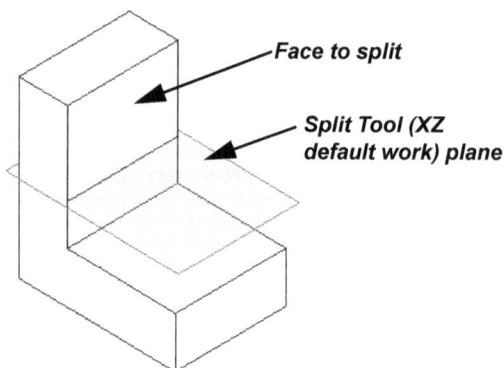

Face to split

Split Tool (XZ default work) plane

Figure 9–17

5. Click **OK** or ✓ to complete the split. Alternatively, right-click and select **OK (Enter)** or press <Enter>.

9.3 Shells

A shell feature is a feature that hollows a solid leaving a specified wall thickness. You can only vary the thickness of the walls between faces if the faces are not tangent. For this reason, you should normally shell the part before you add fillets. The model shown in Figure 9–18 has been shelled to remove the top and side face.

Figure 9–18

Shell features cannot create tapered geometry; they are most often used for models with a constant thickness. Shell features can also be used for castings and molded parts.

General Steps

Use the following general steps to create a shell:

1. Start the creation of the shell.
2. Select the faces to remove.
3. Select the direction of shell removal.
4. Define the thickness of the wall.
5. Complete the feature.

Step 1 - Start the creation of the shell.

In the *3D Model* tab>Modify panel, click (Shell) to create a shell. The Shell dialog box and mini-toolbar open as shown in Figure 9–19.

Figure 9–19

Step 2 - Select the faces to remove.

With (Remove Faces) selected in the Shell dialog box, or selected in the mini-toolbar, select the model faces to remove. The remaining faces are left as the shell walls. Removing a face creates an opening on that side of the part, as shown in Figure 9–20. If no model faces are selected to be removed, the shell cavity is entirely enclosed in the part, as shown on the right in Figure 9–20.

Original Model

Front Face Removed

No Faces Removed

Figure 9–20

- To restore a face that has been selected for removal, hold <Ctrl> and select the face again.

- To automatically select all of the surfaces that are tangent to the surface that is selected for removal, click ⊘ 🗘 in the mini-toolbar or click **Automatic Face Chain** in the dialog box. Clear this option to select only the selected surface. Figure 9–21 shows the resulting shelled geometry when this option is both enabled and disabled.

Surface to be removed

Automatic Face Chain is enabled.

Automatic Face Chain is not enabled.

Figure 9–21

Step 3 - Select the direction of shell removal.

The shell direction options enable you to define the side to which the shell is added. Any of these options can be selected either in the Shell dialog box using the icon, or in the mini-toolbar by selecting the drop-down list next to the shell *Thickness* value field (🗗▼). The options are described as follows:

🗗 (Inside)	Creates the shell inside the existing part boundaries with a specified thickness.
🗗 (Outside)	Creates the shell outside the existing part boundaries with a specified thickness.
🗗 (Both)	Existing part boundaries define the midpoint of the walls of the new part.

Step 4 - Define the thickness of the wall.

The wall thickness for a shell can be uniform, or you can assign unique wall thickness values to individual faces.

- To assign a uniform thickness, enter a value in the *Thickness* field in the Shell dialog box or mini-toolbar. Expand the *Thickness* field to select from a list of recent values.

A unique face thickness can be added using the Shell dialog box only and not in the mini-toolbar.

- To add unique thickness value to individual faces, click `>>` in the Shell dialog box to expand the dialog box. Select **Click to add** in the *Unique face thickness* area and select a face for which you are defining a unique wall thickness. Enter a dimension next to the selected face in the *Thickness* column, as shown in Figure 9–22. Multiple faces can be selected and assigned a unique wall thickness value. To delete an entry, select it and press <Delete>.

Faces to be assigned unique thickness values.

Thickness of (.5mm) was assigned to the top and bottom faces.

Figure 9–22

Step 5 - Complete the feature.

The ⚠ icon displays in the mini-toolbar for a Shell when the feature cannot be created.

Click **OK** or ✓ to complete the shell feature. Alternatively, right-click and select **OK (Enter)** or press <Enter>.

Hint: Shell Restrictions

The model geometry controls whether a shell can be added to a model or not. Note the following restrictions:

- Two tangent faces cannot have different thickness values. This restriction is generally due to the use of fillets. To apply different thickness values, add fillets after the shell.

- The face being removed for a shell must be surrounded by edges (i.e., not a fully revolved feature). Alternatively, use a closed shell, followed by an extruded cut feature.

9.4 Ribs

Consider using the **Extrude** *command to create rib and web features with closed geometry.*

The **Rib** command enables you to create solid extrusions with open geometry. Typically, a rib is a feature that supports adjoining geometry. The rib can be constructed so that it is parallel to (rib) or perpendicular to (web) the plane of the sketched geometry, as shown in Figure 9–23.

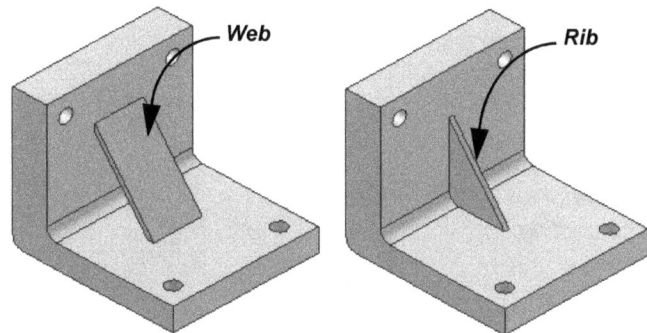

Figure 9–23

General Steps

Use the following general steps to create a rib:

1. Create the rib sketch.
2. Start the creation of the rib.
3. Define the shape of the rib.
4. Define the thickness of the rib.
5. Extend the rib.
6. Define additional features.
7. Complete the feature.

Step 1 - Create the rib sketch.

Rib geometry can be defined by sketching on work planes, planar faces, or existing planar faces. The profile can be drawn so that it does not meet the part. When the rib is created, it is extended to the part, as shown in Figure 9–24. Once the sketch geometry has been defined, you can create the rib.

You can use several entities at the same time to create a series or network of ribs. The profile lines can intersect, but a single profile cannot be self-intersecting.

Figure 9–24

Step 2 - Start the creation of the rib.

The mini-toolbar is not available for creating ribs.

In the *3D Model* tab>Create panel, click (Rib) to create a rib. The Rib dialog box opens as shown in Figure 9–25.

Figure 9–25

Step 3 - Define the shape of the rib.

Select the rib sketch if it is not automatically selected. Click

![icon] (Normal to Sketch Plane) to create a rib perpendicular to

the sketch plane (web) or click ![icon] (Parallel to Sketch Plane) to create a rib parallel (rib) to the sketch plane. Figure 9–26 shows a rib being created both perpendicular (web) and parallel (rib) to the sketch plane of a sketched line.

Perpendicular (web)   *Parallel (rib)*

Figure 9–26

To further refine the direction of the feature, use the appropriate

direction icon (![icon] or ![icon]).

Step 4 - Define the thickness of the rib.

Enter a value for the thickness of the rib or select a value in the drop-down list. By default, the rib is extruded symmetrically on

both sides of the sketching plane (![icon]). To switch the feature creation from both sides to one side of the sketching plane,

select the appropriate direction icon (![icon] or ![icon]).

Step 5 - Extend the rib.

The two options at the bottom of the *Thickness* area specify how the rib terminates. The difference between these extent options is shown in Figure 9–27.

- To extend the rib feature to the part face(s), click ⬜ (To Next).

- To extend the rib feature to a specified distance, click
  ⬜ (Finite) and enter a value for the rib extent.

Figure 9–27

- The **Extend Profile** option extends the profile to intersect the model faces. It is only available when you are creating a finite extension.

Hint: Preview not Displaying

If the preview does not display, it usually means that the geometry cannot be created with the options currently selection, consider changing the direction and extent options.

Step 6 - Define additional features.

For rib features that are created normal to a sketch plane, draft and boss features can be added to the rib during creation. This avoids having to create the features in separate steps.

To add draft to the rib, select the *Draft* tab, as shown in Figure 9–28. Enter the Draft Angle, and specify where the thickness is controlled. Thickness can be controlled at the sketch plane (**At Top**) or at the intersection of the rib and the next feature face (**At Root**).

Figure 9–28

A boss feature can be added to the rib from the *Boss* tab, as shown in Figure 9–29. To create a boss feature, point(s) must first be created in the rib sketch. The point(s) represent the center point of the boss. If points are present in the sketch they are selected automatically. To specify specific points around which to create the bosses, clear the **Select All** option, click

(Centers), and select the points.

Figure 9–29

An example of a boss feature added to a rib is shown in Figure 9–30.

Figure 9–30

Step 7 - Complete the feature.

Click **OK** to complete the feature. Alternatively, right-click and select **OK (Enter)** or press <Enter>.

Practice 9a | Create Shell and Ribs

Practice Objectives

- Create a Shell feature that removes required geometry from the model.
- Add unique wall thickness for selected faces that remain after a shell operation.
- Create a Rib feature from a sketched section.

In this practice, you will add a Shell and Rib feature to create the geometry shown in Figure 9–31.

Figure 9–31

Task 1 - Shell the model.

1. Open **shell.ipt**.

2. In the Modify panel, click ▣ (Shell). The expanded Shell dialog box and mini-toolbar open as shown in Figure 9–32.

Figure 9–32

3. Select the surface shown in Figure 9–33 as the face to remove. Maintain the default 1mm thickness.

Figure 9–33

4. Complete the shell. The model displays as shown in Figure 9–34. The hole in the model did not shell as expected because its surface was not selected for removal.

Figure 9–34

5. Edit the **Shell**. Click (Remove Faces) or click **Faces** in the mini-toolbar and select the surface of the hole to be removed.

6. Complete the shell. The model displays as shown in Figure 9–35.

As an alternative to selecting the surface of the hole as an additional surface to be removed, you can also reorder features. To reorder the hole after the shell, select the hole and drag it after the shell in the Model browser.

Figure 9–35

Unique thickness values cannot be assigned in the mini-toolbar.

7. Edit the **Shell**. Click ⌊>>⌋ to expand the Shell dialog box. This area enables you to specify unique thickness faces.

8. Select **Click to add** in the *Unique face thickness* area and select the face shown in Figure 9–36. Twenty-six faces are selected because they are all tangent to one another. Any one of these faces cannot be assigned a unique wall thickness on its own.

Select this face to add a unique face thickness to.

Figure 9–36

9. Enter **2.5** next to the selected face in the *Thickness* column.

10. Complete the shell. The model displays as shown in Figure 9–37.

Figure 9–37

Task 2 - Create a rib using a provided sketch.

1. In the Model browser, right-click on **Rib Sketch** and select **Visibility** to display this sketch. This sketch will be used to create a rib.

2. In the Create panel, click ⌊⌋ (Rib).

3. Select the sketch as the profile for the rib feature.

4. Click ⬚ (Parallel to Sketch Plane) to create a rib.

5. Ensure ⬚ (Direction1) is specified.

6. Select ⬚ (To Next) as the extent. The dialog box and model display as shown in Figure 9–38.

Figure 9–38

7. In the Rib dialog box, change the *Thickness* to **2.00**.

8. In the *Thickness* area in the dialog box, click ⬚ to add material to the far side of the sketch (based on the orientation in Figure 9–38).

9. Complete the rib. The model displays as shown in Figure 9–39.

Figure 9–39

10. Modify the offset value of **Work Plane 1** to **-50mm**. Note how the rib updates with the change.

11. Save the model and close the window.

Practice 9b

Create Ribs with Bosses

Practice Objectives

- Create a sketch that can be used to create a Rib feature.
- Create a Rib feature with Boss geometry.

In this practice, you will create the model shown in Figure 9–40. To create the geometry, you will sketch the profile of the rib and then using the sketch create a rib with boss geometry.

Figure 9–40

Task 1 - Create the profile sketch for the Rib feature.

1. Open **Complex_Rib.ipt**.

2. In the Work Features panel, expand ▭ (Plane) and select **Offset from Plane** to create a work plane.

3. Select the thin top face of the model as the plane to offset from, as shown in Figure 9–41. Enter **-12.7mm** as the *Offset* value. Complete the plane.

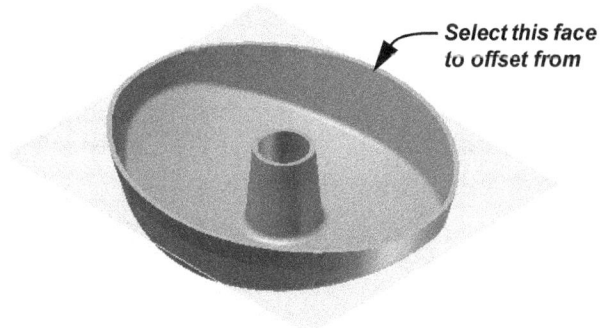

— *Select this face to offset from*

Figure 9–41

4. Rename the new work plane as **Rib Plane**.

5. Create a new sketch on **Rib Plane**.

6. Project the YZ and XZ origin planes.

7. Sketch the six entities as shown in Figure 9–42. Note the orientation of the ViewCube in the image to confirm orientation. Ensure that the horizontal and vertical lines are symmetric about the projected YZ and XZ origin planes and that the central lines are also constrained to the YZ and XZ origin planes. Add the two dimensions shown.

Additional dimensions are required to fully constrain the sketch, however they are not required to successfully create a rib. Rib features automatically project the sketch to the nearest geometry. In creating the sketch for a rib, ensure that you create the correct network, the lengths of the entities are not required.

Figure 9–42

8. Bosses can be added as part of a rib feature. To do this, sketched points must be included in the sketch. Add the six sketch points, as shown in Figure 9–43. The two points that are on the vertical centerline should be symmetric with one another and dimensioned as shown. The remaining four points are aligned at the intersection of the sketched entities.

Add the following 6 sketch points to the sketch.

Figure 9–43

9. Finish the sketch.

Task 2 - Create the Rib feature.

---

1. In the Create panel, click 📐 (Rib).

2. Click 📐 (Normal to Sketch Plane) to create the rib so that it is normal to the sketch plane.

3. Select any one of the sketched entities. A Rib should be previewed on the model. If not, toggle the feature direction using 📐 or 📐 as required until the geometry is displayed.

4. Ensure that 📐 is selected in the *Thickness* area so that the Rib is created evenly on both sides of the sketched entity.

5. Enter **4 mm** as the *Thickness* value.

---

6. Click 🔲 (Profile) and select the remaining 5 sketched entities. The model previews as shown in Figure 9–44. Ensure that you select the sketched entity that lies on the projected YZ plane and not the projected entity.

Figure 9–44

7. In the Rib dialog box, select the *Draft* tab. Draft can be added when creating the Rib feature, instead of as a draft feature.

8. Select **At Top** to ensure that the **4mm** thickness is maintained at the sketched plane once draft is added.

9. Enter **4** as the *Draft Angle* value. Note the small change to the preview as the draft is added.

10. In the Rib dialog box, select the *Boss* tab.

11. Boss features can also be incorporated directly as part of the Rib feature. Bosses are placed based on sketched points in the sketch. Select **Select All** in the Rib dialog box to ensure that all sketched points are automatically selected.

12. Enter **10mm** as the diameter of the boss geometry.

13. Maintain the default offset value of the boss above the Rib.

14. Enter **4** as the *Draft Angle* value.

15. Click **OK** to complete the Rib feature.

16. Toggle off the display of the Rib Plane work plane. The model displays as shown in Figure 9–45. If bosses do not display on the rib along the YZ plane, it is possible that you selected the projected entity and not the sketched line so the sketched points are not being recognized.

Figure 9–45

17. Save the model.

Practice 9c	# Splitting a Face

Practice Objectives

- Create a Split feature that splits a selected face based on a sketched profile.
- Create a Face Draft feature to add draft to a selected face in a model.
- Create a Split feature that trims a solid based on a selected reference.

In this practice, you will use the **Split** and **Face Draft** commands to refine a block-shaped part. The completed part displays as shown in Figure 9–46.

Figure 9–46

Task 1 - Create geometry to define a split.

1. Open **split.ipt**.

2. Sketch, constrain, and dimension the profile for the split on one of the flat faces that contains an arced edge, as shown in Figure 9–47.

Figure 9–47

3. Finish the sketch.

Task 2 - Create the split.

1. In the Modify panel, click (Split). The Split dialog box opens as shown in Figure 9–48.

Figure 9–48

2. Ensure that (Split Face) is enabled and that (Select) for selecting the Faces reference is also enabled.

3. Select the sketch that you just created as the Split Tool reference.

4. Select the face that you used as the sketch plane for the sketch as well as the opposite face as the faces to be split.

5. Click **OK** to split the faces.

6. Select the split surfaces. They highlight individually (below the curve, and above the curve), as shown in Figure 9–49.

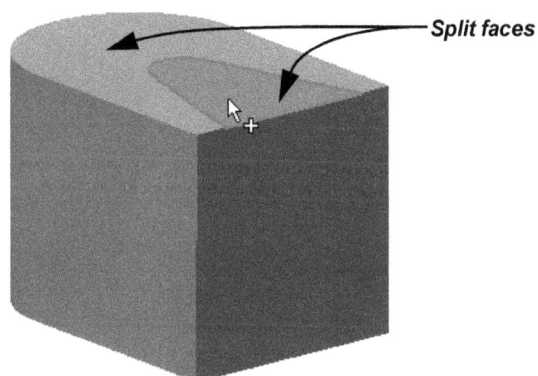

Figure 9–49

Task 3 - Create draft faces.

1. In the Modify panel, click ▨ (Draft) to create a Face Draft. The Face Draft dialog box and the mini-toolbar open.

2. Select the pull direction reference shown in Figure 9–50.

    Click 🔲, as required, to set the pull direction towards the cylindrical end of the part.

Figure 9–50

3. Select the face near the edge, as shown in Figure 9–51. Ensure that the draft angle directions display as shown.

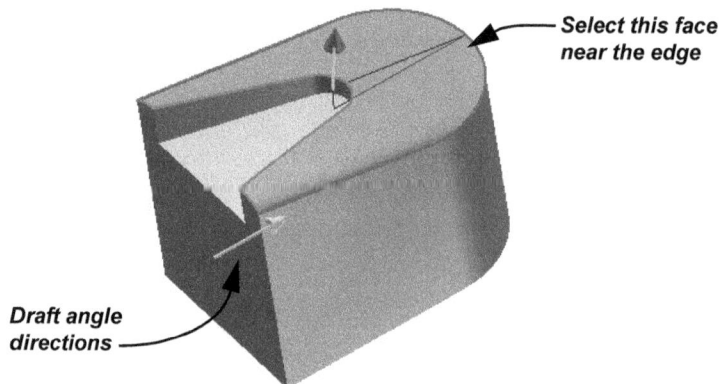

Figure 9–51

4. Set the angle to **10** degrees.

5. Click **OK** to draft the face. The model displays as shown in Figure 9–52.

Figure 9–52

6. Draft the face opposite the side that was just completed.

The small faces that were split from the original faces do not change, but the large faces contain the draft. The edges of the large faces are rounded to enable the blend into the cylindrical face and faces tangent to it.

Task 4 - Create another split.

1. Create a work plane parallel to the bottom face (now H-shaped), inside the part at an *Offset* value of **-57mm**.

2. In the Modify panel, click ▣ (Split). The Split dialog box opens.

3. Click ▣ (Trim Solid), select the work plane as the Split Tool reference, and make the arrow point toward the smaller section, as shown in Figure 9–53.

Figure 9–53

4. Click **OK** to remove that section of the part. The model displays as shown in Figure 9–54.

Figure 9–54

5. Save and close the part.

Chapter Review Questions

1. Which of the following statements is true for creating a draft?

   a. Multiple surfaces can be selected for drafting.

   b. Multiple faces can be selected when defining the pull direction.

   c. Only existing edges on the model can be selected to define the pull direction.

2. Fill in the split options: **Split Face**, **Trim Solid**, and **Split Solid**, with its correct description.

   a. _____ enables you to split faces. The entire part remains as one object, but the faces can be manipulated separately.

   b. _____ enables you to split a part into two bodies along the split reference.

   c. _____ enables you to trim a part. A portion of the part is removed using the toggle direction icons.

3. You can shell the part without removing model faces.

   a. True

   b. False

4. Which of the following is true for shell features?

   a. To create a shell, you must select the face(s) to remove.

   b. A single face that is tangent to another face cannot be removed unless the tangent face is also removed.

   c. A closed shell cannot have walls of varying thickness.

   d. Wall thickness can be added to the inside or outside of a model

5. When creating a shell, how can you leave one side of the part open, as shown in Figure 9–55?

Figure 9–55

a. Use **Remove Faces** in the Shell dialog box.

b. Set the *Thickness* for that face to **0**.

c. Delete the face after the shell has been created.

d. Set the *Thickness* for that face to the negative of the general thickness.

6. What can you do with the **Rib** command that you cannot do with **Extrude** command?

a. Create a surface object.

b. Cut through an existing solid.

c. Select multiple profiles for the feature.

d. Create a solid from an open profile.

Model and Display Manipulation

Learning how to manipulate and control existing and new features in your model provides flexibility in designing and making changes to your models. Tools such as Section and Design views provide additional viewing tools to review the model.

Learning Objectives in this Chapter

- Change the order of features in the Model browser.
- Use the End of Part marker to change the location in which new features are added to a model.
- Remove a feature temporarily from being included as part of the model geometry.
- Create quarter, half, and three quarter section views in a model to help visualize the interior of a 3D model.
- Create and activate custom design views that store display settings for a model.

10.1 Reordering Features

A model is generated in the order in which the features display in the Model browser. In certain situations, the resulting geometry varies, depending on the feature creation order. To achieve the required geometry, you can reorder the features to change the way the part is constructed. To reorder a feature, select it in the Model browser and drag it below or above its current position. You cannot drag a feature above a feature that it references or below a feature that references it.

Consider the following example shown in Figure 10–1. Shell and fillet features are to be added to the model. Due to the order in which the existing features were initially added, the resulting geometry after the addition of the shell is not wanted. Reordering the hole after the shell and adding the fillet before the shell results in the completed part shown in Figure 10–1.

Shell is added, these surfaces are to be removed.

When a shell is added, a wall thickness is applied to the remaining surfaces, including those of the hole.

A Fillet is added. The shell is not applied to features that display after it in the feature list. A fillet placed after a shell might result in incorrect geometry.

Model after reordering the fillet before the Shell.

Figure 10–1

10.2 Inserting Features

By default, when features are added to the model, they are added to the end of the feature list. To insert features at any earlier point, you must move the ⊘ End of Part marker from the bottom of the Model browser to the location at which you want to insert a feature. You can use this technique when you need to create a feature earlier in the design process. Use any of the following techniques to move the End of Part marker:

- Right-click a feature in the Model browser and select **Move EOP Marker**. The ⊘ End of Part is placed after the feature.

- Select and drag the ⊘ End of Part marker in the Model browser to the location at which you want to insert a feature.

Figure 10–2 shows an example of a model and its Model browser before (left-hand side) and after (right-hand side) moving the ⊘ End of Part marker. Once moved, all of the features below it are temporarily removed from the model and a new feature can be added.

Figure 10–2

To return the ⊘ End of Part marker to the bottom of the Model browser use one of the following techniques:

- Right-click ⊘ End of Part and select **Move EOP to End**.

- Drag the ⊘ End of Part to the bottom of the Model browser.

10.3 Suppressing Features

As you work on a complex part, you might find it difficult to identify or select features in the graphics window. You can simplify the appearance of a model by suppressing a feature to make it temporarily invisible. To suppress a feature, right-click on it in the Model browser and select **Suppress Features**, as shown on the left in Figure 10–3. If you suppress a feature, all of its dependent features are also suppressed. Suppressed features and any of its dependent features are displayed in gray and are crossed out in the Model browser, as shown on the right in Figure 10–3.

*You can select features for suppression directly in the graphics window if the **Select Features** feature priority setting is set.*

Figure 10–3

To unsuppress a feature, right-click on the feature in the Model browser and select **Unsuppress Features**. The dependent features that were suppressed are also unsuppressed.

Hint: Rule Based Suppression

Using a feature's Properties dialog box, you can establish rule based suppression. To access the dialog box, right-click the feature, and select **Properties**. In the *Suppression* area of the dialog box, you can set the appropriate situation for suppressing the feature. The suppression options are shown in Figure 10–4.

Sets a feature to always be suppressed.

Sets a dimensional condition on if a feature is suppressed. Only dimensions associated with the feature can be used.

Suppress
- [ ] Always
- [✓] If
  - d7
  - < ▾
  - 2

Figure 10–4

If a suppression condition is set, you must unsuppress it to return it to the model. Just unsuppressing the parent geometry does not resume it.

10.4 Section Views

Section Views help visualize a 3D model by providing a section view of it. There are three types of Section Views that can be created. Figure 10–5 shows these views and the selected planes required to create them.

Full Model View

Half Section View

Sectioning
plane

Quarter Section View

Three Quarter Section View

Sectioning
planes

Sectioning
planes

Figure 10–5

How To: Section a Part

1. In the *View* tab>Appearance panel, select the type of section view in the drop-down list, as shown in Figure 10–6.

Figure 10–6

Instead of entering an offset value, you can dynamically section the model by clicking the left mouse button and dragging the cursor.

2. Select the plane to section about and if required, enter an offset value from the selected plane. Click ⇨ to continue if creating a quarter or three quarter section view.
3. For quarter and three quarter section views, select an additional plane to section about. Select the second plane, and if required, enter an offset value from the selected plane.
4. If required, flip the section by right-clicking and selecting **Flip Section**.
5. To modify the offset from a selected plane, drag the direction arrow or enter a value in the mini-toolbar field. If multiple planes were selected to define the Section View (i.e., Quarter and Three-Quarter Section Views), right-click in the graphics window and select **Virtual Movement>Section Plane x** (where x is the section plane that you want to modify, 1 or 2) to switch the active plane. Use one of the techniques to move the plane, as required.

To change the scroll increments when modifying section plane placement using the scroll wheel in the mini-toolbar field, right-click and select **Scroll Step Size***, enter an increment value, and click* ☑️ *.*

6. Right-click and select **OK (Enter)** or click ☑️ to complete the view.
7. To return to a view of the entire part, select **End Section View** in the Section View drop-down list.

Section views are temporary unless used in conjunction with Design views. Once you select **End Section View**, the created section view is lost and must be recreated if required again. If created in a Design view do not select the End Section View to maintain the Section View in the Design view.

Once created, a section view cannot be redefined and you would need to recreate it to make changes.

10.5 Design Views

A representation of the part's display can be saved using a Design View. Model configuration settings that you might want to save include: part color, work feature (not origin features) and sketch visibility, camera position, section views, orientation, and zoom level. Any of these settings can be saved using a Design View.

How To: Save a Design View

1. Right-click on the *View* folder and select **New**, as shown in Figure 10–7. Additional views are created to capture alternate configurations. When a new view is created it is automatically set to be active.

As of Autodesk Inventor 2017, models created with a default template contain four additional default Design Views. For models created prior to 2017, only a single Master Design View is provided in the default template.

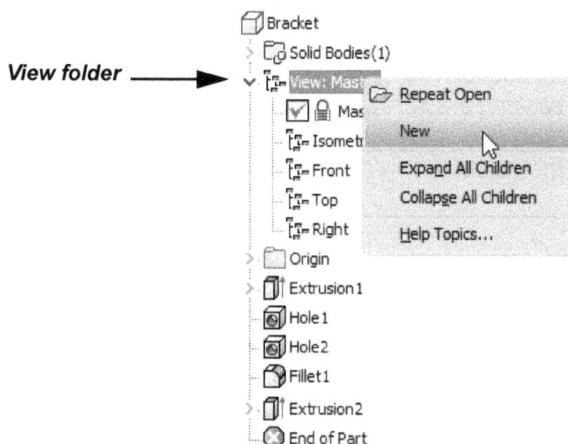

Figure 10–7

2. Configure the view display (e.g., change the part orientation, set a section view, set the part color, toggle off the visibility of work features or sketches, or change the camera position).
3. Rename the Design View. Select the new view, click again (do not double-click) and enter a descriptive name for the view.
4. (Optional) To lock the design view, right-click on the view name in the Model browser and select **Lock**. Locking restricts you or others from making changes to the design view representation.

Design Views can be used when creating drawing views.

To display an alternate Design View, right-click on its name in the Model browser and select **Activate**. Alternatively, you can double-click on its name.

Practice 10a | Section and Design Views

Practice Objectives

- Create section views using a work plane as the cutting reference.
- Create a Design View to capture a model's view display.

In this practice, you will work with a part model and create both Section and Design Views in your model. The model that will be used is shown in Figure 10–8.

Figure 10–8

Task 1 - Create design views in a model.

1. Open **Bracket_Display.ipt**.

2. In the Model browser, right-click on the **View** node and select **New**.

3. Expand the **View** node of the Model browser. A new **View1** Design View is created and is set to be active (indicated by the checkmark).

4. Select **View1**, and then select it again to rename it. Enter **Quarter Section View** as its name, as shown in Figure 10–9.

Figure 10–9

5. Select the *View* tab>Appearance panel and expand the drop-down list associated with ⊞ (Quarter Section View). The command displayed might vary depending on which command was last selected.

6. Click ⊞ (Half Section View), as shown in Figure 10–10.

Figure 10–10

7. Select **XY Plane** in the Model browser. In the offset prompt that displays you can enter an offset value to reposition the section plane. For this section, leave the value at 0.00 in. The model displays as shown in Figure 10–11.

Figure 10–11

8. Right-click anywhere in the graphic window and select **Scroll Step Size**. Accept the default value of .25 in and click [✓].

9. Place the cursor in the *Offset* entry field and scroll the middle mouse button. Note that the sectioning plane moves in .25 in increments to progress you through multiple section views.

10. Alternatively, you can hover the cursor over the offset direction arrow and drag it. The drag uses a smaller increment to produce a more gradual sectioning movement.

11. Click [✓] to complete the section view at its current offset value.

12. In the Appearance panel, expand the view types and click [⊞] (End Section View) to cancel the section view display.

13. In the Appearance panel, click [▦] (Quarter Section View).

14. Select **XY** Plane in the Model browser. In the offset prompt that displays, accept the 0.00 in offset and click [⇨] to continue to the selection of the second plane.

15. Select **XZ** Plane in the Model browser. In the offset prompt that displays, accept the 0.00 in offset. The model displays as shown in Figure 10–12.

Figure 10–12

16. Right-click and select **Flip Section.** Continue to flip faces to obtain the sectioned view shown in Figure 10–13.

Figure 10–13

17. Right-click and select **Three Quarter Section View**. Because two planes would also be required to create a three quarter view you can quickly switch between these two views in the shortcut menu.

18. Return to the **Quarter Section View**.

19. The last plane to be selected is active. To activate the first cutting plane for modification, right-click in the graphics window and select **Virtual Movement>Section Plane 1**. Drag the section plane or modify the offset value in the mini-toolbar to change the plane placement.

20. Right-click and select **OK (Enter)** or click ✓ to complete the definition of the Section View.

Once created, a section view cannot be redefined, you would need to recreate it to make changes.

21. Double-click on **Master** in the **View** node in the Model browser. The model display returns to the original, non-sectioned view.

22. Double-click on **Quarter Section View** in the **View** node in the Model browser. The model displays as sectioned again. The section that was previously created was saved in this view.

Task 2 - Create additional Design Views in a model.

1. In the Model browser, right-click on the **View** node and select **New**. A new Design View is created and is set as active (indicated by the checkmark).

2. Note that the new Design View displays the sectioned view. This is because it was the active view when the new one was created.

3. Right-click on **View1** and select **Delete**. Once deleted, the Master view becomes the active view.

4. Create another Design view.

5. Select it and then select again to rename it. Enter **Color Variation** as its name.

6. Select the *Tools* tab. In the Material and Appearance panel, click 🖌 (Adjust). The appearance editing tool displays in the graphics window.

7. In the appearance editing tool, in the Appearance drop-down list, select **Red**. The cursor displays as a Paint Bucket icon.

8. Hover the cursor over the model so that it highlights, as shown in Figure 10–14.

Figure 10–14

9. Select the model. Click ✓. This assigns red as the color of the model for this Design view. In this case, the color was used to help identify that the view is an informational view and can be used for sectioning the model.

10. Activate the **Master** view and create a third Design View called **Additional Info**.

11. Right-click on **Sketch2** and select **Visibility** to display the feature's sketch.

12. Zoom in on the sketch to change the zoom level and change the view orientation, as required.

13. Return to the Master view. It initially holds the view orientation and zoom level. Return to the model home view using the ViewCube.

14. Return to the **Additional Info** Design View. Note that the view orientation and zoom are stored with this view.

15. Return to the Home view in the Master view.

Task 3 - Add additional solid features to the model.

1. Create a fillet feature on the top edge of **Hole6** as shown in Figure 10–15. Use a radius value of **0.05in**.

Create fillet on this edge

Figure 10–15

2. Once created, return to any of the Design Views that were created and note that the fillet exists in all of the views. Feature creation does not affect Design Views. Design Views only store visual changes in the model, such as color, visual display of work features, sketches, view orientation, and zoom, as well as sectioning changes to the model.

3. Save the part and close the window.

Practice 10b

Feature Order

Practice Objectives

- Change the order of features in the Model browser to obtain required geometry.
- Use the End of Part marker to insert a new feature at a point other than the end of the feature list.

In this practice, you will explore the impact of feature order on a part. You will create a switch plate as shown in Figure 10–16. Once complete, you will reorder and insert features in the part and observe the results.

Figure 10–16

Task 1 - Open and review the part file.

1. Create a new part using the standard imperial (in) template.

2. Create the sketch on the XY plane, as shown in Figure 10–17. Create the sketch symmetrically about the YZ and XZ origin planes.

Figure 10–17

3. Extrude **Sketch1**, **0.25in** away from the sketch plane (behind the model when it is in the Home view). The model displays as shown in Figure 10–18.

Figure 10–18

Task 2 - Create hole features.

1. Create the hole at the top of the Front View shown in Figure 10–19. Create the hole with a diameter of **0.188in**. It should be offset **1.1 in** from the top edge of the extrude and **1.375 in** from the left edge of the extrude, as shown in the Figure 10–19. The hole should cut though the entire part.

2. Create the second hole shown at the bottom of Figure 10–19. Create the hole with a diameter of **0.188in**. It should be offset **1.1 in** from the bottom edge of the extrude and **1.375in** from the left edge of the extrude. The hole should cut though the entire part.

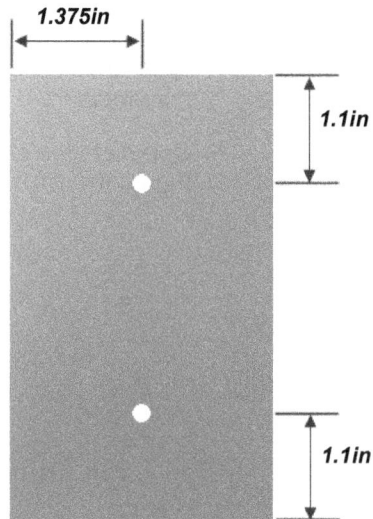

Front View
Figure 10–19

Task 3 - Create an extrude feature.

---

1. Create the sketch shown in Figure 10–20, using the front surface of **Extrusion1** as the sketching plane. Create the sketch symmetrically about the YZ and XZ origin planes.

2. Create an extruded cut feature using the new sketch, as shown in Figure 10–20.

Figure 10–20

Task 4 - Shell the model.

1. In the Modify panel, click ⬛ (Shell).

2. Reorient the view to look at the back of the model and select the back surface as the face to remove.

3. Enter a *Thickness* of **0.063in** in the Shell dialog box or in the mini-toolbar.

4. Complete the shell. The model displays as shown in Figure 10–21.

Figure 10–21

Task 5 - Insert and reorder model features.

Extrusion2 does not display as required. It should not have a wall thickness applied to it. In this task, you will reorder **Extrusion2** after the shell feature to correct this.

1. Delete **Shell1**.

2. Select and drag the ⊗ End of Part   marker above **Extrusion2**. All features below the marker are suppressed, as shown in Figure 10–22.

Figure 10–22

Alternatively, you can also click and drag the ⊗ End of Part marker to the bottom of the Model browser.

3. Recreate the Shell feature.

4. Right-click in the graphics window and select **Move EOP to End**. **Extrusion2** is resumed without a wall thickness, as shown in Figure 10–23.

Figure 10–23

5. Return to the Home view.

6. Create a **0.175in** fillet on the four outside edges of the model as shown in Figure 10–24.

Figure 10–24

7. Orient the model to view its back. Note that the fillet is not applied to the back.

8. Select **Fillet1** in the Model browser. Click and hold the left mouse button and drag **Fillet1**. Try to drag **Fillet1** above **Extrusion1**. Note that the cursor changes to ⊘ as shown in Figure 10–25. This indicates that you cannot move **Fillet1** above **Extrusion1**.

Figure 10–25

Fillet1 cannot be moved above **Extrusion1** because it is its child. **Fillet1** uses the edges of **Extrusion1** as its reference. Therefore, **Fillet1** cannot exist unless **Extrusion1** has already been created.

9. In the Model browser, drag **Fillet1** above **Shell2**. Note that the fillet is now created on the back as well, as shown in Figure 10–26.

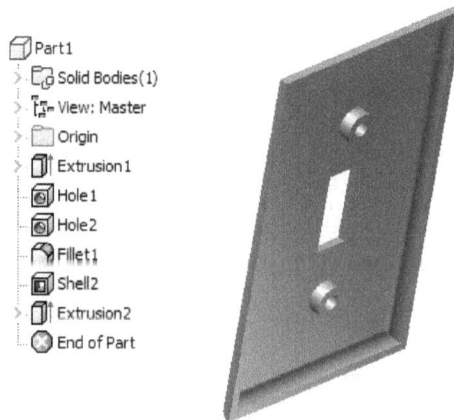

Figure 10–26

10. Save the model. Enter **Switch** as the name of the file.

11. Close the window.

Chapter Review Questions

1. In the example shown in Figure 10–27, **Hole1** is a **Through All** hole and **Extrusion2** is the solid cylindrical feature. What can you do to include **Extrusion2** in the **Hole1** feature (have the hole pass through the cylinder)?

Figure 10–27

   a. Suppress **Hole1** and then recreate **Extrusion2**.

   b. In the Model browser, drag the **End of Part** marker above **Hole1**.

   c. Make **Extrusion2** Adaptive.

   d. In the Model browser, drag **Extrusion2** above **Hole1**.

2. Which of the following statements is true for reordering features in a model? (Select all that apply.)

   a. Reordering enables you to drag and drop features so that you can rearrange the feature creation order.

   b. When reordering, features can be moved anywhere.

   c. Base features can be moved anywhere in the model.

   d. You can insert new features between existing features.

3. Any features below the ⊗ End of Part   marker in the Model browser are still displayed, but you cannot select them as references when creating new features.

   a. True

   b. False

4. If you suppress a feature, all dependent features are also suppressed.

   a. True

   b. False

5. Which items in the Model browser shown in Figure 10–28 are *Suppressed* in the model? (Select all that apply.)

bearing_journal.ipt
   Solid Bodies(1)
   View: Master
   Origin
   Revolution1
   Extrusion1
   Fillet1 (Suppressed)
   Fillet2 (Suppressed)
   Work Plane1
   Extrusion2
   End of Part
   Mirror1
   Hole1

Figure 10–28

   a. Solid1

   b. Sketch3

   c. Fillet1

   d. Fillet2

   e. Work Plane1

   f. Mirror1

   g. Hole1

6. How can a section view be saved with the model?

   a. A section view is saved with the model and can be retrieved in the Navigation Bar.

   b. A section view is saved with the model and can be retrieved in the Appearance panel in the *View* tab.

   c. A section view is saved with the model in a Design View and can be retrieved in the Model browser.

   d. A section view cannot be saved with the model.

7. Once completed, a section view can be modified.

   a. True

   b. False

8. Which of the following can be manipulated and stored in a design view? (Select all that apply.)

    a. Part color

    b. Sketch and feature visibility

    c. Origin Planes

    d. Section views

    e. Model orientation

    f. Model zoom level

Command Summary

Button	Command	Location
	End Section View	• **Ribbon:** *View* tab>Appearance panel
	Half Section View	• **Ribbon:** *View* tab>Appearance panel
N/A	**Move EOP Marker**	• **Context Menu:** In Model browser with a feature selected
N/A	**Move EOP to End**	• **Context Menu:** In Model browser with the End of Part node selected
N/A	**New (Design View)**	• **Context Menu:** In Model browser with the View node selected
	Quarter Section View	• **Ribbon:** *View* tab>Appearance panel
N/A	**Suppress (features)**	• **Context Menu:** In Model browser with a feature selected • **Context Menu:** In graphics window with a feature selected
	Three Quarter Section View	• **Ribbon:** *View* tab>Appearance panel

Fixing Problems

When a parent feature is deleted or modified, its dependent features are affected. This might result in a variety of design problems (e.g., geometry that does not form a closed loop for a solid feature, dimensional changes that result in geometry that cannot be updated, and changes to the model that interfere with other features, etc.). When errors occur, you can use error tracking and recovery tools to correct the design error or accept the errors and correct them later. You might also have to edit other features to correct the error.

Learning Objectives in this Chapter

- Identify the dialog boxes that display when you over-dimension or over-constrain a sketch.
- Use the Sketch Doctor to diagnose and correct failures that occur due to problems in a sketched section.
- Use the Design Doctor to diagnose and correct feature failures that occur for reasons other than problems in the sketch.

11.1 Sketch Failure

In the Sketch environment, an error can occur if you try to over-dimension or over-constrain a sketch. A dialog box, similar to the one shown in Figure 11–1 opens, outlining the reasons for the failed operation. The symbol that displays next to the message indicates the seriousness of the problem.

ⓘ	This symbol (internal white highlight) indicates a partially failed operation.
ⓘ	This symbol (internal yellow highlight) indicates a failed operation.

You can click **Cancel** to cancel the change or click **Apply** to apply the change, investigate, and/or recover the feature.

- In Figure 11–1, the Error dialog box indicates that adding a dimension over-constrains the sketch. You can cancel the command or accept the warning and place a driven dimension.

Driven dimensions are displayed in parentheses.

Autodesk Inventor Professional - Create Linear Dimension

ⓘ Adding this dimension will over-constrain the sketch. Choose Accept to create a Driven Dimension.

| ? | 📋 | | Cancel | Accept |

Figure 11–1

- In Figure 11–2, the Error dialog box indicates that a constraint already exists in the sketch and that the operation has failed (ⓘ). To resolve the problem, cancel the operation.

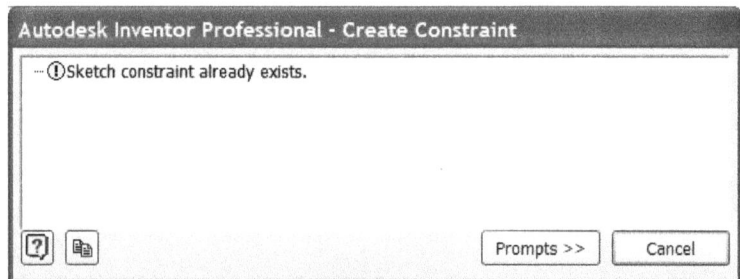

Autodesk Inventor Professional - Create Constraint

ⓘ Sketch constraint already exists.

| ? | 📋 | | Prompts >> | Cancel |

Figure 11–2

Hint: Error Prompts

To control the timing of when error prompts are presented, click **Prompts** at the bottom of the dialog box. Select the required option from the list, as shown in Figure 11–3. These options are not available in all error dialog boxes.

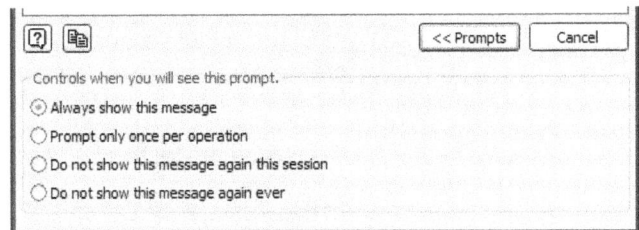

Figure 11–3

11.2 Feature Failure

Sketch Doctor

The Sketch Doctor is an error tracking and recovery tool that examines errors in the sketch that affect feature creation, and also suggests solutions for the problem. For example, your sketch might include errors, such as open loops. As a result, the software might be unable to interpret the sketch when you try to create a feature (e.g., solid extrusion).

If the Sketch Doctor is available, ⊞ displays in the bottom left of the Feature dialog box. Click ⊞ to open the Sketch Doctor dialog box, similar to that shown in Figure 11–4.

When the Sketch Doctor is active, you can pan, zoom, or rotate the part using the function keys (<F2>, <F3>, and <F4>, respectively).

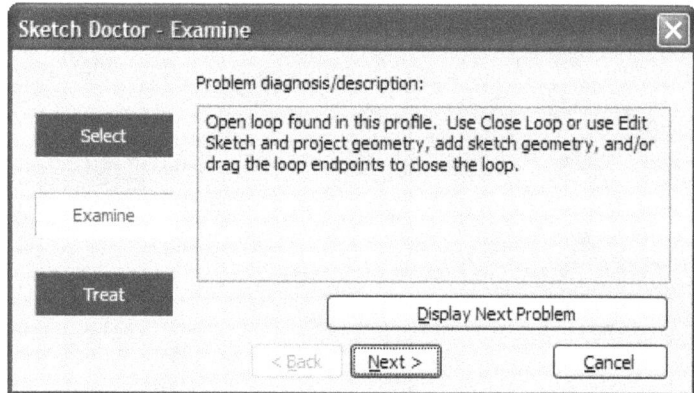

Figure 11–4

Using **Next** and **Back**, you can toggle between three solution steps in the Sketch Doctor dialog box: **Select**, **Examine**, and **Treat**.

- **Select:** Lists all of the errors in the sketch in the *Problem diagnosis/description* area.

- **Examine:** Provides information on the error and suggests solutions. The problem is described in the *Problem diagnosis/description* area, as shown in Figure 11–4. Click **Display Next Problem** to highlight the problem geometry on the sketch.

- **Treat:** Lists the method(s) you can use to correct the problem(s) with the sketch, as shown in Figure 11–5.

Figure 11–5

To correct the error in the sketch, select one of the recommended methods in the *Select a treatment* area and click **Finish**. The various methods you can use to correct the problem(s) are described as follows:

Diagnose Sketch	Enables you to specify which tests to perform on the sketch. 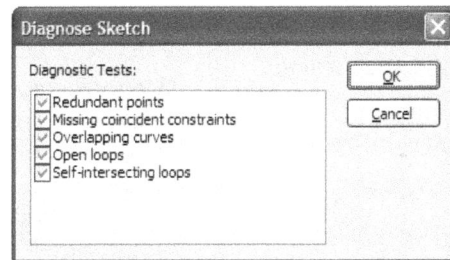
Close loop	Enables you to select sketch entities to close an open loop.
Edit sketch	Returns to the Sketch environment to enable you to fix the problem in the sketch.

Design Doctor

The Design Doctor diagnoses and suggests corrections for when feature failures occurs for reasons other than problems in the sketch. The steps for using the Design Doctor are similar to those used for the Sketch Doctor.

When a feature fails, a Message dialog box similar to the one shown in Figure 11–6 opens, listing the errors that occurred. If more than one error occurs, a failure message displays for each error.

Autodesk Inventor Professional - Update Part Document

ⓘbox.ipt: Errors occurred during update
   ⓘExtrusion2: Could not build this Extrusion

      The attempted operation did not terminate the Toolbody completely by the
   ⓘ specified termination plane and/or part. Change the termination definition or the
      feature (profile) position.

Cancel   Accept

Figure 11–6

When a feature fails, you can perform one of the following operations:

- Click **Cancel** to cancel the operation that caused the failure.

- Click **Accept** to accept the error and correct it later.

In some situations you might also be able to edit the feature directly in the Message dialog box.

Use the symbols that display in the Error Message dialog box to investigate and resolve the failure. The following symbols might display in the Message dialog box:

ⓘ	This symbol (internal white highlight) indicates a partially failed operation.
ⓘ	This symbol (internal yellow highlight) indicates a failed operation.
▽	This symbol enables indicates tips for resolving the failure.
✚	This symbol enables you to open the Design Doctor dialog box to recover the failure.

To fix a failure, select the ✚ symbol and click **Yes** to accept the changes and start the recovery process. The Design Doctor dialog box opens as shown in Figure 11–7.

When the Design Doctor is active, you can pan, zoom, or rotate the part using the function keys (<F2>, <F3>, and <F4> respectively).

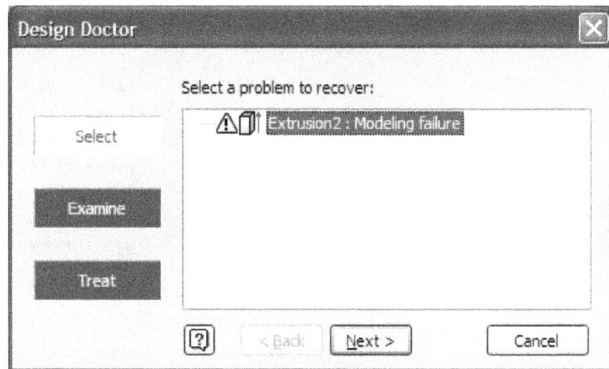

Figure 11–7

Using **Next** and **Back**, you can toggle between the three solution steps in the Design Doctor: **Select**, **Examine**, and **Treat**.

*   **Select:** Lists all of the errors.

*   **Examine:** Provides information on the error and suggests solutions.

*   **Treat:** Lists the method(s) to correct the problem(s).

To fix a feature failure, select one of the recommended methods, as shown in Figure 11–8, and click **Finish**.

Figure 11–8

*⚠ displays in the mini-toolbar for **Fillets**, **Chamfers**, **Shells**, and **Thicken/Offset** commands when the feature cannot be created. Click ⚠ to open the Design Doctor.*

The various methods of resolving a feature failure are as follows:

Edit	Opens the Feature dialog box. Enables you to modify any element and dimension used to create the feature.
Delete	Deletes the failed feature. The sketch is saved and can be reused.
Suppress	Suppresses the failed feature. This method only resolves the failure temporarily. As soon as the suppressed feature is unsuppressed, the failure occurs again.

Failed features are marked in the Model browser with either ⓘ or ⚠, as shown on the left in Figure 11–9. If you close the Design Doctor dialog box before fixing a problem, right-click on the failed feature in the Model browser and select **Recover**, as shown on the right.

Hover the cursor over failed features in the Model browser to display their pre-failure state in the model.

Figure 11–9

Practice 11a | Resolve Sketch Problems

Practice Objectives

- Use the Sketch Doctor dialog box to examine problems in a sketch that are causing an Extrusion to fail.
- Use the Sketch Doctor dialog box to select a treatment option to resolve problems in a sketch that are causing an Extrusion to fail.
- Edit a sketched section to resolve problems that are causing an Extrusion to fail.

In this practice, you will use the Sketch Doctor to diagnose a problem in the sketch.

Task 1 - Create a new part file.

1. Create a new part file with the standard metric (mm) template.

2. Create a sketch on the XY plane. Sketch and dimension the entities shown in Figure 11–10.

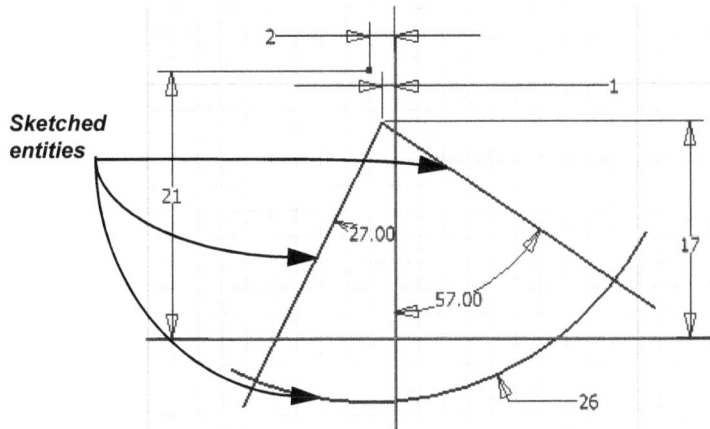

Figure 11–10

3. After dimensioning the sketch, it might look similar to that shown in Figure 11–11. Drag the ends of the lines and arc as required to obtain the sketch shown in Figure 11–10. The sketch is not fully constrained.

Figure 11–11

4. Finish the sketch.

Task 2 - Resolve the error.

---

1. In the Create panel, click ⬛ (Extrude) and set the *Output* to
   ⬛ (Solid). The ⊕ button displays, as shown in
   Figure 11–12, indicating that there are problems with the
   profile.

Figure 11–12

© 2017, ASCENT - Center for Technical Knowledge®

2. Click ⊞ to open the Sketch Doctor dialog box, as shown in Figure 11–13. An open loop is highlighted in the graphics window.

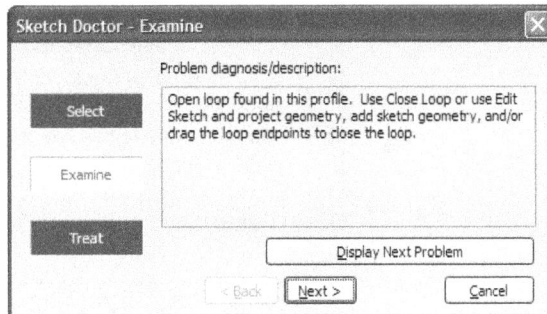

Figure 11–13

3. Click **Display Next Problem**. Another open loop is displayed.

4. Click **Next**. The treatment options are displayed. The Sketch Doctor dialog box opens as shown in Figure 11–14.

Figure 11–14

5. Select **Edit Sketch** and click **Finish**. You are placed in the Sketch environment.

6. Use the **Extend** and **Trim** tools to close the loop.

7. Finish the sketch.

8. Create an extrusion using the sketch and enter **5** mm for the depth.

9. Save the model and enter **sketch_doctor** as the name.

10. Close the window.

| Practice 11b | Resolve Feature Failure I |

Practice Objectives

- Use the Design Doctor dialog box to examine problems causing a model to fail after a dimensional modification.
- Use the Design Doctor dialog box to select a treatment option to resolve modeling problems.
- Edit a feature to resolve problems caused by a dimensional modification.

In this practice, you will find and fix errors using Design Doctor.

Task 1 - Investigate and modify the part.

1. Open **box.ipt**. Review the Model browser to understand the hierarchy of the model.

2. Edit **Extrusion2**. Note that the *Extents* setting is set as **To** and the termination face is set as the back face of the model. Using this *Extents* setting, the entire sketch must land on the termination face when extruded in order to be successfully created.

3. Close the Extrude dialog box.

4. Expand **Extrusion2** in the Model browser and edit **Sketch2**. Change the diameter dimension from *25mm* to **50** mm. Finish the sketch.

5. An error message displays. Expand the nested messages to view the message dialog box, as shown in Figure 11–15. This indicates that the extrusion has failed because the cut is not completely terminated by the termination plane.

As of the printing of this book (March 2017), Autodesk Inventor would not provide access to the Sketch Doctor to resolve a failure unless the dimensional change was made in the sketch. In future releases of the software, access to the Sketch Doctor should be available for dimensional changes made either in the model or in the sketch.

Figure 11–15

Task 2 - Resolve the error.

When the Design Doctor is active, you can pan, zoom, or rotate using the function keys (<F2>, <F3>, and <F4> respectively).

1. Click ✚ in the dialog box.

2. Click **Yes** to confirm that you want to accept changes and begin recovering from the failure. The Design Doctor dialog box opens, as shown in Figure 11–16.

Figure 11–16

3. Click **Cancel** to close the Design Doctor dialog box. Note that the **Extrusion2** feature displays ⚠ next to its name in the Model browser.

4. The failed feature's geometry is not displayed in the model. Hover the cursor over ⚠ **Extrusion2** in the Model browser. The feature is highlighted in its pre-failure state. In large models, being able to highlight failed features in a model is very beneficial.

5. Right-click on **Extrusion2** in the Model browser and select **Recover** to again open the Design Doctor dialog box.

6. Select the problem and click **Next** to examine the causes of the error. For the feature to be created, the entire sketch must land on the termination surface when extruded. Now that the hole diameter has been changed, the feature does not entirely terminate on the single surface.

7. Click **Next** to display the treatment options.

8. Select **Edit Extruded Feature** and click **Finish**.

9. Select the checkbox next to the ⌐ option to terminate the feature on the extended face of the model, as shown in Figure 11–17. Alternatively, you can fix the failure by changing the depth extent to **All**. You must also consider your design intent when resolving errors such as these.

Select this checkbox to terminate the feature on the extended face.

Figure 11–17

10. Click **OK** to close the Extrude dialog box. The model displays as shown in Figure 11–18.

Figure 11–18

11. Save the model and close the window.

Chapter Review Questions

1. The Design Doctor becomes active when a feature failure occurs during feature creation.

    a. True

    b. False

2. What happens when you add a dimension that over-constrains the sketch?

    a. The dimension is added to the sketch.

    b. The dimension is immediately added as a reference dimension.

    c. The Sketch Doctor dialog box opens.

    d. A dialog box opens indicating that the sketch is over-dimensioned.

3. Which of the following indicates a partially failed operation?

    a. ⏱

    b. ➕

    c. ⓘ

    d. 💡

4. Which actions cause a sketch or feature to fail? (Select all that apply.)

    a. Invalid sketch.

    b. Too many sketch entities in the sketch.

    c. Deleting a feature.

    d. Modifying dimensions.

    e. Deleting sketcher references.

    f. Open loop sketch when creating a solid Extrude.

    g. Cut not terminated by the termination plane.

    h. Over-constrained sketch.

5. The failed feature can be the modified feature or a feature that references the modified feature.

    a. True

    b. False

6. What does the **red cross** button indicate if it displays in the dialog box, as shown in Figure 11–19, while extruding a sketch?

Figure 11–19

a. The sketch might have a problem and the Sketch Doctor is available to help fix it.

b. There is applicable information available in the Help files about the **Extrude** command.

c. The sketch selected is not fully constrained.

d. The virtual memory on your computer might be too low for the operation.

7. When adding a dimension that is going to over-constrain the sketch, which options can you perform? (Select all that apply.)

a. Cancel the command.

b. Accept the warning and place a driven dimension.

c. Place the same dimension twice.

d. Replace the conflicting dimension with the new one.

Command Summary

Button	Command	Location
N/A	Recover (Design Doctor)	• **Context Menu:** In Model browser with the failed feature selected

Chapter 12

Sweep Features

Sweep features can be used to create specific geometry that cannot be created using standard extrusions. It enables you to sketch a cross-section and sweep it along a defined path.

Learning Objectives in this Chapter

- Create swept geometry using appropriate path and profile entities.
- Edit a Sweep feature.

12.1 Sweep Features

A Sweep feature enables you to create geometry that cannot be created using an extrusion or revolve. The geometry is defined by sweeping a profile along a path (as shown in Figure 12–1) and can be used to add or remove material.

Sweeps are useful for features that have a uniform shape but an irregular path, such as gaskets and piping.

Figure 12–1

Prior to creating a sweep, a sketched profile and a path must be available for selection.

Open profiles can only be used to create a surface sweep.

- A sweep's profile must be a closed loop sketch to create a solid sweep, as shown in Figure 12–2.

- A sweep's path can be an open or closed sketch. The sketches and geometry in Figure 12–2 show how both a closed and open path can be used. Alternatively, the path can be an existing model edge.

The sweep's path can be a 2D or 3D sketch. 3D sketches are created in 3D space without the use of a sketch plane.

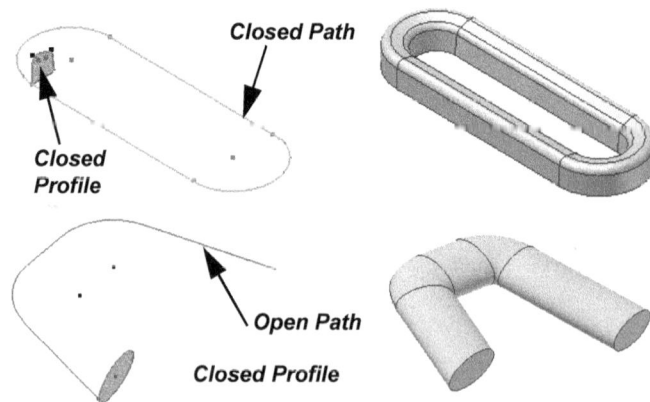

Figure 12–2

- The start point of the sweep is located at the intersection of the profile plane and path. The profile geometry does not need to physically intersect the path.

General Steps

Use the following general steps to create a sweep:

1. Start the creation of the sweep.
2. Select the profile and path.
3. Define the sweep options.
4. Define the type of sweep.
5. Complete the feature.

Step 1 - Start the creation of the sweep.

In the *3D Model* tab>Create panel, click 🐟 (Sweep). The Sweep dialog box displays as shown in Figure 12–3.

Figure 12–3

Step 2 - Select the profile and path.

By default, the ⬚ (Profile) option is automatically active. If a single closed sketch is visible it will be automatically selected, otherwise, select the profile sketch for the sweep. Multiple profiles can be selected, as required.

Select [⌖] (Path) (if it is not already selected) and select the sketched path or an existing solid edge. Once both of these references are selected a preview of the profile being swept along the selected path is displayed.

Hint: Optimize for Single Selection

Enable **Optimize for Single Selection** to automatically advance to the next selector after a single selection is made. Clear this option to be able to select multiple entities for a selection.

Step 3 - Define the sweep options.

Similar to an extrude, a sweep can add and remove material.

Select [⊟] (adds material), [⊟] (removes material), or [⊟] (intersects material options), as required, to define the sweep.

Step 4 - Define the type of sweep.

Path & Guide Rail and *Path & Guide Surface* are the other two types of sweeps that can be created.

Three sweep types can be created. In this student guide, you learn about the **Path** type. Depending on the type of sweep that is selected, the remaining options in this section vary.

- When the Path type is selected, you can select from two remaining orientation options: **Path** and **Parallel**. The difference in the resulting swept geometry for these types is shown in Figure 12–4.

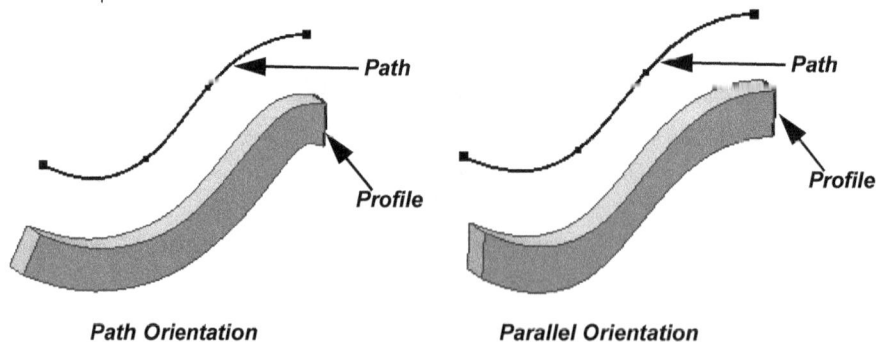

Path Orientation   Parallel Orientation

Figure 12–4

You cannot taper a sweep with a closed path.

*The **Twist** option is only available for Path type sweeps.*

- Tapering sets the angle of the sweep, as shown at the top of Figure 12–5. To taper a sweep feature, enter an angular value in the *Taper* field of the dialog box.

- Twisting sets an angular value to control the rotations of the profile along the entire path from the start point of the path to the end, as shown at the bottom of Figure 12–5. To assign twist, enter an angular value in the dialog box's *Twist* field.

Path

Sweep section

No taper

Positive taper increases the size of the profile along the path.

Negative taper decreases the size of the profile along the path.

Path

Sweep section

No Twist

Twist = 90

Twist = 180

Figure 12–5

Step 5 - Complete the feature.

Once the sweep feature has been defined, click **OK** or right-click and select **OK (Enter)** to complete the sweep feature. Alternatively, you can press <Enter>.

Hint: Sweep Failures

When sweeping a profile on a small fillet or bend, geometry overlap might occur. The software does its best to accommodate this if possible, otherwise, a failure occurs.

Practice 12a | Creating Swept Geometry I

Practice Objectives

- Create swept geometry using appropriate path and profile entities.
- Edit a sweep feature.

In this practice, you will create two sweep features. For both of these features you will sketch their profile entities. However, the path for one will be sketched and the other will be selected. The model will display similar to that shown in Figure 12–6.

Figure 12–6

Task 1 - Open a part file.

1. Open **sweep.ipt**. The model contains a single base feature, as shown in Figure 12–7.

Figure 12–7

Task 2 - Create the path and profile for the sweep.

1. Sketch on a flat surface of the cylinder to create the path for the sweep. Draw and constrain the section as shown in Figure 12–8. Finish the sketch.

*To sketch a line tangent to two circles, start the **Line** command and select and hold the cursor over one of the two circles. While continuing to hold, drag it to the next circle and position the cursor so that the Tangent constraint is visible. Release the mouse button. The same procedure can be used for tangent arcs.*

As of the release of this training guide (March 2017), the tangency to the second circular/arc entity was not being automatically assigned. If required, manually assign the tangent constraint.

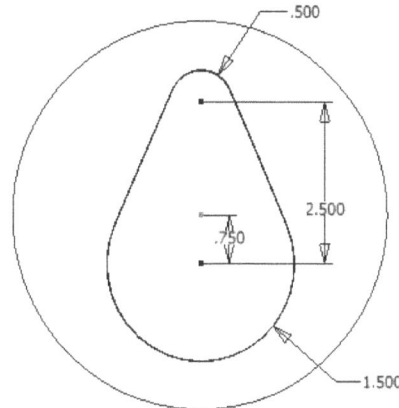

Figure 12–8

2. In the Model browser, select the sketch and then select it again, and rename the sketch as **Path**.

3. Sketch a circle on workplane YZ, as shown in Figure 12–9. This will be the profile for the sweep. When sketching the circle constrain it to a point where the path previously created intersects the YZ workplane. (**Hint:** To constrain the circle, use Project Geometry to project entities in the path onto the sketch plane.) Finish the sketch.

Figure 12–9

4. In the Model browser, select the sketch and then select it again, and rename the sketch as **Profile**.

Task 3 - Create the sweep.

The profile and path have now been defined and the *3D Model* tab is active.

1. In the Create panel, click ⏻ (Sweep). The Sweep dialog box opens as shown in Figure 12–10.

Figure 12–10

2. Ensure that the **Optimize for Single Selection** option is selected. This enables you to select a single profile and the feature immediately prompts you for the Path selection.

3. Select the sketch called **Profile** as the profile for the sweep.

4. Select the sketch called **Path** as the path for the sweep.

5. Maintain the default **Path** orientation option.

6. Click **OK** to create the sweep. The model displays as shown in Figure 12–11.

Figure 12–11

Task 4 - Edit the sweep.

1. Edit the sweep to open its dialog box.

2. In the Sweep dialog box, click [icon] (Cut) to change the sweep feature from a join to a cut. Complete the feature. The model displays as shown in Figure 12–12.

Figure 12–12

Task 5 - Create a new sweep feature that references an existing solid edge.

1. Sketch the arc shown in Figure 12–13 on the YZ workplane. This will be the profile for the sweep. When sketching the section, project the outside top and side surfaces to provide a reference edge to which to constrain the arc. Finish the sketch.

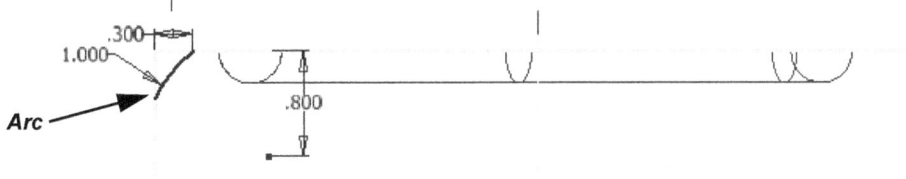

Figure 12–13

2. In the Create panel, click [icon] (Sweep).

3. The new arc will be selected by default as the profile for the sweep. This is because it is the only sketch in the model.

4. Select the existing outside edge of the cylinder as the path for the sweep.

5. In the Sweep dialog box, click 🔲 (Cut).

6. Maintain the default **Path** orientation option.

7. Click **OK** to create the sweep. The model displays similar to that shown in Figure 12–14.

Figure 12–14

8. Save the model and close the window.

Practice 12b | Creating Swept Geometry II

Practice Objective

* Create swept geometry using appropriate path and profile entities.

In this practice you will create two sweep features. The first represents the handle of the dipstick and the second represents the metal rod on the dipstick model, as shown in Figure 12–15.

Figure 12–15

Task 1 - Open a part file.

1. Open **dipstick.ipt**. The model contains two unused sketches and a revolved base feature, as shown in Figure 12–16.

Figure 12–16

Task 2 - Create the sweep for the handle.

1. In the Create panel, click ⟳ (Sweep).

2. By default, the circular sketched profile called **Handle Profile** is selected. Ensure that ⟦⬚⟧ (Path) is selected and select the path called **Handle Path** as the profile to follow.

3. Maintain the default **Path** orientation option.

4. Click **OK** to create the sweep. The model displays as shown in Figure 12–17.

Figure 12–17

Task 3 - Create another sweep feature to represent the rod of the dipstick.

1. Sketch the sweep's path similar to that shown in Figure 12–10 on the YZ workplane. Do not worry about the dimensions or its exact shape.

Figure 12–18

2. Sketch the sweep's profile similar to that shown in Figure 12–19 on the bottom face of the revolved feature. Do not worry about the dimensions or its exact shape.

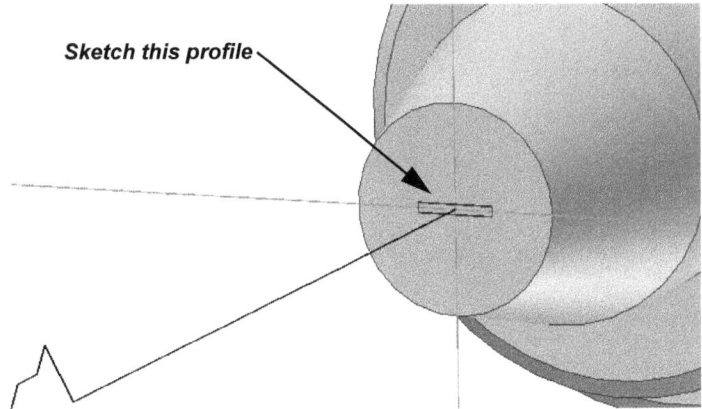

Sketch this profile

Figure 12–19

In this situation, you could have created the geometry as an extrude. However, the section to extrude would need to be a closed section. Using either method, you can create the same geometry. With more experience, you will establish modeling preferences.

3. The profile and path are now defined. In the Create panel, click (Sweep).

4. Depending on how you sketched the profile, you might be required to select it. If so, select the rectangular profile created in the previous Step.

5. Click (Path) and select the path for the profile to follow.

6. Maintain the default **Path** orientation option.

7. Click **OK** to create the sweep. The model displays as shown in Figure 12–20.

Figure 12–20

8. Save the model and close the window.

Practice 12c

Additional Swept Geometry (Optional)

Practice Objective

- Create swept geometry using appropriate path and profile entities.

In this practice you are provided some additional geometric shapes that can be created using a Sweep feature. Create each of these using appropriate path and profile geometry.

Task 1 - Create new parts using a single feature.

1. Create the parts shown in Figure 12–21 using swept features. Start the models using the standard metric template.

Figure 12–21

Chapter Review Questions

1. Which command would you use to create the groove in the model shown in Figure 12–22?

Figure 12–22

   a. **Coil**

   b. **Revolve**

   c. **Extrude**

   d. **Sweep**

2. Which elements must be defined before starting the creation of a Sweep feature? (Select all that apply.)

   a. Profile

   b. Path

   c. Section

   d. Start Point

3. A Sweep feature can be used to either add or remove material.

   a. True

   b. False

4. Which of the following statements for Sweep features are true?

   a. A sweep creates a single feature whose geometry is blended between multiple profiles.

   b. A sweep creates a single feature whose geometry is swept along a defined path.

   c. A sweep can only be added to the model after the base extrusion has been created.

   d. A sweep path must be sketched geometry.

5. You can taper a sweep with a closed path, but you cannot taper a sweep with an open path.

   a. True

   b. False

6. You can twist the path that defines a sweep by entering a Twist value.

   a. True

   b. False

7. How many unconsumed sketches are required to create the sweep feature shown in Figure 12–23?

Figure 12–23

   a. 1

   b. 2

   c. 1 for 2D sweep, 2 for 3D sweep.

   d. A sweep is not based on a sketch.

Command Summary

Button	Command	Location
	Sweep	• **Ribbon:** *3D Model* tab>Create panel

Loft Features

A Loft is a feature that can be used to create complex geometry that blends multiple profiles. Additional control of the resulting shape can be gained by assigning references for the geometry to follow between the profiles.

Learning Objectives in this Chapter

- Create a Rail loft feature using appropriate profile and rail entities.
- Create a Center Line Loft feature using appropriate profile and centerline entities.
- Control the shape and weight of how lofted geometry transitions from adjacent solid geometry.
- Control how lofted geometry transitions between sections.

13.1 Rail and Center Line Lofts

A Loft feature enables you to create advanced geometry by blending multiple profiles. A loft can either remove or add material in a model. There are three available Loft types: **Rail**, **Center Line**, and **Area**. This topic discusses the Rail and Center Line types. When creating a new Loft feature, the default type is a Rail Loft.

Rail Lofts enable you to blend between profiles, as shown at the top of Figure 13–1. As an optional reference, you can further define how the geometry is blended between the profiles by selecting rail entities, as shown at the bottom of Figure 13–1.

Figure 13–1

Similar to a Rail Loft, a Center Line Loft blends between selected profiles; however, control of the geometry between profiles is assigned using a single centerline. The centerline sets the profiles so that they remain normal to a centerline reference, as shown in Figure 13–2.

Figure 13–2

Prior to creating either a Rail or Center Line Loft, sketched profiles and reference entities must be created so that they are available for selection during feature creation.

- Rail and Center Line Loft profiles must be a closed loop sketch (or existing face) to create a solid loft. Open profiles can only be used to create a surface loft. The profiles (sketched or existing face) should represent cross-sections of the geometry that is required to be blended.

- For a Rail Loft, you can control the shape of the loft between profiles. Rails are 2D or 3D sketched curves or existing edges and are optional for feature creation. Each sketch or existing edge that is used as a rail must intersect all profiles and be tangent continuous.

- For a Center Line Loft, a centerline is required. It can be a 2D or 3D sketched curve or an existing edge in the model. Only one center line can be used to create a loft and it does not need to intersect the profiles/sections.

General Steps

Use the following general steps to create a Rail Loft feature:

1. Start the creation of the loft.
2. Define the reference entities.
3. Define the Loft options.
4. Complete the feature.

Step 1 - Start the creation of the loft.

Area lofts are discussed in the Advanced Part course.

Once the profiles and any rail and centerline references have been created, you can start the creation of the loft. In the *3D Model* tab>Create panel, click 🠿 (Loft). The Loft dialog box opens as shown in Figure 13–3.

- To create a Rail loft, ensure that the ⊙ 🠿 (Rails) option is selected.

- To create a Center Line loft, ensure that the ○ 🠿 (Center Line) option is selected.

Figure 13–3

Step 2 - Define the reference entities.

By default, in the *Curves* tab, the *Sections* area is automatically active when you start the creation of a loft. Select at least two profiles to be used in creating the geometry.

- The selected profiles can be either sketched sections or a planar face on existing geometry. Planar faces can only be used as start and end sections.

- If you select a sketch with more than one selectable region, you must select the sketch and then select the region to use.

- To reorder profiles, drag and drop their profile names in the *Sections* area, as required.

Depending on whether you are creating a Rail or Center Line Loft, the selection of the remaining references vary:

- In the *Rails* area, select **Click to add** and select any reference curves that are to be used to further refine the shape of the geometry between profiles. The selection of a Rail reference is optional. As rails are added, the preview updates to display the change.

- In the *Center Line* area, select **Select a Sketch** and select the centerline reference. Once the centerline is selected, a preview displays showing the created geometry. The sections of the loft remain normal to the centerline at all points.

Step 3 - Define the Loft options.

By default, a loft is created so that it adds material to the model. To change this behavior, you can use the following options:

- Click [icon] (Join) to add material.

- Click [icon] (Cut) to remove material.

- Click [icon] (Intersect) to intersect material.

Additional options in the *Curves* tab are described as follows.

Output options	Enables you to create a solid [icon] or surface [icon] feature. Solids must be created by selecting closed curves or a closed face loop.
Closed Loop	Enables you to create a loft that forms a closed loop by joining the first and last selected profiles. This option is not available when rail curves are specified.
Merge Tangent Faces	Enables you to prevent an edge from being created between tangent faces of the feature.

Step 4 - Complete the feature.

Click **OK** or right-click and select **OK (Enter)** to complete the loft feature. Alternatively, you can press <Enter>.

13.2 Advanced Loft Options

Additional options are available in the *Conditions* and *Transition* tabs in the Loft dialog box to better control the shape of the loft. These options are available for all types of loft features.

Conditions Tab

The *Conditions* tab enables you to specify the angle and shape of the lofted geometry when end sections blend into an adjacent solid. Select each item in the list to set its options separately. The conditions that can be set vary depending on the profile geometry and adjacent features. The options are described below. Figure 13–4 shows an example of the options available.

The Conditions tab enables you to set conditions for blending into adjacent solid geometry.

Figure 13–4

Free Condition

The Free condition ( ) is applied to the profiles by default, ensuring that no control conditions are set for the loft for its end profiles, as shown on the left in Figure 13–5.

Tangent Condition

The Tangent condition ( ) is available when the loft profile is an existing face, or when the profile is adjacent to a lateral surface or body, as shown on the right in Figure 13–5.

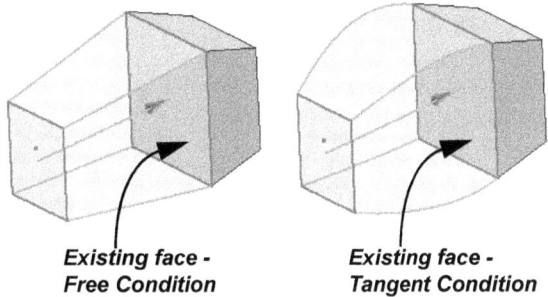

Existing face -
Free Condition

Existing face -
Tangent Condition

Figure 13–5

If the Weight is 0, the Angle is grayed out.

- The *Weight* value sets how far the loft follows the starting profile and angle, as shown in Figure 13–6. A large number gives the angle more influence, so the transition near the profile is more gradual.

A Tangent condition and Weight of 2 has been assigned to the face that is adjacent to existing geometry.

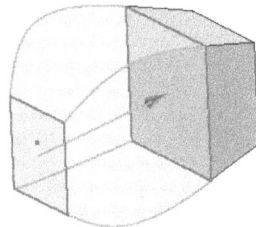

Figure 13–6

Direction Condition

Angular values less than 90 create concave geometry between profiles, while values greater than 90 create convex geometry.

The Direction condition ( ) is available when profiles are 2D sketches. This condition measures the angle of the loft body relative to the plane that contains the profile. Once selected, apply angle and weight to the loft body relative to the profile.

• The *Angle* sets the angular value at which the loft should begin from the profile plane, as shown in the example in Figure 13–7. The default angle is 90 degrees, and the range is from 0.0000001 to 179.99999 degrees.

Figure 13–7

If the Weight is 0, the Angle is grayed out.

- The Weight value determines how far the loft follows the starting profile and angle, as shown in Figure 13–8. A large number gives the angle more influence, so that the transition near the profile is more gradual.

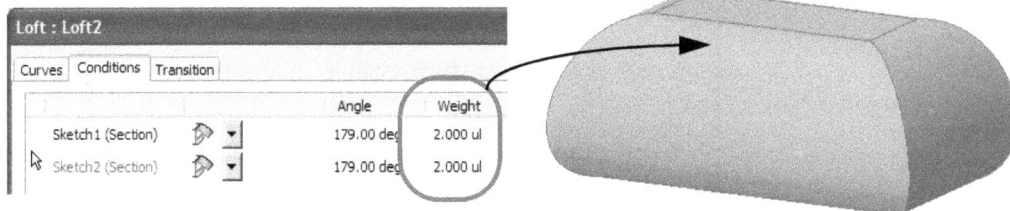

Figure 13–8

Smooth (G2) Condition

The Smooth (G2) condition ( ) (shown in Figure 13–9) is available when either:

- The profile is adjacent to a face to which it can be made curvature continuous, or

- A face loop is selected.

Once the Smooth (G2) Condition is set you can control the angle, direction, and weight to the loft body relative to the profile.

Figure 13–9

Point Conditions

The Sharp point, Tangent, and Tangent to plane conditions for lofts are available when you select a point as the first or last section. The following are the available boundary conditions for points (as shown in Figure 13–10):

- **(Sharp point):** Applies no boundary condition.

- **(Tangent):** Applies tangency, resulting in a round point.

- **(Tangent to plane):** Applies tangency to the point, resulting in a round point. It uses a planar face or work plane as a reference for defining tangency.

Figure 13–10

Transition Tab

The *Transition* tab defines how the Loft transitions from one section to the next. A **Point Set** is a group of points, one on each profile, used to define the edges of the loft. The points in a Point Set are called map points, and the edge of the loft follows the path defined by the Point Set to determine the twist, as shown in Figure 13–11 (four point sets).

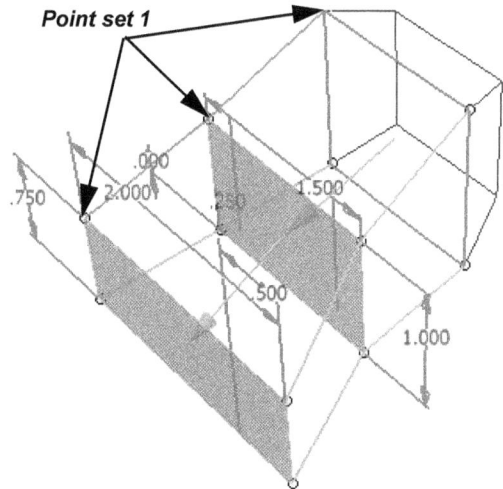

Figure 13–11

By default, the **Automatic Mapping** option is used to calculate this information. You must toggle this option off if you want to manually specify this information. The *Map Point* and *Position* columns list the map points for a point set. You can change the position of a map point by selecting the sketch on which the point lies and select a new location on the sketch. To add a new point set, select **Click to add** in the *Point Set* column.

Practice 13a | Rail Lofts

Practice Objectives

- Create lofted geometry using appropriate profile and rail entities.
- Edit a Loft feature.

In this practice, you will create the model shown in Figure 13–12 using the rail loft feature. Rails will be used to help control the overall shape of the sections that are being blended together.

Figure 13–12

Task 1 - Open a part file and create a loft.

In this task you will open an existing model and create a solid loft feature using sections and rails that have been provided.

1. Open **Rail_Loft.ipt**. The sections and rails required for the loft feature are provided, as shown in Figure 13–13.

3 profiles

4 rails

Figure 13–13

2. In the Create panel, click ⬚ (Loft). The Loft dialog box opens as shown in Figure 13–14.

Figure 13–14

3. Ensure that ⬚ (Rails) is selected.

4. In the *Sections* column, select **Click to add**. Select **Profile1**, **Profile2**, and **Profile3**.

5. Click **OK** to create the loft. The model displays as shown in Figure 13–15. Note that the feature does not follow the shape outlined by the rails, as is the design intent.

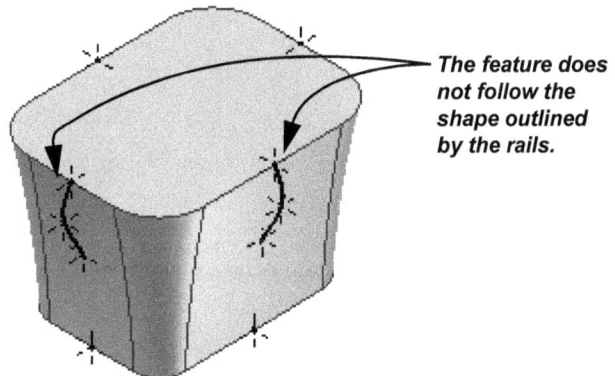

The feature does not follow the shape outlined by the rails.

Figure 13–15

Task 2 - Add rails to the loft.

In this task, you will edit the loft feature and add rails. Rails help control the shape of the loft between sections. When creating rails, remember that they must intersect all sections in the loft.

1. Edit the Loft feature that you just created.

*You can also right-click and select **Select Rails**.*

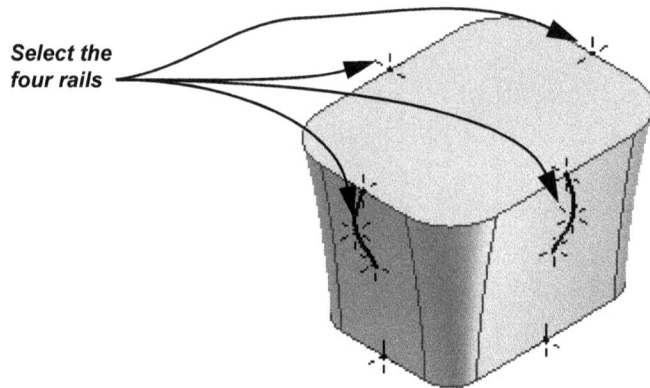

2. In the Loft dialog box, in the *Rails* area, select **Click to add** and select the four rails shown in Figure 13–16. Note that the shape of the loft updates as you select the rails.

Select the four rails

Figure 13–16

3. Click **OK** to update the loft and close the dialog box. The model displays as shown in Figure 13–17.

Figure 13–17

4. Save and close the model.

Practice 13b | Center Line Loft I

Practice Objective

- Create a Center Line Loft feature using appropriate profile and centerline entities to drive geometry based on a selected centerline.

In this practice, you will create the Center Line Loft shown in Figure 13–18. The geometry is generated by selecting two profiles and a single center line reference.

Figure 13–18

Task 1 - Open a part file and create a center line loft.

In this task, you will open an existing model and create a center line loft using the sketches provided.

1. Open **CenterLine_loft.ipt**. The loft's center line and sections have been created for you.

2. In the Create panel, click ⬡ (Loft). The Loft dialog box opens.

3. In the *Sections* area, select **Click to add** and for the profiles for the loft, select **Profile1**, and **Profile2**. The loft is generated by blending between the two profile sketches, as shown in Figure 13–19.

Figure 13–19

*You can also select
Click to Add in the
Center Line area in the
Loft dialog box.*

4. Click ⊙ ⊬⬝ (Center Line) or right-click and select **Select Center Line** to create a center line loft.

5. Select the **Centerline** sketched spline.

6. Click **OK** to complete the loft. The model displays as shown in Figure 13–20.

Figure 13–20

7. Save and close the file.

Practice 13c | Loft Creation I

Practice Objectives

- Create a Loft feature using appropriate reference entities.
- Edit Loft features to change their type and reference entities.
- Control the shape and weight of how lofted geometry transitions from adjacent solid geometry.
- Control how lofted geometry transitions between sections.

In this practice, you will create a loft feature between two existing solid features. You will begin by creating a Rail Loft to compare geometry and then edit this to create a more advanced and customized Center Line loft feature. The final model is shown in Figure 13–21.

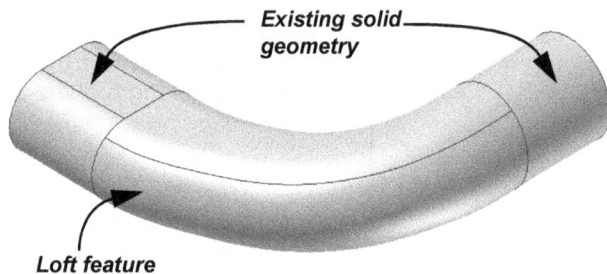

Figure 13–21

Task 1 - Open a part file and create a Rail Loft.

1. Open **loft.ipt**. The model displays as shown in Figure 13–22. The sections and center line you will use to create the loft in this practice have been created for you.

Figure 13–22

2. In the Create panel, click ⬙ (Loft). In the Loft dialog box, click ⬦ (Rails).

3. In the *Sections* area, select **Click to add** and select the two sections (existing geometry) shown in Figure 13–23.

4. In the *Rails* area, select **Click to add** and select the curved sketch, as shown in Figure 13–23.

**Select this
section first**

**Select this
section second**

**Select this sketch
as the rail**

Figure 13–23

5. Click **OK**. The model displays as shown in Figure 13–24 with the **Shaded with Edges** display style set. Note the geometry along the length of the loft.

Figure 13–24

Task 2 - Create a Center Line Loft feature.

1. Edit the Loft feature to display its dialog box.

2. Change the type of loft to a Center Line loft by selecting (Center Line). The sections that were defined for the Rail loft remain selected, but the Rail reference is removed.

3. In the *Center Line* area, select **Select a Sketch** and select the curved sketch (same as that used for the Rail) as the center line reference. You might need to expand the Loft feature and select the curve in the Model browser if it is not displayed in the graphics window.

4. Click **OK**. The model displays as shown in Figure 13–25.

Figure 13–25

Note the subtle difference in the path that the loft geometry takes over the length of the reference curve. This is because with a Rail loft, the rail reference defines the exact path of the loft, as shown on the left in Figure 13–26. With a Center Line loft, the center line reference is a type of rail to which the loft sections remain normal, as shown on the right. Multiple rail references can be used for a rail loft, but only one center line reference can be used.

Rail Loft

Center Line Loft

Figure 13–26

Task 3 - Customize the end conditions for the Center Line Loft.

1. Edit the Loft feature to access its dialog box.

2. Maintain the options in the *Curves* tab. Select the *Conditions* tab. It enables you to control the loft geometry as it transitions from adjacent solid geometry.

3. Expand the drop-down lists and select **Smooth (G2) Condition** for the end conditions for both edges, as shown in Figure 13–27.

Figure 13–27

4. The *Weight* value for both **Tangent** and **Smooth** end conditions can be edited to control how far the tangency/smoothing is taken to establish the condition. By default, the *Weight* for **Edge 14** (right edge) is **1**. Note the effect that this value has on the loft geometry when changed to **2**, as shown in Figure 13–28.

Weight = 1   *Weight = 2*

Figure 13–28

5. Return the *Weight* value for both edges to **1**.

6. Click **OK**. The model displays as shown in Figure 13–29.

Figure 13–29

Task 4 - Edit the dimensions on one of the edges used in the Loft.

1. Expand **Extrusion2** in the Model browser, right-click on **Sketch3** and select **Edit Sketch**.

2. Select the 4 dimension and change it to **12**, as shown in Figure 13–30.

Figure 13–30

3. Finish the sketch. The loft automatically updates, as shown in Figure 13–31.

Figure 13–31

Task 5 - Create transitions to further customize the loft.

1. Edit the Loft feature to open its dialog box.

2. Maintain the options in the *Curves* and *Conditions* tabs. Select the *Transition* tab. This tab enables you to further control the loft geometry as it transitions between the selected sections. By default, transitioning is done automatically by matching points on each section. By manually adding transitions you can further control the shape of the loft.

3. Clear the **Automatic Mapping** option.

This procedure of defining position values on the sections of a loft can be time-consuming, but is valuable when working with differently shaped sections to obtain the required transitions.

4. In the *Point Set* area, if **Set 1** does not already exist, select **Click to add**. The Loft dialog box updates to display a Map Point for each section in the loft.

To define the transition set you select Map Point locations on the edges of each section. Once selected you can refine the position by entering a precise value in the *Position* column. Zero indicates one end of a line entity, .5 the middle, and 1 indicates the other end. Any value between 0 and 1 can be used.

5. Select the approximate location on the left and the right sections as shown in Figure 13–32.

1. Select in this approximate location to place a Map Point.

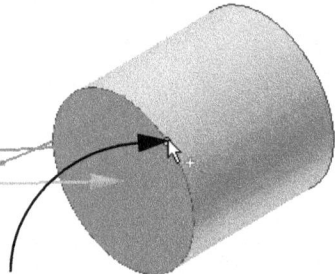

2. Select in this approximate location to place a Map Point.

Figure 13–32

Editing the values can take some time. For this practice, you will select a location and edit the value as you want. The values depend on the selection point on the line and the entities that make up the section.

6. In the *Point Set* area, select **Click to add** to add a new Point set.

7. Select two locations similar to that shown in Figure 13–33.

Add this Point Set

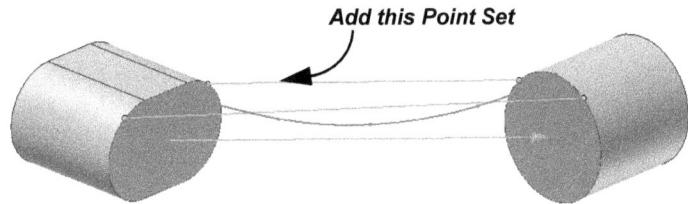

Figure 13–33

8. Continue to add two additional point sets, as shown in Figure 13–34.

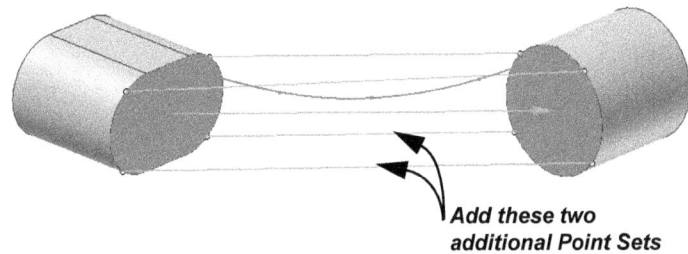

Add these two additional Point Sets

Figure 13–34

9. Click **OK**. The model should display similar to that shown in Figure 13–35.

Figure 13–35

10. Save and close the model.

| Practice 13d | # Loft Creation II (Optional) |

Practice Objective

- Create lofted geometry using appropriate reference entities.

In this practice, you will create lofts features to create the final model as shown in Figure 13–36.

Figure 13–36

Task 1 - Open a part file and review its construction.

1. Open **Razor.ipt**. The model displays as shown in Figure 13–37. The sections you will use to create the lofts in this practice have been created for you.

Figure 13–37

Task 2 - Create a Loft feature to create solid geometry.

1. Create a Rail Loft.

2. In the *Sections* area, select **Click to add** and then select the existing face of the model, **Profile3**, **Profile4**, and the **Endpoint** point as the sections. The preview of the resulting Loft is shown in Figure 13–38. Note that a Rail reference is not required for this loft.

Select this face first

Select the Profile3 section second

Select the Profile4 section third

Select the EndPoint point last

Figure 13–38

3. Select the *Conditions* tab. It enables you to control the loft geometry as it transitions from adjacent solid geometry and the condition at the terminating point.

4. Expand the Edges1 (Section) drop-down list and select **Smooth (G2) Condition** to set the end condition, as shown in Figure 13–39.

Figure 13–39

5. Edit the *Weight* value for **Edges1 (Section)** to control how far the tangency/smoothing is taken to establish the condition. For the new *Weight* value, enter **2**.

6. Expand the Point Endpoint (Section) drop-down list and select **Tangent to Plane** to set the end condition, as shown in Figure 13–40. For the condition reference, select the **EndPoint Tangent Ref** workplane.

Figure 13–40

7. For **Point Endpoint (Section)**, set the *Weight* value to **5**.

8. Click **OK**. The model displays as shown in Figure 13–41 with the work planes toggled off. Note that the connection between the two solid features is not as smooth as it could be.

Figure 13–41

9. Edit the newly created loft feature. In the *Curves* tab, select the **Edge** section reference and press <Delete> to remove it from the loft. This is the solid face reference that was selected as a profile section for the loft.

10. Click **OK**.

11. Create a Rail Loft. Select the two faces shown in Figure 13–42 as the sections for the loft.

Figure 13–42

12. Select the *Conditions* tab. Expand the drop-down list and select **Smooth (G2) Condition** to set the conditions for both edges. Modify the weight values so that the new loft smoothly blends the two solids. If the values are too large the geometry with fail and the resulting geometry cannot be calculated. Figure 13–43 shows the completed model using a *Weight* value of **1.25** and **1.5**.

Figure 13–43

13. Save the model and close the window.

Chapter Review Questions

1. A loft can be used in a model to either add or remove material.

   a. True

   b. False

2. Which of the following best describes the type of geometry that is created using a Loft feature?

   a. A loft creates multiple solid features between each of the profiles.

   b. A loft creates a feature where the geometry is blended between multiple profiles.

   c. A loft creates a feature whose geometry is swept along a defined path.

   d. A loft creates a feature that is rotated around a selected centerline.

3. Which of the following statements for Loft feature is true? (Select all that apply.)

   a. A loft can only be added to the model after the base extrusion has been created.

   b. The profiles for lofts can only be sketched.

   c. Once you select the profiles for the Loft feature, you cannot reorder them.

   d. To use an existing planar face as a section of a loft, you can select the face directly without creating a sketch.

   e. Map points are used to determine the twist of the loft.

4. Which type of loft can be used to create a loft that passes through the three circular sections and is guided along the curve, as shown in Figure 13–44?

Figure 13–44

   a. Rail

   b. Center Line

5. When referencing existing geometry as the start or end section for a loft, which of the following conditions provides access to the *Weight* settings to control its shape, as shown in Figure 13–45? (Select all that apply.)

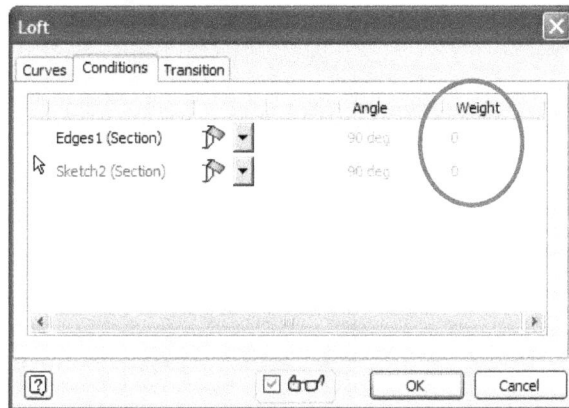

Figure 13–45

a. Free

b. Tangent

c. Smooth (G2)

Command Summary

Button	Command	Location
	Loft	• **Ribbon:** *3D Model* tab>Create panel

Duplication Tools

Incorporating the use of duplication techniques when creating similar geometry enables you to efficiently create models. Duplication techniques can include making multiple copies of an entire model, making multiple copies of a feature, or mirroring geometry.

Learning Objectives in this Chapter

- Create a rectangular pattern of features that translate along a first and second direction.
- Create a circular pattern of features that rotate about a selected axis.
- Create a pattern of features that is defined by sketch points in a sketch.
- Mirror a solid part to duplicate all of its geometry.
- Mirror select features in a model to create required geometry.
- Suppress individual pattern occurrences in an existing pattern.
- Edit Pattern and Mirror features to make changes to the original geometry.
- Delete Pattern and Mirror features from a model.

14.1 Rectangular Feature Patterns

You can create multiple copies of parts or features on a part by creating a pattern. An example of a rectangular feature pattern is shown in Figure 14–1.

Feature to be patterned   **Patterned features**

Figure 14–1

General Steps

Use the following general steps to create a rectangular pattern of features on a part:

1. Start the creation of the pattern.
2. Define the object(s) to pattern.
3. Define the pattern in the first direction.
4. Define the pattern in the second direction, as required.
5. Define additional pattern options, as required.
6. Complete the pattern.

Step 1 - Start the creation of the pattern.

In the *3D Model* tab>Pattern panel, click ⊡ (Rectangular Pattern). The Rectangular Pattern dialog box opens as shown in Figure 14–2.

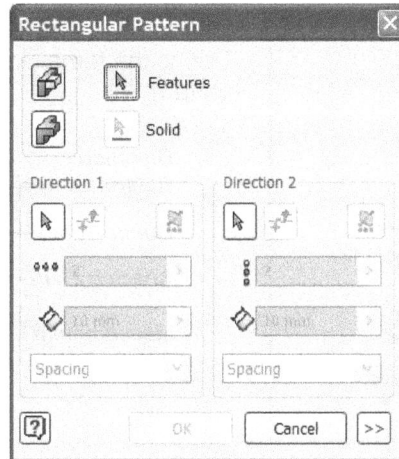

Figure 14–2

Step 2 - Define the object(s) to pattern.

To select the object(s) to pattern, use the options at the top of the dialog box to determine the object type to be patterned:

- Click (Pattern individual features) to create a pattern of individually selected features. This is the default option.

- Click (Pattern a solid) to pattern the entire solid model.

Once the object type is active, select the appropriate feature(s) or the solid model to pattern. Consider the following:

- Work and surface features can also be included in a pattern.

- Dependent features are not automatically patterned if their parent is selected.

- Dependent features cannot be patterned themselves unless the parent feature is selected.

Step 3 - Define the pattern in the first direction.

To define the first pattern path direction, click [cursor icon] in the *Direction 1* area (as shown in Figure 14–3) and select a line, arc, spline, trimmed ellipse, or part edge to define the direction. The path does not have to be linear and it can be open or closed. Define the remaining options in the Direction 1 area to define the pattern:

Figure 14–3

Enter the number of occurrences (including the selected geometry) in the ••• *(Count)* field, as shown in Figure 14–3.

The distance between each occurrence is defined in the ⬦ *(Spacing)* field. How the value is applied to the model depends on the measurement type that is used in the drop-down list shown in Figure 14–3.

- Use **Spacing** to set the entered spacing value as the distance between individual occurrences, as shown in Figure 14–4.

The distance between each pattern feature is 10 mm.

Figure 14–4

- Use **Distance** to set the entered spacing value as the total distance between the first and last occurrence, as shown in Figure 14–5.

The distance between the first and last instance is 45 mm.

Figure 14–5

- Use **Curve Length** to set the length of the pattern equal to that of a selected curve (e.g. line), as shown in Figure 14–6. If this option is used the *Spacing* field is not available. The number of occurrences is equally spaced along the curve.

The instances (5) are equally spaced along the length of the selected curve.

Curve

Figure 14–6

Step 4 - Define the pattern in the second direction, as required.

The allowable reference types are the same for Direction 1 and 2.

To define the second pattern path, click [cursor icon] in the *Direction 2* area and select a different direction reference, as shown in Figure 14–7. The second direction does not need to be perpendicular to the first. Similar to the *Direction 1* area, set the number of occurrences, spacing, and measurement type to define how the pattern is be created in the second direction.

The distance between each pattern feature in Direction 2 is 10 mm.

Direction 2

Figure 14–7

Step 5 - Define additional pattern options, as required.

Consider the use of the *Direction*, *Compute*, and *Orientation* areas in the expanded dialog box (⌗>>) to refine how the feature pattern is generated. The expanded dialog box is shown in Figure 14–8.

Select this button to expand the dialog box.

Figure 14–8

For best patterning results, it is recommended to place the first occurrence on or relative to the start point of the path.

- The Start references in the *Direction 1* and *Direction 2* areas enable you to assign a specific point on the model as the start point for the first occurrence. This can be established independently in both directions, if required.

- The *Compute* area contains options to control how the pattered geometry is calculated. The three options are described as follows:

Optimized	Optimized patterns are the fastest and also the most restrictive. Optimized patterns have the following restrictions: • Features cannot lie on different surfaces. • Features cannot break edges of the part. • Features cannot intersect with each other.
Identical	Identical patterns create identically patterned features. This is the default pattern option. Identical patterns generate the following types of occurrences: • Features that can lie on different surfaces. • Features that can break the edge of the part. • Features that can intersect with each other. • Feature depth of all occurrences is the same value as the pattern leader (regardless of its depth option).
Adjust	Adjusted patterns create occurrences similar to the Identical pattern type while also using feature depth settings. Each occurrence is patterned individually, which increases the computation time for the pattern.

The patterned features in Figure 14–9 show the differences between the **Identical** and **Adjust** compute options. An **Optimized** pattern is explicitly recommended when the pattern results in a large number of occurrences and is used to optimize performance.

Identical Pattern
Slot: The depth of occurrences is identical in measurement (not option) and therefore cuts through all the material.

Hole: The depth of occurrences is identical in measurement (not option).

Hole and Slot were created with the Through All extent option.

Adjusted Pattern
Hole: The initial Hole set to cut Through All. Note that the depth of occurrences is adjusted to take into account the depth setting.

Initial Hole set to Through All extent option.

Figure 14–9

- The *Orientation* area contains options to define how the patterned features are oriented relative to the first selected feature being patterned. The options are as follows:

Identical	Enables you to orient the patterned occurrences such that they are oriented in the same way as the first feature selected for patterning.
Direction1/ Direction2	Enables you to orient the patterned occurrences such that they are the oriented based on either the Direction1 or Direction2 reference paths. Orientation of the occurrences is such that the first feature that was selected for patterning maintains its orientation to the 2D tangent vector of the Direction1 or Direction2 reference path throughout the pattern.

The pattern shown in Figure 14–10 was created by assigning 23 occurrences in *Direction 1* and uses the **Curve Length** measurement type. The **Identical** orientation option was used, which maintains the orientation in the same way as the first occurrence relative as it travels along the curve. The resulting pattern does not produce the required results.

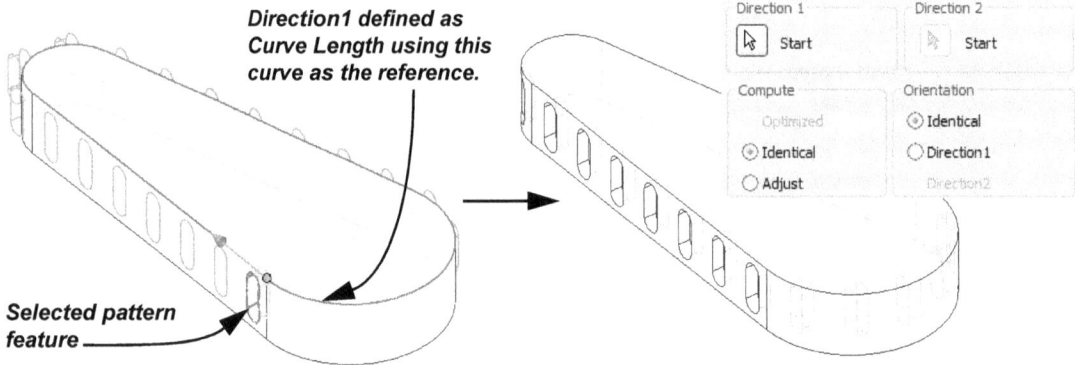

Direction1 defined as
Curve Length using this
curve as the reference.

Selected pattern
feature

Figure 14–10

The previous pattern was edited. A start reference for *Direction 1* was defined (as shown in Figure 14–11) and the **Direction1** Orientation option was set. These edits produced the required results.

Direction1 defined as Curve Length
using this curve as the reference.

Start Point for
Direction1

Selected pattern
feature

Figure 14–11

Step 6 - Complete the pattern.

Click **OK** to complete the pattern. Alternatively, you can right-click and select **OK (Enter)**.

14.2 Circular Feature Patterns

You can create multiple copies of parts or features on a part by creating a pattern. An example of a circular pattern of holes is shown in Figure 14–12.

Figure 14–12

General Steps

Use the following general steps to create a circular pattern:

1. Start the creation of the pattern.
2. Define the object(s) to pattern.
3. Define the rotation axis.
4. Define the pattern placement.
5. Define the pattern orientation.
6. Define additional pattern options, as required.
7. Complete the pattern.

Step 1 - Start the creation of the pattern.

In the *3D Model* tab>Pattern panel, click (Circular Pattern). The Circular Pattern dialog box opens as shown in Figure 14–13.

Figure 14–13

Refer to the Rectangular Pattern topic for more information on selecting features for patterning.

Step 2 - Define the object(s) to pattern.

Similar to a Rectangular pattern, select one of the object types to be patterned (▣ (Pattern individual features) or ▣ (Pattern a solid)) and select the object(s) in the Model browser or in the graphics window.

Step 3 - Define the rotation axis.

To define the axis about which to create the pattern, click ▣ (Rotation Axis) in the Circular Pattern dialog box and select the reference. You can select a cylindrical or conical face, a work axis, or an edge for the pattern axis. If required, click ▣ to reverse the direction of the pattern around the assigned axis of rotation.

Step 4 - Define the pattern placement.

Once objects are selected for patterning and the axis is defined, you can enter values in the *Placement* area to define the pattern.

- Enter the number of occurrences (including the selected geometry) in the ⦙⦙⦙ *(Count)* field, as shown in Figure 14–14.

- Enter the angle between the first and last occurrence in the ◇ *(Angle)* field, as shown in Figure 14–14.

In the example shown in Figure 14–14, a hole is being patterned radially about the larger hole's axis. The values being used are shown in the Circular Pattern dialog box.

Figure 14–14

Step 5 - Define the pattern orientation.

In the *Orientation* area of the Circular Pattern dialog box, select the required pattern orientation.

- Select (Rotational) to ensure that the patterned feature's orientation is rotated, as it extends through the pattern angle.

- Select (Fixed) to ensure that the patterned feature's orientation remains the same as the original feature, as it extends through the pattern angle. When defining a **Fixed** orientation you can change the default Base Point, if required.

Figure 14–15 shows examples of both orientation options that are available.

Rotational Orientation   *Fixed Orientation*

Figure 14–15

Step 6 - Define additional pattern options, as required.

Consider the use of the *Creation Method* and *Positioning Method* areas in the expanded dialog box ($>>$) to refine how the feature pattern is generated. The expanded dialog box is shown in Figure 14–16.

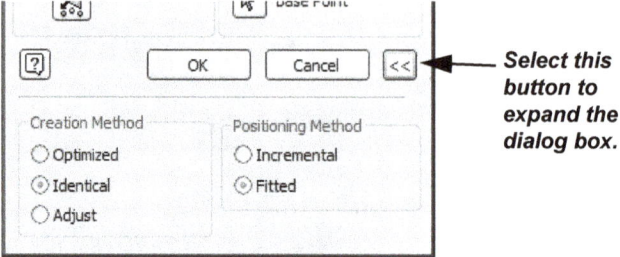

Select this button to expand the dialog box.

Figure 14–16

- The *Creation Method* area contains options to control how the pattered geometry is calculated. The three options are the same as those in the *Compute* area for rectangular patterns. Refer to their description in the Rectangular pattern topic for more information. Figure 14–17 illustrates the differences between the **Identical** and **Adjust** creation methods for a circular pattern.

Identical Pattern: The depth of occurrences is identical in measurement (not option).

Adjusted Pattern: The depth of occurrences is adjusted to take into account the depth setting.

Hole created with the Through All extent option.

Figure 14–17

- The *Positioning Method* area contains methods for positioning the pattered feature in the model. The options are as follows:

Incremental	Enables you to use the Angle value to incrementally define the spacing between the patterned features. For example, an incremental pattern of 3 occurrences at 90 degrees.
Fitted	Enables you to use the Angle value to define the angular range of pattern. The number of occurrences are fit into this value. For example, a fitted pattern of 3 occurrences at 90 degrees.

Step 7 - Complete the pattern.

Click **OK** to complete the pattern. Alternatively, you can right-click and select **OK (Enter)**.

14.3 Sketched Driven Patterns

You can create multiple copies of parts or features on a part by creating a pattern. Examples of a pattern of slots are shown in Figure 14–18.

Slot-shaped cut to be patterned on the face of the cylinder.

Sketched Points added to a 2D sketch to define pattern placement.

Patterned slot-shaped cuts.

Figure 14–18

General Steps

Use the following general steps to create a circular pattern:

1. Start the creation of the pattern.
2. Define the object(s) to pattern.
3. Define the placement sketch.
4. Define the pattern reference.
5. Define additional pattern options, as required.
6. Complete the pattern.

Step 1 - Start the creation of the pattern.

In the *3D Model* tab>Pattern panel, click ⊞ (Sketch Driven Pattern). The Sketch Driven Pattern dialog box opens as shown in Figure 14–19.

Figure 14–19

Step 2 - Define the object(s) to pattern.

Refer to the Rectangular Pattern topic for more information on selecting features for patterning.

Similar to a Rectangular pattern, select one of the object types to be patterned (⬚ (Pattern individual features) or ⬚ (Pattern a solid)) and select the object(s) in the Model browser or in the graphics window.

Step 3 - Define the placement sketch.

To define the placement of the pattern, you must select an existing sketch. The sketch can be a 2D or 3D sketch and must contain sketch points. The sketch points will define the placement of the pattern feature.

Step 4 - Define the pattern reference.

To refine the position of the feature being patterned relative to the sketch points you can optionally redefine the Base Point and Faces for the pattern.

- Select ⬚ (Base Point) in the *Reference* area and select a new point on the feature being patterned. This new point will be used to align the feature with the sketched points for the new pattern.

- Select ⬚ (Faces) in the *Reference* area and select a face on the model to set the occurrence orientation. This reference defines the normal direction for the pattern.

Step 5 - Define additional pattern options, as required.

Consider the use of the *Creation Method* area in the expanded dialog box ($\boxed{>>}$) to refine how the feature pattern is generated. The expanded dialog box is shown in Figure 14–20.

Figure 14–20

- The *Creation Method* area contains options to control how the pattered geometry is calculated. The three options are the same as those in the *Compute* area for rectangular patterns. Refer to their description in the Rectangular pattern topic for more information.

Step 6 - Complete the pattern.

Click **OK** to complete the pattern. Alternatively, you can right-click and select **OK (Enter)**.

14.4 Mirror Parts or Features

The entire solid model or solid model features can be mirrored about a specified plane. This is useful when designing symmetric parts. The model shown in Figure 14–21 was created by designing one quarter of the model and then mirroring the entire model twice.

The geometry is mirrored about this plane.

The geometry is mirrored about this plane.

A dimensional modification made to the original geometry updates the mirrored geometry.

Figure 14–21

How To: Mirror Geometry

1. In the *3D Model* tab>Pattern panel, click ⬓⬓ (Mirror).

2. Define the objects to pattern using the options shown in Figure 14–22.

   - To Mirror individual features in the model, click ⬚ (Mirror individual features). This is the default option.

   - To pattern the entire solid model, click ⬚ (Mirror a solid). In addition to patterning the entire solid, you can select the work and surface features that you want to include.

If you mirror a feature that has dependent features, the dependent features are also mirrored.

Figure 14–22

Enhanced
in **2018**

Fillet features can be mirrored without mirroring their parent feature.

3. Click ⬚ (Mirror Plane) and select a planar face or work plane to mirror about. To select an origin plane, select a plane button (⬚ ⬚ ⬚) or select it in the graphics window or Model browser.

4. Click **OK** to complete the mirroring process once the mirrored part has been defined. Alternatively, you can right-click and select **OK (Enter)**.

A mirrored part and its associated Model browser are shown in Figure 14–23.

This model has been mirrored twice to obtain the required geometry.

Figure 14–23

14.5 Manipulate Patterns and Mirror Features

Suppress Patterns

To suppress a pattern, right-click on the pattern in the Model browser and select **Suppress Features**. To suppress individual pattern features, expand the pattern feature in the Model browser, right-click on the occurrence you want to suppress, and select **Suppress**, as shown in Figure 14–24.

Figure 14–24

- The suppressed occurrence displays in the Model browser with a line across it. To display this occurrence again, right-click on it and select **Suppress** again.

- You cannot suppress the first occurrence (original feature) of the pattern.

Edit Pattern

You can edit patterns and mirrored features at any time by right-clicking on the pattern or mirrored feature in the Model browser and selecting **Edit Feature**.

Delete Patterns

You can delete patterns and mirrored features at any time by right-clicking on the pattern or mirrored feature in the Model browser and selecting **Delete**. All occurrences of the pattern or mirrored feature are deleted except for the original occurrence.

Practice 14a | Pattern Features

Practice Objectives

- Create a rectangular pattern of features that translate along a single direction.
- Create a circular pattern of features that rotate about a selected axis.
- Create a rectangular pattern driven by a curve.

In this practice, you will pattern ribs and holes to create the model geometry shown in Figure 14–25.

Figure 14–25

Task 1 - Open a part file.

1. Open **Air-Box.ipt**. The model displays as shown in Figure 14–26.

Figure 14–26

Task 2 - Create a rectangular pattern.

1. In the Pattern panel, click ⊡ (Rectangular Pattern). The Rectangular Pattern dialog box opens, as shown in Figure 14–27.

Count field

Spacing field

Figure 14–27

2. Click (Features) to toggle it on (if not already active) and select **Rib1** and **Fillet4** in the Model browser.

3. Click (Direction 1) and select the YZ Plane in the Model browser. The pattern previews as shown in Figure 14–28.

If required, change the pattern direction by clicking .

Direction 1

Figure 14–28

4. Set the *Direction 1* in the ⟟ *(Count)* field to **10** and in the ◇ *(Spacing)* field, enter **110**.

5. Expand the drop-down list below the *Spacing* field and select **Distance**. This equally spaces the 10 occurrences over the 110 length.

6. A second direction is not required to create this pattern. Click **OK** to apply the pattern. The model displays as shown in Figure 14–29.

Figure 14–29

Task 3 - Create a circular pattern.

1. In the Pattern panel, click ⟟ (Circular Pattern). The Circular Pattern dialog box opens, as shown in Figure 14–30.

Figure 14–30

2. Verify that 🔲 (Features) is toggled on. Select the hole shown in Figure 14–31.

3. Click 🔲 (Rotation Axis) and select the central hole face for the axis, as shown in Figure 14–31.

Select this hole to pattern

Select this face as the Rotation Axis reference.

Figure 14–31

4. Enter **8** in the ⠿ *(Count)* field and accept the default (360deg) in the ◇ *(Angle)* field.

5. Click **OK**. The model displays as shown in Figure 14–32.

Figure 14–32

Task 4 - Create a second rectangular pattern driven by a curve.

In this task, you will create a rectangular pattern along the outside lip of the model, as shown in Figure 14–33. To accomplish this pattern a point and hole have been created for you, but you will create a curve that will be used to drive the path of the patterned hole.

Figure 14–33

1. Create a sketch and select the top edge of the model as the sketch plane, as shown in Figure 14–34. Project the outside edges that intersect this plane onto the sketch plane. Finish the sketch.

Select this top face as sketch plane for the new sketch. Project the outside edges onto the sketch plane.

Figure 14–34

2. In the Pattern panel, click ⌗ (Rectangular Pattern). The Rectangular Pattern dialog box opens.

3. Verify that ⬚ (Features) is toggled on. Select the hole shown in Figure 14–35.

Figure 14–35

4. Click [cursor icon] (Direction 1) and select the outer curve that was created in the sketch. Ensure that the entire curve around the model is selected, not just a single entity.

5. Set the *Direction 1* in the ••• *(Count)* field to **20**. The preview of the holes reveal an incorrect pattern.

6. For *Direction 1,* expand the Spacing drop-down list and select **Curve Length**. The preview of the holes still reveals an incorrect pattern. Customization of the additional options is required.

7. Click [>>] at the bottom of the dialog box to expand it.

It is recommended that you place the first occurrence on the start point of the path, as was done.

8. In the *Direction 1* area, click [cursor icon] (Start).

9. Select the vertex on the sketched curve, as shown in Figure 14–36, as the reference for the Start Direction. This sets the start point for the first patterned occurrence.

Figure 14–36

10. In the *Orientation* area, select **Direction1** to ensure that the orientation of the patterned holes follows the tangent vector of the curve that was selected as the Direction1 reference.

11. Click **OK** to complete the pattern. The model displays as shown in Figure 14–37.

Figure 14–37

12. Save the model and close the window.

Practice 14b | Mirror a Model

Practice Objectives

- Mirror select features to create required geometry.
- Mirror a solid part to duplicate all of its geometry.

In this practice, you will be provided with the model shown on the left in Figure 14–38. Using mirroring techniques you will create the model shown on the right.

Figure 14–38

Task 1 - Open a part file and mirror features.

1. Open **stand.ipt**.

2. In the Pattern panel, click ▯▯ (Mirror).

3. In the Model browser, select **Extrusion4** and **Fillet5**.

4. Click ▣ (Mirror Plane) and select **Work Plane1** as the mirror plane reference.

5. Click **OK** to mirror the features. The model displays as shown in Figure 14–39

Mirrored features →

Figure 14–39

Task 2 - Mirror the part.

1. In the Pattern panel, click ▯▯ (Mirror). The Mirror dialog box opens.

2. Click ▱ (Mirror solids) to mirror the entire part. The solid model highlights in the graphics window.

3. Click ▱ (Mirror Plane) and select the face indicated in Figure 14–40 to mirror the model about.

Select this face

Figure 14–40

4. Click **OK** to mirror the model, as shown on the left of Figure 14–41.

5. Complete the part by creating another mirror feature, as shown in Figure 14–41.

Figure 14–41

6. Save the part and close the window.

Practice 14c

Mirror Features

Practice Objectives

- Mirror features in a model to create the required geometry.
- Edit parent features in the model and ensure that all mirrored geometry updates as expected.

In this practice, you will mirror and edit features in the model shown on the left in Figure 14–42. The completed model displays as shown on the right.

Original Model

Completed Model

Figure 14–42

Task 1 - Open a part file and mirror features.

1. Open **Brace.ipt**.

2. In the Pattern panel, click ⬚⬚ (Mirror). Ensure that you are mirroring individual features and not the solid.

3. Select all of the solid features shown in Figure 14–43 using either the graphics window or the Model browser. Do not include **Extrusion1** in the mirror or the work features.

Mirror all of the features circled (except Extrusion1).

Figure 14–43

4. Click (Mirror Plane) and select the YZ Plane to mirror the features about.

5. Click **OK** to mirror the feature. The model displays as shown in Figure 14–44.

Figure 14–44

6. Mirror the same features and the Mirror instance about the XZ Plane. Note that by selecting the Mirror feature as the feature to be mirrored, all parent features are also automatically selected. The mirrored model displays as shown on the left of Figure 14–45.

7. Modify the height dimension on **Extrusion4** from *1.5 in* to **2 in** and update the model. The model displays as shown on the right of Figure 14–45. Both the original feature and its mirrored instances update.

Dimensional changes to the original model geometry update in all mirrored instances.

Final Mirrored Geometry

Figure 14–45

8. Save the model and close the window.

Chapter Review Questions

1. The direction references selected to create a rectangular feature pattern must be linear.

   a. True

   b. False

2. The model shown in Figure 14–46 has a pattern of extruded cuts created in one direction. What is the number of pattern occurrences that are defined in the dialog box?

   Figure 14–46

   a. 1

   b. 2

   c. 3

   d. 4

3. Which entities can be used as the rotation axis for a circular pattern? (Select all that apply.)

   a. Work Plane

   b. Edge

   c. Work Axis

   d. Cylindrical face

4. What should you do if the preview of your rectangular pattern is in the wrong direction along a selected path? (Select all that apply.)

   a. Select a new direction reference that is in the correct direction.

   b. Click the **Flip** direction icon in the Rectangular Pattern dialog box to change the direction.

   c. Enter a negative value as the *Spacing* value.

   d. Expand the additional options at the bottom of the dialog box and change the Compute method.

5. The sketch that defines the pattern points in a Sketch Driven Pattern must be created after the **Sketch Driven Pattern** command is initiated.

   a. True

   b. False

6. Which of the following statements are true for removing specific occurrences from within a pattern?

   a. You can suppress the first occurrence of the pattern (original).

   b. You can suppress all but the first occurrence of the pattern.

   c. You can select individual occurrences in the pattern for deletion.

   d. You can use the **Delete** command to delete the first occurrence in the model.

7. Which of the following are valid characteristics of patterned features, when using an Identical Compute method, as shown in Figure 14–47? (Select all that apply.)

Figure 14–47

   a. The created features cannot lie on different surfaces.

   b. The created features can break edges of the part.

   c. The created features cannot intersect with each other.

   d. Feature depth of all occurrences is the same value as the pattern leader (regardless of the depth option set for the feature).

8. Which work feature can be used as a reference for mirroring features?

   a. Work Plane

   b. Work Point

   c. Work Axis

9. You can mirror an entire solid or individual features in a model.

   a. True

   b. False

Command Summary

Button	Command	Location
⬨	**Circular Pattern (feature)**	• **Ribbon:** *3D Model* tab>Pattern panel
N/A	**Delete (entire pattern)**	• **Context Menu:** In Model browser
▷◁	**Mirror (feature)**	• **Ribbon:** *3D Model* tab>Pattern panel
⬚	**Rectangular Pattern (feature)**	• **Ribbon:** *3D Model* tab>Pattern panel
⬚	**Sketch Driven Pattern (feature)**	• **Ribbon:** *3D Model* tab>Pattern panel
N/A	**Suppress (pattern instance)**	• **Context Menu:** In Model browser
N/A	**Suppress Feature (pattern)**	• **Context Menu:** In Model browser

Feature Relationships

Feature relationships are defined as a dependency between features. They are established as you add each additional feature to the model. If the parent feature is modified or deleted, the child feature(s) are affected. Learning how to use feature relationships to your advantage and how to make changes to unwanted relationships is a valuable tool in designing models.

Learning Objectives in this Chapter

- Understand the parent/child relationships that are established when creating pick and place features.
- Understand the parent/child relationships that are established when creating sketched features.
- Use the Model browser and Parameters dialog box to recognize the possible relationships between features in the model.
- Use editing tools to change an existing parent/child relationship in a model.

15.1 Establishing Relationships

Feature relationships are the result of a dependency between features. The independent feature is referred to as the parent and the dependent feature is called the child. When such a dependency exists, the parent feature is used to place or locate the child feature. Feature relationships can be created when pick and place or sketched features are used.

Pick and Place Features

For pick and place features (e.g., holes, fillets, chamfers) you are only required to select placement references to locate a feature. The placement references establish feature relationships between the new feature and the existing features that were used for placement.

- In Figure 15–1, the hole shown on the right was created by referencing the indicated face and the center of the cylindrical extrusion. A feature relationship has now been established between the hole (child) an the cylindrical extrusion (parent).

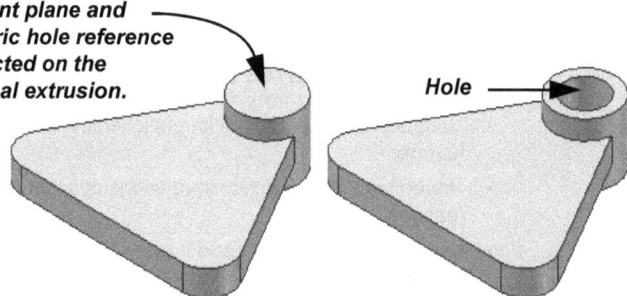

Placement plane and concentric hole reference are selected on the cylindrical extrusion.

Hole

Figure 15–1

- In Figure 15–2, the fillet shown on the right was created by referencing the edge shown. The edge reference establishes a feature relationship with the cylindrical extrusion. A feature relationship has now been established between the fillet (child) an the cylindrical extrusion (parent).

Fillet references this edge

Fillet

Figure 15–2

- In Figure 15–3, the chamfer shown on the right was created by referencing the edge shown. The edge reference establishes a feature relationship with the cylindrical extrusion. A feature relationship has now been established between the chamfer (child) an the cylindrical extrusion (parent).

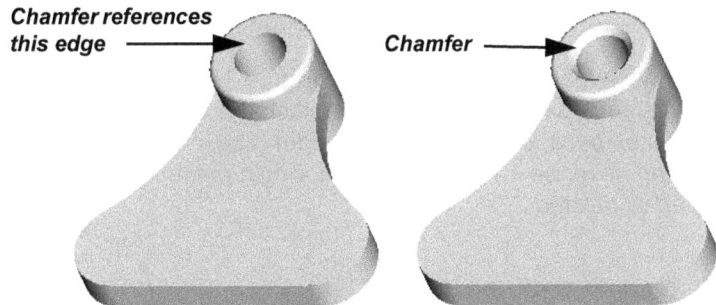

Figure 15–3

Sketched Features

The process of creating a sketched feature results in the creation of feature relationships when the sketch plane and sketch references are selected. Additionally, references might be required for using some of the available depth options.

Sketch Planes

The sketch plane defines a planar reference on which a 2D section is sketched. The sketch plane is then established as a parent of the 2D sketch and any features that are subsequently created from that sketch.

- In Figure 15–4, the sketch plane for a new sketched feature is a face belonging to an extrusion. This makes the new sketch and any feature created from the sketch a child of the extrusion.

Figure 15–4

Sketching References

Sketching references are used to locate sketched geometry. When you select sketching references, feature relationships are established. The sketched geometry is located with respect to these entities using dimensions and constraints. Sketching references can be projected origin or work features, or existing model edges and faces.

Origin work features provide robust sketching references because they can never be moved or deleted.

- In Figure 15–5, the origin planes (YZ and XZ planes) were projected onto the sketch plane for locating the sketch on the model. These references create a feature relationship with the origin plane features.

Figure 15–5

- In Figure 15–6, the cut was located relative to the edge of the square extrusion by assigning a dimension and vertical constraint. The cut is a child of the extrusion and remains in alignment. Additionally, the bottom edge of the base feature was also selected to locate the cut so the base feature is also a parent.

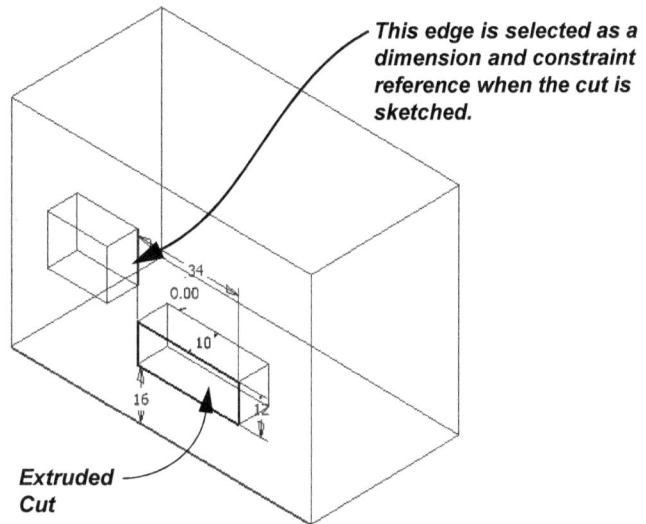

This edge is selected as a dimension and constraint reference when the cut is sketched.

Extruded Cut

Figure 15–6

- In Figure 15–7, the rectangular sketch was located by dimensioning it to the hole and the chamfer. The features created with this sketch are now a child of both the hole and the chamfer.

The rectangular sketch is dimensioned to the center of the hole and the chamfered edge.

Rectangular Sketch

Figure 15–7

It is not recommended that you dimension a feature to another feature that might change later in the design (e.g., fillets or chamfers). If the reference feature is changed or deleted, the new feature might no longer be positioned correctly, or it might fail because it has lost its reference.

Certain geometry creation tools, such as offsetting an existing edge, create an implicit alignment and therefore establish feature relationships.

- In Figure 15–8, the entities at the bottom of the base extrusion are selected as edge references for offsetting. As a result, the new feature is a child of the base feature.

A feature relationship would also have been established if concentric arcs were used to create the feature.

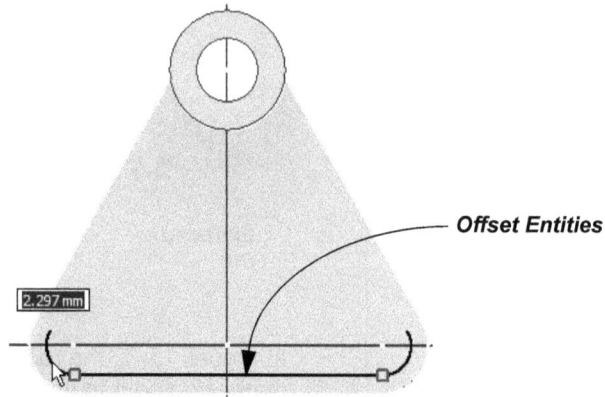

Figure 15–8

Depth Options

Some depth options establish feature relationships. The options shown in Figure 15–9 establish feature relationships because a plane or face is required to be selected as a reference to define the depth.

Depth options can create feature relationships between the new geometry and the reference geometry.

Figure 15–9

15.2 Controlling Relationships

Feature relationships can make models more robust and powerful. Use the following tips to control feature relationships:

- Use the origin features. Since they are never deleted, origin features are useful as sketch planes and sketching references. This establishes the origin feature, rather than a geometry feature, as parents of future features.

- Consider a face carefully before selecting it as a sketch plane. Is it the best selection as a parent for this feature?

- When in the Sketch environment, select references and project from the model in a 3D orientation to ensure that you are selecting the correct references.

- When in the Sketch environment, consider using and offsetting edges, as well as sketching concentric arcs and circles to establish relationships.

- Carefully consider the references before using the **To Next**, **To**, **Between**, or **Distance from Face** depth options. Is this reference the best selection as a parent for this feature?

- Once a pick and place or sketched feature has been created, you can also establish a feature relationship using equations.

15.3 Investigating Relationships

In many cases, you might be required to continue someone else's design or make modifications to a completed model. In such cases, it is important to know how to investigate the model to help understand the existing design and feature relationships. You can use the Model browser and Parameters dialog box to accomplish this.

Model Browser

The Model browser displays all of the features in the model. By reviewing the Model browser, you can understand the hierarchy of the model and understand which features can possibly reference others.

To provide a better overview of the relationships between features, you can right-click on a feature name in the Model browser and select **Relationships**. The Relationships dialog box displays, similar to that shown in Figure 15–10. This dialog box can quickly reveal the relationships between features and enable you to make changes, if required.

*To select features directly in the Graphics Window, ensure that **Select Features** is the active option in the selection filter list.*

The Parents area lists all parent features of the selected feature.

The currently selected feature is listed here.

The Children area lists all child features of the selected feature.

Figure 15–10

- ⟳ **(Make Selected):** Enables you to sets any of the parent or child features as the new selected item.

- ✎ **(Edit Feature):** Enables you to access the Edit Feature dialog box for any of the parent or child features.

Equations

Equations are used in models to control design intent. In doing so, they establish feature relationships. You can use the Parameters dialog box to investigate if equations exist in the model. To open the dialog box, in the *Manage* tab>Parameters panel, click f_x (Parameters) or in the Quick Access Toolbar, click f_x (Parameters). Any existing relationships display in the *Equation* column, as shown in Figure 15–11.

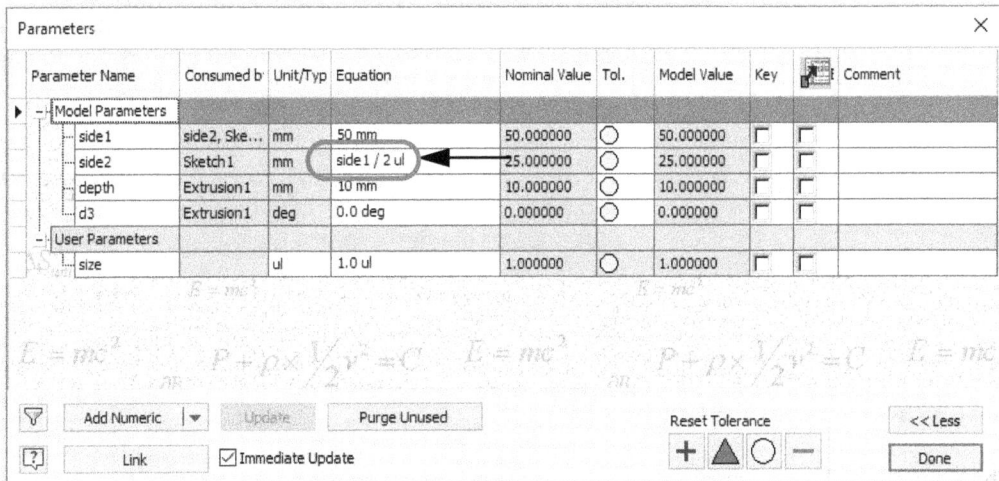

Parameter Name	Consumed b	Unit/Typ	Equation	Nominal Value	Tol.	Model Value	Key	🖼	Comment
Model Parameters									
side1	side2, Ske...	mm	50 mm	50.000000	○	50.000000	☐	☐	
side2	Sketch1	mm	side1 / 2 ul	25.000000	○	25.000000	☐	☐	
depth	Extrusion1	mm	10 mm	10.000000	○	10.000000	☐	☐	
d3	Extrusion1	deg	0.0 deg	0.000000	○	0.000000	☐	☐	
User Parameters									
size		ul	1.0 ul	1.000000	○	1.000000	☐	☐	

Add Numeric ▼   Update   Purge Unused   Reset Tolerance   << Less
Link   ☑ Immediate Update   + ▲ ○ −   Done

Figure 15–11

15.4 Changing Relationships

When the design intent of the model changes, unwanted relationships might occur as a result of modifying or deleting a parent feature. The goal of making a design change is to ensure that not only the feature being changed is modified, but that any children update as expected. Consider using the following editing tools when changes to parent/child dependency are required: **Edit Sketch**, **Redefine**, **Show Dimensions**, **Dimension Display**, **Edit Feature**, and **Delete**.

- **Edit Sketch:** Enables you to access the Sketch environment to define new references or sketch elements.

- **Redefine:** Enables you to change the sketch plane of an existing sketch.

- **Show Dimensions** and **Dimension Display:** Enable you to display feature dimensions and equation relationships in the graphics window. Double-click on the dimensions to change dimensional values or equations in the Edit Dimension dialog box.

- **Edit Feature:** Enables you to access the dialog box that was used when the feature was created. You can define new references or elements in this dialog box.

- **Delete:** Enables you to delete a selected feature by pressing <Delete> or right-clicking and selecting **Delete**. When deleting a feature with children, the Delete Features dialog box opens (as shown in Figure 15–12) which requires you to decide how child features should be handled during deletion.

  - Colors in the dialog box match the colors of the highlighted dependent items in the graphics window.
  - You can clear the options in the Delete Features dialog box (e.g., **consumed sketches and features**, **dependent sketches and features**, etc.) to maintain dependent features and preserve sketches in the model after deletion.

- Ensure that missing child references (identified by ⓘ in the Model browser) are fixed after a feature is deleted.

Delete Features

Additionally delete

☑ consumed sketches and features.

☑ dependent sketches and features.

☑ dependent work features.

OK   Cancel

Figure 15–12

Hint: Missing Sketch Planes

When deleting a feature that also removes the sketch plane of another feature, a Work Plane is automatically created in the model to replace the deleted sketch plane. The new Work Plane is fixed relative to the coordinate system. It is recommended that you replace the Work Plane and redefine the sketch plane to a reference that is relative to the model geometry.

Practice 15a | Change Feature Relationships

Practice Objective

- Use editing tools to efficiently change existing parent/child relationships in a model.

In this practice, you will open the model shown on the left in Figure 15–13 and delete the hole and chamfer. In deleting these features the Delete Features dialog box opens, indicating any relationships to these features. You will deal with these relationships to create the model shown on the right.

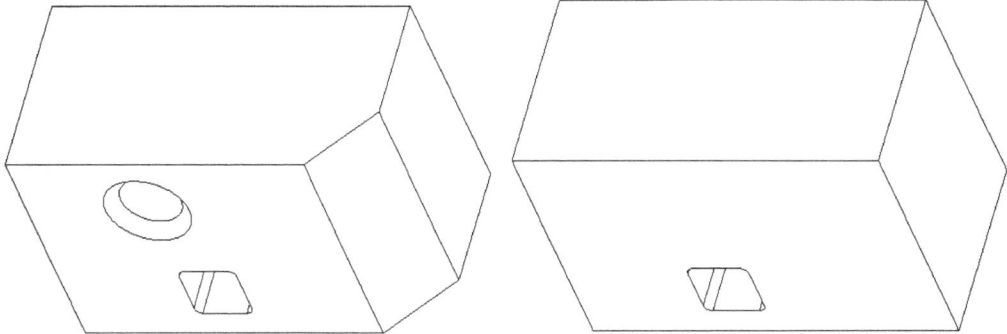

Figure 15–13

Task 1 - Open and investigate a part.

1. Open **pc01.ipt**.

2. Review the Model browser to understand the hierarchy of the model and understand which features can reference others.

3. Display the dimensions associated with **Extrusion2** (square cut) to review its dimensioning scheme. The square cut is located with respect to **Chamfer1** and **Hole1** (dimensioned to the center of the hole and the edge of the chamfer).

4. Modify both **Chamfer1** dimensions to **5.00**. The model before the chamfer dimensions are modified is shown on the left in Figure 15–14, and the model after modifications are finished is shown on the right. The cut has moved to the right as a result of modifying the chamfer. Is this the design intent? Why is it generally not a good idea to dimension the edges created by features, such as fillets and chamfers?

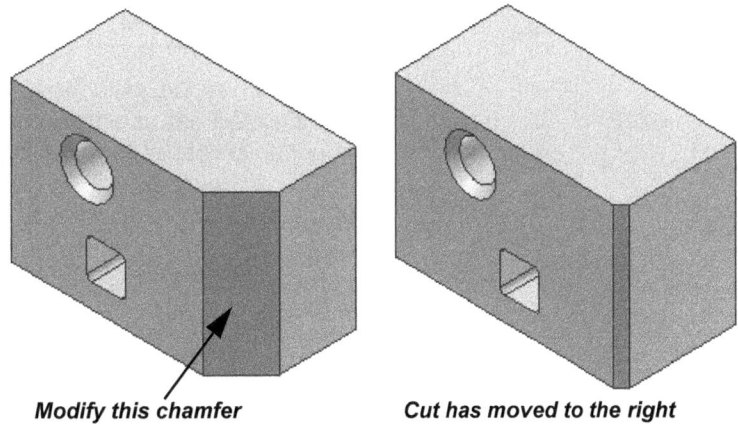

Modify this chamfer   **Cut has moved to the right**

Figure 15–14

Task 2 - Redefine the location of the cut.

1. Edit the sketch for **Extrusion2**. You need to re-dimension the cut.

2. Delete the **50** dimension that locates the cut to the chamfer.

3. The cut is now under-constrained. Add a dimension from the cut to the vertical edge on the left side of the model, as shown in Figure 15–15.

Add this dimension

Figure 15–15

4. Finish the sketch.

5. Delete **Chamfer1**. The Delete Features dialog box opens. The Model browser indicates that **Hole1** and **Extrusion2** are placed on the face that is affected by a chamfer. This face still exists after the chamfer is deleted. Click **OK** in the dialog box. Is the square cut affected?

Task 3 - Delete the hole.

1. Right-click on **Hole1** in the Model browser and select **Delete**. The Delete Features dialog box opens, indicating that the hole has children (dependent sketches and features), as shown in Figure 15–16. To delete the hole, you must fix the references for the dependent feature (square cut).

Delete Features

Additionally delete

☑ consumed sketches and features.

☑ dependent sketches and features.

☐ dependent work features.

[?]   OK   Cancel

Figure 15–16

2. Click **Cancel** to close the Delete Features dialog box and cancel the delete action.

3. Edit the sketch for **Extrusion2**. Re-dimension the cut from the top edge of the base feature instead of from the center of the hole.

4. Finish the sketch.

5. Right-click on **Hole1** in the Model browser and select **Delete**. The Delete Feature dialog box opens, indicating that the hole has referenced consumed sketches and features.

6. The sketch and chamfer do not need to exist without the hole. Click **OK** to delete both features.

7. Save the part and close the window.

Practice 15b

Delete a Sketch Plane

Practice Objective

• Use the Delete Features dialog box such that the dependent sketches and features are not deleted with its parent geometry.

In this practice, you will delete a feature and observe how it affects the sketch plane of another feature. The final model displays in Figure 15–17.

Figure 15–17

Task 1 - Open a part file.

1. Open **redefine.ipt**. The model displays as shown in Figure 15–18.

Figure 15–18

2. Edit the sketch for **Extrusion3**. Note that the sketch for the cut is placed on the top face of **Extrusion2**.

3. Finish the sketch.

Task 2 - Delete Extrusion2.

1. Select **Extrusion2** in the Model browser and press <Delete>. The Delete Features dialog box opens as shown in Figure 15–19, indicating that the highlighted features (**Extrusion2**, **Extrusion3**, and **Sketch3**) will also be deleted. However, the design intent is to maintain the cut.

The colors in the dialog box match the highlighted dependent sketches and feature colors in the graphics window.

Delete Features

Additionally delete

☑ consumed sketches and features.

☑ dependent sketches and features.

☐ dependent work features.

OK   Cancel

Figure 15–19

2. Clear the **dependent sketches and features** option.

3. Click **OK** to delete the **Extrusion2** sketch. The model displays as shown in Figure 15–20 with **Work Plane1** created automatically in place of the deleted face. The sketch was automatically transferred to **Work Plane1** when the original sketch plane was deleted.

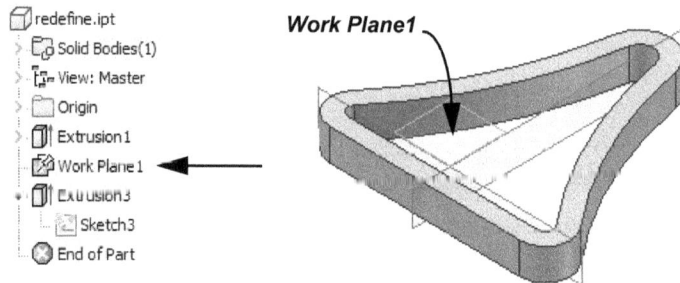

- redefine.ipt
- Solid Bodies(1)
- View: Master
- Origin
- Extrusion1
- Work Plane1
- Extrusion3
- Sketch3
- End of Part

Work Plane1

Figure 15–20

4. It is recommended that you redefine the placement plane of the sketch to select a more stable reference that will truly reflect the geometry. Right-click on **Sketch3** and select **Redefine**. Select the face of **Extrusion1** as the new sketch plane. Delete **Work Plane1**.

5. Save the model and close the window.

Chapter Review Questions

1. A pick and place feature can be the parent of another pick and place feature.

   a. True

   b. False

2. Which of the following actions creates a feature relationship when sketching a feature? (Select all that apply.)

   a. Selecting the sketching plane.

   b. Selecting sketching references.

   c. Creating an offset entity.

   d. Using an existing edge to create a new entity.

   e. Dimensioning the length of a line.

   f. Aligning a new entity with an existing entity.

   g. Extruding to a Blind depth.

   h. Extruding through all surfaces.

   i. Extruding to intersect with a selected face or plane.

3. Which of the following features create a parent/child relationship when created in a model? (Select all that apply.)

   a. Origin Planes

   b. Work Planes

   c. Extrude

   d. Hole

   e. Chamfer

   f. Fillet

   g. Shell

4. Which of the following processes of creating a sketched feature results in the creation of feature relationships? (Select all that apply.)

   a. Selecting sketch planes.

   b. Selecting sketching references.

   c. Selecting depth options.

5. If a parent feature is deleted, which of the following options can be used to change the references to the child feature? (Select all that apply.)

   a. **Edit Sketch**

   b. **Share Sketch**

   c. **Redefine**

   d. **Edit Feature**

6. The Delete Features dialog box opens if you select and delete the hole shown in Figure 15–21. Which of the following best describes why this dialog box becomes available?

— Delete this hole

Figure 15–21

   a. Because the Delete Features dialog box opens when deleting all of the pick and place feature types.

   b. Because a chamfer was placed on the edge generated by the creation of the hole.

   c. Because there are other pick and place features in the model and you need to select the other ones to delete at the same time.

   d. Because the hole was placed as a Coaxial hole and is a child to the extruded cylinder.

7. The (Make Selected) icon the Relationships dialog box only enables you to change the active feature to a listed parent feature. You cannot use it to activate a child.

   a. True

   b. False

Sketching Options

This appendix provides a detailed summary of the options that you can use on the Sketch Ribbon to create a sketch.

A.1 Sketch Geometry Creation Options

All of the sketch geometry creation options are located in the *Sketch* tab>Create panel. Expand the commands to locate all of the options. A summarized list of the available sketch creation options is as follows.

(Line)	Creates straight lines or arced segments. Select two points to create a line. Selecting a third point creates a line between the second and third point. To sketch an arc, press and drag an arced entity from the end point of a line.

Line

Arc segment

(Spline (Control Vertex))	Enables you to sketch a free-form curve. Select multiple points to create the spline. Each point that is placed defines the vertices of the control frame.
(Spline (Interpolation))	Enables you to sketch a free-form curve. Select multiple points to create the spline. The spline is drawn through each point.
(Equation Curve)	Draws a curve based on the entry of an equation.
(Bridge Curve)	Draws a smooth G2 curve between two selected entities.
(Circle (Center Point))	Creates a circle by selecting its center point and a point on its perimeter.
(Circle (Tangent))	Creates a circle based on three lines that you select. The circle is tangent to all three lines. There might be more than one circle that can be drawn for any three given lines. You can control which circle displays, based on where you select the lines. Select the line near the locations at which the circle should touch.

(Ellipse)	Creates an ellipse based on its center, and one point on each of its major and minor axes.
(Arc (Three Point))	Draws an arc based on three points that you select. First select the two end points, then select a point on the arc. The last point determines the center, radius, and included angle of the arc.
(Arc (Tangent))	Draws an arc tangent to an existing line or an arc. Select the end of the line or arc as the start point. The arc is drawn tangent to the selected object. Complete the arc by selecting a second point. When the first point is selected, the object to which the arc is tangent is highlighted in red, and a green dot displays at its end point.
(Arc (Center Point))	Enables you to select three points to draw the arc. The first point determines the center of the arc and the other two points determine the ends of the arc. You can select the end points in either order. After selecting the first point, move the mouse in the direction in which the arc should be drawn.
(Rectangle (Two Point))	Creates a rectangle with its sides parallel to the X- and Y-axes. Select two opposite corners to create the rectangle.
(Rectangle (Three Point))	Creates a rectangle at any angle. Select three points to create the rectangle. The first two points that you select define one side and the third point locates the opposite side.
(Rectangle (Two Point Center))	Creates a rectangle along the X and Y axis. Select two points to create the rectangle. The first point defines the center of the rectangle and the second point defines the outer corner.
(Rectangle (Three Point Center))	Creates a rectangle at any angle. Select three points to create the rectangle. The first two points define one side and the third point locates the center.
(Slot (Center to Center))	Draws a slot by selecting three points. The first two points define the entire length of the slot between its centers, and the third selection defines the slot's thickness.
(Slot (Overall))	Draws a slot by selecting three points. The first two points define the entire length of the slot and the third selection defines the slot's thickness.
(Slot (Center Point))	Draws a slot by selecting three points. Select the center point of the slot, followed by the center point of one arc and finally select a point to define the slot's thickness.

(Slot (Three Point Arc))	Draws a slot by selecting four points. The first three points define the arc length and radius of the slot and the fourth selection defines the slot's thickness.
(Slot (Center Point Arc))	Draws a slot by selecting four points. The first three points define the center point of the arc, its arc length and radius of the slot. The fourth selection defines the slot's thickness.
(Polygon)	Draws regular polygons, where all sides and all angles are the same. Like rectangles, polygons can be drawn with a series of lines, but it is easier to draw using this specialized command. There are two options for drawing polygons: **Inscribed** and **Circumscribed**. **Inscribed** uses a vertex between the two edges to determine the size and orientation of the polygon. **Circumscribed** uses the midpoint of an edge to determine the size and orientation of the polygon.

(Chamfer)	Adds an angled corner. The size of the chamfer is determined by distances along each line from their intersection, or by a distance and an angle.
(Fillet)	Adds an arc to create a rounded corner, and dimensions the arc. The 2D Fillet dialog box enables you to specify the radius of the fillet.
(Point)	Adds points to the sketch.

A.2 Sketch Editing Options

All of the sketch editing options are located in the *Sketch* tab>
Modify and Pattern panels. A summarized list of the available
options is as follows.

(Move)	Moves objects more precisely and enables you to copy sketch entities.
(Trim)	Removes the segment to the nearest intersection in each direction from the point selected. If an intersection only occurs in one direction, the end of an object is removed. If intersections occur in both directions, the center of the object is removed.
(Scale)	Enlarges or reduces the size of sketched entities by entering a scale factor as a multiplier.
(Copy)	Copies source entities to one or more new locations in the sketch. No relationship is established between the newly copied entities and the source.
(Extend)	Continues an object to meet the next object in its path or to close an open sketch.
(Stretch)	Stretches sketched entities. It enables you to stretch constrained geometry while maintaining its constraints. The select-and-drag technique cannot be used to manipulate constrained geometry.
(Rotate)	Rotates objects at a specified angle. You have the option of making a copy of the objects while rotating them.
(Split)	Splits an entity (line, arc, or spline) based on an intersecting entity (entity, work plane, or surface).
(Offset)	Creates parallel shapes with another object tool.
(Rectangular Pattern)	Creates copies of entities in two directions. The directions do not need to be perpendicular to each other.
(Circular Pattern)	Creates copies of entities about an axis.
(Mirror)	Copies entities across a center line.

A.3 Sketch Constraint Options

All of the sketch constraint options are located in the *Sketch* tab> Constrain panel. A summarized list of the available constraints that is as follows.

(Coincident)	Makes two selected points coincident. If the centers of two circles, arcs, or ellipses are selected, the objects become concentric. If a point and an object are selected, the point lies on the object or along the extension of the object.
(Collinear)	Makes selected entities lie on the same line.
(Concentric)	Makes selected arcs, circles, or ellipses have the same center point.
(Fix)	Fixes a selected point or object relative to the default coordinate system (Sketch environment 0,0,0).
(Parallel)	Makes two selected entities parallel to each other. This constraint can be applied between two lines or ellipse axes.
(Perpendicular)	Makes two selected entities perpendicular to each other. This constraint can be applied between two lines or ellipse axes.
(Horizontal)	Makes a line horizontal or aligns two selected points horizontally.
(Vertical)	Makes a line vertical or aligns two selected points vertically.
(Tangent)	Makes the selected items tangent. The objects do not need to touch to be tangent.
(Smooth (G2))	Makes selected entities continuous in curvature.
(Symmetric)	Makes selected lines or points symmetric about a reference line. To apply this constraint, select the first line or point, select the second line or point, and select the line of symmetry.
(Equal)	Makes selected lines the same length or all of the selected circles and arcs the same radius.
(Edit Coordinate System) (Constrain panel drop-down list)	Moves or rotates the coordinate system to any location on the sketch plane.

A.4 Dimension Type Options

A summarized list of the dimensioning types that can be used to constrain a sketch is as follows.

Linear	Select the entities to dimension. Move the cursor to the required location for the dimension and place the dimension using the left mouse button.	
Center	Select two entities. Move the cursor to the required location and place the dimension using the left mouse button. To place an aligned dimension, place the dimension at a point along a line that joins the two entities that are being dimensioned. An aligned icon ( ) displays. Click the left mouse button, move the cursor to the required location, and click the left mouse button again. An aligned dimension displays. You can also right-click and select the location for the dimension when you are placing it.	
Arc Length	Select the arc, right-click, and select **Dimension Type>Arc Length** and then place the dimension.	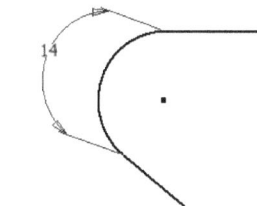

Radius/ Diameter	Circles default to a diameter dimension. An arc defaults to a radius dimension.	
	To dimension a circle with a radial dimension, right-click and select **Radius**. Move the cursor to the required location and place the dimension using the left mouse button.	
	Use the same technique to dimension an arc with a diameter dimension. Right-click and select **Diameter**.	
Angular	Select lines **A** and **B** and place the dimension using the left mouse button. The resulting angle depends on the placement location of the dimension.	
Tangent	Select arc **A** and move the cursor onto arc **B** so that ⌀ displays. Select arc **B** and place the dimension using the left mouse button.	
Revolved	Sketch half of the cross-section of a revolved feature. The diameter dimensions are created by selecting the center line of the revolved cross-section and then selecting the geometry, right-clicking, and selecting **Linear Diameter**.	

Primitive Base Features

Base features can be created in two ways. You can use a workflow that creates a sketch using the *Sketch* tab and then use the feature creation controls to create solid geometry. Alternatively, you can select from a list of predefined Primitive types that refine the workflow process by initiating the sketch entity and feature types for you.

Learning Objective for this Appendix

- Create a base feature using Primitive features.

B.1 Primitive Base Features

Primitive features can also be used as secondary features.

A set of four primitive features; **Box**, **Cylinder**, **Sphere**, and **Torus** are provided to enable you to create these standard 3D shapes quickly and easily. These commands bundle together many of the steps that are completed manually when sketching a base feature so that they are done for you. Figure B–1 shows examples of the primitive features.

| *Box Primitive* | *Cylinder Primitive* | *Sphere Primitive* | *Torus Primitive* |

Figure B–1

Use the following steps to create a primitive base feature:

1. Select the Primitive type.
2. Define the sketch plane.
3. Sketch the extent of the Primitive.
4. Define the depth and direction, if required.
5. Complete the feature.

Step 1 - Select the Primitive type.

By default, the Primitives panel is not displayed in the ribbon. Right-click on the ribbon and select **Show Panels>Primitives** to add the panel.

To create a primitive, select a type in the *3D Model* tab> Primitives panel. The available types include ⬛ (Box), ⬛ (Cylinder), ⚪ (Sphere), and ⊙ (Torus). The Primitives panel always displays the last accessed type.

- If the required type is not displayed on the Primitives panel, click ▼ under the current option and select the required type in the expanded drop-down list.

Step 2 - Define the sketch plane.

Similar to a sketched base feature, you can select the sketch plane before selecting the primitive type.

Once the primitive type command has been activated, you can select the sketch plane from the Model browser or from the temporarily displayed origin planes in the graphics window.

Step 3 - Sketch the extent of the Primitive.

The model is reoriented into a 2D view and you are prompted to sketch the geometry. The required steps to sketch the geometry are dependent on the type of primitive being created. In all cases, if you fully place the geometry without using the dynamic input fields, the primitive is created without a 2D dimension scheme. To assign a dimension scheme you need to return to the sketch and edit it to add dimensions. The procedure to sketch and include dimensions for each type, is as follows:

Box	Click to place the start point of the box. Do not click again to place the opposite corner of the box. Enter a value in the highlighted dynamic input field (do not press <Enter>), press <Tab>, and enter a value in the next dynamic input field to fully define the size of the box. Press <Enter> to complete the box.
Cylinder	Click to place the center point of the cylinder. Do not click again to place the outer extent of the circle. Enter a value in the dynamic input field for the diameter of the circle and press <Enter>.
Sphere	Click to place the center point for the sphere. Do not click again to place the outer extent of the sphere. Enter a value in the dynamic input field for the diameter of the sphere and press <Enter>.
Torus	Click to place the center point of the torus. Do not click again to place the outer extent of the torus. Enter a value in the dynamic input field for the outer diameter of the torus and press <Enter>. Enter another value in the next dynamic input field for the diameter of the torus geometry and press <Enter>.

Step 4 - Define the depth and direction, if required.

Box and Cylinder primitives are created using the Extrude feature whereas Sphere and Torus primitives are created using the Revolve feature.

Once you have pressed <Enter> to finalize the final dimension of the primitive, the feature's dialog box, mini-toolbar, and a model preview are displayed, as shown in Figure B–2 for the Sphere primitive.

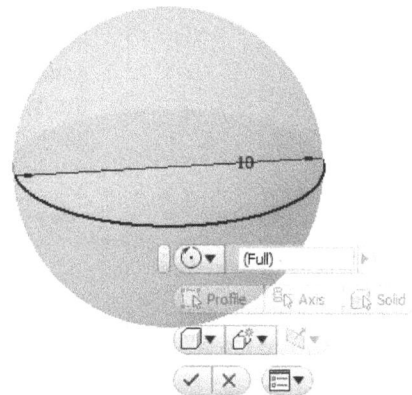

Figure B–2

The sketch is automatically selected as the profile and, in the case of the Sphere and Torus primitives, it also assumes the reference axis to revolve the geometry. The Box and Cylinder primitives enable you to further define the depth and direction of the feature. This is done by either working in the dialog box or in the mini-toolbar, as shown in Figure B–3.

The Depth and Direction can be defined in either the dialog box or mini-toolbar.

Figure B–3

Step 5 - Complete the feature.

Click **OK** or ✓ to complete the primitive base feature and close the dialog box and mini-toolbar. Alternatively, right-click and select **OK (Enter)** or press <Enter>. The Model browser updates to list either the Extrude or Revolve feature.

Hint: Adding Dimensions

If you place the sketch of the primitives without using the dynamic input, the resulting primitive sketch does not contain dimensions. To add dimensions or assign specific constraints, right-click on the feature in the Model browser or in the graphics window and select **Edit Sketch**.

Practice B1 | Creating a Primitive

Practice Objectives

- Create a new part model using a predefined template.
- Create a Box primitive as the base feature.
- Sketch the extent of the required primitive shape so that dimensions are automatically assigned.
- Define the depth and direction options to complete the primitive feature.

In this practice, you will use a primitive shape to create a base feature in a new part file. The final geometry in the model is shown in Figure B–4.

Figure B–4

Task 1 - Create a new part model and sketch its geometry.

1. Create a new part file using the standard metric (mm) template.

2. If the primitives panel is not displayed in the ribbon, right-click on the ribbon and select **Show Panels>Primitives**.

3. In the *3D Model* tab>Primitives panel, click ⬚ (Box). The Origin planes are temporarily displayed.

4. Select the XY Plane in the Model browser or graphics window. The plane is reoriented into a 2D orientation to sketch the geometry. Note that you are still in the *3D Model* tab and not in the *Sketch* tab.

By default, the Origin Center Point is projected onto the XY sketch plane. However, because you are not in the *Sketch* tab, you cannot project any further reference entities or create any explicit constraints or dimensions.

5. Start the sketch by moving the cursor to the projected Center Point, as shown in Figure B–5, and click to place the point.

6. Move the cursor to the approximate point shown in Figure B–5 to define the extent of the box, but DO NOT click.

Start the box here

11.736 mm

17.878 mm

Select corner

Drag cursor to this approximate location but do not click.

Figure B–5

7. The dynamic entry field for the horizontal dimension is active. Enter **30**. Do not press <Enter>.

8. Press <Tab> to activate the dynamic entry field for the vertical dimension.

9. Enter **10** and press <Enter> to complete the section. The dimensions display on the sketch. The only control over the location of the box is relative to the projected Center Point.

10. The model is reoriented into its default orientation and the Extrude dialog box, mini-toolbar, and a model preview are displayed, similar to that shown in Figure B–6. The section is automatically set as the *Profile* and has been extruded to a default depth.

*By Default, the display of the Mini-Toolbar is toggled off. To toggle on its display, on the View tab, expand **User Interface** and enable the **Mini-Toolbar** option on the list of interface items.*

Figure B–6

Do not press <Enter> after typing the depth value. After typing the value, pause for a few seconds and the model will update with your changes.

11. A default depth value and direction is assigned for the Box primitive. Set the depth to **15**. This can be entered in the Extrude dialog box or in the mini-toolbar.

12. Once a value has been entered, right-click and select

    OK (ENTER) or click 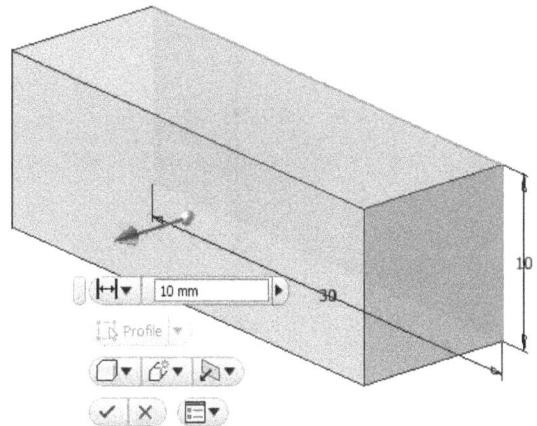 in the mini-toolbar. Alternatively, click **OK** in the feature dialog box.

13. Hover the cursor over the ViewCube and click (Home) to return to the model to its default 3D orientation. The model displays as shown in Figure B–7.

Figure B–7

14. Save the file as **Primitive_Box** and close it.

Additional Practices I

This appendix provides additional practices that can be used to review some of the functionality that was previously covered.

Practice C1 | Part Creation

Practice Objective

- Use the required features to create the models shown in the provided image.

In this practice you are provided images of part models that you are to create using the feature creation techniques that you have learned in this student guide. Minimal instruction is provided.

Task 1 - Create the parts provided.

1. Create the part files shown in Figure C–1 using the standard metric (mm) template. The dimensions of these parts have been omitted to help you understand that the software is a design tool. Once the model has been built, dimensions can be modified as required. Remember the perceived design intent of the model while building the parts.

Figure C–1

2. Create the model shown in Figure C–2 using the standard English (in) template and the dimensions shown.

Figure C–2

3. Create a new part file using the standard English (in) template. Create the part as shown in Figure C–3.

    •   As the starting point, create the triangular sketch first and then extrude it. Use work features to assist in creating the remaining geometry.
    •   To create the Ø.50 peg with a single extrusion, sketch the profile on a work plane located below the bottom face of the part.
    •   The bottom of the circular hole is not visible in the Isometric Home view shown in Figure C–3.

Consider renaming the work features as you work through the practice to help identify their purpose in the model.

Figure C–3

4. Create the new part shown in Figure C–4 using the standard metric (mm) template.

Figure C–4

5. Create the new part shown in Figure C–5 using the standard metric (mm) template.

Figure C–5

6. Create a new part called **hubguard** using the standard metric (mm) template. Create the extrusion so that it displays in the Isometric Home view as shown in the upper right corner in Figure C–6.

SECTION A-A
SCALE 1 : 1

Figure C–6

7. Create a new part called **chamfer** (as shown in Figure C–7), using the standard metric (mm) template. Consider the following design intent suggestions when creating feature relationships:

- Should the holes be revolved sketched cuts or holes?
- Should the holes be created as individual features?
- Is there an easy duplication technique that can be used to ensure that all of the holes are dependent on one another?

Figure C–7

8. Create the part shown in Figure C–8 using the standard metric (mm) template. Use sweep features as required.

SCALE 1.50 : 1

SCALE 1.50 : 1

R25
R30
R5
R10

SECTION B-B
SCALE 1.50 : 1

Part13

Figure C–8

9. Create a new part using the standard metric part template. Model the geometry so that the completed model displays as shown in Figure C–9. The overall diameter of the model is 60mm and its height is 30mm. To design the remainder of the model, use a dimensioning scheme and dimensions that are appropriate.

Figure C–9

*A complete model (**Housing.ipt**) has been included in your practice files for you to review, if required.*

Hint: The small holes around the exterior are tapped with the following thread type:

- ANSI Metric M Profile

- Size 4

- Class 6H

- Designation M4x0.7

- Right Handed

Practice C2

Creating a Sweep and Loft

Practice Objective

- Open the provided model and create additional sweep and loft features.

In this practice, you will add sweep and loft geometry to the part shown on the left in Figure C–10. The completed model is shown on the right.

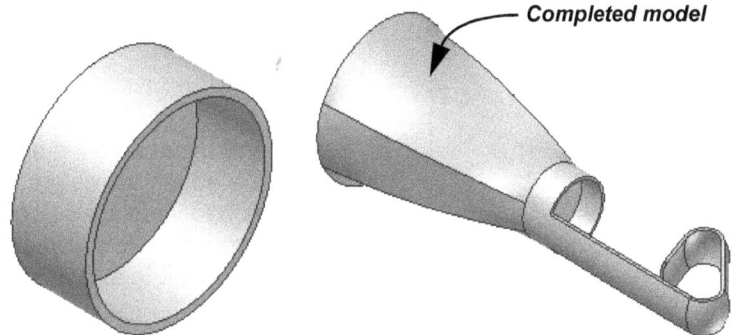

Figure C–10

Task 1 - Open a part file.

1. Open **project.ipt**.

Task 2 - Create the sweep profile.

In this task, you will create the sweep feature shown in Figure C–11.

Figure C–11

1. Right-click on the thin surface of the model shown in Figure C–11 and select **New Sketch**. The sketch displays as shown in Figure C–12.

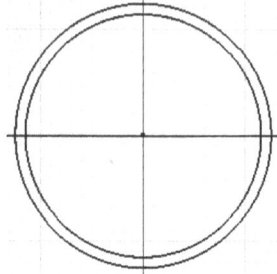

Figure C–12

2. Sketch and dimension the section as shown in Figure C–13. Project the edges as required. Ensure that the end points of both sketched lines are coincident with the edges of the sketch plane. Create a vertical construction line through the center and use it to add a Symmetry constraint for the two sketched lines.

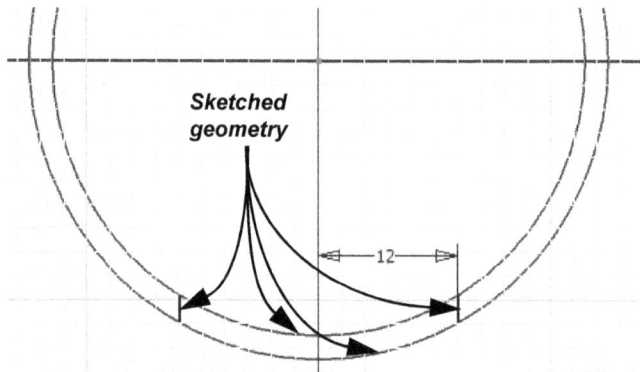

Sketched geometry

Figure C–13

3. Finish the sketch.

Task 3 - Create a sweep path.

1. Create a work plane through the line shown in Figure C–14 and at **180** degrees to the XY Plane. The work plane displays as shown in Figure C–14.

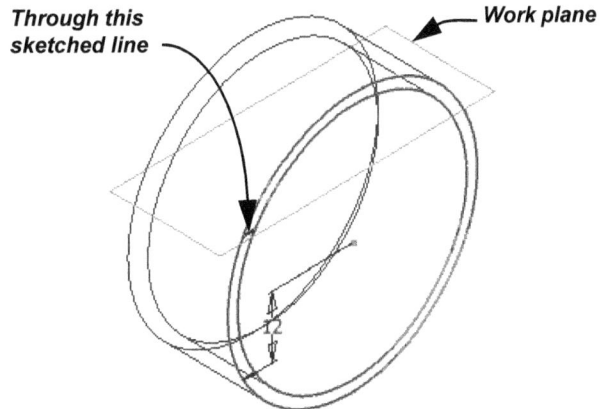

Through this sketched line — *Work plane*

Figure C–14

2. Right-click on the new work plane in the Model browser and select **New Sketch**. The sketch displays as shown in Figure C–15.

Figure C–15

3. Project the end point of the line shown in Figure C–16 onto the sketch plane.

Project the end point of this line

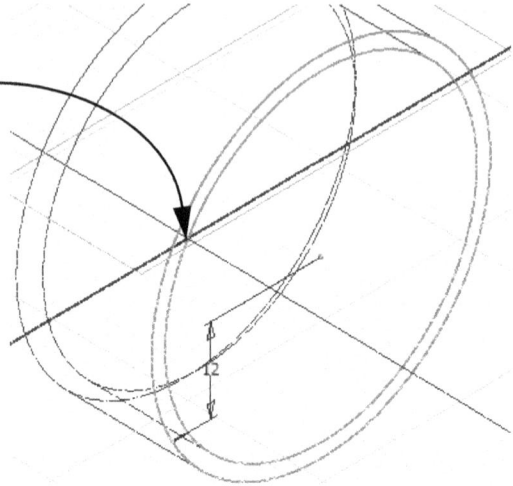

Figure C–16

4. In the Navigation bar, click ⬚ (Look At) and select the work plane you created in the Model browser. The sketch displays as shown Figure C–17.

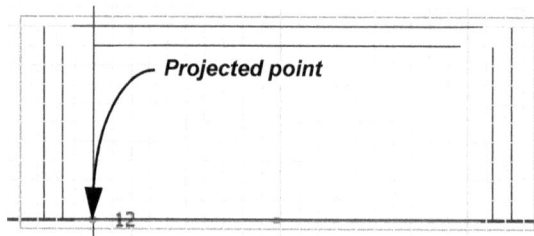

Projected point

12

Figure C–17

5. Sketch and dimension the section as shown in Figure C–18. The two arcs have the same radius. Start the geometry from the projected point. Reorient the sketch using the ViewCube if your orientation is different than that shown in Figure C–18. The start point of the sweep must be located at the intersection of the planes for the profile and path.

Figure C–18

6. Finish the sketch.

7. Create a **Sweep** feature with the sketched profile and path that you just created. The model displays as shown in Figure C–19.

Figure C–19

Task 4 - Create a loft feature.

1. Create a work plane parallel to and **55** mm from the bottom face of the first extrusion, as shown in Figure C–20.

2. Create a work plane parallel to and **145** mm from the bottom face of the first extrusion, as shown in Figure C–20.

Bottom face

Figure C–20

3. Sketch and dimension the rectangular section on the first work plane, as shown in Figure C–21. Apply the Symmetry constraint about the XY and XZ planes.

Project the XY and XZ planes onto the sketch plane to locate the geometry.

33

37

Figure C–21

4. Finish the sketch.

5. Sketch and dimension the circular section with a **110** mm diameter on the second work plane, as shown in Figure C–22.

Project the Origin Center Point onto the sketch plane to locate the geometry.

Figure C–22

6. Finish the sketch.

7. Create a loft feature using the bottom face of the first extrusion and the two sketches, as shown in Figure C–23. Use the *Conditions* tab to set the transition between the existing model and the loft geometry to be tangent.

Figure C–23

The model displays as shown in Figure C–24.

The work planes are not shown in Figure C–24.

Figure C–24

8. Save the model and close the window.

Index
